WHEN BUSINESS EAST MEETS BUSINESS WEST

The Guide to Practice and Protocol in the Pacific Rim

Christopher Engholm

JOHN WILEY & SONS, INC.

New York • Chichester • Brisbane • Toronto • Singapore

For
Nancy Lee Woolsey

In recognition of the importance of preserving what is
written, it is a policy of John Wiley & Sons, Inc., to have
books of enduring value published in the United States
printed on acid-free paper, and we exert our best efforts
to that end.

Library of Congress Cataloging-in-Publication Data:

Engholm, Christopher.
    When business east meets business west: the guide to
practice and protocol in the Pacific Rim / by Christopher Engholm.
        p.   cm.
    Includes bibliographical references and index.
    ISBN 0-471-53033-6 (cloth)
    ISBN 0-471-53034-4 (paper)
    1. Business etiquette—Pacific Area.   2. Intercultural
communication—United States.   3. Cross-cultural orientation—United
States.   I. Title.
HF5389.E53   1991
395′.52′099—dc20   91-12204

Printed in the United States of America

10 9 8 7 6 5 4 3 2 1

Foreword

The mythical Pacific Rim is no longer something in the imagination of international marketers who dream of selling to the multitudes of the East. The old attitude of selling oil to fill the lamps of China has vanished with the hard realities of marketing to Asians who are not always willing, or able, to buy. In the decades since World War II, however, East Asia has emerged as an economic powerhouse and Asia's "mini-dragons" are well on their way to freeing themselves from their colonial legacies, soon to emerge as competitors to American manufacturers and potential partners in production and trade. We have witnessed the swift rise of Japanese know-how and influence in the Asia-Pacific region as we entered the final decade of the American Century. To quote from a recent *Forbes* article, "Asia is no longer on the threshold of becoming an important economic power. It's here now."

Today, Japan's trade and investment in Asia have expanded to the point of near hegemony in the region; only in the Philippines does the United States retain number-one standing in total trade volume, though that position is soon likely to be lost to the Japanese as well. As world trade continues its division into three huge trading blocs—Asia-Pacific, North America, and Europe—the countries of the West now face the stark reality of defeat in the trade war against Japan, at least in the Asia-Pacific, the fastest growing trade bloc of the three. If this happens—and most observers predict it will—Japan's economic strength could become invincible in the other two blocs as well. As Chris Engholm successfully demonstrates, it behooves entrepreneurs, executives, and commercial officers in the West to come to grips with why we have failed in Asia—and how we can turn the trend around in our favor. What have we done wrong? What can we learn that will improve our competitiveness in the booming Pacific Rim?

This book offers answers and solutions. From my own experience conducting business in Asia and training American executives to do better business there, I have seen first-hand our multifarious shortcomings in Asia vis-à-vis Japanese and ethnic Chinese businesspeople. Our problems in Asia are sometimes traceable to our products, our technology, and our after-sales service, but these problems are almost always accompanied by our *inability to cross into Asian business culture and do business the way our Asian customers do.* As the author states in this book, Western executives often don't *know* their customers—their needs, their preferences, their cultural traits, and their unique style of communicating and negotiating.

This book succeeds in a variety of ways. First, it points out the "soft" problems in our competitive position in Asia, many involving etiquette and protocol for doing business the way Asians do. Second, it presents a generic style for approaching Asian business opportunities that works wherever business is conducted in Asia. Third, it offers all of the detailed information that could possibly be needed to impress Asian hosts, correctly observe local rituals and dining manners, and deal with the culture shock of living and working in Asia. It's all here, and it's presented in a quickly readable manner that busy executives will appreciate. The sooner they absorb and implement the advice given here, the sooner we can expect to see our trade position in the Asia-Pacific take a turn for the better. As the Chinese proverb chides: "If we do not change our direction, we are likely to end up where we're headed."

DIANA ROWLAND
Rowland and Associates
San Diego, California

Preface

*Only relics of the 19th century and the
hopelessly uninformed would lump Asians
together and speak of "orientals," and of
"Eastern thought."*

LUCIAN PYE

As part of my research for this book, I undertook a "Pacific Circle" airline flight to ten capital cities of the Asia-Pacific. Most of them were not new to me; I had conducted business in many of my scheduled stopovers. But my research and my time rations required me to visit all ten cities in *one month*. Quite unlike Matsuo Basho (1644–1694), the greatest of Haiku poets, who traveled "the narrow road to the deep north" on foot, carrying a bamboo walking stick, my road would be traveled by plane, train, and automobile. One can't help but acquire a unique perspective on the Pacific Rim during a trip that goes around the full circle. Cultural snapshots of people, places, and encounters get burned into the visitor's psyche. This book is a revisiting, so that I can share all that I've learned from my research and experience.

As investment swirls into Thailand, the Philippines, and China, new outposts have emerged as links in North American companies' Asian strategy. Today's executives do business with peoples of many cultural areas of Asia and thus, as Fred Katayama writes in *Fortune,* they have to "cope with the sharp difference in style and behavior that divides East from West and East from East." Although many writers have identified Chinese traditions as the cultural bond among Pacific Rim nations, striking differences exist in their values, commercial behavior, and social etiquette. The height of civility in one place may be the epitome of rudeness in another. Each destination requires a huge investment of preparatory time and effort, to sift through the eclectic literature on business practices, protocol, and taboos of that part of the Pacific Rim. In training people for crossing into Asian business cultures, I have found that, even if a book covers the entire region and gives current information, it's written for leisurely travelers, not for businesspeople. Western executives need a business etiquette guide for Asia that acknowledges the sometimes profound differences, but also underscores the similarities, in business behavior between Asian cultures. North Americans could then cross into these diverse cultures adroitly, without years of preparation.

This book tells what's acceptable, and not acceptable, throughout all of Asia; in many ways, it is an "accidental tourist" guide. Its goal is to lessen the impact of a place and its people (within the context of doing business), allowing one's concentration to be focused on competitive advantage rather than the pitfalls of a potential faux pas. I've intentionally made the book more than a guide to manners and customs. I've organized it to facilitate both a *conceptual understanding,* which one needs to comprehend the diverse value systems of Asia, and an *appreciative understanding* of the resulting behavior patterns, which foreigners encounter in commercial environments. The book will, I hope, help readers to anticipate and formulate negotiating strategies, thereby enhancing their position vis-à-vis competitors.

Whether Asian counterparts are Malay or Mandarin, Taiwanese or Thai, the book reveals everything businesspeople need to know to better communicate, negotiate, and conduct themselves with propriety. There is even advice on how to host an Asian delegation, if one's Asian hosts should decide to pay a return visit. The material here has been "test-driven" with executive-level audiences and refined to incorporate their questions and suggestions. Many of the book's best anecdotes come from participants in my seminars, who have shared their Asia-visit stories with me.

The three Parts of the book focus on (1) cultural values and business behavior—the cultural origins of Asian values, and how they surface in the commercial landscape; (2) communication and negotiation—the greeting rituals throughout the region, and how Asians communicate and negotiate with Westerners; (3) business etiquette and protocol throughout the Pacific Rim—how to conduct oneself in Asia when dining, giving gifts, socializing, and hosting Asians.

The hardest part of writing a complete and concise guide to business protocol for the Asia-Pacific has been to be brief. To any critics who might accuse me of leaving out important details, I can only say that, unfortunately, the omission simply could not be avoided. When I began my research, my first interviewee, a Chinese magazine editor in Hong Kong, told me perfunctorily: "A book about business practice and protocol throughout Asia would be impossible to write. It can't be done." I chalked the comment up to Chinese pessimism and went ahead and wrote the book anyway—not for skeptics or critics, but for businesspeople bound for Asia.

We live in an age of information overload and I felt I should try to condense my message so that it can be read in about as many hours as it takes to cross the Pacific on a flight from the United States. Luckily for me, the Concorde doesn't fly that route.

Acknowledgments

A book like this is the product of interviews and research, as well as first-hand experience. Numerous people shared their insights, experience, and humor with me; each was a unique contribution for which I am indebted. In this regard, I would like to thank (in random order) the following people.

Saiman Hui, for answering my questions about the Hong Kong–China relationship; Andrew Grossman, for educating me on the ways of business in Korea; Patrice Mawhinney, for talking with me about expatriates in Taiwan; Jackie Gannon, for revealing to me the secrets of success for foreign businesswomen in Asia; Zhong Ding, for helping me to comprehend and appreciate China's business culture, and sharing with me his always incisive analysis of it; Sheila Yue Mei Luo, for her insights about Chinese politics; Diana Rowland of Rowland & Associates, for her insights into Japanese business etiquette and problems in intercultural communication; Steve Willard and his wife Merce, for their insights into doing business in the Philippines and the problems and joys of the Anglo-Asian mixed marriage; Jack Lewis at the University of Southern California, for inviting me to join the faculty at the International Business Education and Research (IBEAR) program; Ping Li, for his insights about China's economic policy; James Wen, for his comments on Asian politics and international banking; Gregory Tsang, for his comments on Chinese business practice; Lin C. Hoong, for talking to me about the government–business relationship in Malaysia; Hong-Chul Ahn, for answering my questions about Korean gift-giving and business practice; Todd Michael Banks, for his advice and encouragement both as a friend and business partner in Asia; Nancy Madison, for enlightening me on the art of translation and interpreting; Thomas Bikson and Scott Warmuth for their generous introductions; Nigel Bonny, for sharing with me his experiences working and traveling in Asia; Tom and Nancy Woolsey, for their support; Barney and Yvonne Engholm, for their encouragement; Jeanie Engholm and Helen Bloomfield, for typing the manuscript; Al and Mary Kern, for granting me the use of their company's word processing and laser printing facilities; my agent, Julie Castiglia, and my editor at John Wiley & Sons, Ted Scheffler, who has the patience of Job.

CHRISTOPHER ENGHOLM

Del Mar, California
August 1991

Contents

PART I

The Tao of Asia Business
People—Nations—Values

PART II

AsiaSpeak
Status—Formality—Trust

PART III

The Book of "Li"
Etiquette—Ceremony—Protocol

Appendixes

WHEN BUSINESS EAST
MEETS BUSINESS WEST

PART I

THE TAO OF ASIA BUSINESS
PEOPLE—NATIONS—VALUES

It is not good for the Christian health
To hustle the Asian brown
For the Christian riles
And the Asian smiles
And he weareth the Christian down.

At the end of the fight
On a tombstone white
With the name of the late deceased,
and the epitaph drear:

A fool lies here
Who tried to hurry the East.

RUDYARD KIPLING

CHAPTER ONE

Why Cross "The Great Waters"?

In dealing with another person,
the whole secret of success is
finding the right way of approach.

First you must rid yourself of all prejudice;
and, so to speak, let the ideas and values
of the other person act upon you without
restraint;

Then you can establish contact with the other,
understand him, and gain power over him.
In this way you can undertake
the most dangerous things, such as
Crossing the Great Waters, *and succeed.*
ADAPTED FROM THE ANCIENT CONFUCIAN
BOOK OF CHANGE (THE I CHING)

American business has begun to
recognize that its largest
and fastest growing markets
are in the Pacific.
BERNARD K. GORDON, PROFESSOR OF POLITICAL
SCIENCE, UNIVERSITY OF NEW HAMPSHIRE

Managers and entrepreneurs of the West no longer enjoy the luxury of a choice in becoming involved in the markets of the Asia-Pacific. The Pacific Rim—that formidable linkage of export-led economies driven by tireless workers and shrewd industrial strategy—has emerged as the most important new frontier for business endeavor in the world. As a trade bloc, the Asia-Pacific is the world's largest market, a vast region of consumers and industrial end-users with seemingly limitless financial capability to purchase goods from the West.

The numbers are truly monumental. Three hundred billion dollars in trade—70 percent of the world's total—now crosses the Pacific annually; that is, Asian trade grows by an astonishing $3 billion a week! The six largest banks in the world are in Asia, as are six of the world's ten largest ports. One hundred and eleven Japanese firms are included in the Global 500, and 11 South Korean firms have joined this illustrious group. Japan's economy, second only to that of the United States, produces annually an average of 13 percent of the world's gross domestic product. The Commission on Integrated Long-Term Strategy predicts, however, that China's fast-growing economy will eclipse Japan's by 2010, based on a conservative Rand Commission estimate that China's economy will grow at a rate of just under 5 percent a year.

Japanese investment in the Newly Industrialized Countries—Hong Kong, Singapore, South Korea, and Taiwan—is increasing 50 percent per year; in Indonesia, Malaysia, the Philippines, and Thailand, the rate is 100 percent per year. (Total Japanese investment in Asia between 1951 and 1989 amounted to $40 billion.) Taiwan alone has announced plans to invest $300 billion to upgrade its infrastructure over the next six years. Even Vietnam has entered the investment sweepstakes, approving 193 joint ventures, worth $1.3 billion, with non-Communist countries since 1987. New jobs are being created throughout the region, enlarging the ranks of Asian consumers who have disposable income to spend on Western imports. The "dragon" economies of Asia not only represent burgeoning markets; they also offer Western companies an endless supply of relatively low-cost skilled labor, venture capital, and leading-edge technological know-how.

North America and the Pacific Rim

No country has shifted its corporate focus from the Atlantic to the Pacific as swiftly as the United States. Surprisingly, the United States, since 1983, has conducted more trade across the Pacific than across the Atlantic. United States exports to the Far East have grown 1,200 percent since 1960, constituting a larger percentage of U.S. export growth in a shorter period of time than in any other region of the world. Of America's 20 largest trading partners, eight are now in the Pacific region. Our yearly trade with Asia was $77 billion in 1978; now, it's well over $200 billion annually and growing rapidly. In 1988, U.S. exports to Singapore, China, Taiwan, Korea, and Hong Kong increased, on average, by an incredible 40 percent over the previous year.

Canada, too, is extending and intensifying its economic links in the Pacific Rim. Canadian businesses, which had sold under $5 billion worth of goods to Japan in 1975, sold more than $9 billion worth of goods there in 1989, a formidable 60 percent increase over 14 years. Canada's total trade with Taiwan stood at $48 million in 1975; now, it's over $1 billion annually—low compared to U.S.–Taiwan trade, but expanding rapidly nonetheless. Another trend will ensure Canada's key role in Asia-Pacific trade. Over 25,000 Hong Kong businesspeople have relocated in Vancouver since the Tiananmen Square uprising in China in 1989, bringing with them $3 billion in cash investment. Locals have nicknamed the city "Hong Couver," because of the influx of Chinese money and culture. Vancouver is fast becoming a new pearl in the Pacific Rim necklace of business capitals, soon to rival Singapore as a regional center for corporate and financial operations. Like a tail wagging a dog, the city of Vancouver will eventually serve to unite all of Canada with the dynamic economies of Asia. If the Canadian government manages these new trade relationships adroitly, the economic benefit to Canadian firms will be significant.

Our relationship with the *people* of the Pacific Rim has also broadened and intensified. Flows of capital, technology, and merchandise parallel movements of salespeople, students, immigrants, and tourists. The number of travelers who now cross the Pacific has grown by 20 to 30 percent a year over the past four years, and trans-Pacific travel will equal one-third of world air traffic by 1992.

Asian-Americans represent a growing cultural and economic presence. Now numbering between 6 million and 7 million, Asian-Americans are the fastest growing, wealthiest, and most educated minority population in America. Harvard's freshman class each year averages 12 percent Asian-Americans. The University of California Berkeley's student body is 25 percent Asian-Americans, and Massachusetts Institute of Technology's (M.I.T.) is 22 percent. "All these trends," says Richard Drobnick, Director of the International Business Education and Research (IBEAR) program at the University of Southern California, "increase the interpersonal contact between the U.S. and Pacific Rim nations in a variety of overlapping roles as competitors, customers, suppliers, partners, classmates, and neighbors."

The High Price of Ignoring Asia

The benefits of participating in the Pacific Rim's economic takeoff are obvious. The corollary is: companies unwilling or unable to participate will discover increasing difficulty in obtaining necessary components of comparative advantage—fresh sources of working capital, breakthrough technologies, burgeoning consumer markets, inexpensive skilled labor, and leading-edge manufacturing and management know-how from Asia. The time for pondering whether to participate in the Pacific Rim's economic miracle has passed; the time for making the investment of time and resources necessary for permanently engaging in Pacific Rim opportunities is well underway.

"Euro-Centricity": Our Downfall?

Too many North American companies place too little priority on the Asian market, when planning their global corporate strategies. The current trend is to curtail efforts in Asia and concentrate on the nascent opportunities of Central and Eastern Europe and the post-1992 European Economic Community (EEC). This improvident shift in strategic focus disregards fundamental and verifiable facts concerning geographic, demographic, and economic comparisons between Europe and Asia.

The Asia-Pacific region is *twice* the geographic size of Europe and the United States combined. Half of the world's population lives in Asia and, more importantly, by the year 2000, *two-thirds* of the world's inhabitants will live in Asia. The European population is expected to have shrunk by then to about 6 percent of the world's population. At its current rate, U.S.–Asian trade by the end of the 1990s will be *double* that with Europe. John Naisbitt and Patricia Aburdene, in *Megatrends 2000,* tell us that "Asia will have 80 million new consumers by the year 2000." On the other hand, they predict only 11 million net new consumers in Europe. Workers in Hong Kong, Korea, Singapore, and Taiwan save as much as 35 percent of their earnings; if this rate is maintained, Asia will remain the world's main source of business capital into the next millenium. As for Europe, what country besides Germany could match the combined cash reserves now held by Japanese and Taiwanese banks, which amount to over $150 billion?

Our lack of staying power in Asia is unfortunate, because Asian customers maintain a preference to buy American. "American businessmen are not aggressive in taking advantage of our natural favoritism toward American products," says John Ni of Taiwan's Industrial Development and Investment Center. The Japanese face a historical obstacle among Asian buyers, traceable to Japan's invasion and occupation of Asian countries during World War II. As the U.S. share of the total Asia-Pacific market gradually slipped, during the late 1980s and early 1990s, from 38 percent to about 25 percent, the slack was taken up by European and Asian suppliers. The Japanese, for example, will soon be shipping more of their exports to Asia than to America, and Taiwan's trade surplus with Asia now surpasses its surplus with the United States. During the second half of the 1980s, the U.S. trade deficit with Asia hovered around a whopping $80 billion a year; with Japan, it has come down from $50 billion in 1987 to a slightly more manageable $38 billion in 1990.

Happily, America's trade deficit with Asian countries has been declining in 1989–1991, in part because of a weaker dollar that makes our exports cheaper for Asians to buy, but also because American manufacturing companies have become leaner, more efficient, and more quality-conscious. They have also begun to focus their resources on breaking into, and holding onto, overseas markets, including high-growth markets in Asia. With each passing year, American firms sell more to Asia, increasingly from their Asia-based factories. If current trade trends continue, the United States will actually achieve trade parity with both Japan and Taiwan by 1993. Our past experience in trading with Asia cautions us, however, not to count our dollars before they're deposited. If we are to continue to improve and *sustain* our balance of trade with Asia, we must persevere in our effort to penetrate these markets for years to come.

The World's Toughest Market

The list of entrepreneurs or companies that decided to exploit Pacific Rim opportunities covers millenia. Roman West and Chinese East started doing business together via the Silk Road long before the birth of Christ. Millions of Chinese emigrés, and globalized Japanese trading companies, have tried to exploit the East since the Opium War. Many of them possess family connections there, share the same language, and know the values, behaviors, and methods of Asian business interaction. Neophyte North Americans and Europeans, attempting to serve themselves a piece of the Pacific Rim pie, discover that the region is terribly competitive. Cultural insularity among Asians intensifies the difficulties for Westerners. "We like doing business with each other," says a Chinese friend of mine. "We have a way of doing business that we are comfortable with and Westerners don't always fit in." Jack T. Sun, president and executive director of Taiwan's Pacific Electric Wire & Cable Company adds: "Most Chinese trust only their own people, and not anybody else." In short, the Pacific Rim is a tough market marked by extreme ethnocentricity, ingrained government business collusion and corruption, old-boy networks, and diverse cultural barriers.

To make matters worse, North American corporations' competitors, especially those in Asia, ensure that their representatives enter Asian markets familiarized with the cultural values, negotiating behavior, and business protocol of their customers. Most importantly, large numbers of them master the local languages of their customers—Chinese, Thai, Tagalog, Bahasa Indonesian, or English. These firms make a clear effort to learn Asian idiosyncrasies and taboos; North American firms tend to do little to train representatives who must cross into Asian cultures. "We go to great pains in the U.S. to study a market before entering it, but in Asia and the Pacific Rim, we seem inclined to skip this step because market research requires us to go back to school to learn what we think are 'exotic' cultures and languages—which is frankly difficult," writes Michael Tomczyk in *Export Today.*

Once in Asia, North Americans commit blunders ranging from the excusable—like the American negotiator who gestures an obscenity to his Malay customers when he pounds his fist into his palm, or the company that delivered 500 "funeral notices" (Christmas cards written in red ink) to its Japanese partner—to the more profound but subtle errors in intercultural communication— like wrongly concluding that a verbalized "yes" may be a polite "maybe," or that a smile means satisfaction rather than embarrassment. A typical failure is to not recognize Asian negotiating tactics or important nonverbal cues like lack of eye contact, laughter, and, most significant of all, the use of silence. These cultural signs might be neglected without effect when one is the buyer, but a seller who ignores them cannot succeed. Asians would never have been able to penetrate North American markets if they had not first learned and adjusted painstakingly to doing business the Western way. There are 15,000 Japanese MBAs in the United States studying to be marketers for Japanese firms, a testament to the firms' desire to know the American consumer in order to sell to the U.S. market. If businesspeople do not learn the Asians' way of doing business before attempting to penetrate Pacific Rim markets, their efforts will be self-defeating.

When East Meets West:
A Clash of Business Cultures

Our failures in Asian markets are cultural as often as they are entrepreneurial. Our frank and personable executives often offend their more reserved and face-conscious Asian counterparts. They tend to enter Asia without the slightest notion of its history, values, or style of communication, and therefore fail to "network," Asian-style. With all of their rhetoric about "networking," Western businesspeople don't form in the East the long-term personal connections that result in successful business dealings. There are many reasons for this, but the primary one is probably impatience: to the Westerner, time is money. Westerners need to understand that time is also an investment, especially when business relationships are being forged in Asia. Westerners continue to fail to establish these bonds with any frequency, and become irate when they see business opportunities handed to those who have succeeded in building bridges to the East.

Divergent value systems are at the root of the clash between Asian and Western business practices. The typical Westerner, for example, learns to be an individual, to be *self*-motivated. A Westerner competes with others, is not adept at operating cooperatively, and approaches problems by seeking practical solutions, regardless of their impact on others. The typical Asian, taught to think of the collective before the self, functions *interdependently*. An Asian seeks solutions that preserve *harmony* among all parties. Western business agreements often come after two parties fight for their interests. Asians try to reach agreement through compromise, with the parties seeking a mutually beneficial arrangement that will continue to prosper when the deal is done. Westerners consider consensus decision making antiquated, a woeful waste of time in an era requiring immediate response to change; they seek a specific result from a single contractual agreement. Asians emphasize the value of engaging in numerous business transactions over the long term and of remaining partners, in a bond of reciprocity, respect, and trust.

Another sphere of business discord between East and West is created when egalitarian-minded Westerners fail to recognize the extremely hierarchical, rigidly ranked nature of most Asian societies. Unequal social status is hard for Westerners to accept; similarly, it's hard for Asians to accept the fundamentally equal social status among North Americans. Asians seek *prestige* rather than *recognition* for accomplishments. Concerned about status in the group and about reputation (face) in the eyes of coworkers, Asians are not likely to seek personal credit for achievements or to publicize their success. Asians must abide by certain unwritten rules of conduct pertaining to status; Westerners have greater freedom to be individuals. Westerners are trained to be informal instantly, or as soon as possible, with a business client, to establish rapport and a personal connection. Asians maintain a high level of public formality in doing business, and will let down their guard only during informal business and social meetings.

Asians' business reality is obscured by an oblique matrix of complex ritual designed to reinforce status differences, protect face, and ensure that village/corporate/national traditions (they're all merged) are preserved and passed on to new generations. Westerners appreciate spontaneity, wit, and congeniality; the Asians measure a person by whether he or she observes rules of social protocol, especially those rules that reinforce deference to superiors.

By knowing something about Asian business culture and protocol, businesspeople can create advantages for themselves and their company. However, the task of "knowing something about Asian business culture" means more than merely learning to sip hot *sake*, eat rice with chopsticks, and bow to an Asian host at the appropriate obeisant depth. I contend that many North American executives could increase their competitiveness in Asia by sharpening their *intercultural communication* skills and by learning the rules of Asian social and business etiquette. When businesspeople have the gamut of skills needed to successfully cross cultures in the Asia-Pacific, they gain what I call the Etiquette Edge.

What Is the Etiquette Edge?

The Etiquette Edge refers to more than learning the customs and manners of a foreign business environment. As the world's manufacturers narrow the gap between the traditional areas of advantage, a company with the ability to cross cultures, communicate with people in foreign regions, and negotiate long-range overseas partnerships based on reciprocal trust will have an edge over its competitors. Before North American firms encountered competition from Japan, Korea, and Taiwan in their attempt to sell in international markets, few took seriously the notion that the "style" of an offer has bearing on success overseas. Since 1970, however, America's competitive advantage has narrowed vis-à-vis competitors in Asia and Europe. Today, success often depends on "who you know" and what connections are maintained in Byzantine bureaucracies abroad. Because business in Asia involves a high degree of ritual and reciprocity, an inappropriate response to a traditional custom can blow a deal and derail years of carefully laid plans.

One hears, time and again, how an Asian customer rejects an American vendor or business partner, who may be offering the lowest price, best service, or highest quality, because an alternative partner has become a trusted friend or has been referred by another Asian business associate. Acceptance into Asia's diverse business cultures, and strong relationships with businesspeople there, are advantages that equal, or even outweigh, many of the traditional factors in a firm's competitive advantage, such as lowest price, after-sales service, and quality of products.

To attain an Etiquette Edge, one must master a series of intercultural communicating and negotiating "competencies." Among them are the following desirable skills:

- Resolving conflicts and impasses while safeguarding a partner's face (reputation);
- Communicating ideas, humor, and individuality through an interpreter;
- Perceiving and comprehending nonverbal facial expressions and body language (called "belly language" in Japan);
- Exchanging technical know-how with Asians, without giving up proprietary information.

No one is born with these skills, and most executives visiting Asia for the first time are unaware of their shortcomings in crossing borders gracefully. Reading guidebooks helps; experience helps even more. This book is a cultural guide, and should be taken along on Asian trips. Relevant parts can be reread before attending a banquet, visiting a home, hosting an Asian delegation, or negotiating a contract. The book will, I truly believe, enhance performance *and* profits, help in building a wide network of business relationships, avoid costly blunders in social situations, improve communication and international business negotiation, help with becoming a more informed and more sensitive guest in Asia, and enhance the sense of fulfillment that accompanies working and living in Asia. The book offers the most important advantages an executive can have: commercial style, and strategy suited to Asian business culture.

The Pacific Rim: A Kaleidoscope of Contrasts

What the West has traditionally called "The Orient" is a region comprised of nations that are striking in contrast, geography, ethnicity, religious traditions, standards of living, and degree of exposure to Western culture. Let's debunk the antiquated and hollow term, "The Orient," and, along with it, "oriental character," "oriental cooking," and "the oriental mind." Lucian Pye, the illustrious Asia scholar at M.I.T., quoted earlier, is correct: there is no "lumpen" Pacific Rim. The *only* generalization that seems permissible is that nearly all Asians share the physical characteristic of black hair.

The ten countries we are discussing contrast geographically more than they compare. Singapore is the size of the Bronx, Japan is the size of California, and China is slightly larger than all of the United States. Indonesia is nearly as wide as the United States but is made up of 13,500 islands, some as small as an iceberg. Climates vary as much as geographic size. It snows in Seoul and Beijing in the winter; Indonesia, Singapore, and Malaysia simmer at about 80 degrees virtually every day of the year.

Then there's the village versus the city. Nine out of ten Hong Kong residents and all Singaporeans live in urban areas. The populations of Japan, Taiwan, and South Korea are about 75 percent urbanized; the Philippines, 50 percent; Malaysia, 38 percent; and Thailand, 20 percent. (The United States is 80 percent urban.) Asians contrast in income as well, spanning the extremes of wealth and poverty. The Japanese earn about $23,000 annually; Hong Kong Chinese, $8,160; Thais, $930; Filipinos, $700; and Mainland Chinese, $250. At Asia's low end, workers in Indonesia can be hired for as little as 14 cents an hour. The Japanese enjoy one of the highest standards of living and probably the best health care in the world; only 12 percent of Indonesia's 170 million people enjoy access to clean water, and only two of every five Indonesian newborns live to the age of five!

Japan in the Age of *Yutori*

"Japan today is an intensely globalized society," says Bruce Sterling, coauthor of *The Difference Engine,* "with sky-high literacy, very low crime, excellent life expectancy, tremendous fashion scene, and a staggering amount of the electronic substance we used to call cash." What better introduction to Japan, which the Japanese call *Nihon,* or *Nippon.* The first thing a visitor realizes, walking through today's Tokyo, is that a consumer revolution is underway and it features the emergence of Japan's new middle-class consumer. DINK (dual-income-no-kids) families navigate the sprawling cityscape in search of products considered off-limits to them five years ago, before the dawn of the present era of *yutori,* or "spare money." "Trade barriers are starting to come down, and the [Japanese] consumer is starting to spend like crazy," says Maureen Smith at the U.S. Department of Commerce.

Few North Americans realize that, by 1984, the Japanese spent an average of $583 each (16 percent of their income) to buy American-made products, while Americans spent only $289 each (2 percent of their income) on Japanese products. American exports to Japan rose 34 percent in 1988, 18 percent in 1989, and 8 percent in 1990. (In 1990, Japan's exports to the United States declined.) Japan is hardly restricting its purchases of U.S. goods to raw materials and foodstuffs. In 1988, Japan bought more manufactured goods from the United States ($22 billion worth) than Germany and France combined. Half of these purchases were labeled "high tech" by the Department of Commerce. These statistics suggest that, although the Japan market may be expensive to succeed in, it's definitely not closed. ·

The Japanese are romancing the West. One of the most popular shows on Japanese television is called "USA Express," a human-interest window on American culture. Our free-booting "culture" —music, fashions, and movies—seems our hottest export to Japan. Tom Cruise is a sex symbol. NFL football warm-up jackets pass in the crowd every few seconds.

Even rap music—called *rappu*—has arrived, sung in Japanese by local bands outfitted in the latest U.S. ghetto-wear. Favorite foods among Japanese teenagers now include ice cream, sherbert, hamburgers, and pudding. Bewildered Westerners won't stand more than a few seconds in downtown Tokyo before someone offers to assist them in finding a destination.

South Korea: Moving Upmarket Rapidly

People measure Korea's progress toward modernity by the number of new, wide bridges that span the Han-gang River skirting Seoul, now one of the world's ten largest cities. A few years ago there were three bridges; now there are 17, with more on the way. The Daehan Life Insurance Building (called "Golden Tower") that towers above Seoul is Asia's tallest building, a symbol of Korea's will to be part of the Pacific Rim economic miracle.

Korea's own economic "miracle" is the product of hard work, guided industrial policy, and loans, mainly from the United States. Korea still depends on the United States to purchase 40 percent of its exports. Exports soared by 30 percent in 1986 and 1987; wages rose 40 percent between 1986 and 1988. Economic growth has rebounded to 8–9 percent in 1991, after a slump in 1989 to 6.7 percent. Prices and wages, however, are locked in a vicious cycle that will fuel an inflation rate of 8–10 percent through 1992. With the reunification of North and South Korea, the country could become the Germany of Asia, its economic might now ominous even to Japan. There are more PhDs in Korea per capita than anywhere else in the world.

Korea is a 600-mile-long peninsula the size of Virginia and has a restless population, North and South combined, of 45 million people. At night, a visitor may see fistfights on Seoul streets between drunken executives. I asked a student on a bus about this and he shrugged: "Koreans fight a lot." Riot police wearing U.S.-issue green fatigues, helmets, and boots, and equipped with tear gas bombs and clubs, interrogate students emerging from the subway. Koreans are not always friendly to Westerners, especially Americans. I had been warned: Keep to yourself and avoid confrontation. Americans may even be the target for tossed garbage and vegetables. A defense-industry friend instructed me: "Wear a Canadian flag on your shirt. They love Canadians." Korea seems to exist in a state of continuous military alert. During a Civil Defense Drill held on the 15th of every month, yellow flags appear on buildings, sirens blare, and citizens make their way to shelters located in the city's underground walkways. Korean males serve a mandatory three-year stay in the military. The country spends 6 percent of its gross national product (GNP) on defense, the same percentage as the United States. Widened highways in

South Korea double as emergency airstrips, to be used in case of attack from the north. In 1991, a tumultuous year, student protests and numerous self-immolations were carried out to demand the ouster of President Roh Tae Woo. In the coming months, South Korea's government will have to find solutions to the problems of promoting economic growth, controlling inflation, and moving the political apparatus of the government further in the direction of democratic reform.

Taiwan: Under Pressure to Import

Once called Formosa, Taiwan (population 19.8 million) is an island about the size of Holland. The Taiwanese live under an authoritarian government, still run by Chinese Nationalists who fled the Mainland during its takeover by the Communists in 1949. Martial law was finally lifted in 1987, after being in force since 1949. Taiwan is the 12th largest trading nation in the world.

Fantastically productive, Taiwan's 316,712 factories are mostly small and family-run; 85 percent of them employ fewer than 50 workers. Taiwan is cash-rich, second only to Japan—and Japan has six times as many people. An economic powerhouse with a timid demeanor, Taiwan has amassed $69 billion in cash revenue. The Taiwan stock market does as much trading as both the New York and Tokyo exchanges. The Chinese penchant for speculation may be the cause. At the Wall Street Restaurant in Taipei, the tables feature built-in television monitors for following stocks during the meal.

Although 120 countries don't recognize Taiwan diplomatically, Taiwan exports to virtually all of them. After 1949, the Chinese Nationalist Embassy in Washington became the Coordination Council for North American Affairs, Taiwan's unofficial embassy in the United States. Most officials are "retired," a status that serves to maintain the facade of nonofficial relations between the United States and Taiwan.

Ironically, the Taiwan–China relationship grows stronger every day through formal and informal trading. Recently, 50,000 seamen from Taiwan sailed to China without proper visas, to visit relatives for an important holiday. Both countries turned a blind eye. A recent Gallup poll shows that 65 percent of Taiwan's citizenry would welcome open trade between the Mainland and Taiwan. Offering an olive branch to the Mainland mandarinate, Taiwan's President Lee Teng-hui formally ended the "state of war" between the Communist Mainland and Taiwan in May 1991.

Hong Kong: A Borrowed Place on Borrowed Time

Long ago, the British found Hong Kong's deep-water harbor perfect for mooring their large clipper ships. In 1842, China gave the island-port to England as a victory prize of the Opium War, a gesture that Queen Victoria's Foreign Secretary, Lord Palmerston, accepted with derisive laughter. (It was not with laughter that Prime Minister Margaret Thatcher relinquished Hong Kong to China in a treaty signed in 1984!)

Hong Kong has become the world's greatest entrepôt trading center, its second busiest port, and its third largest financial center, with more Rolls-Royces per inch than anywhere else. Hong Kong possesses the world's biggest air cargo terminal and the second largest futures market. About the size of New York City, with 40,000 (mostly small) enterprises, Hong Kong is, as the cliché goes, a schoolroom for the study of free-market capitalism. There is duty on only five commodities coming in, and no duty on goods going out.

Hong Kong is also a gateway to the Chinese market. Between 2 million and 4 million Mainland Chinese workers are now employed by foreign-invested enterprises in Guangdong Province, the entry point from Hong Kong, and 30 to 40 percent of China's foreign-exchange income comes from, or through, Hong Kong. Hong Kong manufacturers have transferred whole industries to South China, to reduce labor costs; for example, 80 percent of Hong Kong's renowned toy industry now manufactures in China. However, the "Pearl of the Orient" will, in 1997, become a Special Administrative Region of the People's Republic of China (P.R.C.). No city or country on earth lives under more uncertainty than Hong Kong. Hong Kong is a city, as Chinese poet Han Su-yin wrote in *LIFE* in 1959, "on borrowed time in a borrowed place." The approaching year of 1997, an *Insight* guidebook waxes,

> was blotted out of the collective psyche . . . a non-thing to be never spoken of . . . in the economically fat years of the sixties and seventies . . . then it bubbled to the surface in mid-1982 with the lead up to Prime Minister Margaret Thatcher's visit to Peking.

Because of China's crackdown on pro-democracy student demonstrators in 1989, few Hong Kong businesspeople believe that the "One Country, Two Systems" policy will preserve laissez-faire capitalism on the island. Although Hong Kong is a window that looks out on Chinese consumers, it is entirely dependent on the Mainland for its raw supplies and food. China has become Hong Kong's largest trading partner and its sole source of inexpensive labor, but is also its greatest political nemesis.

China: "To Get Rich Is (Still) Glorious"

From Hong Kong, visitors cross the border at Shenzhen into the People's Republic of China (P.R.C.). All visitors and traders crossed the bridge at Lowu, when China first opened to the West. "When you carried your luggage across the bridge, you entered another world," recalls David Zaidner, a commodities trader. "You disappeared into China. For a week or two, you heard nothing whatsoever about the outside world. Anything could happen to you—and no one would have known. It was eerie, stepping over the brink of civilization." China's GNP growth of 10 percent during Deng Xiao-ping's reforms outstripped virtually every other country in the world. The Chinese continue to get richer. In prosperous East China, 5 percent of the people are members of "10,000 Yuan Households," earning more than $2,700 a year.

China is a scenically beautiful country. Even after the Tiananmen Square Massacre in 1989, its vast, untapped market continued to lure the business suitors of the world. However, it is one of the roughest places to do business, if only for its lack of Western comforts. The little irritations of business mount quickly for the faint-of-heart. No one queues; the Chinese scrimmage instead. They stampede to get on trains and airplanes, and into taxis. At most hotels, visitors can forget room service. Highways are perennially under construction. Air pollution in cities like Chongqing singes the lungs. Hepatitis outbreaks hardly get reported. Dirt, grime, stench, and smoke-filled meeting rooms are the business environment, and complaining is fruitless.

Recently, I was in Chongqing, accompanying the director of Asian marketing for American Plant Growers, Inc. We sat cramped inside a CAAC (Civil Aviation Administration of China) jetliner preparing for takeoff. Suddenly, the air ducts began spewing white mist that filled the fuselage. It turned out to be disinfectant; there had been an outbreak of lice in the city!

Singapore: Hong Kong's Understudy?

The Singaporeans are second to the Japanese as the most prosperous people in Asia. The island, 26 by 14 miles small, freed itself from British colonialism in 1963 and became part of

Malaysia. Two years later, it split off from the Malaysia Federation and declared itself the Republic of Singapore. Singapore, meaning "The Lion City," has an immigrant society. On its streets, Malay, Tamil, Mandarin, Hokkien, Cantonese, and English are spoken, as well as a combination of them all, called Singlish. Residents of Chinese descent make up the majority, about 75 percent of the population. Fifteen percent are Malay; 7 percent are Indian. As in other Southeast Asian societies, those of Chinese descent control the economy; one in four of this group in Singapore is an entrepreneur. Few Malays or Indians participate to a great extent in Singaporean high corporate culture.

Lee Kuan Yew ruled the country from independence until 1990. His "speak softly but carry a big stick" leadership style was a unique blend of ancient Confucian patriarchy and English gentility. Not a single slum area exists in Singapore, to spoil the fantastically cosmopolitan (some would say artificial) atmosphere. Shopping complexes, outdoor cafés, or cricket clubs appear at every turn. Virtually everyone who wants a job has one. Officialdom seems corruption-free. The economy grows 10 percent a year. The government doesn't run at a deficit and possesses large cash reserves. Singaporeans save 42 percent of their money, more than any other populace in the world. Foreigners are made to feel welcome in Singapore, unless they're caught jaywalking, smoking in a public place, littering, or smuggling narcotics.

Singapore is a city where people look over their shoulder. Infractions of the most mundane kind bring steep penalties. A speeding ticket, for example, can result in heavy fines and loss of a driver's license. Antigovernment political positions can bring severe punishment and imprisonment. "In Singapore, rules are made to be changed, but not broken," says a taxi driver of Chinese descent. The Malay, Tamil, and other minority communities are largely disenfranchised from the power hierarchy. These groups perceive Singapore as a multiethnic society; the government strives for a Chinese society. Mandarin is the chosen language for business and education.

A shortage of labor is a problem for the city-state. As Hong Kong utilizes Chinese labor by building factories in southern China, Singapore will have to import Indonesian labor, to expand and become less dependent on the multinational corporations that fuel much of Singapore's growth. This prospect involves surmounting the cultural antipathy that exists between Malay and Chinese people throughout the region. No one doubts, however, that Singaporean businesspeople will rise to the challenge. Indigenous entrepreneurs are already setting up private ventures by the hundreds, in a surge of investment in higher technology companies inside Singapore and across its borders.

Thailand: New Flashpoint for Export Manufacturing

Bangkok, the capital city on the Chao Phraya River, is called, like Los Angeles, *Krung Thep,* the City of Angels. Visitors hear the *"Sawadee"* welcome at the hotel, and see the graceful hands raised into the prayer-like *wai.* Three-wheeled *tuk-tuks* sputter through the gaseous Bangkok air. The balmy heat soothes, the legendary Thai hospitality calms the nerves. One hears the phrase *"Men Pai Ren"* at every turn. It translates to: "No problem . . . never mind . . . it doesn't really matter." Western expatriates lounge around the pool in the late afternoon, the envy of those freezing in Manchuria or cramped into crooked apartments in Taipei. In Bangkok, business and pleasure have fused.

Besides the sensual benefits of being in Thailand, there are extremely attractive incentives for businesses to invest in the country. Thailand has become the new site for low-cost manufacturing for export—labor can be hired for as little as 27 cents an hour (though the average wage paid to workers in foreign-owned factories is $160 a month). The government supports business and does everything in its power to attract foreign investment; 30 percent of its exports originate from foreign-owned factories. The Japanese, who invested $3 billion in Thailand in 1989, open five new factories a week, on average. The increase in investment flows has paid off so remarkably that little Thailand may soon become a Newly Industrialized Country. Thailand achieved a 12.2 percent economic growth rate in 1988, 11 percent in 1989, and 9.7 percent in 1990, with exports growing over 30 percent each year. A "bloodless" coup in February 1991 has not disrupted the economic takeoff.

Malaysia: A Bright Future Assured by Resources

This lush peninsula about the size of England is divided geographically among Sabah, Sarawak, and the Malaysian Peninsula, where the capital, Kuala Lumpur, is located. Sabah and Sarawak are 400 miles offshore in the South China Sea (see page 2). Malaysia is roughly the size of Japan but has only 17 million people. Roadside stalls serve *satay,* cubes of meat dipped in a spicy peanut butter sauce. Islamic minarets and onion-shaped cupolas rise above the traffic of motorcycles and taxis.

Malaysia is a major world producer of tin, rubber, lumber, palm oil, gold, and petroleum. It is also the third largest producer of semiconductors. Malaysia has one of the highest standards of living in Asia. GNP growth is high. The country doubles its exports every three years; over 50 percent of its exports are electronic goods and components. The telephones work. The roads are good. Malaysia is currently privatizing hundreds of companies in finance, agriculture, and utilities—a massive sell-off, 30 percent of which is tagged for Malay, rather than Chinese, ownership. Foreign investment commitments have rocketed tenfold over the past two years, for a total of $9 billion in 1989 alone.

The population is 47 percent Malay, 33 percent Chinese, and 9 percent Indian. As expected, the Chinese run the business and the Malays, who are predominantly Moslem, run the official government, centered in Kuala Lumpur. The Indian population works mainly in the rubber industry and as doctors and lawyers. Malaysians speak Bahasa Malaysia, but educated urban Malays speak the Queen's English, usually impeccably. Although city buses are filled with blue-frocked girls just off work at Seiko, women generally wear the *purdah,* an Arab-style robe; few women wear a veil. Islamic fundamentalism is strongest in the northern states, where whippings and canings are carried out against those found guilty of imbibing alcohol or participating in illicit sex. Malaysia is a democratic monarchy run by seven sultans, one of whom acts as king. Buddhist, Christian, and Hindu minorities in Malaysia live in constant fear of Islamic religious revival, which could exclude them from the mainstream of Malaysian culture and politics.

Indonesia: Weaning Itself from Oil Dependence

With 10 percent of its population, or 18 million people, qualifying as middle class, Indonesia has the rather unlikely distinction of possessing the second largest middle class of consumers in Asia, second only to Japan. The country's 13,677 "Spice Islands" comprise the world's largest archipelago, known to geographers as the 3,000-mile-long Malay Archipelago, the fabled "East Indies" during Europe's Age of Discovery. Indonesia is identified with the Polynesian-looking faces of its people, its multiple dialects, a village way of life, and an enormous population. The population includes over 300 ethnic groups; Batak, Balinese, Badui, Dayak,

Javanese, and Overseas Chinese are only a sampling. Strewn across this tropical Babylon are 250 to 400 mutually unintelligible languages and dialects. Indonesians are the fifth largest population on earth.

The capital of Jakarta, on the island of Java, is the focal point of Indonesian business and decision making. A military-based political system has run Indonesia for 25 years under the tutelage of President Suharto. Rumor has it that about 2,000 Moslem men in Jakarta make all of the important political decisions for the entire country. They are virtually all Javanese, drive last year's Mercedes-Benz, and speak English. The people of the outer islands wage a continuous battle to hold on to control of their resources and wealth, coveted by the leaders in Java.

These tight-knit bureaucrats have grown increasingly pragmatic in recent years, trying to deregulate the country's economy away from petroleum, via foreign investment, and to reduce cronyism and the rampant corruption among government officials that has embarrassed Indonesia's leaders and tarnished the country's image for decades. (Mrs. Tien Suharto, the president's wife, was once dubbed "Madame Tien Per Cent" by the Indonesian public.) They have smashed monopolies. Foreign investment, mainly from Korea and Taiwan, is rising. Indonesian labor costs roughly the same as labor in Thailand and China but produces surprisingly high-quality goods.

The country's manufacturing sector is currently growing at 10 percent a year. The war in the Persian Gulf has encouraged foreign oil companies to return to Indonesia, because of increased demand for Indonesian oil. A conspicuous absence of Chinese investment in Indonesia is attributed to the leftover sentiment aroused when millions of Chinese were slaughtered by the Japanese leadership, in the aftermath of the 1965 Communist coup attempt. The whole Chinese population of Indonesia was accused of being Communist organizers of the coup. Indonesians of Chinese descent wield great clout in Indonesian commerce. Two strains of Chinese people live in Indonesia; the *Peranakan* were born there and are totally assimilated into Indonesian culture, and the *Totoks* are newcomers to the archipelago and continue to pay personal allegiance to the P.R.C.

The Philippines: Thriving on Uncertainty

Since their People Power revolution in 1986, the Filipinos have proven to be indomitable survivors, enduring seven coup attempts,

The Ubiquitous Chinese

The "sojourn" of Overseas Chinese, called the *Nanyang,* began over a thousand years ago. Now, 47 million Overseas Chinese live outside of Mainland China; they make up 10 percent of the population of Thailand, 2.5 percent of that of Indonesia, and 80 percent of that of Singapore. They have invested in farms, rubber estates, copra plantations, timber, shipping, and merchandising. In Malaya, they became traders, supplied most of the mineworkers, and soon owned one-third of the mines. In Thailand, they have worked in tin and tungsten mines, on rubber plantations, and as shopkeepers and traders. In both Thailand and Indonesia, they have dominated the retail industry; in Thailand, 80 percent of the country's rice mills have Overseas Chinese owners.

The Overseas Chinese are not cohesively unified; among themselves, they maintain strong cultural biases and prejudices. The Hong Kong Chinese tend to view other Overseas Chinese as less worldly and unsophisticated. Chinese from Singapore and Taiwan privately label the Hong Kong Chinese as "carpet baggers."

Some of the world's richest people are Overseas Chinese. Li Ka-Shing, reputed to be the wealthiest man in Hong Kong, owns Canada's twelfth largest oil company and Hong Kong International Terminals, which controls half of the shipping traffic through Hong Kong harbor. Y. K. Pao, a Hong Kong shipowner and real estate financier, purchased the Omni Hotel chain in the United States for $135 million in 1988. Y. C. Wang owns Taiwan's Formosa Plastics Group, which had sales of $5.8 billion in 1988. Y. Z. Hsu, from Taiwan, has had comparable success in textiles.

In some Asian countries, most notably Indonesia, Thailand, and Vietnam, discriminatory laws against the Chinese have been ratified, not on racial bases, but to target them as capitalists who might monopolize strategic industries.

◆

a calamitous earthquake and volcano eruption, economic downturns, power outages, and strikes. Over 50 million people live on the Philippine Islands archipelago, and they speak over 70 mutually unintelligible languages and dialects. The English language was brought to the islands by American occupiers in the early 1900s, to replace the grating phonology of Tagalog (Filipino) as the language of business. In the Philippines, *pinoy* (Filipino) culture mixes with a long Spanish heritage and modern American consumer culture. A popular Filipino saying summarizes the

Asia's Language Blocs: The Key to a Polyglot Marketplace

Human divisions in Asia are less racial than they are linguistic. Over 1,000 languages are spoken in the region. The Sinitic, or Sino-Tibetan, category is the largest language group in Asia, and Chinese languages are the largest subdivision. More people speak Mandarin than any other language on earth.

- Mao Tse-tung declared Mandarin (*Putunghua,* "the common language") the national language of China. Dialects other than Mandarin—Fukienese, Amoy, Hakka, and Cantonese, for example—are spoken by 20 percent of the population. The Taiwanese speak Mandarin, English, and a Chinese dialect that locals call Taiwanese.

- The Cantonese dialect is spoken in Hong Kong and by most overseas Chinese. Educated Hong Kong Chinese usually understand some Mandarin, and speak English as a second language.

- In Indonesia, 70 percent of the population speaks Bahasa Indonesian. Bahasa Malaysian is the language of Malaysia.

- In Singapore, the government uses "China language" (Mandarin), but English remains the language of business and management. Singapore's multiethnic and polyglot population also speaks Malay, Tamil, and a number of Chinese dialects.

- Filipinos learn to speak Tagalog, the national language, and English. Filipinos are the third largest English-speaking population in the world.

- The Korean language is a member of the Ural-Altaic language group. It is similar to Turkish, Mongolian, and, possibly, Finnish. Koreans speak and write Korean, which evolved from ancient Chinese. However, during the Japanese occupation of Korea (1910–1945), all schooling was in Japanese. Most Koreans over 45 can read both Japanese and Chinese.

◆

country's three centuries of Spanish rule and four decades of American colonialism: "It was like 300 years in a convent and 40 years of Hollywood."

American culture and values have penetrated deeper into Philippine society than into any other country in Asia. The Philippines is the only Christian, English-speaking democracy in Asia, which may explain why the United States enjoys a dominant market share. Unfortunately, because of perennial threats to its political stability, the Philippines is the riskiest country in the region for a foreigner who wants to live, work, or invest there. As a result of Japanese firms' moving their processing and assembly work to the Philippines, foreign investment in the islands tripled during 1988, and exports rose 27 percent.

The Five "Realms" of Asian Business Practice and Protocol

Geography plays only a minor role in the cultural makeup of Asia. Although the region can be divided into distinct cultural spheres, including Chinese and Moslem traditions, these divisions do not follow national or geographic boundaries. Visitors may deal with a Malay *or* a Chinese person in Singapore, Kuala Lumpur, or Jakarta. In Bangkok and Manila, you will deal with a Thai and a Filipino person, respectively, as often as a businessperson of Chinese descent.

Businesspeople traveling throughout Asia will find they are dealing with five distinct cultural areas. These are *not* bound by geography, but by beliefs, behavior, culture, and social mores. These areas, which I call "realms," correspond nicely to the religious philosophies that have left their legacies in Asian nations— Confucianism, Shintoism, Islam, Buddhism, and Catholicism. (Hinduism, with its Brahmanic code of behavior, monotheistic underpinnings, and concept of reincarnation, has also left its mark in Southwest Asia, but, because Westerners rarely deal with Indians in doing business in Asia, I have opted for only five realms.)

Each realm has distinct business practices and social etiquette. Western businesspeople need to be acquainted with all of them, to effectively cross commercial borders in the Pacific Rim.

1. Confucian Asia (China, Taiwan, Hong Kong, South Korea, Singapore)

Confucian Asia is East Asia minus Japan. China, Taiwan, Korea, Hong Kong, and Singapore have Confucian-style business practice and protocol. I have already mentioned the influence of China on these other countries: they not only adopted China's style of government (the lineage state) and methods of rice cultivation, but these peoples also stand under a common umbrella of customary law and ritual. This code of law and ritual was spelled out in China's ancient philosophical literature, which originated with the works of Confucius (551–479 B.C.).

The Confucian *Analects,* a body of notes compiled by the philosopher's disciples, may have been the first etiquette manual ever written. Advice ranges from cutting food into small bites (so chopsticks can be used instead of knives) to receiving old friends (with joy). Beyond their advice on etiquette and ritual, the *Analects* propound the rules for governing oneself through life. Confucianism is not China's religion; it is a practical code of conduct to follow in everyday life, a manual for managing human relationships harmoniously. One core rule acknowledges that there are superiors and inferiors and states that superiors must act with virtue (*te*) and inferiors must obey their superiors. One should be dutiful toward one's parents and elders, reciprocal in one's obligations, respectful of human dignity, and fair toward all. Confucianism inculcates servility, frugality, abstinence, and diligence. It recognizes hard work, patriarchal leadership, entrepreneurial spirit, and familial devotion.

2. The Island Empire of Japan

Japan is a "realm" of business practice and etiquette unto itself. Although Japan's state religion was traditionally Shintoism, early rulers did not suppress Buddhism or Confucianism. Most Japanese are a Buddhist-Shintoist-Confucian blend, in their religious outlook. Modern Japanese put great stock in their eclectic religiousness. Factories have animistic shrines and protective deities. Shintoism contributes the ideal of loyalty to one's clan, group, or company. In the tradition of the Shintoist Samurai warriors, the Japanese value sacrifice for the sake of their leaders, whether in government or business, and apologies and atonement for one's mistakes or breaches of responsibility. Buddhism contributes the ideal of mentorship, in the master/disciple model of Zen Buddhism, as well as the ethics of frugality, silent meditation, and formality. Confucianism instills values of duty and family piety. Together, these value systems contribute to Japan's success and make Japan a unique realm.

3. Moslem Asia (Indonesia, Malaysia, Singapore)

The "original people" (*Orang Asli*) migrated to the Malay Peninsula from South China. Proto-Malays, who brought seafaring and navigational skills to the region in 2000 B.C., were followed by Deutero-Malays, whose farming skills and self-contained village organization were to influence Malay ethnic patterns for centuries. Their system of social custom and tradition, later given the name *adat* in Malaysia and Indonesia, is equivalent to the Western notion of common law. *Adat* culture became Moslem culture after the Islamization of the region in the 13th century. Maritime trade spread *adat*/Moslem culture as far east as present-day Mindanao. This southernmost island of the Philippines is Moslem to this day; the rest of the Philippines is Christian.

The Crescent of Mohammedanism was always mightier than the Cross of Christendom in Southeast Asia. As early as 1292, Marco Polo discovered Islamic trading communities in Sumatra. Islam had replaced the Hindu kingdoms of the region by the 13th century. The spread of Islam started with the rise of Malacca, a locus of trading and commerce in Southeast Asia. Malacca began as a market and a pirate center; its officials levied tolls from passing vessels, bound for India with cloves, nutmeg, mace, and other spices. Through trade, Malacca became the diffusion point for Islamic religion in the region. Like a gentle breeze, Islam blew across Southeast Asia and supplanted Hinduism and Buddhism. When Malacca fell to Portugal in 1511, it became the staging ground for Portuguese attempts to stamp out Islamic rule and trade in the region. Islamic leaders moved to the Sumatran state of Acheh, which then became the major trading entrepôt between Indian and West Asian Moslems. For the next century, Islam outstripped Catholicism in its spread over the archipelago. Where trade was conducted by Moslems, there went Islam. Islamic traders were the missionaries of the faith, and Islamic rulers, who were also the leading merchants and chief wholesalers, controlled supply and prices. Islam soon assimilated the region's other religious clans, often associated with Indonesian/Malaysian mysticism. Islam never actively converted these populations; it brought them into the fray as fellow traders.

Mounting resistance to the incursion of Western values since the 1920s has resulted in a revival of Islamic fundamentalism in Indonesia. Islamic values and precepts are used as models for society, the economy, and politics, not to mention business intercourse and protocol.

Whether in Malaysia, Indonesia, or Singapore, or on Mindanao in the Philippines, Moslem Asians live by the laws of the *Koran,* which forbids certain activities and declares certain food unclean. Moslem women observe strict rules as to their behavior, dress, and social roles. In general, Moslem Asians pride themselves on their loyalty and devotion to Allah and see themselves as part of the "brotherhood" that makes up the Islamic world. Islam does not separate religion from commercial activities or from politics and government.

4. Buddhist Asia: Thailand

Thailand is the only country on the Pacific Rim that is overwhelmingly Buddhist, which makes the country a unique realm. (Although we will not discuss its business practice and protocol, the Southeast Asian country of Burma shares many similarities with Thailand, including the fact that its population is almost entirely Buddhist.)

Buddhism can be summed up in one simple belief: "All life is suffering." The interpretation given in Thailand is that everyone should be tolerant and easygoing, because material things and personal achievement don't matter much in the grand scheme of life. One's well-being is more important than one's career position. One's economic status is the result of *karma* accumulated over the course of past existences. Buddhism's five major commandments are:

1. Do not take life.
2. Do not steal.
3. Do not commit adultery.
4. Do not tell untruths.
5. Refrain from intoxicants.

Most Thais follow all but the last one pretty closely. They live by the Buddhist principle of following a middle path, avoiding extremes in business and social life and in their opinions. Thais are neutralists. Because of their Buddhist values, they are frugal and they see time as cyclical, which diminishes any reason for rushing. Thais enjoy more personal freedoms than Koreans, Chinese, Taiwanese, and most other Asians. In Buddhism, life and work are separated figuratively and literally. If a task isn't a pleasant one, it's not considered worth doing; one's well-being is more important. This is not to suggest that the Thais don't work hard; they do, and this is one of the reasons foreign investment has rapidly increased.

5. Asia's Catholic Corner: The Philippines

Three different cultures coexist in the Philippines—Filipino, Hispanic, and Chinese. Filipino values are the result of centuries of village agriculture, based on tribal kinship; 300 years of exposure to Spanish Catholicism; almost 50 years of exposure to American free enterprise; and an enduring Chinese presence in every large industry. Although the islands' Western appearance and English-speaking businesspeople may give an impression that Filipinos are more "like us" than other Asians are, let me caution that traditional business practices and an indigenous code of protocol remain in place. A "culture capsule" in the following chapter explains why this area is a realm of Pacific Rim protocol unto itself.

CHAPTER TWO

Getting to Know
Pacific Rim Customers

On the crowded platform at Shibuya-ku subway station in Tokyo,
I was standing behind a Japanese schoolgirl. She wore a blue-and-
white sailor-style uniform. When I noticed that she was reading a
book in English, I peered over her shoulder. The title on the open
page read: "Where Does Pizza Come From?" Another title read:
"Why Do People Marry in June?" The book was called *New Light
English.* She turned the pages, reading eagerly: "Why is Thirteen
an Unlucky Number?" "Where Is Santa Claus a Woman?" "Why Do
People Shake Hands?" I thought about children in the West. Were
they reading primary-school Japanese-language books with page
titles like: "Why Do Children Bow to Their Parents?" "Why Is the
Number Four an Unlucky Number?" "Why Do Women Wear Red
to Get Married?" Among all my contacts and acquaintances in the
United States, I know only a handful of adults, let alone children,
who can read Japanese, and fewer still who could answer simple
cultural questions about the East. By contrast, from early in childhood, many Asians, especially the Japanese, possess a deep understanding of Western culture.

Is the West "Culturally Illiterate"
about the Pacific Rim?

Almost any book about running a business states the cardinal
requirement for entrepreneurial success: *know your customer.* How
can businesspeople pretend to *know* customers in Asia, when they
hardly notice the differences among them and don't comprehend
the stark contrasts that exist in their histories, values, and business
methods? To follow the first rule of marketing—to know the customer—in this region of extreme social, political, and cultural
diversity is no easy task.

A Pacific Rim Cultural Literacy Quiz

To measure your general knowledge of Asian society and culture, write on a piece of paper your answers to the following questions. The maximum point score is given at the end of each question. When you have completed all the questions, check your answers against those given below, and enter the points you've earned in the "Score" column. Total your points and look up your score in the rating categories at the end of the answers.

	Maximum Points	Score
1. What will happen to Hong Kong in 1997?	1	_____
2. What is the name of the most famous hotel in Singapore? (Starts with R, but it's not Ritz.)	1	_____
3. What is the language of business in the Philippines?	1	_____
4. What is the most prevalent religion in Japan?	1	_____
5. What is the only man-made structure that can be seen with the naked eye from the moon?	1	_____
6. What does *guanxi* mean in China?	1	_____
7. Which is the only country of Southeast Asia that was not colonized by Europeans?	1	_____
8. What is a "wat" in Southeast Asia? In what country is Ankor Wat located?	2	_____
9. What religion is practiced in Indonesia?	1	_____
10. What does ASEAN stand for?	1	_____
11. How many Overseas Chinese are living outside of Mainland China: 7 million or 47 million?	1	_____
12. Do people drive cars on the right side or the left side of the road in Japan? In Korea?	2	_____
13. What is meant by the Chinese expression "A nail in the eye"?	1	_____
14. What is the equivalent of a *geisha* house called in Korea?	1	_____
15. What Chinese dialect is spoken most widely in Hong Kong?	1	_____
16. In "The King and I," Yul Brynner played the king of which Southeast Asian country? Who is the current king of that country?	2	_____
17. Does one use a spoon to eat soup in Japan, or raise the soup bowl and sip?	1	_____
18. Is it acceptable to blow one's nose at the dinner table in Korea?	1	_____
19. How do they say "Bottoms up" in Japan? In Korea? In China?	3	_____
20. Should visitors expect to dine with chopsticks or with a knife and fork in Thailand? In Malaysia?	2	_____
21. In what country is the Tea Ceremony still practiced? Where did the ceremony originate?	2	_____

22. Should guests offer to share the cost of lunch in Korea? Elsewhere in Asia?   2   _____
23. Should travelers or hotel guests or diners tip everyone who performs any service, when in the People's Republic of China? In Hong Kong?   2   _____
24. In what countries are the following brands of beer brewed: Tsingtao? Kirin? South Pacific?   3   _____
25. Is it acceptable to mix other food with rice in Japan? Elsewhere in Asia?   2   _____
26. When seated next to a Korean during a meal in Korea, is it proper to fill (or refill) his or her glass? Pour his or her soy sauce?   2   _____
27. What is a *karaoke* bar?   1   _____
28. On the morning after a night-before social blunder, committed while intoxicated with Japanese coworkers at an after-work company party, must the offender apologize?   1   _____
29. Where is soju (a rice wine) predominantly served? *Maotai*? *Sake*?   3   _____
30. Should a gift given by a Korean friend be opened in the person's presence?   <u>1</u>   _____

      45   _____

_____

Answers: 1. It will come under Chinese sovereignty; 2. Raffles; 3. English; 4. Shintoism; 5. Great Wall of China; 6. Inside connections, or clout; 7. Thailand; 8. A temple; Cambodia; 9. Islam; 10. Association of South East Asian Nations; 11. 47 million; 12. They drive on the left side in Japan; on the right side in Korea; 13. A pain in the neck; 14. A *kisaeng* house; 15. Cantonese; 16. Siam (now called Thailand); King Bhumipol; 17. One raises the bowl with the right hand, then holds it with both hands and sips, or slurps to cool it; 18. Only if the nose-blower wants to clear the table and eat alone; 19. *Kanpai,* in Japan; *Konbae,* in Korea; *Gambei,* in China; 20. In both places, diners are given a *spoon and fork;* knives and chopsticks are not used; 21. Japan; China; 22. An offer to "go Dutch" is rude anywhere in Asia; the person who invites, pays; 23. In China, tipping is not universally expected; in Hong Kong, it is; 24. China; Japan; New Guinea; 25. Other food should not be mixed with rice in Japan; anywhere else in Asia, they may be mixed; 26. Yes; yes; 27. A drinking place in Japan, in which visitors may be asked to sing their favorite song; 28. No, because this behavior is somewhat expected; 29. Korea; China; Japan; 30. No; the Korean friend will be embarrassed.

Ratings—
Points Scored

40–45	Congratulations! You're on your way to becoming an expert in Asian business practice and protocol.
30–39	You may be prepared to do business like a pro in some countries, but you'll be handicapped in others.
20–29	You're off to a good start, but need to expand and update your Asian cultural literacy, to interact comfortably and avoid embarrassing moments.
1–19	Your hopes for business success in Asia are at high risk of failure; consider an in-depth study of Asia, before doing business in the region.

Westerners who do business in Asia learn that its peoples have some basic similarities but they have very different cultural characteristics. Anyone who serves Asian markets successfully has to be something of a chameleon. Most Westerners, unfortunately, take the view that the Asia market is the Asia market is the Asia market, and what difference does it make whether the prospect is in Korea, China, or Thailand. These same people would never announce a decision to "break into the Western Hemisphere market." Without specifying the United States or a regional American market, or the Canadian, or Brazilian, or Caribbean, or another particular market, the notion is absurd.

Westerners' perception of the European Economic Community (EEC) is quite different. To North American marketers, the EEC is a collection of highly differentiated nations and cultures. Most businesspeople interested in European ventures can easily answer: Where is the biggest bike race in Europe held? Where does the Pope live? Where is the running of the bulls? What will happen in Europe in 1992? Equally elementary cultural questions about Asia draw a blank look and silence. Westerners compare poorly to Asian businesspeople's level of cultural literacy about the United States. This chapter will help with cultural literacy regarding the Asia-Pacific, which will lead to better knowing and serving Asian customers.

Asians, Through Western Eyes

During a seminar that I conducted on etiquette and protocol in Asia, an executive in the audience asked: "Can't Asians at least meet us halfway? Can't they learn something about the way the West does business, rather than us learning how they do business?" The fact is, before the Japanese, Koreans, and Chinese began conducting large-scale business in North America, they *did* learn our commercial ways and they continue to study them. The 15,000 Japanese students who receive MBAs in the United States each year won't be looking for jobs with American companies. They're learning Western business ways in order to serve their companies back home. When in Asia, Westerners are on Asians' home turf. The Asians are often the customers, and the Westerners' product or service may be available from one of their own or a neighboring country's businesses. Why should they be expected to meet the Westerners halfway?

North Americans tend to arrive in Asia with an attitude that their way of doing business is the "right" way, and Asians' way is strange and bizarre. In their scenario, with some Western instruction and assistance, perhaps the Asian way will become less "peculiar," more efficient and *sensible*. Politically, everyone in the world seems to want to emulate North America; shouldn't Asians then have the same attitude toward conduct of business and international relations? Those who venture into Asia with this attitude can usually be seen leaving the region, face hidden by clutching hands, moaning, "Why is this happening to me?"

They haven't understood that business in Asia is conducted the way *Asians* conduct business, and that WILL NEVER CHANGE. North Americans persist in expecting Asians to someday *become* Westerners. Is this doctrinaire? Yes. Is it good business? Not at all.

Good Ol' Yankee Ethnocentricity

Because of a collective cultural illiteracy regarding the Pacific Rim, many Westerners rely on stereotypes and myth, when dealing with Asians. As recently as 1980, a majority of Americans surveyed in a Gallup poll believed that people in China had a higher standard of living than people in Singapore, South Korea, and Taiwan. In the same poll, which surveyed a national sample of Americans, the most common descriptions of Asia were: "crowded with too many people," "undeveloped," "[a place of] political unrest," and "dirty, with poor sanitation." Only 4 percent of the respondents thought Asians "peace-loving" and only 3 percent agreed with the descriptive "well dressed." The West has been slow to acknowledge that the East is capable of modernity. An old European adage seems to color Western thinking: "Nothing changes in the East. Better fifty years of Europe than a cycle of Cathay."

As of 1982, only one U.S. government trade representative could speak Japanese; in 1991, there were three, as reported in the *Los Angeles Times*. Numerous Asians have graduated with honors from Harvard, Yale, M.I.T., and Stanford, many with advanced degrees. How many Americans could even read the admission exams for Tokyo University? This state of affairs will continue to cripple us in crossing intercultural barriers.

The *Unreal* Asia: Famous One-Liners

There's little mystery as to the origin of warped perceptions of Asians. Skewed reports on Asia's inhabitants began when Marco

Polo visited six Sumatran kingdoms and wrote that one was occupied by men with tails! Sir Stamford Raffles, the father of Singapore, who spent 17 years traveling throughout Southeast Asia, labeled Islam a "robber-religion." The first Protestant missionary to Siam, Karl Frederick August Gutzlaff, said that the Chinese "delight to live in wretchedness and filth" and that they are "indifferent to religious principles."

The Myth of the Lazy Native

Malays have long been perceived as indolent, largely because they have not participated in business enterprise as aggressively as the Chinese. Europeans, who also became indolent in the enervating tropical heat of equatorial Asia, arranged for an army of local servants to satisfy their every need. Neither the British nor the Dutch were encouraging "native initiative" when they poured opium into Malaysia and Indonesia until as late as 1924. Across the South China Sea, Spanish colonialism, which featured slavery, taxation, and forced labor, crushed the Filipinos' natural industriousness and entrepreneurship. The Spaniards, who eschewed manual labor, sought noble status through the management of debt labor on *encomiendas* (large plantations granted to colonizers along with their native inhabitants), and encouraged gambling. In hindsight, Filipino "indolence" was passive resistance against a cruel colonial invader.

The "Yellow Peril"

The "ingenious Chinese" were respected early as the inventors of paper, pasta, gunpowder, the compass, and houses that sway in the event of an earthquake. But when an influx of Chinese immigrants threatened American labor, they became a "Yellow Peril." "The 'little yellow man' is . . . working ruin and desolation all over this great empire," recorded the minutes of the House of Representatives in 1886. The "Chinaman" smoked opium, played the lottery, and stole jobs, said the propagandists. To their credit, American employers and traders thought the honest, upright, hard-working, frugal, peaceful, and industrious "Chinaman" was good for business!

Then Hollywood took over. As portrayed on screen, Chinese worked in restaurants and laundromats, wore their hair in a pigtail, had big buck teeth, and gambled like fiends. They looked alike. They were daft, superstitious, lazy, and unmanageable, as depicted in movies like *The Good Earth* and *Red Dust.* Unlike the Japanese, portrayed as ruthless and cunning, the Chinese were redeemingly cute and harmless. China, according to the 1935 film *Oil for the Lamps of China,* represented hordes of easy customers eager for American products. Charlie Chan personified Confucian "wisdom," which he propounded in nongrammatical English.

Mainland China's propensity for countertrade and barter arrangements to finance purchases has, unfortunately, worsened foreigners' condescending perceptions. I recently participated in a meeting at which, in the presence of a Chinese businessperson, a prominent American executive asked: "How are the Chinese going to pay for this technology—with rice or what?" This type of offensive remark stems from cumulative misperceptions of Asian cultures. I answered the executive's question by saying that China's economy was the fourth largest in the world, and a letter of credit for $1.5 million could be easily obtained.

The Japanese have been popularly portrayed as clever and vicious, with eyes for world domination, as though the history of the 1930s and 1940s was a permanent rerun. Gilbert and Sullivan's "Mikado" is the best known example of "Japanism." Imported from Victorian England, this spoof of Japanese culture seems more comfortable for some people than realisms such as Japan's domination of the financial world. In the 1960s, jokes about "Japanese quality" were popular. Within one generation, Japan took the lead in quality products; rather than compete heartily, some Americans reignited fears of a Japanese "grand design" to dominate the world, this time economically rather than militarily ("They're still trying to win the war"). A recent survey indicated that many Americans still think the Soviet Union presents a threat to U.S. security; however, *twice* as many think Japan is more of a threat, economically. Increasingly, Japan is used as a scapegoat for America's economic problems.

Asians have long been labeled "inscrutable" by Westerners who saw no reason to get to know them. The current Western press, and even some authorities on correct usage, have fueled misperceptions of Asians by lumping Chinese, Japanese, Vietnamese, Korean, Filipino, and Cambodian communities under one label: Asian-Americans.

It's time the ethnic caricatures and generalizations held, consciously and subconsciously, about the peoples of the Asia-Pacific were dislodged and replaced with images and archetypes that are closer to reality. Asians are *individuals,* and cannot be filed under handy headings. This chapter aims toward an understanding of

Asians' unique predicaments, pressures, and values—and toward an end to stereotypes.

Culture Capsules: The *Real* Asia

I begin my seminars on etiquette in Asia with a series of "culture capsules"—nutshell descriptions of the historical experience and resulting values and national character patterns of each Asian nationality. I always give one caveat about the culture capsules: To discuss "the Japanese" or "the Indonesians" as if all people in a culture are exactly alike is patently absurd. Individuals are, by nature, unique. Generalizations never apply in all cases, especially when individuals in a country vary in exposure to other cultures to the degree that Asians do. *The following national character sketches are, therefore, only a starting point* for a better understanding of the personality traits of TYPICAL Asian customers—how they make decisions, perceive foreign businesspeople and products, and are likely to behave in a business relationship. The more "traditional" (unaffected by Western cultural influence) an Asian is, the more that person will match the composite described; the more westernized, urbanized, and internationalized an Asian is, the more that person is likely to vary from the composite. The culture capsules are intended as a point of reference for understanding the values and priorities of Asian businesspeople. (Readers with scores of 40 and higher on the cultural literacy quiz may want to merely skim the capsules for review.)

Culture Capsule: The Mainland Chinese

As the mother culture of East Asian society, Chinese culture was superior in every way. China's name, *Zhong Guo Ren,* means "the people of the Middle Kingdom." Their collective world view places the Chinese at the center of "all below heaven" (*tian xia*) and at the apex of civilization, surrounded by "barbarian" cultures that occupy the periphery. In Chinese creation myth, the universe was created by Pan-gu, a cosmic being. When Pan-gu died, his limbs metamorphosed to create the natural world. Human beings were cooked up in an oven by the goddess Nü-gua. Some humans were burnt black and some were underdone and turned out white. Those done just right turned out yellow—the

Chinese. This Sino-centricity would not have been destructive if China had not let its size, power, and influence go to its head. When the industrial age took hold in Europe, the Chinese refused to consider that the outside world might someday influence their existence. This is the Middle Kingdom syndrome. As the Japanese author Akito Akira has written: "Those who did not share the Chinese view were irrelevant to it."

The Chinese lost their elitist isolation when foreigners invaded and occupied China's port cities during the 19th century. Foreign subjugation and Chinese resistance to the Western technology being acquired quickly in neighboring countries resulted in a national feeling of inferiority in China. China refused, for example, to adopt the bronze cannon, which might have defended the country from foreign imperialist invasion, because to do so would have been an admission that China did not have technological, as well as cultural, superiority over all outside "barbarians." Delusions of "great power" status eventually gave way to a leap-frog mentality—an urgent pragmatism to achieve modernization overnight—among China's modern leaders. High economic growth and a higher standard of living have come to the Chinese, but money and resources have been wasted because of imprudent decision making. China suffers now from what I call "state of the art disease," a tendency to want leading-edge technology rather than appropriate technology.

Most Chinese remain distrustful of foreign ideas and culture and are suspicious of outsiders. For centuries, China has tried to acquire Western technology without losing the Confucian philosophical, spiritual, and moral values that anchor Chinese civilization. The Chinese have a word for the dichotomy between Western materialism and Chinese spiritualism: *t'i-yung*. *T'i* means "substance," "essence," or "pure values"; *yung* means "utility" or "means to an end." *T'i* is more prized than *yung*.

China's current policy is to acquire the technology of Western modernization without importing Western culture. However, the medium *is* the message. Fax machines and satellite receivers are contradictions of efforts to block out the values and culture that come over the airwaves. The Chinese slogan advocating this current strategy is *nei jin, wai song:* "Repression within, harmony with the outside." The collapse of Communism in Central Europe and the *perestroika* reforms in the Soviet Union have isolated China from the world community. Its current strategy has become increasingly risky to China's effort to become a key player in the world economy.

Against this background toil the Chinese manager and the bureaucrat. Officials know the limits of their turf. Provincialism pervades their country's economy and their government's policy; leaders in the provinces recently rejected Beijing's new Five-Year Plan. The Chinese are uncertain about the direction and pace of reform. Surrounded by political uncertainty and economic dilemmas, Chinese decision makers hesitate to take responsibility. The buck never stops. Typical bureaucrats eschew taking responsibility but love to wield authority—and obtain the fringe benefits that come with their jobs. Someone else higher up always has responsibility. Regarding authority, the traditional saying is: "The higher the monkey ascends, the more exposed are his parts."

The Chinese feel a deep compulsion to reach positions of authority because they are synonymous with gaining access to scarce resources. Power does not always equal responsibility. Because no one will take responsibility, decisions are often delayed; the early provincial system of time-consuming "documentary travels" is still alive and well.

Some highly placed Chinese officials, who have a reasonable fear of political reprisals, live by the Taoist credo of *wu wei* (activity in nonactivity): responsibility is to be delegated efficiently to underlings so as not to dilute the enjoyment of superiority. "He shall excel who never strives," Lao Tze advises; "Who strives shall not excel."

Chinese managers maintain a risk-averse management rationale. Given the unpredictability of political and economic reform in China, managers feel powerless to manage their companies. Ubiquitous party favoritism, corruption, and bureaucratic incompetence seed feelings that any new project is destined to fail.

A manager's wage in China is $900 per year, plus $300 in possible annual bonuses. This low wage is reason for seeking the noncash benefits obtained through *guanxi,* informal back-door connections.

Culture Capsule: The Taiwanese Chinese

The Mainland's mandarinate ruled the Kuomintang until its defeat by the Communists in 1949. Mainland nobility started arriving on the island of Formosa in the early 1940s, long before the final fall of Chiang Kai-shek. Taiwan's Old Guard has controlled Taiwan ever since. Although reforms in the 1940s broke the Chinese dictatorship in Taiwan, animosity between mainlanders and Taiwanese has never faded completely, even as Taiwan's population has grown from 8 million in 1951 (including 2 million mainlanders) to 20.6 million in 1991.

For four decades, Taiwan's legislature and National Assembly have been dominated by Mandarin-speaking parliamentarians (commonly dubbed "Old Thieves" by critics) set up the Nationalist government in exile. They have never had to face election, and they do not speak the Taiwanese dialect spoken by 85 percent of the island's population. Taiwan's road to constitutional reform has not been a smooth one; the 1991 debate over whether to hold public elections of high officials resulted in fistfights, on the Assembly Hall floor, that put two National Assembly members in the hospital. Happily, experts predict that a new, elected National Assembly will be in place by the end of 1991.

Mainland China is backward economically; Taiwan, the second most *cash*-rich country in the world, with $69 billion in foreign exchange reserves, suffers economic awkwardness. Subsidized loans, expertise, military protection, and grants from the United States fueled Taiwan's takeoff. America's role in Taiwan's economy can be expressed numerically: of Taiwan's $10.9 billion trade surplus in 1988, $10.4 billion was with the United States. The formula for the Taiwan miracle, as stated by Robert Elegant, has been: American aid plus American purchases plus Chinese talent plus Taiwan's Confucian work ethic. The average wage is now over $17,000 a year.

Most of Taiwan's companies are small family-run businesses. Their entrepreneurial, superresourceful, export-driven managers tend to distrust officialdom and are leery of anyone outside their immediate family. Most Taiwanese companies, often limited to family members, have between 5 and 15 employees. As Taiwanese entrepreneurs become more sophisticated and more global, the West will witness the further internationalization of Taiwanese money as well as accelerated, government-guided, technological upgrading of Taiwan's largest companies.

Culture Capsule: **The Hong Kong Chinese**

Hong Kong was the destination for Cantonese and Fukienese Chinese fleeing war, famine, and political reprisal in Mainland China, especially during the civil war that culminated with the Communist victory. Among those who fled were some of China's hardiest capitalists, and they found fertile ground for cultivating enterprise in British-run, laissez-faire Hong Kong.

Today's Hong Kong businesspeople possess a Western education, have a fully internationalized perspective, and have been thoroughly exposed to the West via mass media. They are likely to be well-heeled and well-traveled, and to have family members living abroad. Although fully acquainted with Western business practices and contract law, they share a business network with other Chinese inside and outside of Hong Kong, and conduct some non-Western transactions, that is, based on relationships rather than formal contracts. Victor Chung, age 45, is an example. He lives in Orange County, California, but travels across the Pacific ten times a year to confer with family members who run different aspects of the "family business"—30 small companies pulling in $100 million annual sales from computer assembly, trading, tobacco farming, and apparel manufacturing.

Every Hong Kong businessperson is preparing, in his or her own way, for 1997. During a three-year period, 150,000 Hong Kong professionals and skilled residents fled for safe haven abroad. The exodus of dollars from Hong Kong will come in 1996–1997, after another business cycle is completed but before control of Hong Kong passes to China. Although pessimistic about Hong Kong's future, most businesspeople acknowledge that they're powerless to change China's internal political system. Only 25 percent of the people in Hong Kong believe that the "One Party, Two Systems" concept can be preserved; 70 percent think China will not honor it after 1997.

Two factors spell doom for Hong Kong as we know it today. First, in China, decisions are made and materials are allocated through the back door, via *guanxi* connections. Second, power and politics on the Mainland are governed by influence and family connections rather than by financial contract and legal right, as in Hong Kong. These two fundamental differences between the societies will spell disaster. Former Prime Minister Lee Kwan Yew of Singapore fended off the influence of Mainland Communists. The Hong Kong Chinese yearn for a leader like Lee, to hold the line against the Chinese in 1997. Could Hong Kong renege on its treaty with China and arm itself for independence instead? China experts in Hong Kong point to China's population and army and say: no way.

Culture Capsule: The Koreans

Korea was dubbed *Chosun*—the Land of Morning Calm—in 2333 B.C. by its first ruler, Tangun. Unfortunately, the history of the Korean people has been anything but calm. Korea has suffered

a long and violent history of humiliating foreign invasions and occupations. Koreans are euphemistically known as a "people of
many sorrows." In their folk songs, birds don't "sing," they "cry."
Bells don't "ring," they "cry." Streams sound like they are "crying."
The relentless scenes of people weeping in TV and radio soap
operas border on the ridiculous. Where does this pathos originate?
A victim of its geographic position, Korea is a rabbit-shaped mass
of land that dangles like a piece of bait into the Yellow Sea on the
east and the Sea of Japan on the west. The country is vulnerable to
Japan from the south and China from the north. I doubt that any
other country has endured such a history of abuse and has still
achieved independence. The Chinese conquered the northern region of Korea in 108 B.C.; the Koreans retook it in 313 A.D. Mon-
gols invaded Korea in 1259 and remained until the Koreans drove
them out in 1368. Japan took its turn in 1592. From the 1600s to
the 1880s, Korea became the "Hermit Kingdom." In 1876, Japan
began to force open Korean ports to initiate trade; in 1910,
the Japanese took total control of Korea as an occupying force,
until the Japanese defeat in 1945. The United States then occupied the South (below the 38th parallel) and the U.S.S.R. occupied
the North. The Korean War (1950–1952) began when troops from
the North, backed by China, attacked the South.

   If one fundamental aspect of Korean character were to be singled out, it would be the ingrained value called *hahn,* the deep-
seated feelings of rancor, frustration, shame, and insecurity, bred
of centuries of oppression, that have given Koreans a national
sense of inferiority. *Hahn* has been harnessed by Korea's postwar
leaders into a tremendous national motivation to achieve, to save
face for the republic among the world's community of nations.
Koreans accepted the country's authoritarian government because
they felt it would bring modernization, power, and security—the
long-awaited national redemption. And it did.

   Koreans' work ethic is not Christian, Confucian, or Japanese in
origin; it is generated by *hahn* and it is found in women as well
as men. Korean women have suffered under foreign occupation as
much as their menfolk have suffered in the wars. For example,
Korean women were rounded up and taken to the front to be
"playthings" for Japanese troops. It is said that "the *hahn* of a
Korean woman can frost the middle of summer."

   A typical Korean is a complex cultural composite: Confucian,
Shamanistic, Buddhist, and Christian. Roughly 60 percent of
Koreans are Buddhist or Buddhist-Confucian, 25 percent are
Christian, and almost all of them remain partly Shamanistic.
(Christians account for only 1 percent of the population in Japan

and the figure is even less in China.) The huge, dark, Christian churches that rise out of the Seoul cityscape are startling. Christianity in Korea quickly associated itself with the independence movement against the Japanese, thereby winning hearts and minds. As a voting bloc, Christian Koreans will enjoy a majority by the year 2000, and their dominance will surely move the country toward democratic reform.

In Korea, the aristocracy is much more competitive and less unified than in China. Conflict and competition sometimes supersede harmony. Extremely class- and status-conscious, Koreans divide themselves along class lines; the elite occupy bureaucratic, business, and academic positions. Koreans' social stature is based largely on education and family ties, and fits into a hierarchy of dependent relationships based on loyalty. Good-natured, generous, humorous, emotional, sentimental, and short-tempered, the typical Korean views the West with some reservation and ambivalence. Koreans maintain a deep Confucian sense of duty to family, state, and company. A militaristic discipline pervades all levels of Korean commercial endeavor. Ranking and obedience to authority are ingrained early; military training is required for all Korean men.

Few Horatio Alger stories come out of Korea. Upward mobility usually depends on nepotism or personal affiliations, yet everyone strives to gain top positions of power and influence. Tenacity, talent, and hard work are needed to get anywhere. Only one out of four Korean students is accepted into the freshman class of Korean universities.

Koreans have discovered that the most secure jobs are found at companies affiliated with *chaebols* (corporate conglomerates). These firms offer employees lifetime employment and high social standing. However, antipathy toward the *chaebols*, which are family-controlled and highly favored by the government, has fueled labor uprisings in Korea since the early 1980s. Korea's manufacturing industry is controlled by as few as 30 *chaebols*. "In Japan, the company gets rich," says Choe Dong Soo, senior analyst and manager of Korea Investor Service. "In Korea, only the company owner gets rich." Nearly every Korean resents the pervasive power of the *chaebols*.

Culture Capsule: The Japanese

A metaphor for Japanese character is the *daruma* doll, a bottom-weighted papier-mâché figurine that returns instantly to an upright position when pushed or punched. Visitors to Japan's futuristic capital today find it hard to believe that Tokyo was totally destroyed two times; by an earthquake in 1923 and Allied bombings in 1942. Except for part of the Tokyo Station building, the red-brick buildings of old Tokyo have completely vanished. The Japanese are survivalists, as well as team players.

For the most part, the only language spoken in Japan is Japanese. The country is an island culture of almost total ethnic homogeneity, where collective unity is easily enforced. The Japanese pride themselves on the *uniqueness* of their race, to the point of harboring a *uniqueness* complex. Articles in the Japanese press state baldly that the inherent qualities of the "traditional Japanese mind" make the Japanese uniquely suited to perform production tasks that other national groups cannot. In one article, a tradition of cleanliness (inspired by Buddhism) and of discipline (inspired by Shintoism) was credited for Japan's prowess at maintaining the cleanest "clean room" for producing the most defect-free computer microchips. The tradition starts, one article contends, with the habit, taught in childhood, of leaving one's shoes at the door of one's home, and is symbolized by workers' nightly soaking bath in a deep tub called an *ofuro*.

Groupthink means team values. Japanese companies' values are virtually identical to those of the pre-Meiji rice-cultivating village. In a classic study, "The Spiritual Structure of Modern Japan," by Professor Kamishima Jiro, these early village values are compared with those of modern Japanese corporations. The village emphasized economic independence and self-sufficiency, through group solidarity. Shintoism focused villagers on *Matsuri*, or festivals, which gave group members a sense of emotional unity through strict adherence to ritual. The villages, like modern Japanese companies, were managed by a gerontocracy—leaders who had the benefits of experience and age. Elders are thought to be natural leaders; youths must wait until they are older and more experienced, before they are given their chance to lead.

Many experts, besides Professor Jiro, have observed that a Japanese company is a "secondary village" in its organization and system of values. As in the rice-farming villages of ancient Japan, tasks are separated among people who are bonded socially. They may drink together after-hours, recreating the festival-like atmosphere and togetherness that marked their ancestors' Shinto rituals. Seniority in the Japanese company is based on length of service, just as leadership in the early village was based on age and experience. The large family feudal system has declined, but universities and large companies have replaced it. Individual worth is tied to the importance of the company or the school, in Japan's economy. On the rice farms, everyone had to be a generalist and learn every aspect of the operation, from planting to harvesting. The same system exists in Japanese companies today.

Japanese workers and managers are hired into entry-level positions directly out of college. Pay raises and promotions are automatic. *Nenko-joretsu* is the wage system based on seniority; status and seniority are tied to length of service. *Shushin Koyo* is the lifetime employment system. Participation in after-hours gatherings with coworkers, to foster harmony and cooperation, is expected. Loyalty to the company surpasses the family bond. Workers take responsibility and then accept blame, to protect their superiors from loss of face. They know they can influence decisions, but the ultimate decision comes from the top. Because Japanese managers tend to originate from the rank-and-file, they know the trials, tribulations, desires, and dreams of employees.

Japanese managers make an active commitment to preserve harmony, through intricate social rituals like gift giving, bowing to superiors, and using honorific language to show deference. They keep opinions to themselves, rarely expressing true feelings (*honne*) and voicing instead *tatamae* feelings, those revised to harmonize with public opinion. Fearing exclusion from the group, managers concentrate their energy on saving face for themselves *and* their opponents and counterparts. Status, the benefits of high position, and seniority all derive from length of service. Japanese managers humbly decline to take credit for personal achievements, even when credit is due. They cooperate with their coworkers in every way, to get the job done without the boss's involvement in any mistakes and hitches along the way. Individualists are not welcome; every person in the group is responsible to lend a hand in achieving the group's objectives. Where do Japanese values of group loyalty and cohesiveness originate? The Japanese learn early that the whole is more than the sum of its parts. During the *samurai* period, Japan's *daimyo* led the *Ie*, a warring family, and would sacrifice all for the *ie*. Today, the *ie* is the company. All workers—like modern-day samurai warriors—defend the *ie*.

Culture Capsule: The Singaporeans

No people on earth are more willing than the Singaporeans to do business the Western way. Their intention is to sell to the West. Foreigners are likely to deal with highly educated,

English-speaking, ethnic Chinese who have a surprisingly cosmopolitan character. Although many Singaporeans feel Big Brother watches their every move, the level of government meddling in daily business is light, relative to Korea, China, or Indonesia. "It's a one-party state, not a dictatorship," says Robert Bradfoot, managing director of Political and Economic Risk Consultancy, Ltd., in Hong Kong and Singapore. "That one party runs the state very much the way IBM would." Only Hong Kong's government is more laissez-faire about regulating business. The typical Singaporean speaks English and believes Hong Kong Chinese are elitist for not doing so. Singaporeans, currently cash-rich, represent an untapped source of working capital to Western entrepreneurs.

Singapore is a multiethnic city-state where power is vested among those of Chinese descent. Fear and suspicion persist between Malay-dominated Malaysia and Chinese-dominated Singapore. The breakup resulted from separation of Malay/Singaporean Chinese and Singaporean/Malaysian Malays. The jokes still told about the "lazy Malay" hurt the feelings of Malays, who do work hard. Many of Singapore's Chinese worry that Malays are multiplying in number. (Some Malays believe this fear is behind Prime Minister Lee's courting of Hong Kong Chinese to relocate in Singapore.)

Singapore's leaders say they seek Hong Kong brains and wealth. Singapore's declining birth rate and increasing emigration to Western countries, where higher-paying jobs are available, have drained the country of many of its best thinkers. Attractive immigration policies are being offered to residents leaving Hong Kong, but most of them are heading for Canada, Australia, or America. They readily cite the drawbacks of Singapore: too much government control over business; too much restriction in civil laws; lack of freedom of speech; censorship of the press (The Asian *Wall Street Journal* has curtailed publication in Singapore, in protest); and a ubiquitous and all-too-watchful secret police.

Singaporeans realize they're rich, compared with their Asian neighbors, but maybe not as free. Singapore's social policy is anti-individual; the prosperity of society as a whole is paramount. The typical Singaporean is pragmatic, skillful, logical, and productive. Personal sacrifice to achieve the city-state's goals is emphasized. The enforced values are Confucian: thrift, industry, and social cohesiveness.

However, the government claims that Confucianism is on the wane in Singaporean society. The self-analyzing Singaporean intelligentsia debate whether the society should be founded on

Confucian values and ethics or on a more modern code. This question arises almost daily in the press, under headlines like: "Five Confucian Principles Our Factories Have Eradicated Completely" or "What It Is To Be Chinese." Professor Lim Chong Yah, of the Economics and Statistics Department at the National University of Singapore, alleges that Confucian business and social practices have been eradicated in Singaporean society.

Few would concur with him, however, when he insists that government positions in Singapore are not held by a privileged ruling class rather than by fairly and popularly elected officials; or that family connections do not play a significant role in company promotions to management level; or that Singaporeans are not reluctant to speak out and voice their opinions; or that there doesn't exist a Confucian-steeped scale of social prestige, with officials at the top and merchants at the bottom.

The typical Singaporean willingly trades some of what Westerners might define as inalienable rights, in exchange for an extremely high standard of living and a clean, crimeless urban environment.

Culture Capsule: The Malaysians

"Nothing much has changed in Malaysia over the last five years," said a Malaysian woman at the end of a visit there. She was referring to the country's development program, government corruption, and racial discrimination by ruling Malays against Chinese Malaysians. During colonial times, too few indigenous laborers were available to mine tin, tap rubber, or harvest the British plantations. Foreign labor, mainly Chinese and Indian, was brought in to help. The British left Malay customs and religion intact, except for a few offensive features of the culture, like arranged marriages and the subjugation of women. Malay rulers were allowed to hold their positions, at least symbolically. The British educational system created an educated class of the Malay elite, who, working alongside their colonial masters, attained positions of real influence in the government bureaucracy.

A Malay is a Moslem who speaks the Malay language and conforms to Malay social customs. The strict protocol of praying five times a day tends to unify each Malay with the community. Moslem laws are observed, regarding what is *haram* (forbidden), like eating pork and drinking alcohol, and what is *mukruh* (allowed, but not encouraged), like smoking, eating crabs and shellfish, and touching dogs (they are considered unclean). Malays hope to make the *hajj,* a pilgrimage to Mecca, thereby gaining great respect in the community. Education stresses knowledge of the Koran, but the Koran does not make much distinction between the sacred and the secular worlds. Malays are interested in trade and commerce to the degree that the whole community benefits.

As Moslems, the Malays are committed to the protocol of *budi,* which has two forms. As individuals, they observe *adab,* the responsibility to show courtesy in word, deed, and action to all people at all times. As members of society, they observe *rukun,* acting in ways that encourage social harmony in the family, community, and society as a whole. Asian Moslems are more passive than Middle Eastern Moslems. Malay *tid'apa* is the equivalent of Thailand's *mai pen rai;* both express indifference to the mundane tasks of daily life. "Malaysians and Indonesians, in particular," writes Lucien Pye, "embrace the non-Islamic ideal of tranquility and avoid agitating the inner psychic state of others."

Tell that to the newcomer Chinese Malaysians! They were perceived by the Malays as holding allegiances to Mainland China. The Malays chose to segregate the Chinese and Malay populations, because the small number of Malays would be threatened with extinction if the Chinese were permitted to become equals in the society. After the Communist Liberation in China, the political/guerrilla threat to Malay intensified and became the impetus for Malaysia's break from Singapore. Large numbers of Chinese Malaysians then looked to China as their motherland, and not to the Malay Peninsula.

Malay officialdom continues to discriminate against the Chinese Malaysians. Malays fill freshman classes at universities, and more qualified Chinese cannot find a place. In the business world, Malays will get the best lease locations in new buildings; Chinese applicants get what's left. Malays buy cooked food from Malay vendors, not from Chinese, out of fear of contamination from pork. Because the Malays believe the Chinese often cheat in business, they avoid partnerships with them. Strict limits on Chinese school enrollment, job availability, and government representation might be reminiscent of South African apartheid (which Kuala Lumpur denounces regularly), were it not for the fact that the Chinese prosper in Malaysia, as they have since Chinese migrations from South China to the peninsula began. The Malays administer the functioning of society; the Chinese Malaysians virtually run the business community and literally control the economy.

Culture Capsule: The Indonesians

Although Indonesia is the most populated Moslem country in the world, its national emblem, ironically, is the Garuda, a mythical bird in the *Hindu* pantheon of gods. Indonesia is mentioned in the Hindu holy book, the Ramayana.

Indian trade in the islands began during the second century A.D., and Islamic traders initiated commerce with Indonesia during the fourth century. In the 14th century, the Hindu Period had its Golden Age, and the religion of Islam took root in North Sumatra and later spread to Java. The people of Java, and its capital Jakarta, are almost all Moslems; Bali's 2.5 million people are mostly Hindu.

Originating from early village organization, the cooperative village harmony (*Mmsyawarah*) is imbedded in Indonesian character and culture. Tens of thousands of Indonesian villages are organized under the tradition of mutual assistance (*gotong royong*), a system based on an ancient model of joint responsibility and cooperation. When a person, family, village, or, for that matter, state, is in trouble or need, the people nearby drop their own work to give needed assistance, without pay or coercion. This emphasis on harmony permeates social, commercial, and national affiliations. *Suku,* social adhesiveness among all ethnic groups, was made possible by the tolerant, all-inclusive doctrine of Islam and was further guaranteed by Indonesia's fervent nationalism. Indonesians are Indonesians first and members of their ethnic groups second.

Instilled in Indonesia's population are the values embodied in the Pacscilla, a five-point manifesto for Indonesian politics and social life: belief in one supreme god (any god is fine); a just humanity; the unity of Indonesia; democratic rule by representation; and social justice for all Indonesians regardless of ethnicity.

Like Malays in Malaysia, the Indonesian Malays believe there are no "single monkeys"—people who are islands unto themselves. Indonesian Malays are nonindividualistic and cooperative rather than competitive or self-interested. They adhere to proscribed group behavior and individual duty (*fardu kifayah*). One duty is to never sever relationships due to altercation. Compromises are made to keep the group together, and materialism and worldly pleasures are denounced in favor of communal values. Indonesian Malays are against the pursuit of wealth and power for their own sake, but continue to believe in hard work, industry, and self-reliance.

Responsibility to family, friends, and community takes precedence over economic advancement ("People are more important than possessions"), and the deepest sentiment (*kesayangan*) is reserved for kin and other close relationships. Obligations toward blood relatives (*darah,* meaning "blood") are primary, especially in the parent–child bond, under Islamic law. Indonesian Malays have a fatalistic acceptance of their lot, life's events, and the economic conditions of their country. Whether a typhoon strikes or someone is late to a meeting, the comment, delivered with a shrug, is the same: "*Inshallah*" (it's God's will).

Culture Capsule: **The Thais**

Through the fortunes of history and the will of its people, "Muang Thai" ("the Land of the Free"), unlike any of its neighbors, has remained free from domination by colonial powers throughout its history. The French, who had arrived in Siam (Thailand's early name) by 1662, brought with them Roman Catholic missionaries assigned to convert all of Eastern Asia. The two countries exchanged embassies, but a nationalist plot in Siam forced the departure of the French in 1688. In 1664, Siam and the Dutch East India Company signed a trade treaty, but Siam sidestepped Dutch rule. In later centuries, a Chinese monopoly on trade blocked out the British, Japanese, and Americans.

Three things distinguish Thai culture: rice, Buddhism, and monarchy. Rice farming is the leitmotiv of Thai life and history; it patterns social structure and emphasizes group farming based on cooperative, voluntary village organization. Thais tolerate individualism, but find comfort in being part of a group.

Nearly all Thais are devoted Buddhists, which makes them almost inhumanly tolerant. The Thais are called "the Danes of Asia," because of their mild and friendly disposition. No one in Thailand seems to be in a hurry; like Buddhism's Wheel of Life, time itself is cyclical rather than linear. Thais accept the authority of those in positions of power, believing that these people must have acquired the *merit* to deserve such power, through successive past lives in which they progressed to a state of *karma* closer to Nirvana. However, Thais expect those in power to care for the commonfolk in the ways a parent looks after a child.

Thais are humble, patient, good-humored, and tolerant, and they live austerely, without ostentation. They eschew conspicuous displays of intelligence, wealth, or talent. They accept their lot in life; passing through this life is, after all, an experience that will be repeated for them many times before they enter Nirvana. Thais are considerate of their superiors and show them respect (*griengjai*). Separation of work from private life and family comes first. Thais maintain a rather short-term horizon as businesspeople, perhaps as a result of having concentrated in the past on the trading of commodities rather than the manufacturing of finished products.

A typical government official in Thailand is from a socially prominent family, received a master's degree overseas, married wisely, and has been hired into a position because of personal or familial connections. Recently, working for a private company has become more important than working for the government. Ethnic Chinese are present in all Thai social classes except those identified with government and military positions. Although only one out of every ten Thais is of Chinese descent, the Chinese control the business community as owners of the banks and prominent factories. Every Thai will admit that Chinese money runs Thai politics. For all practical purposes, then, the Chinese seem to be running Thailand. The Chinese have learned not to ruffle Thai feathers, however, and the relationship between Thais and Chinese in Thailand is a smoother one than in Moslem Asia.

Culture Capsule: The Filipinos

Early Filipino tribal society was organized along kinship lines. After colonization by the Spanish, Catholicism was superimposed on this kinship-based social system. The blood-brother covenant, when mixed with the *compadre* system of Spanish Catholicism, produced enormous families based on both blood line *and* godparenthood. Alliances were created among those who were related by blood and among those "ritual kinfolk" linked together by ceremony. Family and group membership was all-important, and exclusion from the group became the Filipinos' worst fear.

These and other ancient values survive in modern Filipinos. They respect their elders, defer to superiors, and show kindness and tolerance to underlings. Favors are reciprocated. Filipinos are group-conscious. They expect trustworthiness from *compadres* and kin. Family and group connections are relied upon to produce tax breaks, kickbacks, and elusive contracts.

This nepotism applies to politics as well. Corazon Aquino, who won the presidency on a platform of popularism, is the offspring of one of the largest sugar plantation families in the Philippines. Without family connections or political influence, an aspiring leader has little chance of success. The colonial experience of the Philippines included the electoral process, which was reinforced by the traditional patron–client relationships already present; connections became vital even with the electoral process. Filipinos say: "An American politician kisses babies. In the Philippines, we finance their education." The Philippines has been, and will continue to be, a place where family interests and national interests are too often the same thing.

To Filipinos, a sense of self-esteem, or face, is essential. *Hiya* refers to shame, the loss of face. Filipinos avoid conflict to avoid *hiya,* and they go to great lengths to protect others from *hiya.* Filipinos have a deep respect for fellow humans, regardless of rank or status. Even panhandlers on the street are rejected with "Patawarin Po" ("forgive me, sir"). The Filipinos' regard for self-esteem is mirrored by their code of personal honor. For example, *amor-propio* (love of self) demands that self-respecting Filipinos honor their guests with hospitality and not accept open criticism passively. To confront or accuse is to attack a Filipino's sense of *amor-propio*—a serious affront that often results in violence. Although Filipinos may feel a natural willingness to share within their group (*pakikisama*), they know that many relationships, especially those in business, involve debts of gratitude (*utang na loob*). Filipinos avoid people who do not reciprocate a favor (a *walang utang na loob*). They feel a profound patriotic duty to their nation, and they are willing to sacrifice for it, a feeling called *pagkabayan.* National identity, however, is marked by conflicting origins: Filipinos may not consider themselves Asians nor do they consider themselves Westerners.

CHAPTER THREE

The Six Commandments of Asian Commercial Practice

The American way [of business] is, "Hey, it's costing us $5,000 to $6,000 to send you on this trip; you'd better get the business." The Oriental idea is, "We're 2,000 years old, and we want to build a relationship and learn all about you and all about your facilities."
JOSEPH DORTO, CHIEF EXECUTIVE,
VIRGINIA INTERNATIONAL TERMINALS

Eastern and Western business practices differ in many ways. I've boiled down the differences to six Asian commercial practices, six "commandments." If ignored, these practices can sabotage any encounter between businesspeople from the East and the West. By keeping the six commandments of Asian corporate culture in mind, Westerners will sidestep many of the pitfalls and headaches they might otherwise experience in doing business in the Pacific Rim. To understand the rationale behind Asians' business behavior, which might, at times, seem strange and inscrutable, especially during a first venture into the region, remember that Asian counterparts are following these six commandments:

    I. **The collective comes first**.

    II. **For every person, a social rank and station**.

    III. **Let there be harmony (at least on the surface)**.

    IV. **No person shall "lose face."**

    V. **Relationships first, business later**.

    VI. **The rules of propriety and ceremony shall prevail**.

These principles are behind most of the Asian social etiquette and business protocol discussed in coming chapters. A detailed look at each commandment will show how unorthodox and out-of-step Western business practices are, when compared to those of Asia.

The Collective Comes First

The nail that sticks up gets hammered down.

CHINESE PROVERB

A friend of mine, John, speaks fluent Japanese and works for a Japanese real estate development company in Tokyo. When the company planned to build a hotel in Florida, John was dispatched to Miami to solicit bids for the proposed hotel from construction companies. The bids came in and the Japanese developer hired a U.S. construction firm to begin the project. Soon after, the developer pulled the plug on the American construction firm and told John to hire a Japanese construction company that had just set up an office in the United States. John and the U.S. construction company were shocked. The ground-breaking for the hotel had been covered in the press. The first checks had been cut. Construction was underway. The Japanese real estate developer didn't care. The Japanese construction company's price had come in way over the U.S. company's bid, but the developer was going with "one of our own." The developer announced that a hefty cancellation fee would be paid to the U.S. construction company, if it would peacefully walk away from the deal.

John returned to Tokyo to see the company's executives in person. He told the president of the company, "We have fair competition in the United States. You can't cut out the American company this late in the process or the government in Florida will get involved!" No one would listen. The construction would be performed by a Japanese company and that was that.

The most common complaint among North American businesspeople who have done business with Asians is that Asian business groups tend to be closed toward foreigners' participation in their business activities. Nearly every North American entrepreneur I interviewed for this book had a tale similar to John's, involving Asian commercial discrimination and exclusionary practices in dealings with foreign companies. These accusations were confirmed by the Asian businesspeople with whom I spoke. In general, businesspeople from the "realms" of Asia have a way of conducting business that Westerners don't share. The Asians feel a sense of comfort in doing business among themselves—not only with people they know personally, but with those who share their national, ethnic, corporate, and/or social background.

Asians identify strongly with their group, which might be their immediate family, kin-group, company, or ethnic group. They derive an enormous sense of pride in their unique national and ethnic backgrounds. When people from varied backgrounds ventured to the New World, they created highly diversified, melting-pot societies in North America; most Asians remain bound to clearly defined social groups based on kinship, village of birth, ethnicity, schools attended, and employer.

The ethos of collectivism in the region goes back to antiquity. The Chinese word for "everyone" is *daiya,* or big family; the Chinese word for "nation" is *gwojya,* or country-family. A clan *(hsing)* was subdivided into families sharing the same surname, and the surname, the group identification, precedes the given name—a reversal of Western practice. After their death, clanspeople were worshipped, as an expression of allegiance to the heritage of the clan group. In more recent times, Chinese clans became secret societies and, usually, associations of people who had the same surname. These groups are still popular in Singapore and Hong Kong and in some Overseas Chinese communities. Business relationships among members of these associations interlace all over the Pacific region; instead of a centrally located home office, their tether is personal and familial connections.

Asians depend on their group members for their survival; as independent individuals they are powerless, especially in the realm of business. Asian businesspeople are *team* players. Their success in business depends as much on group affiliation as on skill and talent; they must have close friends in high places. The highest achievers in a class of Japanese graduates will be hired for positions in business and government; the remaining graduates will pull strings for each other throughout life. In Korea, high school classmates, military cadets, and members of a university class become bonded for life; they will continue to work together as a unified group, regardless of their positions in business and government.

Here's an example of how tight-knit and pervasive these "old boy" business networks, called *Dong chang saeng,* are in Korean society. Korea's 1961 coup d'état was carried out, for the most part, by members of the Eighth Class of the Korean Military

Academy. After the coup, each member of the academy's Eighth Class, whether involved in the coup or not, was invested with power and clout in Korean society. On the down side, if members of a prominent group don't support a member of the group, they risk being rejected and being branded a *sangnom* ("nonperson").

Without membership in a prominent business group, Filipino entrepreneurs stand little chance of success. Roughly 80 Filipinos control 450 of the country's major corporations, and six families control 90 percent of the economy. The success or failure of a Filipino depends largely on access to this elite group of business-people. A Filipino, however, can expand and/or create a group by using the *compadrazco* system—taking on new family members through godparenthood. A godchild is called an *inaanak,* or created sibling. Every Filipino businessperson seeks to have a community leader as his or her child's godparent, because the relationship expands the parent's job references and political clout. I once met a mayor of a small town in the Philippines who said he had 739 godchildren! Bureaucrats in the Philippines are under constant pressure to respond to their kin-group and ignore the wishes of others, including their superiors. Filipinos use the term *pakikisama* to describe the human capability to coexist, to behave as comrades or brothers, to act together as a family team. *Pakikisama* requires the individual to sacrifice personal welfare for the sake of the society as a whole.

All Asian cultures feel a certain amount of antipathy toward those who break out of the group to pursue individual goals. In the Japanese language, the word for "I" is *watakushi,* which also means "private" or "personal." Its antonym, *oyake,* means "public," "the group as a whole," or "the common good." Thus, *watakushi* has a veiled negative connotation—"to seek one's own interest," or "selfishness." The group should come first, and individuals should place group interests before their own. The typical East Asian has little room to disengage from the social structure in order to become his or her own person or rise above a particular station in the group. Some people break the molds of the hier-archy, but they often pay the price of becoming outcasts. Even if they achieve great success, they are often never again fully accepted.

Fear of being ostracized by one's group is the motive for the rigorous process parents undergo in Japan and Korea, to enroll their child in a top preschool. Acceptance into a top high school and university is even more demanding. Once they join a com-pany, Korean and Japanese workers spend several evenings a week participating in drinking sessions with their coworkers. Two things are going on here (besides the drinking). Members of the group are exhibiting their loyalty to the collective by bonding with the other members, by getting chummy and personal. But these sessions coerce individuals into following group directives; to fail to do so would be to risk exclusion and rejection, something equal to leaping toward the bottom of the economic pile. A Japanese worker depends on the group for ascent into the hierarchy; workers who have group support get promoted and move into positions of greater prestige.

Asian business groups find ultimate expression in corporate conglomerates. These affiliations of companies and their suppliers (*keiretsu* in Japan; *chaebols* in Korea) are monopolistic industrial groups that wield vast control over the national economies. The conglomerates are cross-owners of each other's stock, which frees them from the management-by-stockholder syndrome of the West. Japan has 12,000 companies grouped in *keiretsu;* their sales equal 25 percent of Japan's total gross national product (GNP). Korea's conglomerates command collective sales totaling 90 percent of the country's $231 billion annual GNP. Because companies in a conglomerate are guided by interlocking directorships and often hold stock in each other, they enjoy a high degree of stability, which affords them the additional luxury of managing with a long-term view. Subcontracted suppliers that are part of these huge industrial conglomerates pitch in to achieve the highest possible productivity for the group. In stark contrast to companies in the West, an Asian company will lay off its workers and break up its group only as a last resort. Even during slowdowns, unemployment in Japan remains about 3 percent. Idle workers are transferred to other companies affiliated with the *keiretsu* or *chaebol,* a practice that enables companies in Korea and Japan to offer workers the security of lifetime employment.

Preservation of the group implies protectionism. Japan's fierce opposition to foreign participation in its economy has resulted in 1,000 times more Japanese money being invested in the United States than American investments in Japan. While Sony buys Columbia Pictures and Matsushita gobbles up MCA, T. Boone Pickens can't even buy a controlling share of a relatively miniscule Japanese auto-parts manufacturer called Koito Manufacturing Company. When Koito's president, Takao Matsuura, was asked by the *Los Angeles Times* (Nov. 19,1990) whether General Motors, the world's largest auto company, would get a seat on Koito's corporate board if GM, rather than T. Boone Pickens, were to invest in the company, Matsuura replied: "Very difficult. [GM would] find out how we receive orders from our Japanese customers; I can't imagine such a situation. We'd never let them put in an officer." That one statement says it all. The welfare of the group, in this case Toyota's corporate conglomerate, comes before the interests of outsiders. Pickens has now sold his 26 percent interest in Koito; the auto-parts manufacturer spent $14.4 million, mostly for legal fees, to fight him off.

The corporate groups travel well, as my friend John found out first-hand. Over 400 Japanese auto-parts makers flocked to the United States when the big Japanese automakers first set up plants on American soil. The *keiretsu* system is being brought by Japanese companies to foreign countries, and these companies will conduct business in an exclusionary manner just as they do in Japan.

Can a foreign company become an insider in Asian business groups? Yes; business success in Asia *depends on* becoming a member of business groups.

How to Gain Membership in Asia's Business Groups

- Observe the social customs and commercial rules of an Asian culture, as a first step in gaining membership in the indigenous business community. Many foreigners, especially newcomers, make the mistake of openly criticizing local business procedures—for example, the slowness of business decision making or a byzantine distribution system—and decrying restrictions that seem illogical and inefficient. Business in Asia is a personal, in-group activity that, until recently, was almost entirely closed to strangers. Great patience is needed. "Many foreign enterprises," says author Shuji Hayashi, "expect instant membership in a club that has been closed for centuries." Doors will not open quickly, but, with perseverance, they will open eventually.

- Contact an Asian liaison who can gain introductions into appropriate business groups. The pack of foreigners who populate the foreign clubs and spend their evenings complaining about the terrible business environment in Asia should be avoided. Social time should be spent instead with Asians who can act as a bridge to the business community. (Chapter 4 has more advice on using Asian consultants as introducers.)

- Avoid becoming a member of one group or faction in a local business community and ignoring the others. Connections should cross faction lines, and good relations with all of the relevant industry groups should be nurtured. Rival factions and groups may shun a Westerner who is close to their competitors. Feedback on responses among the members of the business network should be gathered constantly.

- Don't ask an Asian individual to act independently, on behalf of a Western company. By associating with foreigners (outsiders) too closely, an Asian's loyalty to his or her group (a company or a country, or both) may be questioned by the Asian's colleagues.

- Exhibit discretion and confidentiality. Asian "groupthink" can defeat Westerners in Asia because businesspeople connect *and* they conspire. No statements should be made in a person's absence that would not be made in the person's presence, and ongoing business discussions should be strictly confidential.

For Each Person, a Social Rank and Station

Among mankind there are necessarily differences in elevation; it is impossible to bring about universal equality.

I CHING

Most Westerners have probably heard that Asian society is highly status-conscious and hierarchical. Egalitarian-minded Westerners often forget that Asian societies place high priority on recognizing a person's social standing and behaving accordingly. In business, a Westerner's insensitivity to levels of status gradation can have disastrous results. For an American delegation visiting Taiwan, disaster drove up in a limousine.

The Taiwanese often use both a limo and a van for transporting delegations of business visitors from the West. The CEO of the Western company will ride in the limousine; the rest of the delegation will ride in the van. This selective treatment backfired when an American delegation, calling on a company in Taipei, balked at the unequal treatment. Its members "rotated leaders" so that each of them could have a ride in the limo. The Taiwanese were offended and considered such frivolity badly misplaced. The blunder was an affront to the hierarchical system on which Chinese culture and business are founded. The

American delegation projected itself as immature, insensitive, and unaccountable.

Early Chinese society was divided into four classes; from highest to lowest, they were: scholars, farmers, artisans, and merchants. China's rulers were chosen from the scholar gentry; the work of "brains" was thought more important than that of "hands," and scholars who passed a battery of examinations rose to high bureaucratic positions. Because of the importance of food, farmers occupied the second rung on the status ladder. Artisans were third; they produced necessary goods with their hands. Merchants, who produced nothing and were only intermediaries, were at a low level of the hierarchy, a notch above prostitutes and grave diggers. Merchants caught trading outside the country were subject to severe penalties. For example, the penal code in China during the Ching Dynasty decreed that a merchant who went to sea to trade goods, or who moved overseas to conduct trade, could be punished by beheading.

The vertical ranking of people by age and gender is a tenet of Confucianism. Women are subordinate to men, and younger people should obey and show dutiful respect to their parents and elders. Even today in Asia, age connotes experience, seniority, and high status, no matter how much actual merit the person possesses. In Confucian thought, people are not created equal; they fit into well-defined slots in an elaborately ranked hierarchy of social position and authority. In Korea, for example, *yangban,* the aristocratic elite class, is at the top of the hierarchy; *sangnom,* mentioned earlier, is at the bottom; and all other classes and occupations are positioned between these two extremes.

Asians' social position traditionally begins with early education and crystallizes before entry into college. Adults' social rank depends on family background, school attended, and employer's size and stature. Status orientation has so many gradations that few people will occupy an identical status position. Rarely will two people meet who are exactly equal to each other in rank and status; almost invariably, one person will have to defer to the other. For example, it is said in Indonesia that every person has a station in life and that no two Indonesians occupy the same social stratum—there are *no* social equals. "Everything [about Indonesian business] is patriarchal," an Indonesian computer specialist recently told writer Paul Burnham Finney. "You go to the 'father' to get things done." When twins are born in Thailand, the first one born is awarded higher status than the second!

Social ranking explains why Asians value business cards: they are a starting point for decisions on how much comparative status an acquaintance possesses and therefore how much deference is required. Foreigners, even after hundreds of years of economic intercourse between East and West, remain outside this status system. Little or no accommodation for outsiders exists in Asian business or social hierarchies. (Chapter 4 pursues this topic further.)

How to Plug into Asian Corporate Hierarchy

- Find out exactly where an Asian counterpart fits into his or her corporate hierarchy. This information will provide insight into the person's decision-making authority and enlightenment as to proper behavior when in the person's presence. The order in which an Asian delegation enters a room or their seating order in a meeting may indicate the rank and status of each member. Deferential treatment will be given to individuals of superior status and respectful phrases will be used in their presence. Informal channels might amplify data on Asian colleagues, including what exactly the titles on their business cards indicate as to their level of authority.

- Boost the status of any negotiators and expatriates who are sent to Asia, to put them on equal footing with a higher-level Asian businessperson. Letterhead stationery and business cards should clearly define their positions, so that their high status can be gauged quickly on the Asian side.

- Train negotiating teams to function in a more hierarchical manner than they would use in North America. Seniority levels and individual roles for team members should be defined, and the team should choose a leader or "captain." Other team members should practice *not* jumping in with their opinions and passing along all of the team's communications at the negotiating table through the team leader. Hierarchy should be stressed and the Western notion of majority rule downplayed. Team members should defer to the team leader in their verbal statements and in their nonverbal gestures. (Chapters 5 and 6 offer more points on communicating in Asia.)

- Emphasize any difference in status, whether higher or lower, between Western visitors and Asian counterparts. Social and business intimacy in Asia usually occurs between superiors and subordinates, not between those of relatively equal rank and status, who may be rivals. Asians feel more comfortable in relationships between persons of unequal status, with one person deferring to the other. Westerners are just the opposite. They feel uncomfortable in unequal relationships and at ease dealing with social equals. Westerners must adjust to being treated either as royalty *or* as inferiors.

Let There Be Harmony (At Least on the Surface)

The Chinese have been called the "Greeks of Asia," because of the widespread influence of their culture and values. The Greeks, however, sought *truth* in their philosophical pursuits; the Chinese sought *harmony*—harmony with the natural world and harmony among people. Their desire for harmony originated on the rice farms of ancient China and spread across Asia. The rationale was practical. Conflict, harmony's opposite, could reap disaster for an entire community; when people fought, they starved. Without harmony within a communal village, how could villagers unite to build irrigation canals that would conserve precious water? Without cooperation, who would tend the fields to prevent famine? To survive, the members of ancient village communities had to work together harmoniously. Throughout Asia, the need for harmony and an absence of conflict affected every aspect of village organization and decision making. In a crucial contrast, when pioneers conquered the North American wilderness centuries later, single-household families farmed the land, independent of their community.

In Asian commercial practice, the collective (the company) must have the cooperative effort of its employees if it is to survive. Conflicts that threaten to dissipate team unity remain unspoken. Bad news that is likely to disrupt harmony is suppressed. If an impasse arises, a third-party mediator is called in to resolve the problem through indirect arbitration; no one gets hurt or humiliated.

Unfortunately, Asians often achieve harmony at the expense of truth. At informal after-hours business meetings, Japanese executives express *honne*—literally, their "true mind." During the formal meetings, they express only their *tatamae* feelings, those acceptable for public announcement, and they hide all other reactions. Small drinking parties in Japan, called *nigikai,* often follow *tatamae* negotiations, to try to discover whether proposals are going to be formally accepted. Koreans use the word *hukmak* to mean the truth one feels behind the facade that is presented publicly. Rarely do outsiders get a glimpse of *hukmak* or *honne* when doing business in Asia, and this is a source of endless frustration for foreign businesspeople.

To preserve harmony in the decision-making process, Asian businesspeople usually approve or reject proposals unanimously, but only after behind-the-scenes positioning guarantees that no one will get caught taking a stand on an opposing side. Consensus decision making is called *nemawashi* in Japan, *barangai* in the Philippines, *pummi* in Korea, and *muafakat* or *musjawarah* in Indonesia. Most Asian negotiators prediscuss their bargaining positions in private, to prevent face-threatening disagreements from erupting out in the open, especially when foreigners are involved. Few decisions are made by a single person, without group consensus or approval. Teams of factotums negotiate positions and discuss proposals behind closed doors before the real negotiations take place. Small family-run enterprises, located mainly in Taiwan and Hong Kong, are an exception.

Nemawashi literally means "binding roots" and refers to the task of transplanting a tree. One digs a hole around the tree, gently trims the roots, and then makes the transplant, greatly reducing the shock to the tree by proper preparation for the move. Haroshi Ishi, Senior Research Engineer at Nippon Telephone and Telegraph Human Interface Laboratories, has given a good thumbnail sketch of the *nemawashi* system.

> Decision making in Japan is a collective process involving many people. The person pushing a plan spends a lot of energy to gain consensus before the formal decision. Before the proposal document is sent around, he explains the plan to everyone concerned at informal meetings and through personal contact. He tries to get the tacit agreement of others, and this effort decreases the possibility that the plan will not be supported. Getting a consensus beforehand is a key to success. . . . *Nemawashi* means that all the people who approve the plan at all levels will have the feeling of participation in formulating it; this makes it possible to implement the plan more smoothly.

The *pummi* system in Korea is patterned closely on the Japanese system; consensus decision making among Malays, however, is a shade different. In Indonesia, decision making is done through *muafakat* (agreement) and *musjawarah* (settlement by open discussion)—an onerously lengthy forum in which all points of view are expressed and then endlessly clarified and restated, until a unanimous decision finally reflects compromise by everyone. The majority does not prevail; the objective is to fuse all viewpoints. The final decision often goes in favor of the party who can continue to argue the longest!

Why do Asians use *nemawashi* and similar decision-making systems? To shield decision makers from responsibility. Because the interest of the collective is paramount, no one wants to take too much credit for a success or any blame for a failure. When the locus of authority is obscure, any one person or division in a company is protected from blame or embarrassment. The identity of the approver remains vague whether the outcome of the plan is good or bad. Bad decisions have a negative impact on a manager's career anywhere in the world; in Asia, it can be risky for a manager to receive acclamation as well, because the manager may appear to be "out for himself." An opportunistic Korean manager, for example, may become the target of fellow managers' derision, lies, collusion, and deceitful tactics, directed toward discrediting and dislodging the opportunist from his or her position. A revenge plot is called *moryak*. Once under group attack, the victim cannot expect colleagues' overt support. History provides a famous example of Asian-style collective decision making that hid the decision makers. Consensus decision making brought Japan progressively into World War II. During the postwar Tokyo war crimes trials, no *one* Japanese individual could be blamed for initiating the chain of events that resulted in Japan's entry into the war. Through consensus decision making, potential conflict and loss of face are avoided, and harmony among the team is preserved. No one feels left out *or* too much in the spotlight.

How to Play a Part in Preserving Harmony

- Never ask for a final decision within the context of an initial meeting attended by multiple Asian negotiators. A meeting with foreign negotiators is purely ceremonial, until proper *nemawashi, pummi,* or *muafakat* has taken place without the foreigners present.
- Don't assume overt democratic decision making by Asians, rather than the consensual decision making that takes place

behind the scenes. "How many of you are in favor of painting the factory green?" is a foolhardy type of question.

- Forewarn Asian negotiators by providing an agenda for an upcoming meeting. The Asian team will have to discuss any new proposal behind closed doors, before offering any feedback. No member of the Asian team will risk an improvident public position on the wrong side of an issue.

- Plug into the decision-making chain, to ensure that consensus making moves along quickly. A whole network of individuals must be massaged, to achieve approval on a proposal. Western buying decisions are usually made by an end-user alone. In Asia, three entities are typically involved in a decision to purchase: the end-user, a governmental body that oversees such purchases, and the relevant financial institution that is funding the purchase. "Push" (from below) and "pull" (from above) produce the synergy necessary to get a contract approved. In an ideal situation, the officials overseeing a specific industry in the Asian country are urging end-users under their aegis to acquire the Western product being offered, and end-users are calling on these same officials to allow them to purchase the product. Fewer government barriers must be overcome in Japan, Taiwan, and Hong Kong than in other countries in Asia, but the "push–pull" approach holds true in any country where a vertical decision-making hierarchy exists.

- Take care not to "go around" anyone by going directly to the person in charge, in an attempt to speed up decision making. The bypassed person's assistance may be needed later—and may be withheld.

No Person Shall "Lose Face"

What exactly is involved in protecting and preserving face in Asia?

- In Korea, a hard-working manager comes under attack and is brought down by a conspiracy of fellow managers, who disgrace him for trying to climb higher on the company totem pole.

- A Japanese distributor hired by an American company fails to sell the company's product in Japan. The distributor pays the U.S. company $100,000 a year on its contract, so that the U.S. company won't suffer a loss of reputation.

- The foreign owners of the Shanghai Hilton announce a party to celebrate the opening of the 20-story hotel near the Bund. They invite representatives from the construction company that built the hotel, as a special show of thanks. They forget to invite members of the Shanghai Tourist Bureau, who played a role in obtaining official approval of the project. Unfortunately for Hilton, the tourist bureau is in charge of arranging *all* of the foreign tours to Shanghai, none of which they put up at the new Shanghai Hilton.

These cases illustrate the vicissitudes of saving face in Asia.

In societies where collectivism (rather than individualism) is pronounced, exclusion from the group is feared more than any punishment; alternatively, respect and admiration are synonymous with power and status within the group. Face in Asia refers to the amount of acquired respect that a person has earned. In China, *mian-zi* (face, or reputation) is like a credit card. The more face, the more respect or deference is shown.

In Asian business culture, the will to acquire and save face results in tolerance of vagueness, untruths, and nonverbal messages such as long silences, in communication patterns. Formality, conformity, and mimicry of social forms prevent embarrassing situations that can rob face. Politeness prevents conflicts over issues involving the respect due to another person who may have more face, or more status. The result is that most Asians are extremely sensitive to criticism, especially when expressed in the company of their peers or superiors. They tend to conform to their group (for safety in numbers) and to wage conflicts behind the scenes. Only after an adversary is defeated can a conflict finally come to light—ideally, without loss of face for anyone. Koreans are said to fear loss of face (*ch'aemyon,* in Korean) more than the death of a spouse.

How Westerners Can Save Face

- Abide by Asia's rules of polite protocol; they exist to prevent open conflict and confrontation that can result in loss of face. Among the face-saving rituals and protocols that can be expected to take place are bowing, profuse apologies, formal turn-taking during negotiations, deferential but obligatory toasts at meals, and tedious but necessary company speeches and toasting at banquets.

- Conduct necessary "facework," to keep business relationships primed. Gifts should be given often, and respect should be shown to those who enjoy high status but lack what may be considered meritorious skills and expertise. If a business relationship must be severed, the Asian participant should be allowed a safe retreat, so that he or she doesn't lose face among peers, because of Western indelicacy. Above all, any breakup should remain polite and controlled, if for no other reason than to avoid a reputation as *bu gei mianzi,* the Chinese expression for someone who embarrasses others or causes them to lose face.

- Never reprimand an Asian in public or openly accuse him or her of a misdeed. *Malu,* an Indonesian term meaning to strip someone of face and status by denouncing the person in the presence of coworkers, prevents any later retelling of a face-saving version of what happened.

- Apprise your audience of your intentions through informal channels, when announcing new plans or making government statements. Any statements that might offend or embarrass anyone can then be reworded or deleted. Emperor Akihito did this recently, before making a formal apology to Korea, on behalf of the Japanese people, for the atrocities Japan committed against the Koreans during its occupation of their country during World War II.

- Resolve all conflicts privately, present problems without placing any blame, and be as indirect and inoffensive as possible when discussing problems or mishaps. In Asia, hints and insinuation are used for conflict management, not the verbal bludgeoning that heads the list of Western methods. More gets done faster, when no individual is made to look bad.

- Consider appealing to Asians to protect *your* face, in order to resolve a conflict. Herb Rammrath, senior managing director of General Electric Plastics-Pacific, accompanied a sales representative to see a Japanese customer. The customer had refused to accept a recent price increase, and Rammrath, like his rep, was answered with an adamant "No." As he got up to leave, Rammrath mentioned that his boss would be greatly disappointed with him, because of his failure to sell the price increase. The Japanese customer, sympathizing with Rammrath over his impending loss of face, said, through the interpreting sales rep, "Okay, I accept, but just this month."

Relationships First, Business Later

Fundamental sincerity is the only proper basis for forming.relationships.

I CHING

Most North American businesspeople think of building a "business relationship" abroad as a rather straightforward task in which any cultural differences can be easily overcome through informality, "eye-to-eye" talk, and having a few drinks together. In Asia, the meaning of a "relationship" is much deeper.

The government of ancient China depended on a system of client–patron relationships (*kan-ch'ing*) to maintain stability throughout the vast provinces of the country. At the village level, to have "good *kan-ch'ing*" was to have a sense of well-being, a feeling of being at ease, in a relationship with, say, a landlord. Those who had good *kan-ch'ing* would help each other rather than compete. For example, to get his rent, the landlord was dependent on the goodwill of the tenant. If the tenant normally paid the rent but could not pay the entire amount, he would open negotiations with the landlord. If there had been a drought or a flood, or if rain came at the wrong time of the year, or insects plagued the crops, the landlord's obligation to the tenant demanded that rent be postponed, as needed for the tenant to survive. If good *kan-ch'ing* existed, the landlord would not press for the rent and the tenant would pay up in bountiful years. Relationships and good *kan-ch'ing* remain vital in Asian business cultures today.

The Japanese concept of *kone*, like *guanxi* in China and *bapakism* in Indonesia, means "personal connections"—bonds that sustain an informal system of exchange of goods and services through networks of personal relationships. Asians maintain their business relationships through reciprocal exchange of gifts, favors, and promotions. *Guanxi* relationships among Chinese businesspeople, wherever they are located, can be described as ingratiating personal relationships that impose multiple obligations on the respective participants. These relationships can stem from the town in which one's parents were born, the university one attended, or a direct familial tie.

In the P.R.C., the entire economic system of supply and demand is based on an informal distribution network; the movement of goods and services occurs within a weblike series of interpersonal channels based on *guanxi.* The monetary value of goods is often subordinate to the clout one has, within the distribution network, in terms of *guanxi* relationships. These relationships form the backbone of decision making, promotions, and resource allocation. China's dependency on *guanxi*-style networking tends to reduce, if not nullify, official regulations concerning internal trade and economic exchange. *Guanxi* is the reason why managerial positions in China are filled with a family's members, friends, and coworkers, rather than with well-qualified people, and why many Chinese university students who are the offspring of high officials get to study abroad. Nonetheless, *guanxi* relations, like their equivalent throughout Asia, can make things happen when and where they otherwise might not.

Relationships are based on trust, dependency, and obligation, but reciprocity is their lifeblood. Asians carry around a ledger in their heads. They know exactly what debts are owed by themselves and by others to them, at any given time. The ledger of reciprocal debt never gets balanced; relationships are expected to remain in a dynamic state, with one person or the other always wanting for a favor, to be reciprocated at some future time. A debt owed in the Philippines must be paid back "with interest." Indebtedness *(utang na loob)* requires returning a favor slightly more valuable than the one received. In Japan, *on* is a favor granted to someone, often regardless of whether the favor is requested, that imposes a debt of gratitude *(giri)* on the recipient. *On* compels one to repay and, like *utang na loob,* can be a great burden on the unwilling receiver. The Japanese spend as much time giving *on* as they do trying to avoid receiving it. Receiving favors implies an *obligation (uiri,* in Korean) that must be reciprocated.

Duty and obligation generate relationships among Malays too, but these are not the relatively simply *quid pro quo* relationships of *guanxi* or *on–giri.* Most Moslem relationships are paternalistic, like that between the student and the Islamic teacher/priest, who is the medium between the believer and the divine. No set rules of obligation exist, yet the Moslem Asian can marshal great and impassioned support for his agenda, by calling in debts of those who owe allegiance to him.

When a reciprocal relationship includes a dependent and a bene-factor, it becomes imbued with what the Japanese call *amae* (*aniu*, among Koreans). *Amae* is the principle of mutuality that helps to make business transactions smooth; the same word is used to de-scribe the attitude of a child toward its parents. Any *amae* relation-ship involves a dependent subordinate and a superior—and these paternalistic relationships are sought-after, rather than avoided, by buyers and sellers in Asia. Sellers look after their buyers' every wish; in return, they receive loyal business from the buyer. Writing in the *Harvard Business Review,* Kuniyasu Sakai has likened the Japanese buyer–seller relationship to that of the ancient *samurai* warrior and his lord, the *daimyo,* to whom he remained loyal unto death. "From the day a subcontractor accepts the first contract—probably from a small subsidiary of one of the giant companies—it has given up its freedom, it is told what to make, when to put it on line, and how much it will get for it on delivery." Moreover, the loyalty and obligation run deep. Unlike its American and Canadian counterparts, a Japanese supplier will rarely accept an order from a customer's competitor.

Lingering personal or business debt is distasteful to Westerners, who consider such ongoing commitments to reciprocity an invasion of privacy and an infringement upon personal liberty. In the West-ern ethos of social equality, no person should be overly indebted to another. Because ongoing indebtedness of any kind is a cause for anxiety, Westerners tend to be "instant reciprocators" in business dealings that involve trade-offs. In Asia, repayment of a favor is always delayed, especially if the acquaintance or business relation-ship is new. To pay back a favor quickly is an antagonistic gesture, because it connotes reticence or unwillingness to become attached or involved with the other party and to forge an ongoing obligatory relationship. Balanced reciprocity implies that the relationship has ended, that one person or the other has opted to discontinue the association. By delaying the balancing of debt in a relationship, Asians sustain their friendships and business partnerships.

Some well-known Japanese phrases illustrate the point. *Arigato* means "thank you," but the Japanese often substitute *sumimasen* when they offer their thanks. Literally, *sumimasen* means "not yet finished," or "I am indebted to you for a kindness I have not re-turned." *Sumimasen* underscores the ongoing nature of a relation-ship by identifying the speaker as the indebted beneficiary of the other person's kindness. *Sayonara,* the Japanese word for "good-bye," carries a similarly open-ended meaning: "Until we meet again."

Asians perceive business relationships, and business contracts, *holistically.* One dimension of the relationship can't have equanimity, to the exclusion of all others. Here's an example. Japan has recently threatened to withhold further investment in U.S. government bonds, in response to trade sanctions proposed by the United States to counter Japan's continuing trade imbalance with America. From Japan's point of view, the underwriting of $600 billion of U.S. debt, mostly through the purchase of bonds, is reciprocity enough, in exchange for the gargantuan trade imbalance. American negotiators have resisted linkage between Japan's trade imbalance and the underwriting of U.S. debt. From the Japanese perspective, however, both issues are *inseparable components of the total relationship* between the two countries. The issues bear on each other, within the context of "trade" negotiations. In a business relationship, an Asian may feel the relationship is solid while the Westerner feels the Asian hasn't lived up to the letter of the contract. A wise Westerner will view the total collaboration with a macro lens when trying to solve micro problems.

How to Turn Business Relationships into Profit

- Foster relationships, connections, and the right friends and allies in the right places. Without them, a foreign firm has little chance of comprehensive business success in Asia. Foreign firms and their representatives are expected to build business relationships and networks based on *amae,* or the local equivalent, as Asians do. With a hit-and-run approach, a foreign firm won't be invited to enter into ongoing relationships and won't be able to foster *nagai tsukiai,* the Japanese term for a long and trustful relationship.

- Invest in people and in relationships with them. "My experience with making money in Asia," said Steve Willard of Willard & Associates, an international business consultancy, "is you go to Asia and build relationships first. You don't try to close deals and do things fast. You build relationships. You're helpful. You establish expertise. You take your time and you invest in people."

- Be prepared for a trial test, once you've invested in people. Sun Tzu writes, in *The Art of War:* "Test them to find out where they are sufficient and where they are lacking." Doing more than is promised on the trial test will go far. The trial test might be as insignificant as a $5,000 order, but that

$5,000 may become, over the years, hundreds of thousands of dollars in annual orders if the test is performed well.

- Don't introduce contracts and lawyers until the final phase of negotiating. At the beginning of a business relationship, they're secondary to the bond of *personalized trust* between the parties. A short letter of understanding, drafted between the partners without the assistance of lawyers, can serve to show trust.

- Perform favors for potential Asian business partners, to generate connectedness and indebtedness. Reciprocity is the key to relationship-building in Asia, and no favor is forgotten. Modern Asians don't consciously think about reciprocity in Confucian terms, but reciprocity and obligation lie behind most of their actions. Their response and their loyalty to serving the needs of a Western colleague are conditioned by whether the Westerner responds to them reciprocally—in a proprietary and civilized manner. The approach might require having coffee with a stuffy old bureaucrat before every meeting held at a certain ministry, thanking him profusely, and presenting him with a small gift. Walking by him to the meeting would be more comfortable, but he will almost certainly be needed at some point in the future.

- Don't rush to reciprocate favors; you don't need to "tie things up" immediately. A state of unequal or imbalanced reciprocity is expected. The future will bring balance through another exchange.

- Obtain references and solicit endorsements from Asian customers, to enhance trust among new customers. Asians do not make a habit of accepting business solicitations from businesspeople to whom they have not been formally introduced. (Chapter 4 has more tips about introductions in Asia.) Business relationships in Asia generalize across countries. A Malay Chinese associate may be able to connect a Westerner with a Chinese associate in Thailand or Hong Kong or the Philippines.

- Nurture and covet business relationships in Asia by visiting people often and keeping track of them as they move within an organization or from job to job. Asian business associates will be influenced by attention to their emotional needs. I have, at various times, researched colleges in America for an Asian friend's daughter, sponsored a friend's sister so she could emigrate to the United States, and found employment for the United Asian associates who have come to the United States to live.

• Remember that *price* may not be Asians' most important criterion in a buying decision. North Americans tend to think that they'll win or lose a bid because of price, and that a lowest-price offer will win a contract. To their consternation, an Asian company may pay 20 to 30 percent *more* than their bid, to purchase from a supplier that represents a personal connection. Buying decisions are based on a *relationship*. In a typical case, complaints were circulating in Malaysia about a Japanese company that purchased a $20,000 piece of equipment from a Japanese supplier and shipped the equipment all the way to Kuala Lumpur, instead of buying an $8,000 identical piece of equipment from a Malaysian company located in Kuala Lumpur.

• Ascertain what outstanding obligations are on a potential Asian partner's debt ledger, *before* entering a binding business relationship. The ideal partner to team up with is one who has a lot of favors coming in. The backlog of unpaid reciprocal debt may become an indirect benefit as the business relationship progresses.

The Rules of Propriety and Ceremony Shall Prevail

Do not look at what is contrary to propriety;
Do not listen to what is contrary to propriety;
And do not make any movement that is contrary to propriety.
                                                    CONFUCIUS

Early Chinese writings, especially ancient Confucian treatises such as the *I Li* and the *Ji Li*, outlined the rules of court ceremony and ritual. The Chinese word *Li* (propriety* or etiquette) originally meant "sacrifice"; the French word "etiquette" derives from

---

* To ensure a full understanding of the meanings of the word propriety, I offer the *Random House Dictionary* definition:

PROPRIETY: 1. Conforming to established standards of good or proper behavior or manners. 2. rightness or justness. 3. *the proprieties,* the conventional standards of proper behavior; manners.

the rather superficial "decorum." Since Confucian times in Asia, etiquette has referred to the appropriate behavior for specific types of human relationships; etiquette ordains how people of similar and dissimilar *status* should relate to one another. Politeness is a ritual of technicalities that choreographs, for public view, the fixed relationships between inferiors and superiors that are considered essential to the preservation of Chinese society.

In ancient China, the "correct performance of ritual," Lucian Pye says, "produced the highest type of power." Power and authority were vested among those few elites who participated in the ancient court ritual and ceremonies. A large part of the emperor's function as the "Son of Heaven" was to perform the requisite rites and rituals required of his station. Through strict adherence to ritual and propriety, Chinese citizens were inculcated with a sense of morality, a code of ethics, and a keen knowledge of what was proper. The Confucian code of ethics and propriety virtually abnegated the need for an extensive body of civil law in China. People stayed in line by adhering to the code of what Confucians considered "virtuous." A person imbued with virtue (*te*) had a conduct of grace and refinement and was completely versed in the rules of propriety.

Outside of East Asia, ritual and protocol are no less central to business and social intercourse. In Malaysia and Indonesia, equivalent tenets are based on Islamic law. In fact, the governments of these countries have had to respond to their people's demands for strict observation and enforcement of Islamic customs and practice—for example, separate dining areas for men and women at universities, and partitioned classrooms. Islamic standards are so high in these countries that the common people seem in constant apology to their superiors for possible violations of tenets of Islam.

Although Confucius advocated the making of money to the best of one's ability, he believed the proper bases for business relationships should be trust and righteousness, enforced by ritualized etiquette and ceremony. Commercial relations and contracts were to be based on deeper, virtuous principles such as probity and loyalty, sincerity, and benevolence as embodied in Confucianism. Business partners were admonished to be morally upright, refined in behavior, and strict observers of proper rituals and ceremony when they conducted business.

Given the Asian priorities of a hierarchy and the need to save face, it follows that strict rules of politeness and protocol will be observed by those who desire not to offend those in positions of authority. Observance of proper protocol protects face by helping to avert open conflict. Because loyalty to the group is dominant, the ancient rituals that instill the group with a feeling of cultural uniqueness will remain in force, despite modern influences from the West. Asian businesspeople have learned to do business in the West sans rituals and ceremonies, but they still play central roles in indigenous business practice in Asia. Rituals that express deference and respect to superiors should be learned and observed by foreign businesspeople who are trying to sell their wares and services to Asian buyers.

"Among the functions of propriety," said Confucius, "the most valuable is that it establishes harmony." The foreigner in Asia should consider the converse: the *nonobservance* of propriety causes discord and discomfort, and is felt subliminally as a threat to the collective. In Korea, a person who fails to observe proper protocol is labeled a "nonperson" *(sangnom)*, the lowest-level social Neanderthal. Part of the payment of respect and honor to an Indonesian is made by absorbing the many inconveniences the person might bring to the relationship (tardiness and interruptions) and the heat of the climate, among other downers. To fail to accept them without comment would be *kurang ajar,* bad manners.

North American businesspeople who behave insensitively to cultural creeds and customs find themselves barred from the networks of indigenous businesspeople who offer the connections needed to prosper in Asia. "The foreigner does not wish to spend his time in talking empty nothings," wrote Arthur Smith in his book, *Chinese Characteristics,* in 1894. ". . . [T]o [the foreigner] time is money. In most of Asia, people have an abundance of time and little, if any money." He concluded: "[W]ith [the foreigner's] predisposition to dispense as much as possible with superfluous ceremony because it is distasteful, and because the time that it involves can be used more agreeably in other ways, it is not strange that the foreigner . . . makes a poor figure in comparison with a ceremonious Chinese." He could have added "or other Asians." There is no need to "go native," but the unwritten local rules of propriety must be observed in the interest of cementing strong, long-term business relationships based on trust and accountability.

Why Participate in Asian Ritual and Ceremony?

A U.S. trade official has answered: "Asians will usually reciprocate what you bring to the table in *form* with the equivalent in *substance.*" (The italics are mine.) No simple *quid pro quo* holds true in all negotiations, but playing by Asian customers' rules of business practice and protocol offers a comparative advantage over competitors who ignore them. Participating means becoming familiar with traditional greeting rituals, Asian communication patterns, negotiating tactics, dining and drinking etiquette, gift giving, and ceremonial events, among other aspects of being a culture-sensitive guest. These are all detailed in the chapters of Part II, to help even those who are visiting the Pacific Rim for the first time to conduct themselves like Asia-Pacific commuters.

PART II

ASIASPEAK
STATUS—FORMALITY—TRUST

CHAPTER FOUR

Making a Stellar First Impression

> *When you see a stranger, suspect him to be a thief.*
>
> JAPANESE PROVERB

Picture yourself meeting someone for the first time at a cocktail party in the West. How do you form your first impression of the stranger?

If you're like me, you note the person's appearance and clothes, and you listen to his or her words. You respond positively if the person is affable and possesses a sense of humor; you sense honesty if the person looks you in the eye when speaking to you. In general, Westerners appreciate individual personalities and distinctive idiosyncrasies, and make a judgment as to whether a person is friendly and informal. If dialogue goes smoothly and a sense of connection is developing, we might then ask "What do you do?", meaning "What occupation or profession are you in?"

Up to this point, we have accepted the other person as a social equal; the person's business experience and family background have played virtually no part in forming our first impression. We already know we like the person, we feel comfortable with our social communication, and we only glance at the person's business card when the inevitable exchange finally comes. Our employers and the positions that we hold in our respective companies remain secondary to more immediate personal and psychological considerations, as we solidify our first impression of each other.

We couldn't be differing more from our Asian business counterparts.

First Impressions in the East

Generally, when two Asians meet, the considerations that form their first impression of each other are wholly different from those that predominate in the West. The importance of hierarchy and status, and the priority of social ranking, as described in the previous chapter, are played out when two Asians meet each other for the first time. Whether the strangers are Korean, Japanese, or Chinese makes little difference. Both parties need a quick definition of who has higher status and rank in the social order. From the moment two strangers meet in Asia (this rarely happens without a formal introduction, arranged by a third party), they must move fast to ascertain which of them has to *defer* to the other. Asians do not believe people are inherently equal, as Westerners typically do. The differing degrees of social stature must be revealed at the outset of the meeting, so that both parties will know how to speak to one another and how to behave properly.

The problem is best illustrated by language usage. Most Asian languages contain honorific pronouns and idioms of speech that attenuate the level of intimacy being expressed. One's speech must be geared to whether an encounter is with someone of higher or lower status. Asians use a host of different pronouns, when addressing people of disparate social rank, age, and gender. A Thai person, for instance, can choose from eleven different words for "you," to reflect the status and gender of an acquaintance. Anywhere in Asia, a bureaucrat who wishes to sever what has become a personal relationship with another official might suddenly adopt a formal and impersonal form of speech, when communicating with the official. The status adjustment is accomplished immediately, through language alone. Perfect strangers in Asia do not strike up conversations in bus shelters or bars. They don't know how to *address* or speak to one another, because they don't know which of them has an inferior (or superior) rank, or whether they might, by sheer coincidence, be social equals. When two Asians, meeting for the first time, cannot quickly discern which one of them possesses the higher status or ranking—and, therefore, who should defer to whom—explosive arguments can result between these two people who don't know each other at all! In Korea, fistfights break out between strangers fairly frequently, over this issue.

To measure and compare status in the decisive first moments of an encounter with a stranger, an Asian tries to answer a number of questions as quickly as possible, in an exactly reversed order of the social information gathering done in the West. The Asian asks silently, as the encounter proceeds: What kind of language is this person using? Am I being deferred to, or am I expected to defer? What level of formality is being displayed? Am I picking up all the clues of high or low ranking? What do posture and manners indicate about this person's social background? How deep was the bow or *wai* to me? Am I getting the disrespectful look-in-the-eye or the respectful downward glance? Where did this person go to school and from what city do the family ties originate? The Asian pays special attention to the stranger's age; the older the person, the more respect and deference must be shown.

Possibly the most important question the Asian asks is what company the person works for. A person's prestige rises according to the size of the employer, not the specific nature of a position; an engineer at Nissan may have more status than an astrophysicist at a small R&D company. The Japanese will often state the name of their company before their own name, when introducing themselves, especially to other Japanese people. They may not even mention what they do at the company; the more important fact is that they are members of a large and reputable organization. In most large East Asian firms, the length of employment at a company is an indicator of level of seniority and of salary, because length of service is linked to pay.

An Asian's schooling may affect his or her status as much as any other factor; school ties become business and political connections in later years. Speech patterns can be evidence of erudition and education level; the more educated a Korean person, the more frequently Chinese derivatives will appear in conversational expressions. A final status barometer is family and social connections. Koreans might even ask about a person's *pon* (ancestral home, where the family originated) and *kohyang* (place of birth).

Once the status difference is defined, the two acquaintances can communicate: a first impression has been formulated and an exchange of ideas can begin. In short, the purpose of the first impression, between two Asian strangers, is to find out where each of them fits into the group—their relative positions in the social hierarchy. In contrast, the purposes of the first impression among Westerners are to discover the distinctive personality traits of the individual as a separate entity *outside* the group, and to make assessments about the person's compatibility and commonality with oneself.

Why Sparks Fly When Asians and Westerners Meet

Can there be any rapport when Asians and Westerners meet, given that they assess others using such widely disparate criteria? Both parties inevitably try to reveal to each other aspects of themselves that the other does not necessarily value. The Westerner wants to show off unique personality traits; the Asian is busy explaining an employer's prosperity and a personal length of employment. The Westerner is flippant toward formalities of greeting and insensitive to the Asian's strict adherence to unwritten rules of social conduct based on rank and status. An attitude of immediate openness and informality may be underlined by casual dress, posture, and speech—all of which embarrass and may offend the more formal and introverted Asian. Moreover, the Asian recoils at the Westerner's presumptive touches—the pat on the shoulder, or the man-to-man poke in the ribs, as if the Westerner were a family member.

When North Americans realize that they are not "getting through" to Asians, they get irritated. They don't want to participate in mysterious and time-consuming greeting rituals, pointless nonbusiness conversations, uncomfortably long silences, and dealings with people who seem to make a career of acting distant and impersonal. The Asian, meanwhile, grows uncomfortable with the Westerner's recital of personal achievements. The Asian will not give reciprocal information until this new acquaintance has been proven trustworthy.

An Asian's trust may not be easily earned by a Westerner. Asians usually perceive Westerners through the narrow lens of stereotype, reciprocating Westerners' perceptions of Asians, described in Chapter 2.

"Homo Westernicus," Through Asian Eyes

On the surface, Asia appears to be infatuated with things Western, from high-tech to high fashion. Asians appear to envy our social freedoms and high standard of living, our advanced technology and means to high productivity. Among young people in Asia's capital cities, North America is a primary source of music, fashion, art, and literature. What could evidence this infatuation with Western culture more than the recent gathering of *600* Japanese press photographers at a Tokyo airport to greet Bubbles, Michael Jackson's pet monkey. Michael wasn't even there! However, Asians' animosity toward foreigners, and things foreign, coexists with their infatuation.

Many Japanese, for example, believe that Westerners, mainly Americans, are materialistic, coarse, self-indulgent, and luxury-loving. With their origins in formalistic societies that value self-effacement, obligation, and conformity to the group, many Asians feel North Americans are vulgar and crass in their self-seeking approach to achievement and success. Many Moslems believe Westerners are overly aggressive (because we eat too much meat) and take themselves far too seriously. For the Moslem, the evil triad of modernization, urbanization, and international commerce amounts to a genuine assault on the purity of life Moslems attempt to achieve. In response to the perceived threat to their cultures that is embodied in Western cultural imports, nearly every Asian country has, at some time in the recent past, mobilized "anti-Westoxication" campaigns, to prevent the West from exporting its vices, which range, say the promoters of these campaigns, from drug abuse to pornography, cigarette smoking, and smuggling. Even AIDS in Asia is generally thought to be a "foreign disease" from the West. The *Economic Daily* in China recently compared the threat of AIDS to that of capitalism, another "infectious disease" that is partly blamed for the 1989 protest movement in China. The "loving-capitalism disease" was described as *aizibing,* a homonym for Acquired Immune Deficiency Syndrome.

Americans' behavior in Asia doesn't always help. At the 1988 Summer Olympic Games in Seoul, U.S. athletes broke out of line during the opening ceremonies to wave signs that read HI MOM! I'M HERE, stole a statue of a lion's head, and kicked in the door of a taxi.

The Malady of "Asia Fever"

More relevant to business relationships is the way many of our business representatives pursue the Pacific Rim market. Their short-term perspective has become the germ of Asian business-people's most debilitating generalization about Westerners: the Western businessperson suffers from "Asia Fever," a tendency to enter the Pacific Rim mystified about the market and in search of the "big deal"—a foreign speculator in quest of the mother lode. Asians joke all the time about how Westerners are in a big

A Westerner's Checklist for a Stellar
First Impression in Asia

Follow these tips and suggestions, when meeting people in Asia for the first time, whether at a cocktail party or a business meeting, or in a formal third-party introduction. They will distinguish you from the stereotypes of foreigners that exist in Asia and will accelerate your acceptance as a foreigner who is willing to observe the local rules of social intercourse.

- Observe cultural greeting rituals, and exchange business cards.
- Remain formal with Asians for a longer period than you would with North Americans.
- Emphasize your position and function in your company.
- Seek common ground during initial conversations. "Non-task soundings" (also known as small talk) are no waste of time in Asia. Explore similar schools, technical knowledge, business experience, and mutual business associates. Forge a link.
- Conceal personal idiosyncrasies until the second or third meeting; don't strive for informality in speech, apparel, or posture during a first meeting.
- Don't ape an Asian counterpart. Be Western and be yourself, but recognize that personal assessments of you will be based on your status and position in your company, rather than your congenial and convivial nature.
- Include nonbusiness topics in your conversation. Your family is a place to begin. Inquisitiveness regarding your family ("Are you your wife's first husband?") and your income may seem intrusive at first, but don't register surprise or alarm. It is only an attempt to ascertain your status and social background. To find out whether you are *subai* (content with life), a Thai might ask you about your health and personal happiness—questions that catch some foreigners off-guard. Ask the same type of questions in response, but be prepared for Japanese and Koreans to be more reserved in discussing family matters than are other Asians.
- Be selective, when narrating your past. Asians are sometimes perplexed when a North American describes his or her family situation, which may be unorthodox from an Asian perspective. My own experience is a case in point. My parents divorced when I was young. Both remarried, and now the two couples socialize together regularly. Asians get rattled, when I try to explain this situation. Their replies are usually along the lines of, "Americans are very open." I never can tell whether they

mean that my four parents are open-minded and experimental or that *I* am too open, in revealing my background. A North American telling a tale about his third wife might elicit a similar reaction.

- Don't name-drop in Asia. Businesspeople in North America do it to impress and find common ground with new acquaintances. Koreans are especially sensitive to name-dropping, because they consider names private and sacred. If you want to drop a name, describe the company you have dealt with, and let your Asian acquaintance ask whom you know at the firm.

◆

hurry, and bent on *extracting* short-term benefits from business opportunities rather than collaborating with business partners over the long term. "I think Americans are very McDonaldized," says Jimmy Lai, a prominent Hong Kong businessman and founder of the Giordano clothing store chain. "If they're hungry, they want to eat right away. Whatever they want to do, they want results right away." North Americans tend to seek deals that can be concluded quickly, effortlessly, and inexpensively.

Japanese business suitors in Asia, by and large, are willing to spend the time, energy, and money to get to know Asian customers and their specific needs, often making repeated visits in their effort to win a contract. Conversely, we are perceived as being in Asia only temporarily, for short assignments or a business stopover. The Hong Kong Chinese complain: "Too many North Americans take the 'seagull approach' in Asia. They send a marketing guy who flies over here, soils up the coast, and then flies away."

Business Matchmaking in the Pacific Rim

A consultant with a Canadian real estate firm attended one of my seminars and later asked me for advice in dealing with a number of Hong Kong real estate companies that had remained reticent to hire him as a marketing consultant. He articulated his frustration at not getting hired by the Hong Kong Chinese whom he had dealt with at these companies. I asked whether he knew any of these people from past business endeavors or social ties. He said "No." He had met with the Hong Kong representatives periodically, and they had inquired about his services; he made a sales presentation and quoted them his price. He was at a loss as to why he had not been hired. My advice was simple: "Do a freebie for one of these Hong Kong guys, in order to get a reference." Without an introductory reference that he could use in pitching his services to Hong Kong's tight-knit real estate community, he was never going to be hired. He was still an outsider.

The same general advice applies to all industries in every country of Asia. Personal introductions and references *must come from other Asians* in the business community. No Western business will get very far without them.

"Networking" and "Cold Calling": Dirty Words

The only way to expand a business network and appropriate social milieu in Asia is via formal introduction by an Asian counterpart who sees a clear purpose in making the introduction. The Western phenomenon of business networking (attending cocktail parties and meeting business partners) is only nascent in most of Asia. Business connections occur at the initiation of an Asian associate—usually a friend who can trust the Westerner's handling of the meeting, and who knows what opportunities are appropriate and compatible with the Westerner's interests. Introductions are not made lightly; they are made for a reason. The more reasons Asian colleagues see, for introductions to others, the better off the Westerner will be. Cold-calling potential customers is a strictly Western business practice. Author Robert Marsh's advice about cold-call introductions in Japan is valid for Asia in general: "Cold contacts, without a proper introduction and out of the blue, are not effective with the Japanese. Someone reputable should introduce you, speak on your behalf, say who you are, emphasize your advantages and interests."

Introductions: A Grave Responsibility

Asians take any introduction very seriously. The business relationship generated by a formal introduction reflects on the personal integrity of the introducer. An American businessman recently bungled a real estate deal in Asia. To save his own face, the Asian introducer was impelled to pay back all of the losses incurred by the Asian associates (friends) to whom he had introduced the American. The American is still considered a friend, but his Asian counterpart no longer introduces him to *anyone;* the

American can't figure out why he's not getting any more referrals. The word is out: he can't be trusted.

Sometimes, before introducing someone, the Asian introducer (often a close friend) may state that the credibility of the other party can't be guaranteed and that the introducer won't be taking responsibility for the relationship that might be forged. If a contact, or even a close friend, sees no reason why a particular Westerner and a particular stranger should be introduced, the introduction won't happen. Comfortable? No. Part of introduction protocol in Asia? Yes.

Consultants as Matchmakers

A consultant can be a good liaison, but Westerners must beware of the "chopstick syndrome," the tendency to hire an Asian person to represent a company because "he has a cousin in Taipei" or "his uncle is well-connected in Kuala Lumpur." A consultant should be hired because of the person's verifiable potential to introduce a company to the highest echelon of potential customers and relevant government officials. A consultant's value should not be measured by estimated *costs,* but by the estimated *savings* of money, time, and resources spent on gaining fast entry into a desired Pacific Rim market.

An example from my own experience illustrates how a trained consultant/introducer can be a valuable asset to a company. As a manufacturer's agent for a large American company, I decided to attend a "Purchasing Mission" from an East Asian country, for the purpose of introducing to potential Asian customers the high-tech products that I represented. I solicited the assistance of a consultant (who was also an old friend). He had been raised in the country from which the mission was coming, and he had connections with the country's consulate, a cosponsor of the mission. Before the arrival of the mission, he set up a formal meeting with the visiting delegation, to be held, in private, after an opening VIP reception. The conference started the next day, and it soon became apparent that the most important Asians were suspiciously absent. "Plane delayed," was the excuse. The American executives who had paid to attend were irate. The delegation finally arrived late in the afternoon, and our meeting was held as preplanned. We made great strides in setting up a major purchase of products, all because of the prior arrangements made by my well-connected consultant. (The delegation hadn't been delayed at all. They had made a stop in Las Vegas en route to the conference!)

Etiquette for Introducing Others in Asia

- Introduce two people to each other in Asia only when there is a clear purpose for making the introduction.

- Don't introduce high-status Asians to low-status Asians (drivers, servants, and secretaries, for example) unless there is a clear purpose for doing so: "Mr. Kim will be your exclusive driver during your stay here, and I thought that I should introduce him to you."

- Remember that names are personal and private. A Korean, for example, may not say the Westerner's name, during an introduction to another Korean. The Westerner is expected to take over the introduction once the Korean has stated a place of origin and an occupation or status. When more than two Koreans meet, the persons who don't know one of the other parties will be asked, by the person they know, to introduce themselves. They will then say their names and pass their cards to the stranger, whose name is not uttered by the "introducer."

Demystifying Pacific Rim Greeting Rituals

Business greetings in Asia can become awkward. The Asian will be trying to effect a Western-style greeting, and the Westerner, an Asian-style greeting. Both acquaintances may appear clumsy and feel uncomfortable. A Japanese person initiates the handshake of the informal West just as the Westerner tries out a carefully practiced bow. The hand coming up meets the head going down, and both greeters, feeling stiff and goofy, try to recover from the cartoon scene they've just played out.

The first time I introduced an American executive to one of his Korean counterparts, I spent 45 minutes preparing the American to meet the Korean in the traditional manner: bowing, passing his business card with both hands, speaking quietly, averting constant and direct eye contact, sitting straight in his chair, with his feet on the floor, controlling wild arm gestures, and so on. When we arrived, Mr. Kim emerged from the entrance to his company dressed in a Western suit; he smiled and reached out to shake hands with my well-prepared client. "How are you doing? Nice to see you!" Mr. Kim observed none of the traditional Korean formalities my client had rehearsed; he was completely adept at dealing with Westerners and had spent much time in the United States. However, many Asian businesspeople possess no international perspective, and will expect to be greeted in the style that is familiar to them. A savvy Westerner will be prepared to greet Asians in both the Western way and the Asian way, and will be flexible about which one suits an occasion.

Greeting People Asian-Style

- Step back, if necessary, to allow a two-to-three-foot greeting space. Say "Hello, it is nice to meet you," or the equivalent, in English or in the local language. (See Key Phrases . . . on page 99.) State your name and company. If another person has begun the introduction, state your name and company anyway, because an Asian introducer may NOT state your complete name when introducing you. Then bow, if you are in Japan or Korea; *wai,* if in Thailand; *salaam,* if meeting a Malay; or *namaste* if meeting an Indian. (These gestures are explained below.) The Western handshake may be substituted for these traditional greeting gestures; take a cue from others present and from the person you are meeting. Don't be alarmed if your Asian acquaintance, imitating other Westerners, grabs your hand firmly and says heartily, "Hi there, I'm Mr. So-and-So. Nice to meet you!" This practice spreads with every passing day in Asia.

- Pull out your business-card case (a nice new one, made of rawhide) from your shirt pocket or inside coat pocket. Don't carry your cards in a wallet in your pants pocket or bury them in a travel case. Pull out one of your cards, hold the case in the palm of one hand, and offer the card with the fingers of both hands. Your new acquaintance should receive your card with its printing presented for reading (upside-down to you). Take your new acquaintance's card with both hands and continue to hold it with two hands as you read it. Read all of it, and indicate that you are impressed with the person's job title; your acknowledgment of the implied status is a compliment and a courteous gesture. In Japan, new acquaintances are flattered when someone admires a person's job position, an eloquent phrase, or a remarkable achievement, by uttering a long *"hai . . .,"* in comprehending acknowledgment.

- Spark conversation using the information on the person's business card, referring to the company, the job function, or the company's location. Don't leap into an informal Western-style conversation revolving around current events, your impressions of the person's country, or a joke you heard recently. Stay close to the cards at the outset. Try to avoid asking the person to repeat his or her name, if you did not hear all of its syllables. Unless the name is a phonics puzzle and a mispronunciation may be offensive, read the name aloud from the business card, and then ask whether you have pronounced it correctly. (Asians may have trouble pronouncing your name; North Americans have many countries of origin and, consequently, many variations of multisyllabic names. Say your name clearly, when you introduce yourself. Asians will be equally reluctant to ask for a repeat pronunciation.)

- After conversation has been ignited from information on the business cards, place your new acquaintance's card carefully in your card case, for safekeeping. If you've met a group of people in a meeting room, I recommend spreading their business cards in front of you on the table, in an arrangement that corresponds to their seating locations. Addressing each person by name is easier, with the cards for reference. Avoid scribbling notes on others' business cards, and don't fiddle with them or shuffle them disrespectfully.

Addressing Asians by Their Proper Titles

An Asian businessperson's title should be used whenever possible. In polite usage, "you" as an address is limited, especially with executives, PhDs, and medical doctors. Instead, "President Kim," "Dr. Wang," "Director Liu," and so on, is proper, even when a first-name address is used in return. Asians realize that, in Western society, a person is addressed by given name, after initial formality wears off, but the practice in most of Asia is to address colleagues using their surname indefinitely, and Westerners should not cross over to first-name address. If an Asian acquaintance prefers "President Smith" or "Mr. Smith," then "Call me Sam" may be seen as denigrating the Westerner's status. Public officials in the Philippines may not be addressed by their names at all; only titles are allowed: "Mr. Secretary," or "Mr. Mayor," or, for the wife of the latter, "Mrs. Mayor"!

A special note: In Thailand, a royal title may appear after a name on a business card. P.O.C. *(Phra Ong Chao)* stands for "grandchild

When, Where, and How to Bow

When a person bows in East Asia, he or she may be expressing, to another person, gratitude, devotion, congratulations, sympathy, loyal service, or apology, or may be simply saying hello or goodbye. The ritual of bowing imbues any event or encounter with formality and ceremony. Bowing is most prevalent in Korea and Japan, and, to a much lesser extent, among traditionally minded Chinese in China and Taiwan. Businesspeople in Singapore do not bow. Bank customers in Japan are bowed to as they approach a teller; a Japanese person may bow into the phone when talking to a superior! A shopper may be bowed to by an employee at the entrance to a Japanese department store. (Japanese-owned stores in Singapore tried to transfer the tradition to their stores there, but Singaporean customers reacted negatively to such obsequiousness, preferring lower prices instead.)

Rather than bow to Westerners, most East Asians will greet them with a handshake and what I call a "shadow bow," a slight dip of the head and shoulders. Most Western executives play it safe and use the shadow bow rather than a full-fledged bow. Korean and Japanese businesspeople formally bow to each other and to Westerners who speak their language and have achieved a level of assimilation into their culture. I recommend shaking hands at a first meeting and participating in the bowing ritual at later meetings, especially among high-status executives and officials in Japan and Korea. Elsewhere in Asia no bow is needed.

- To bow in Korea: keep the back straight, palms on buttocks (women fold the arms in front of them), and bow from the waist. Keep the feet together and the legs straight.

- To bow in Japan: keep the hands at the sides, palms open and facing the thighs (women fold the arms loosely just above the waist).

- In both Korea and Japan, the deeper the bow, the more deference is expressed. A bow should always be as deep, or slightly deeper, as that of a counterpart of equal status.

- Koreans will rarely bow more than once. The Japanese, however, may bow numerous times to emphasize their respect, humility, or deep apology.

of the king," M.O.C. identifies a child of a P.O.C., and there are other designations. The significance of any unfamiliar letters after a Thai's name should be queried. The person (or better yet, someone else) should be asked about proper address. The title without the name is usually preferred.

Projecting a Specific Title

Western business titles can be misleading. A "vice president" may be one of numerous senior salespeople or heads of divisions; an "executive assistant" may pour coffee and take dictation; a "sole proprietor" may be the president of the company and its *sole employee*. In Asia, where job titles are accurate indicators of status and rank, titles like "consultant," "photographer," "writer," or "engineer" may be considered vague. In Japanese and in Korean, for example, entirely different words are used to describe a fiction writer and one who produces nonfiction. Western job descriptions should be made as specific as possible—"Nuclear Reactor Shielding Engineer" is more acceptable than "Engineer." Any mystery in a title will only invite misunderstanding of specific capabilities.

Greetings and Introductions in China

When introducing people in China, Hong Kong, and Taiwan, and people of Chinese descent in Singapore, higher-ranking persons are introduced before those of lower rank; an older person comes before a younger, and women precede men. Handshakes are acceptable with both men and women; hugs, kisses, or a pat on the back as a display of bonhomie are not, except between very close friends.

A Chinese surname comes first, then the middle name, and lastly, the given name. Mr., Mrs., Miss, or the person's title, can be added to the person's surname. A man named Liu Wei-da could be addressed as Mr. Liu or Director Liu, according to his business card *(ming pian)*. The term *Tongzhi* (Comrade) is back in vogue as a form of address in post-Tiananmen China, for men *and* women. Tongzhi should be used sparingly and without being flippant. Mr. Liu might be addressed as Liu Tongzhi.

A Chinese person may add Mr. or Mrs. to a Westerner's *first* name: "Mr. Fred," for Fred Smith. Throughout China, I am known as "Mr. Christopher." My advice is always to correct the Chinese person before the misnomer sticks, but, in my case, Christopher is a lot easier for a Chinese person to say than Engholm.

When a Chinese person comes to the West, he or she may reverse the names, in an effort to seem more Western, and thoroughly confuse everyone who has learned that Chinese surnames come first. At a first meeting with a Chinese person in the West, the surname should be clarified; it may not appear first on the business card. The Asian may also have adopted a Western first name for use in the West; a friend of mine named "Zhong" uses "John" when he is in the United States; a woman named "Wan" chose to be "Wendy."

Surnames of Chinese husbands and wives do not match; Chinese women keep their family name when they marry. Children take the surname of their father.

In Taiwan, many people have Christian first names and Chinese surnames, as a result of decades of Western missionary activity on the island. A man named Ho Cheng may become Johnny Ho Cheng, and may be called Johnny Ho, or Mr. Ho.

Japanese Names and Introductions

Traditionally, a Japanese delegation introduces its junior members first, and its senior members in ascending status order; this custom has been changing, with increasing exposure to the West. Most Japanese greet Westerners with a handshake and a shadow bow and will not expect a formal bow in response. When meeting older businesspeople of high status, Westerners should observe the Japanese greeting ritual by bowing, saying their name, and then exchanging business cards *(meishi)*. Even among very close Japanese friends, touching gestures like bear hugs and pecks on the cheek are considered an invasion of private space.

Like native American names, Japanese names often denote natural objects or phenomena: *komatsu* is a small pine or sapling; *okuma* is a great bear; and *yamashita* means under the mountain. When written in Japanese, the person's name will appear with the surname first and given names second. When a Japanese person has his or her name romanized on a business card, for use in the West, the given name will come first. Place Mr., Mrs., or Miss before the surname, or add "san" (Honorable Sir, Honorable Madame) as a suffix to the surname. Mr. *or* Mrs. Tanaka could be addressed "Tanakasan." However, do not add "san" to your own name or address members of your own team using "san"; use Mr. or Mrs., or the appropriate title.

Korean Names and Introductions

Elders and superiors are introduced first in Korea. Most Korean men expect a handshake rather than a bow. Urbanized Korean women often shake hands with Westerners but bow to Korean men. The safe route is to allow a Korean women to initiate a handshake. If she doesn't, then a shadow bow is in order.

There are only 200 or so family names in Korea, half of which are rare. One out of four Koreans is named Kim and more than half are named Kim, Lee, or Park. Korean names begin with the family name, follow with the clan or generation name, and end with the given name. The generation name is shared by one's brothers and cousins, and, if the family chooses, by one's sisters, and is represented by a Chinese character that has an auspicious meaning. The Korean generation name helps to delineate the family branch of origin, which bears on the status ranking in the community. A Korean's third name, often given at baptism, is not a legal name. When Koreans spell out their names in the romanized alphabet, they sometimes reverse the order of names, so the surname may have to be queried. Only the surname is used, with Mr., Mrs., or Miss preceding it or *Songsaeng-nim* (respected person) as a suffix. As in China, Korean wives do not take their husband's name. Mr. Park's wife will answer to "Mrs. Park," but is referred to by Koreans by her original family name.

A Korean husband refers to his wife in numerous ways, depending on the rank of the person he is speaking to. Oddly, the most respect-imbued title for referring to one's wife is reserved for introductions to the *lowest* ranking people the husband meets. Russell Howe, author of *The Koreans,* tells us that unfortunate foreigners who are learning the Korean language "often make the mistake of referring to their wives by the most respectful term, thinking that this translates Western ideals of equality; what it is taken to mean, of course, is that the Westerner is treating the corporation president as though he were a waiter." *"San,"* the honorific term in Japan, translates as *"ssi"* in Korea and is used in the same manner—as a suffix to the family name of men and women.

Introductions in Malaysia and Indonesia

Elders are introduced before younger persons, and women before men. Urban Malays, whether in Indonesia, Malaysia, or Singapore, will be accustomed to shaking hands with Westerners. Men greet each other by bowing slightly, shaking both hands, or shaking the right hand. Women usually don't shake hands; Western women should simply shadow bow and smile. The traditional Malay greeting gesture is the *salaam* (raising the right hand up to the heart), especially when meeting elders. The *salaam* means, "I greet you from my heart." To show respect when greeting an elder, a young person may bring both hands to the heart while the elder will usually raise only one.

Malay names are a little more complicated than those elsewhere in Asia. For example, a Malay man is named Hamid bin Algadri. His friends probably call him Hamid. Malays in Malaysia might address him as Encik Hamid and those in Indonesia, Bapak Hamid (both translate to "Sir Hamid"); both terms mean "father." The connective bin in his name means "son of," and Algadri is his father's name, not his surname. Bin is usually dropped. Thus, Hamid bin Algadri may be called Mr. Hamid Algadri, or Mr. Hamid.

An example of a Malay woman's name is Kemala binti Among-pradja. Her friends call her Kemala. Proper address for a Westerner is Miss Kemala or Mrs. Kemala, depending on her marital status. Binti means "daughter of" and Amongpradja is her father's name. Her father's name is usually dropped, however, when she marries; at that time her name is combined with that of her husband. If Mrs. Kemala is married to Mr. Hamid, she can be addressed as Mrs. Kemala Hamid. Malays might call her Puan Kemala; *puan* is the term for a married woman in Malaysia. In Indonesia, Ibu (literally, "mother," but translated as "Madam") can be added to an adult woman's name. Mrs. Kemala could be properly addressed as Ibu Kemala. When in doubt regarding address of a Malay friend, it's best to ask and to write the name phonetically on the person's card, to avoid having to ask again.

A person of Indian descent in Southeast Asia should be greeted with the *namaste* (put the palms together at chest level and do a shadow bow). Indian men will shake hands but Indian women may not. Indians' last name, or surname, can be preceded with Mr., Mrs., or Miss.

Names and Greetings in Thailand

Among Thais, lower-status people are introduced first—the receptionist before the CEO, the child before the wife. Thai businesspeople will shake hands with visiting Westerners, but the traditional greeting is the *wai.*

As with the bow in Japan, the *wai* can mean almost anything: Thank you; Greetings to you; I've made a mistake; Have mercy on me; You are my superior; I am indebted to you; I am sorry. To *wai*, for social equals: form a temple with the fingers, holding them close to the body *at chest level,* then shadow bow. Inferiors might raise the fingers to the level of the nose, or, for total obeisance, lower the forehead to just below the thumbs. The lower the head and the higher the palms are raised, the more respect is expressed. Inferiors *wai* first; when the elderly wife of an important official enters a room, a Western visitor should *wai* to her before she acknowledges the visitor. Monks do not return a *wai;* neither does a king or queen. If a Westerner is arrested, he or she should definitely *wai* a lot to the officer, to indicate apology. A *wai* from a waiter or an office clerk can be acknowledged with a smiling nod rather than a *wai.* The rule for *wai*ing is: if someone of equal or greater status *wai*s, then *wai* back; otherwise, stick to the handshake for men and the smiling nod for women. Never return a *wai* to a child, for example, when meeting the son or daughter of a business associate. Thais believe doing so will shorten the child's life! A good rule to follow: don't *wai* to a person under the age of thirteen.

Surnames have been used in Thailand only for the past fifty years. The Thai given name comes first, followed by the family name, and Thais address each other using the *given* name or title, not the surname. For example, the director of the Information and Promotion Service Division at the Office of the Board of Investment in Bangkok is Vanchai Mahatanankoon. Western visitors are relieved to be able to call him Mr. Vanchai, using his given name and not his family name. As for Thai women, Asoka Soonthornsaratoon can be addressed as Mrs. Asoka. Introductions require stating only the person's given name, not the long and unwieldy family name. "Khun" means Mr., Mrs., or Miss and can be used as a prefix to any person's first name, as in Khun Asoka. However, a person's title, as in Manager Asoka, is preferable to Khun.

Filipino Introductions

A Filipino should be greeted by raising the eyebrows and then letting them fall as eye contact is made and the greeter smiles. This gesture means "hello." Nearly all Filipinos will shake hands, but foreign men should let Filipino women initiate the gesture. A greeting to an elderly woman in the Philippines is a kiss on the cheek or the traditional *manolo* (the greeter takes the elder's hand and touches it against his or her forehead, while leaning toward the elder). It might be wise to postpone these to the second or third meeting with the elder person. Sir or Ma'am is appropriate address to a superior; use Mr., Mrs., and Miss with those of similar station.

When and Where to Be Punctual

Most Asians expect punctuality, even in seemingly laid-back Southeast Asia. Indonesia, for example, is hardly a sun-drenched, tropical, mañana land, as Vice President Dan Quayle found out during a recent visit there. Because his tennis match with a dignitary in Australia ran overtime, the VP arrived in Indonesia two hours overdue. The following morning, the front-page headline in the *Jakarta Post* bellowed: QUAYLE ARRIVES BEHIND SCHEDULE. From a public relations standpoint, most would agree the blunder fell short of Quayle's domestic gaffes, but the careless prioritizing cost him dearly among Indonesia's officialdom. Here are some other tips on timeliness:

- Spread out appointments in any urban area; traffic can be horrendous in Asian cities, and many addresses are hard to find, even for taxi drivers.

- Expect Filipinos to be late for nonbusiness-related appointments; they will not want to appear too eager to enjoy the hospitality being offered.

- Be punctual in Thailand, but expect Thais to be slightly late; if an appointment is not *sedouak* (convenient), then it's *my sedouak* (not convenient), and the Thai won't be on time.

- Arrive on time for Korean dinners and sightseeing, but don't get hot under the collar if you have to cool your heels a while before your guest or host arrives. Punctuality in Korea is often lax for nonbusiness-related meetings.

- Be on time or early in Singapore and Hong Kong. People there are sticklers for punctuality.

- Be punctual to all meetings in Malaysia and Indonesia, especially if the meeting is with someone of superior status. Be present, as a show of respect, when a Malay VIP arrives, even though the Malay is not punctual. A Moslem who arrives late may wave off the tardiness with a phrase like: "Nobody knows what Allah will bring." Getting irritated is pointless, even when your Indonesian associate constantly shows up late and still expects you to be on time. If an invitation to an official function requests arrival 15 minutes early, be there as requested. The purpose is to have the guests on hand when the VIPs arrive. Don't make appointments on Friday, the Moslem day of prayer, when government offices close at 11 A.M.

In Taiwan and China, punctuality is somewhat of a nonissue; a car and driver will likely pick you up at your hotel, for banquets, factory tours, and meetings.

Meeting Elders in Asia

Elders are revered in Asia, and should be shown unlimited respect and constant attention. They often sway opinions about business deals, regardless of any cold comparisons of product specifications. The rules of conduct toward elders are important:

- Stand up when they enter a room.
- Greet them in a traditional manner, before greeting anybody else.
- Put out a lit cigarette when an elder enters the room, and don't smoke or drink alcohol in the elder's presence without asking his or her permission.
- Don't recline in a chair or cross your legs when seated within an elder's view; sit upright, with feet on the floor and knees together.
- Remove your sunglasses when speaking to an elder, even when outdoors.
- Never raise your voice in an elder's presence.

A Little Language Competency
Goes a Long Way

The language of international trade, says an old adage, is the language spoken by the customer. When a foreign marketer arrives in a country and is unable to utter "hello," "goodbye," and "thank you" in the local language, the marketer/guest may be considered remiss in preparing for crossing into the country and its culture. Unfortunately, the overwhelming majority of Western marketers in Asia expect their Asian customers to overlook their collective lack of Asian language competency. Asia marketer Michael Tomczyk believes, as I do, that "Language is one of the reasons why Pacific Rim–U.S. trade is so one-sided. [Asians] speak our language but we don't speak theirs!" The problem is that fluency for all Pacific Rim business communities requires learning *seven languages:* Mandarin, Cantonese, Japanese, Korean, Thai, Bahasa Indonesian, and Bahasa Malaysian. Mastering one Asian language is a mental marathon, besides being extremely time-consuming and expensive. North American firms, for the

Key Phrases That Help Break the Ice

Nothing puts an Asian host at ease like an effort by his foreign guest to speak a few words in his language. Try to arrive in an Asian country with a command of the key phrases listed below. (I have not listed Filipino phrases in Tagalog because the language of business in the Philippines is English.)

	Good Morning	Good Afternoon	Good Evening
Mandarin	*Nǐ zǎo*	*Nǐ hǎo*	*Wan-an*
Cantonese	*Jóu Sahn*	*N'ang*	*Jóu Táu*
Japanese	*Ohayo gozaimasu*	*Konnichiwa*	*Konbanwa*
Korean	*Annyong hashimnika*	*(same)*	*(same)*
Thai	*Sawat dee khrap (for men)*	*(same)*	*(same)*
	Sawat dee kha (for women)	*(same)*	*(same)*
Indonesian	*Selamat pagi*	*Selamat siang*	*Selamat malam*
Malaysian	*Selamat pagi*	*Selamat petang*	*Selamat malam*

	Please	Thank you	Excuse Me
Mandarin	*Chíng*	*Shyieh-shyieh*	*Duay bū qǐ*
Cantonese	*Ching Néih*	*Dò Jeh*	*Deui M̀jyuh*
Japanese	*Dozo*	*Arigato gozaimasu*	*Sumimasen*
Korean	*Chushipshio (means "please give me"; for buying)*	*Kamsa hamnida*	*Sille hamnida*
Thai	*Dai prod*	*Khob khun khrap (for men)* *Khob khun kha (for women)*	*Kho prathartoad*
Indonesian	*Silakan*	*Terima kasih*	*Permisi*
Malaysian	*Tolong*	*Terima kasi*	*Maafkan saya*

	Yes	No	Goodbye
Mandarin	*Duay*	*Bū duay*	*Zaì jìan*
Cantonese	*Haih*	*M̀haih*	*Joi Gin*
Japanese	*Hai*	*Iie*	*Sayonara*
Korean	*Ne*	*Aniyo*	*Annyong ikeiseyo (person leaving)* *Annyong kaseyo (person staying)*
Thai	*Krub (for men)* *Kha (for women)*	*Mai khrap (for men)* *Mai kha (for women)*	*Sawat dee khrap (for men)* *Sawat dee kha (for women)*
Indonesian	*Ya*	*Tidak*	*Selamat*
Malaysian	*Ya*	*Tidak*	*Selamat tinggal*

most part, have not made it a priority to train their employees in Asian languages. Dr. John Graham, a professor and consultant who has worked for Ford Motor Company, says that the auto manufacturer employs 1,000 people to conduct its business with Japan, including the transfer of production technology *from* Japan. How many of these people speak Japanese? "You can count them on one hand," said Graham, during a recent lecture on Pacific Rim business.

North Americans have been lucky: English is the lingua franca of international business transaction throughout Asia. However, as Tomczyk suggests, this bit of luck hardly lessens the need for Western marketers to learn the languages of their Asian customers. Can a North American buyer really justify purchasing products from an Asian delegation that has to pitch a sale solely through an interpreter? Businesspeople *can* succeed in Asia without local language fluency, but knowledge of a few phrases is essential, to indicate an appreciation of the customer's language and an inclination toward more communication on common ground.

Getting Names Translated

An irritating formality, but one that must be *done correctly the first time,* is to obtain a good translation of a Westerner's name for each country in which he or she will travel. In Asian languages, some Western names sound funny, and many names can't be easily translated at all. Tom Carcel, who lived and worked in Japan as a marketing representative for an American pharmaceutical firm, complains that when his Japanese colleagues added the familiar *"san"* (meaning honorable) to "Tom," his name became *"Tomasan,"* which sounds like the Japanese word for "testicles." Says Tom: "It was a heck of a way to introduce myself."

I quickly discarded an early translation of my name into Chinese. The final two characters, if mispronounced, could have been construed as "bend over and penetrate." *That* would have been a heck of a way to introduce myself!

There are two different routes for translating a proper name into an Asian language; it can be done phonetically or ideographically. If the name does not translate well phonetically (it sounds poor in the Asian language), it can be translated as an idea rather than for its pronunciation. For example, the name Eve translates poorly into Chinese; it sounds awful in Mandarin. A euphonic substitute would be its translation as "Evening."

Phonetic translation is common for Japanese and Korean; for Mandarin or Cantonese, characters will be employed that carry meanings of their own, in addition to denoting phonetic sounds. For the Philippines, Western names stay untranslated; the language of business is English. The same is true for Indonesia and Malaysia, except in dealing with Chinese-speaking businesspeople. A translation of a name into a specific Chinese dialect (Mandarin or Cantonese) would then be required.

For Chinese dialects, it is best to have a name translated phonetically first, and, *if possible,* employ characters that hold special meanings as well. Sir David Wilson, Governor of Hong Kong, has what the Chinese consider "good characters." His name is translated phonetically but, within the word for "Wilson," he has changed one character so that his name in Chinese means "to protect everybody's credit." Chiang Kai-shek's name meant "middle" or "right," and was written to combine with characters that meant "to arrange or manage a country." Margaret Thatcher's characters mean "distinguished." Singapore's former Prime Minister Lee Kwan Yew's name means "to glorify country and/or family."

Western names do not translate well into Thai; most sound odd and are difficult for Thais to pronounce. It may be advisable to pick a common Thai name that has a similar sound. My name, Chris, sounds like the Thai name "Grits," meaning the powerful spear thrown by a well-known Buddhist god.

Two warnings are in order here. First, when translating a name, a wise Westerner solicits the services of an Asian translator whose *native language* is the language targeted for the translation. To use an inappropriate translation of a name in Asia can be terribly embarrassing. As soon as Asian hosts hear it, they will want to argue endlessly about how to change it. Two or three opinions on the translation should be collected from other native speakers of the language, before business cards are printed.

Second, it's NOT a good idea to wait, and have business cards printed in Hong Kong. The risk of error is greater, and the whole arrangement is a terrible headache to endure at the outset of a business trip to Asia.

To get cards printed in Asian languages, most people look under "stationers" in the Yellow Pages; an Asian language printer can usually be found in the Asian community of a large urban area. The older style—printing the translation of a name on the reverse side of the card—seems to be on the wane. Today's card carries printing on only one side. The name is printed with the translation right underneath it. The card should also include the name of the company (in English), the card carrier's title and address, and relevant phone numbers, a telex number, and a fax number, all with the appropriate country code.

Becoming Fluent

Are some Asian languages easier to learn than others? After Bahasa Indonesian and Bahasa Malaysian, the Japanese language is probably the easiest Asian language for Westerners to master conversationally. First, the language sounds exactly as it looks, when romanized, and does not require tricky accents and intonations as Mandarin and some other languages do. Second, it contains hundreds of words borrowed from English, which can be learned overnight simply by modifying their pronunciation, like *rah-shah-wah* (rush hour).

Written Japanese is a different matter. The Japanese borrowed their writing system from the Chinese; it's currently comprised of a few thousand Chinese characters called *kanji,* which take schoolchildren 12 years of memorization to learn, in addition to two other sets of simple phonetic characters (*kana*) called *hiragana* and *katakana.* Because many Japanese actors and entertainers never finish formal schooling, they have to read their lines phonetically, in *kana,* sometimes not even knowing what the words mean; many are technically illiterate because they can't read *kanji.*

Chinese and Korean languages borrow few freebies from English. Foreigners have to start from scratch. A single word in a Chinese dialect may have five or more completely different meanings, depending on how the word is pronounced. (The modern "pun," I'm sure, finds its origin in China, where it fuels comic performances to this day.) The long-term rewards of learning Chinese, however, are worth considering. Japanese and Korean, among other Asian written languages, are based on traditional Chinese characters. Someone who masters Mandarin can make some sense of the newspapers in Seoul, Tokyo, or, for that matter, Ho Chi Min City. However, the three languages are *not* interchangeable. Korean grammar, for example, is similar to Japanese, not Chinese.

Mandarin, which everyone in China and Singapore can understand, is easier to learn than Cantonese, which is spoken by most people in Hong Kong. "The only reason to learn Cantonese is if you are marrying a Cantonese-speaker and want to get to know the relatives," a friend of mine advises correctly.

The Korean language is easier to learn to read than to speak. *Hangul*, the country's alphabet, is phonetic rather than ideographic and can be learned in a few hours. Most of the letters are actually diagrams of how to form their sounds with the mouth. The ingeniousness of the system warrants Korea's *Hangul* Day (October 9), a holiday celebrating the alphabet. Unfortunately, Korean newspapers still use Chinese characters to save space.

Getting Started Toward Fluency

The most efficient way to learn any Asian language is to spend a year in Asia, concentrating on becoming conversationally fluent. Most North Americans who are truly fluent in Asian languages have supported themselves by teaching English while in Asia. Short of relocating in Asia, a language tutor can be found for about $30 an hour. Community-college courses are increasingly available for learning Japanese and Chinese, and many forward-thinking American corporations have set up in-house language training programs. Unfortunately, no "one-minute solution" exists for acquiring Asian language competency. All of the "instant fluency" tape sets and television tutorials now available still require Herculean effort, to reach true fluency.

CHAPTER FIVE

Where *Yes* Means *Maybe* and *Maybe* Means *No*

Calamity comes by means of the mouth.
CHINESE PROVERB

This chapter begins with a true story, a "case study" of what not to do. I was one of two American sales representatives preparing to make a presentation to a delegation of East Asians (it doesn't matter which country they were from) on a buying mission in the United States. Our late-evening meeting had been arranged on short notice. The other representative was from a division of Nippon Electric Company (NEC) located in the United States. He was about 55; because I was younger, I deferred to him and asked that he make the first presentation to the seven Asian officials.

I'll always regret that I did.

Within 20 minutes, his (our) audience had dwindled from seven to three people; delegates became disinterested, bored, or non-plussed with Mr. X's presentation and personality. An underling from the Asian delegation approached me and whispered impatiently, "When will this man be finished?"

"I don't know," I sighed.

When the audience had shrunk to just two delegates, the others having exited the meeting room for meetings with other Western representatives, Mr. X finished and departed as well. What had gone wrong? Why had Mr. X's presentation—one he had delivered innumerable times to American audiences—failed so abominably with this Asian audience? Why didn't he "get through" to them?

I had witnessed the debacle start-to-finish; I knew the answer. Mr. X failed to observe rules of *intercultural communication* that can help Western representatives bridge the communication ravine that divides business East and business West.

Anatomy of a Communication Snafu

Mr. X's lack of intercultural communication caused him two kinds of problems. His first set of mistakes pertained to his verbal communication—called *spoken language,* by experts in cross-cultural communication. Mr. X made the wrong use of words and phrases to communicate ideas, information, opinions, and emotions. His second set of mistakes pertained to nonverbal communication, or *silent language*—the realm of communicating that includes gestures, posture, eye messages, and proximity boundaries.

Mr. X's *spoken language* problems are described below and given a wider perspective in the rest of this chapter. His second series of mistakes, the nonverbal or silent language ones, are analyzed in the next chapter.

When Mr. X initiated the business discussion, he offered *no small talk.* He launched his sales presentation without exchanging business cards or asking a single question about the companies and government agencies that the delegates represented. This was considered depersonalizing and haughty. No personal connection was made, no common ground was located. Moreover, he offered no apology for calling a late meeting with the delegation or thanks for their attending it on short notice.

He spoke in *large blocks of language* that his interpreter could not translate accurately; his audience soon lost the thread of his presentation and became fatigued.

He spoke authoritatively and directly in *a loud voice* that offended the Asian delegation's more sensitive communication style. They expected a *seller* of products to behave in a more deferential manner to potential *buyers* of the products.

Mr. X replied with *a frank (and impolite) "No,"* in response to requests to transfer NEC technology to the Asian country. The reply was considered too blunt and offensive; few Asians, as we will see, say "no," even when they communicate a negative response.

He *misread euphemisms.* The Asian delegates voiced their general disinterest in the NEC product in statements like: "We will consider this further," and "We think this is a very advanced technology, relative to our needs." Mr. X failed to facilitate two-way discussion about what the Asians' needs *were,* by asking questions and offering positive feedback.

To support his claims, he *depended on a videotape.* A video can be effective in a sales presentation. Unfortunately, Mr. X let his run uninterrupted for 15 minutes and the sound track was in English! Members of the audience began to excuse themselves one after another. Instead of stopping the videotape to break the monotony, Mr. X became irritated at his Asian audience for not paying attention to it. He turned his body away from them, in a posture that expressed resentment!

Why Westerners Clash with Asians in Verbal Communication

The communication problems that Mr. X personified are *cultural* in origin, not necessarily symptoms of incompetence. When they try to communicate, Eastern and Western cultures clash for three primary reasons, all worth looking at closely.

Frankness versus Face

The clash of communication styles starts with Westerners' penchant for frankness and Asians' need to preserve and protect face. North Americans use a direct, rather impersonal, and often confrontational approach when they speak with business associates, whether at home or overseas; they maintain that business discussion is not to be taken personally. Quite the opposite, Asians relate to their business associates in a very personal manner; they maintain that business relations *are* to be taken personally. Hints and hidden messages in gestures and euphemisms are meant to convey what may be offending a listener, but they often go unnoticed by the untrained Westerner, to the consternation of the face-conscious Asian.

Asians value politeness and the maintenance of respect and trust between partners. The Japanese use the term *sasshi* to describe the compassion and sensitivity one must show another person, if a good feeling or mood (called *kimochi*) is to imbue an encounter between two people. North Americans are typically less sensitive and emotionally involved than Asians, when communicating in a business setting. North Americans are typically task-oriented and time-efficient; unfortunately, Asians, throughout the Pacific Rim, have little respect for frank and aggressive people because such behavior is associated with rustic or ill-bred character. People who are too direct and assertive may be considered not only impolite but downright risky to associate with. The confrontation they often provoke can permanently mar or destroy relationships between businesspeople and corporate groups.

Confrontation versus Compromise

Westerners' frankness and pragmatic communication style might be tolerable to Asians, if we did not go a step further and make confrontational debate our favorite mode of discussing ideas with business associates. Two North Americans discussing a political conflict may lash out at each other repeatedly, before they decide to agree, disagree, or change the subject. *Debating* an issue is, for Westerners, half the fun of resolving it. Unfortunately, we tend to carry over the debating style when discussing business in Asia.

In the Asian style of discussion, individuals present their ideas, then allow others to do the same. All parties seek common ground on which to stake a compromise without ever having to overtly reject each other's ideas openly. Jeffery Shapard, cofounder of the Two-Way Information Communication System (TWICS), a cross-cultural electronic network that links Japanese communicators with people abroad, is keenly aware of the resulting communication clash. His comments are revealing.

One of the biggest conflicts in communication style between Japanese and people from EuroAmerican cultures is that of confrontational debate as a vehicle of discussion. When, for example, our Japanese participant sets forth a set of ideas and is suddenly attacked by some American members of the online discussion group, he is put into a defensive position. The American members may not actually disagree with him, but may merely be taking opposing positions for the sake of discussion, engaging in an intellectual sport typical of Western communication style. However, [the Japanese person] may feel that his personhood is being attacked, as he is not used to separating his ideas from his personality. . . . Why should he waste his time when the rules of the game are such that one side wins and the other loses, rather than both sides learning and moving together to some middle ground, especially when it appears that those he is talking with have already made up their minds that they are, in fact, correct and he is wrong?

This communication rule generalizes for all of face-conscious Asia: An attack on an Asian's personal ideas will likely be interpreted as an attack upon his or her personhood, which can prevent the achievement of harmony and mutual understanding between communicators.

When conflicts occur during a negotiation, Asians will usually grow more silent, using their posture to indicate their discomfort. They may reply in abstract terms, avoiding the issue by smiling and suggesting that another topic should be discussed. Conversely, North Americans like to get conflicts out in the open, defending themselves overtly and aggressively. Believing such frank debate crass and lacking in subtlety, Asians disclose less and less, and resist entering the argument. Thus, Westerners' transparent approach to resolving conflict results in an additional clash that may stifle communication and threaten further business relationships in Asia.

Personality Differences

Smooth conversations between Asian and North American executives may be sabotaged by personality differences as well as differences in professional background and experience. Over half of Japan's company directors possess a background in engineering. Most American company directors know little about engineering; one-third of them are lawyers, one-third are accountants, and the rest rose through the ranks as managers. North American marketing people have trouble trying to communicate with engineers at their own companies! The marketing people typically approach problems and express themselves creatively and informally; the engineers are typically logical and analytical in their communication style and problem solving. The divergence is multiplied when creative, extroverted managers and marketers from the West sit down to communicate with more formal and procedure-oriented engineer-types in Asia.

Most Westerners who go to Asia as expatriates can be characterized as extroverted people; they are corporate superachievers, self-motivated dealmakers, and cross-cultural adventurers. The Asians they meet tend to be more introverted and conforming. The extroverted Westerners reveal their personalities openly and informally; the Asians practice restraint, and they seem evasive and defensive to the North Americans. The loquacious Westerners may be regarded in Asia as all-talk-and-no-substance.

A fundamental difference, psychologically, between Westerners and Asians, was described to me by Steve Willard, a business consultant and corporate trainer who has a background in psychology. When Westerners meet new people, they quickly allow the new acquaintances to become informal and chummy with them. They even expect such behavior in those they meet. However, they don't permit new acquaintances to experience their innermost private self unless a longer-term relationship develops; even then, they will probably protect their private self. Overall, Westerners become informal rapidly, but are rarely willing to let down their defenses any further, after the informality is established. They prefer to maintain a "business familiarity" with their business associates, rather than permit them to see their innermost character, conflicts, hopes, dreams, and desires.

Most Asians maintain a heavy façade of formality during first meetings (how heavy, depends on whether the person is from more formalistic North Asia or less formalistic South Asia). However, *once they deem new acquaintances appropriate and acceptable*—that is, trustworthy—they take them straight through their exterior defenses to their innermost self. Westerners who are admitted beyond Asians' defenses find themselves in the most private zones of the Asians' emotional life. Confidence about intimate problems, personal struggles, kids, and family, as well as business endeavors can catch startled listeners off guard. Many of the expatriates whom I interviewed for this book had been surprised repeatedly at the intimate thoughts and feelings shared with them by their Asian associates. Some Westerners become uncomfortable and clam up, when conversation gets too personal and unrelated to business. North Americans, although glib and informal at the start, are often reticent about allowing Asians (or anybody else) to share their deepest emotions and personal dilemmas. Some Asians wonder whether North Americans *have* an emotional self; more than a few Asians have decided that the personable-from-the-start Westerner is a "paper carp hanging in the May wind with its huge mouth open and nothing inside," as intercultural expert Mitsuko Saito says. The hollowness disappoints Asians who want to forge a personal bond alongside the business bond.

North Americans who have become privy to Asians' inner self must be extremely sensitive and careful. A glib or sarcastic comment can be devastating to the confiding person and will be considered a betrayal of trust, which can sever the business relationship and create lasting resentment.

"ASIASPEAK": Communicating Asian-Style

The first time I witnessed communication differences between East and West was as a photographer shooting a wedding. The

How Asians Communicate with Each Other

Facilitating Through Feedback   When Asians negotiate, they give feedback to the speaker. Japanese conversations, for example, are punctuated with pauses during which feelings are checked and positive *hais* and affirmative nods occur. Frequent nodding, to indicate comprehension (*aizuchi*, in Japan), is a courtesy to the speaker and facilitates communication. In China, one hears, "*duay, duay, duay*"; in Korea, "*dai, dai, dai*"; and in Indonesia, "*ya, ya, ya.*" Through an interpreter, these short affirmations *sound* and *feel* stronger than they are; three "*hais*" in a row, when interpreted, sound pretty decisive: "Yes. Yes. Yes." Often, Westerners can't figure out what's feedback and what's a formal "Yes."

Anticipating Listeners' Reactions   Conversation among Asians is a constant assessment of feelings and reactions, a monitoring of the relationship at hand. Listeners' reactions are anticipated, to avoid saying something they will not agree with. Speakers can adjust their statements according to the feedback they are receiving. In Japanese, Korean, and Chinese languages, the verb and its tense occur at the end of a sentence, not near the beginning as in English. Should a speaker sense that his or her listeners do not react positively to something that is being said, the speaker can easily change the meaning of the sentence before reaching its end. For example, when a person comments in English, "I like the idea of the proposal," listeners know the person "likes" the proposal, from the wording at the start of the sentence. In East Asia, a person might say, "The idea of this proposal, I . . ." (here, the speaker checks for positive nonverbal feedback), and then can choose to conclude with any of the following: " . . . I like," " . . . I don't like," " . . . I liked," " . . . I would like if . . . ," and so on.

Throughout Asia, a person who delivers bad news directly and assertively, without considering the reaction of the listener, is thought to be a sort of social cretin. In Korea, for example, someone who repeatedly worsens another person's mood (*kibun*) by delivering bad news that the person should know about, may be shunned in the future and even cut off from former relationships. Negative reports, manufacturing mishaps, and similar bad news may be concealed, to protect someone's *kibun,* especially if the someone is a higher-status person. The same sequence occurs in Japan, for a different reason—to protect oneself from criticism. Bad news in the Philippines is concealed to protect the way one is esteemed by a superior; underlings find every way possible to pass along bad reports, without being held responsible for their negative impact on their superiors. Go-betweens are often utilized to break disconcerting news.

Speaking Around the Point and Never Saying "No"   When a meeting in Asia is concluded, each negotiator (especially in Japan) desires to have achieved three goals: unanimity of opinion; solidarity (the issues have not divided the group); and saving face (no individual who disagreed has been embarrassed). No one wants to offend another person by rejecting his or her idea or position. Thus, much negotiating in Asia is a process of expressing a position and listening to a counter position, with neither side openly rejecting the other's successive positions along the way. Eventually, the two sides come together in compromise. No one gets hurt. The business relationship prevails unscathed, because no one has had to say "No" directly. When it comes to saying "No," Asians throughout the Pacific Rim have created an art form—the oblique "No."

Here's a *partial* list of the ways Indonesians say "No," gathered by Cathie Draine and Barbara Hall in their book, *Culture Shock: Indonesia:*

1. *Belum* (This means "no," for unstated reasons.)
2. *Tidak usah* ("Don't worry about it; it's not necessary.")
3. *Lebih baik titik* ("I'd rather you didn't do that.")
4. *Tidik boleh* ("I can't, because I haven't been given permission.")
5. *Tidak senang* ("I'm upset or unhappy with it [or with you].")
6. *Tidak terima* ("You've got to be kidding!")
7. *Jangan* ("Don't! The sky will fall!")

A similarly long list could be created for every Asian culture.

◆

groom was Anglo-Saxon and the bride was Japanese. During the reception, the wedding guests polarized into two groups, one on each side of a large room. In the Japanese group, the guests were bowing to each other, the men were exchanging business cards, everybody was speaking quietly and politely, younger people were showing deference to older people, and no physical contact, wide gesticulating, or roaring laughter could be found. On the American side, the pictures were completely different. People shook hands firmly, spoke loudly, guffawed, called each other by their first name, hugged and touched each other, and waved at one another with wide hand and arm gestures. I've witnessed the same polarization when Asian and Western businesspeople socialize.

Skills for Better Communication with Asians

To communicate across cultures, Westerners need to develop some interactive skills that can help in gaining conscious control over the communication patterns that are spontaneous and natural in the West and are communication barriers in Asia. These techniques, called *intercultural communication* skills, include:

1. Communicating effectively through an interpreter;
2. Not taking "yes" to be an affirmative commitment;
3. Facilitating two-way discussion through "active" listening;
4. Substituting clear, direct diction for idioms and slang;
5. Fostering safe (rather than unsafe) rapport.

These skills will help with communicating, negotiating, and building strong friendships in Asia and, indeed, around the world.

Conveying a Message Through an Interpreter

People who aren't fluent in the language of Asian customers have to depend on interpreters at all times, whether negotiating or socializing. The only country in Asia where an interpreter will NOT be needed is the Philippines. However, guests must speak slowly, because their accent may be difficult for Filipino business partners to understand. A good proportion of the Korean business community speaks English, and most educated Thais can speak English to some degree. Everywhere else in the Pacific Rim, however, communication is done through an interpreter.

Words, ideas, humor, intelligence, and personality are entrusted to the interpreter. All that I have said about building strong business relationships in Asia may have sounded relatively easy to do; because of the need to communicate solely through an interpreter, such an endeavor is hardly a simple proposition. I have witnessed few foreigners in Asia who understand how to be interpreted well. To be clearly understood, Westerners must know how to get their messages clearly interpreted. Most people who have problems "getting through" to Asians blame their interpreters; I teach my seminar participants that *they* must take responsibility for getting their message better interpreted.

Knowing That "Yes" Is Not Always an Affirmative Answer

In 1969, President Richard Nixon traveled to Japan to meet with Prime Minister Eisaku Sato, to request a curb on Japan's textile exports to the United States. The Prime Minister replied: *"Zensho shimasu"*—literally, "I will do my best." Nothing was ever done to stem the flow of textile exports to America, and Nixon was reported to have accused Sato of being a liar. Such linguistic gymnastics on the part of the Japanese have been dubbed, by

Checklist for Being Interpreted Well

- Limit sentences to 20 to 30 words. Write the script out and edit it so that it can be spoken in short sentences. The shorter the sentences, the less likely the audience will lose the train of thought or feel overwhelmed.

- Pace the text in triplets. Whenever possible, split statements into three parts, with the last phrase being the "punch" line. Rather than saying: "The product is perfectly reliable in all of our tests, and it can be safely operated by your factory personnel . . . it's the best option on the market today," give the first fact: "This product has been shown to offer excellent reliability in all of our tests." Let the interpreter translate. Then add: "The product can be safely operated by your factory personnel." Let the interpreter translate. Give your clincher: "In conclusion, the research I have presented to you proves that this product is the best option on the market today." When the interpreter finishes translating this line, heads will be nodding in total comprehension. If the interpreter had to grapple with the all-in-one version, the audience would likely become bored and preoccupied.

- Be redundant. Roughly 70 percent of a translated message fails to pass through an interpreter to an audience. Much of what passes through will be comprehended only hazily, because your words will have been denuded of their emotionally and culturally conditioned content by the process of translation. It doesn't hurt to *reiterate* important points and check for nods of comprehension.

- Find and train a good interpreter. The best way to find an interpreter is through referral. Call business colleagues and ask whether they have used an interpreter whom they would recommend. If that doesn't work, call the American Translators Association, in Ossining, New York: (914) 941-1500. The organization represents hundreds of certified interpreters and translators for all languages, many of whom have special expertise—microbiological terminology in Burmese, for instance. The organization can refer you to one of its chapters located in your area or overseas, and will send you a personnel directory.

  To "train" an interpreter means to rehearse the presentation with the person well before the scheduled departure for Asia. No interpreter will be able to translate all the required technical terms without opening a dictionary; this groundwork should be done at home, not in front of an Asian audience. If *any* humor, irony, or special verbal twist appears in the presentation, make sure the interpreter has found the right nuance to translate it, rehearses it, and knows the body and facial language needed to deliver it, so that the audience gets the message clearly and responds favorably. Some Westerners work with their interpreters for two or three weeks before leaving for Asia.

- Do not begin another phrase until the interpreter has finished translating the previous one. Westerners often forget, especially when things get heated during a negotiation, that, no matter what they say, only the statements conveyed by the interpreter will be understood at all on the Asian side. They often get angry and cut in before the interpreter has finished translating their earlier sentence. The Asians will sense that the foreigner is angry about something, because of the accompanying gestures and expression, but a chopped-off message will come through garbled.

When speaking through an interpreter, look at the person to whom you are "speaking" and not at the interpreter. This phase can be more comfortable than your delivery in English, when you are looking at a listener who cannot understand your language. Rehearse eye contact as part of the pretrip training.

- Expect Asian counterparts not to trust the interpreter. Don't trust theirs, either. Instruct your interpreter to break into the dialogue to retranslate what the Asians' negotiator has said, if the translation is faulty or if the tone of the statement has been modified in any way. The oldest trick in the book is to *pretend* to be uncomprehending of a language, in order to listen in on unguarded conversations. Stay out of earshot, when discussing sensitive topics among colleagues. The trick can work both ways, but few North Americans have the language skills needed to use it.

- Have your interpreter debrief you after each meeting. Interpreters often overhear significant utterances on the Asian side that you should know about.

◆

author William Lutz, "doublespeak": a "language that pretends to communicate but really doesn't." However, Asian circumlocution is not as Orwellian as Westerners would like to think. "Yes" may mean "maybe" in Asia, and "maybe" may mean "no," but that doesn't mean that Asian counterparts aren't communicating. They're doing it in the language of *AsiaSpeak*. When Westerners learn to decipher it, AsiaSpeak can be comprehended like any other language.

A friend of mine who works for a Japanese boss was in the habit of saying "No" when she meant "No." Her boss became increasingly irritated and finally asked her to be more indirect. He told her that, if she wanted to say "No," she should do it by using hints, euphemisms, and nonverbal gestures, which, he felt, would have a less abrasive effect on others in her office.

Paul Norbury and Geoffrey Bownes have written on this topic perceptively in their book *Business in Japan.* They point out that camouflaging one's true feelings and intentions, as Asians do in conversation and negotiation, is not necessarily duplicity. The impetus for Asians' vagueness is actually sensitivity to their listener. Filipinos invited to a social occasion may say "Yes" to the invitation just to be courteous, when they know they will not be there. They will feel that to refuse the request would hurt the inviter's feelings and rob him or her of face (*hiya*), and they will avoid this outcome even if it means telling an untruth.

Listening for "No."   Westerners doing business in Asia can't take "Yes" for an answer *anywhere* in the Pacific Rim, without thorough verification and cross-checking to ensure that the "Yes" you have heard was not a "polite yes" that really meant "No." A "polite yes" aggravates foreigners, who eschew verbal guessing games; Asians are equally disturbed when foreigners can't take a hint or read the signals that are common usage. A typical dialogue might be:

Westerner's Question: Has my proposal been approved?

If the intended reply is "No," any one (or more) of the following polite replies may be given instead. They are tactical replies synonymous with "No."

The Conditional "Yes":	"If everything proceeds as planned, the proposal will be approved."
The Counter Question:	"Have you submitted a copy of your proposal to the Ministry of Electronics?"
The Question Is Criticized:	"Your question is difficult to answer."
The Question Is Refused:	"We cannot answer this question at this time."
The Tangential Reply:	"Will you be staying longer than you originally planned?

The "Yes, but . . ." Reply: "Yes, approval looks likely, but . . . ." In Japan, the reply will actually end with "but . . ." (*desu ga*). Your interpreter will translate the "but . . ." as "but maybe not" or something similar.

The Answer Is Delayed: "We will know shortly." In Japan, you may hear that your proposal is being considered "*kakyuteki sumiyaka,*" or "with the greatest expedition possible," which, of course, means with almost no expedition at all.

Another answer might be a stone-cold silence. A disconcerting silence often substitutes for a direct, potentially offending "No," during a negotiation that has devolved into a squabble. Silence is a cue to back off and change the subject.

Facilitating Two-Way Discussion

How does communication get running smoothly in a meeting in Asia?

By *facilitating*—a fancy term used by communication experts for "positive feedback" or "active listening." The challenge is to get two sides talking *with* each other rather than *at* each other. Both sides have to communicate through an interpreter, which can make any discussion, even one between old friends, awkward and disconcerting for both parties. The tips in the following sections will get discussions in Asia off to a good start and keep them running smoothly.

Interject Questions.   Because of the language barrier, the best way to encourage the Asian side to explain its product needs, technological know-how, or interest in a proposal, is to ask questions—*lots* of them.

Westerners should enter *every* meeting in Asia, whether formal or informal, with a long mental (if not written) list of inquiries to be answered by Asian partners. Asians may well consider it impolite to be interrupted with a tangential comment or opinion, but *not* with a relevant question about their presentation; the questioning is perceived as attentive listening, which is appreciated. If the

Checklist for Uncovering the Truth

- Listen for euphemisms that may mean the opposite of their literal translation. A few of the most commonly heard euphemisms are: "I'll check on it and do whatever I can." "It's difficult." "We have to study the matter further." "I'll do my best after talking with my superiors." They *all* usually mean "No."

- Repeat the position of the Asian side and ask for confirmation, if you don't believe a "Yes." (In the Philippines, you can even ask whether the "Yes" is a "formal yes" or not.) If your counterpart hedges, then "Yes" probably meant "Maybe." Back off quickly, to avoid embarrassing anyone, and change the subject.

- Meet informally with a lower-ranking member of the Asian negotiating team, who might reveal the true situation to you over drinks. You might back into your questions, observing, for example: "Your superior must not like my proposal very much, because he did not attend the discussion today." Self-effacing questions often elicit refreshing (and true) responses, like: "Oh no, not at all. He's considering it with colleagues tomorrow, in fact."

- Appeal to the Asians' conscience. Asians have a deep sense of moral integrity. The Japanese like to say that they are *ryoshinteki na minzoku,* or motivated by their conscience: "Even if others do not know, Heaven knows, and I myself know." With this obligation to know the truth, an appeal can be made to the person, who has a duty to be truthful to others and to self. This approach can be implemented for resolving conflicts or getting what is rightfully deserved from Asian counterparts. Appeal to their sterling integrity. When nothing else works, go to the highest-level person you can reach, and ask for a proof of personal integrity in the form of the straight answers you're looking for.

◆

meaning of a sentence is not clear, the interpreter should immediately be asked for clarification. A good way to do this is to restate the point made and inquire whether the information has been received correctly. The idea is to break up the monotony of an interpreted conversation by interjecting relevant questions. They turn the one-way presentation into a dialogue, which helps to personalize the meeting and to get the two sides exchanging information and ideas rather than merely taking turns delivering them.

Slow *Way* Down.   Westerners often destroy the *kimochi* or *ki-bun* (mood) of a meeting by replying too quickly and offhandedly, in their attempts to appear forthcoming. Asians spend a good amount of time formulating a complete idea or opinion, which they convey seriously to the Westerners. They are surprised when the North Americans comprehend and respond immediately, and rather inarticulately, after formulating only a "snap judgment." The Asians feel let down and become irritated that the North Americans do not dedicate equal energy and time to their comments. Asians work out their ideas completely so that they can be communicated clearly and succinctly. The Westerners' ideas arrive at their mental doorstep in long, wordy translations that must be reassembled into logical sequence before they can be comprehended. The Asians, naturally, may feel more comfortable just listening. A savvy Westerner deliberates before replying, to get relevant ideas in order, and knows that the pause before responding will not be perceived as not having an answer. A person who takes time before replying will be considered thoughtful and intelligent, not unprepared or elusive.

Use Soft Rebuffs and No Personal Accusations.   The Western habit of confronting problems head-on can be offensive and even terrifying to Asians. Issues of face and group harmony are involved.

Wrong: "I don't know what the problem was. Your Mr. Yamada assures me that he sent the FAX, but I never received it."

Acceptable: "There must have been a problem with our FAX communication, because I never received the FAX that Mr. Yamada sent to me."

One person should never be singled out for blame. If and when the culprit is discovered by the Asian side, appropriate measures will be taken behind the scenes.

Never Be the Bearer (or Source) of Bad News.   Missionary Paul Crane has written, about foreigners in Korea: "One of the greatest errors that a foreigner commits is the lack of recognition and appreciation of the *kibun* [mood] in dealing with Koreans." Foreigners forget that frank discussion of negative topics is considered impolite and offensive, throughout Asia. A thorny topic should be broached first through a go-between who can deal with the problem in the appropriate manner through indirect channels. Problems get resolved faster this way than if a whole team of Asian negotiators is confronted with a dilemma head-on.

Compliment and Congratulate the Whole Group.   To give credit for something personally puts individuals on the spot. Asian businesspeople form a tight-knit group in which individuals shun criticism as well as excessive commendation that can separate them from the group. The "company" should be complimented, and thanks should be expressed to the "organization."

Offer an Apology When Necessary.   Asians offer apologies much more frequently and willingly than do North Americans, who tend to deny blame and give excuses when things go wrong. Asians, especially the Japanese, tend to "take the rap" and accept blame with profuse apologies, rather than offer excuses. North Americans' unwillingness to apologize unnerves Asians. In the negotiation scene in the movie *Black Rain,* the irreverent New York cop, Nicksan (Michael Douglas), is reprimanded for allowing the escape of a Yakuza gangster. The Japanese police chief says: "You don't have to drink the tea, but you *should* apologize." Nicksan can't believe his ears and refuses to "take the rap." Westerners who indirectly cause a situation to go awry should admit fault and apologize. They won't be culturally conditioned for this kind of resolution, but, to save face and get off the hook, it's the fastest route.

Don't Show Anger Openly.   Although their patience may be tested, why should Westerners remain passive and cool, never holler, and "never let an Asian see them sweat"? Impatience with a Thai indicates an incompetence to understand the problem, a lack of *suparp* (politeness), and a disposition that is *jai rohn,* which means hot-headed and aggressive. Filipinos inherited the Spanish ability to hide and control their emotions. In China, to show anger is to lose face. "If heaven and earth cannot sustain / Their violence for a day; / How foolish is that man, and vain, / Who gives his passions play!" said Lao Tze.

Don't Be a Boaster.   North Americans' career mobility depends on moving up a very competitive corporate ladder; a little tooting of one's horn and some back-stabbing are part of the game. We tend to take credit for our accomplishments and boasting of them is an accepted part of business socializing, especially with one's boss. "Americans tend to suffer the 'Gee, I'm great' complex," says Christine Houston, a partner with Korn Ferry International who works in Tokyo. "We're taught to be individualists and to emphasize ourselves. That attitude just doesn't cut it [in Japan]." Throughout Asia, self-adulation is considered a violation of unwritten laws of humility. If boasts are made in the presence of Malays, for example, they think the boaster is *sombong* (proud and arrogant). Filipinos may apply to a boaster the term *pabalatbunga* (skin of fruit), meaning skin-deep or superficial; they judge people more by *loob* (inner self) than by worldly accomplishments. As for the Chinese, their saying is: "The smaller the mind, the greater the conceit."

Asian hosts may *test* their guests' humility. I was once introduced to a Chinese delegation as an author of a book about doing business in China. The delegation became very interested in me and one member said, "You must be a very great expert on China business." I took that as a cue to reply, "The more I know about China, the less I understand." The statement was greatly appreciated; from that moment on, I was accepted by the delegation as a friend. Mei Yaochen's advice, in Sun Tzu's *The Art of War,* can be applied to personal or company accomplishments: "Great wisdom is not obvious, great merit is not advertised."

Resolve Delicate Issues via a Go-Between.   Almost any impasse or misunderstanding can be ironed out by meeting informally with a person outside the negotiation setting. Any potential sticking point during a negotiation can be diffused by saying, "I like the idea." Later, the point can be brought up after hours. Efforts to protect everyone's face and sidestep potentially embarrassing conflicts will be appreciated, especially in Indonesia, China, and Malaysia, where government policy and business interests are represented by different negotiators. Often, it becomes obvious that *they* don't agree with each other.

Avoiding Idioms, Slang, and Too-Direct Diction

Negotiating through an interpreter in Asia can be, to quote T. S. Eliot, an "intolerable wrestle with words and meanings." Words are symbols encased in layers of consciously and subconsciously felt meanings and interpretations; it's easy to be fooled by a linguistic illusion that plain and clear words have been translated for Asian listeners into terms of identical meaning. The idioms Westerners use to communicate—"right off the bat," "playing hardball," and "two strikes on them before they even

started," to cite a few deriving from the game of baseball—
rarely translate at all into a foreign language. Allied to these
crippling linguistic problems is the tendency for Asians to communicate indirectly and politely, using ambiguous words and insinuation. Against these obstacles, it's amazing we communicate
at all in Asia!

The reminders in the following sections will help get messages
through Asian barriers faster and as close to their original form as
possible.

Translations: The Right Words May Have Wrong Meanings.
Often, the same word has an entirely different connotation when
translated into an Asian language. The Japanese might describe a
suggestion or proposal as *mondai,* a problem. The English word
"problem" has a negative connotation that is not present in *mondai,*
which means simply, "something that will need further study." Before registering a negative emotional reaction to words and
phrases, Westerners should consult their interpreter for help in
understanding the words' connotations.

Loaded Words.   Some words, when conveyed through an interpreter, can attain a dagger quality. I was once seated at a banquet table near an American woman who asked a Chinese official
whether China has a problem with "racism." That word, along
with "abortion," "massacre," and "corruption," is what I would
call "loaded," in speaking with Chinese. I interrupted the conversation and changed the interpretation of the word "racism" to
"discrimination." Some Westerners have a tendency to use steel-
claw language as hyperbole in their conversations. Replies to questions will be more forthcoming if subtle rather than extreme
words and phrases are chosen.

Unconditional Statements or Questions.   When more than
one Asian negotiator is present at a meeting, ambiguity in the
Asians' statements must be accepted. Questions should not be
phrased so that the listener has to answer yes or no. The listener's
opinion should be asked. For instance, to the question "Is the
project one that you can accept?" the reply will be an ambiguous
"Yes," out of politeness rather than truthfulness. "Do you understand what I have said?" will be answered "Yes" invariably, because to say "No" might offend the questioner or indicate a lack of
intelligence on the part of the listener. Instead, the listener can
be asked whether it might be advisable to illustrate a point again,

in a different way. Does the proposal answer all of his or her questions? Does it seem appropriate to anticipated needs?

Idioms.   Western idioms don't translate into Asian languages; and interpreters may not have heard the current "in" phrases. "Man, that's rough," and "I can't believe my eyes," are examples of common idioms that might cause confusion. Diana Rowland tells a funny story about an American and three Japanese associates who were having drinks in the stern of a yacht cruising around Tokyo Bay. One of the Japanese men said: "If it weren't for taxes, the budget would be no problem." The American replied: "Well, in that, we're all in the same boat," and guffawed. The Japanese looked puzzled. One of them then said: "Yes, . . . we *are* in the same boat. Did you want to take a different boat?"

Westerners can *bet on it: talking turkey* with Asians, *peppering their rap* with culturally bound slang, jokes, and idioms, will leave Asian listeners *out in left field* —they may even think the speaker is *out to lunch. Capiche?*

Humor: It May Not Travel Well.   In translation, sarcastic humor may backfire. No sardonic or snide comments should be made in reference to any Asians, in any conversation. Filipinos are especially sensitive to humor directed at them; a good policy is to avoid commenting on others' appearance or character completely. Asian acquaintances may take the lead in making innocent swipes at individuals or companies. Koreans love to joke in this way, but the territory where jokes are acceptable may be closely defined. Joining in could be risky: seemingly private comments soon become public in tight-knit Asia. The Chinese say: "Words once released cannot be recaptured by the swiftest steeds."

This advice goes for speeches as well. The Western practice of opening a speech with a good joke falls flat because of the translation needed. A speech to a culturally *mixed* crowd offers some flexibility. Communication expert John Condon, in the opening remarks to his speech at the Intercultural Encounters with Japan Conference in Tokyo in 1974, gave an imitatable example:

> If this were an all-U.S. audience, I might begin with a joke. If this were an all-Japanese audience, I might better begin with an apology. Since we are a mixed group, let me begin by apologizing for not making a joke.

Voice Volume: *Decrease* It for Emphasis.   The loud voice— and the uproarious laughter—of the typical Westerner is probably

Successful Salespeople

The best salespeople I have known or heard about in Asia follow a few simple rules of selling-style.

- They're always prepared with current information about their industry, their products, and their customer's company. They don't lose composure, when asked to respond to the same questions over and over, because they realize that repetitive inquiries indicate a rising interest level rather than a delay tactic.

- They do not rely on the glamorized or hyped-up image of their products as presented in brochures, videos, or commercials. They concentrate on highlighting the high quality and unique specifications of their products, and on explaining how certain items offer unique benefits: increasing productivity, controlling quality, conserving energy, and so on.

- They promote their products truthfully. They avoid using hyperbole or sensationalizing the facts, because they realize how much homework their Asian customers will have done before the meeting.

- They do not deride competing products or exhibit comparison advertisements, which are prohibited under industrial agreements in many Asian countries.

- They bring along 15 to 20 extra copies of their sales proposals; it isn't always easy to find a photocopier or a person to operate it, in many developing countries of Asia.

- They type out their opening sales presentation in short sentences, and give each member of their audience a copy. This *guarantees* full understanding of what they say and substitutes for "reports" summarizing what they have said, which Asian career negotiators in their audience must submit later to superiors who could not attend. They rehearse with their interpreter beforehand. They *read through* the presentation, sentence by sentence. Rather than make a "pitch," they stay close to the original materials, to ensure total clarity in the translation process.

- They assign their negotiation team different parts of the presentation, to prevent tedium and delineate a clear role for each member of their delegation.

- They present all prices and specification figures in written form, to prevent misunderstanding of verbalized numerical figures, which could disrupt the smooth flow of their presentation.

- They know where their company is going—its strategic direction—in the next ten years, especially as it relates to the Pacific

Rim. They respond to Asians' desire to forge a long-term relationship with a foreign company.

- They discuss more than business with their Asian customers. As
part of every business meeting, preferably at the start and at the
end, they ask about the welfare of their customer's family: "Are
the children in college now?" "Is your wife feeling better?" and
so on.

◆

the characteristic that most offends Asians. North Americans'
habit is to raise their voice when they are not being understood
or not getting their way. The Asians understand *what* was said
only after the interpreter's rerun. *How* it was said may make
them recoil and become quiet, to avoid a confrontation. The
higher an Asian's status, the less volume is used in speech. A
gentle, soft-toned voice should be used for normal speech; as the
importance of the topic increases, the speaking volume should
decrease. A *quiet* voice gives emphasis, not a loud one. Even if
asked to repeat points for the tenth time, the speaker should not
turn up the volume, for clarity. It will shatter the mood of the
meeting.

Safe Rapport: A First Step in Building Trust

How much time do North Americans spend conducting small
talk with a potential customer, before turning the conversation to
business? Most North Americans claim they spend roughly five
minutes conversing about nonbusiness topics, before moving the
conversation to matters of business; the typical Japanese, Korean,
or Filipino might spend *one or two days* conversing, building trust,
and socializing.

Small talk has a double role: to create the ambiance of *congeniality* Asians find necessary to conduct business, and to build
trust among Pacific Rim contacts so that they will enter into
business deals and introduce other business opportunities and
contacts. Many North Americans are unwilling to participate in
small talk and unable to do it well. It requires taking an interest
in the place and people, being an interviewer, delicately prodding a host to divulge interesting truths about his culture. Small
talk, or constructive information gathering, is useful in acquiring
"free" information about the Asian company's relevant product
lines, its experience working with foreign companies, its position
in local/central bureaucracy, and its proprietary technological

know-how. The indigenous technical capabilities of the country, the nature of the decision-making bureaucracy in a particular industry, and competitors' activities in the country are all worth some small-talk time. This information can be obtained freely in the process of getting to know a business partner personally, through rapport.

Things to Know about a Host Country

A general knowledge of a country being visited—its government leaders, basic geography, political system, and economic structure—is essential. Its major newspapers and magazines should be reviewed, for briefing on the country's current sports figures, movies, and television personalities. Westerners should know their own country's foreign policy position vis-à-vis their host's country (in order to field questions about it). Most importantly, they should know a host country's sensitive spots, so they can steer clear of "unsafe" topics.

Conversing Confidently: Safe (and Unsafe) Topics for Rapport

People's Republic of China

- Talk about the "Warring States Period" (c. 453 B.C.) versus the "Warlord Period" (1911 to 1949), and other aspects of China's tumultuous history, but omit the Cultural Revolution and the 1989 crackdown on protesters.

- Ask for details about current economic policy and management reforms.

- Don't bring up religion, sex, abortion, or the collapse of Communism around the world.

- Refer to China as the People's Republic of China, not Red China, Mainland China, or Communist China; refer to Taiwan as the Province of Taiwan, not the Republic of China, because the Chinese officially consider it a province of the People's Republic.

- Avoid making vehement statements criticizing the Old Guard or the Tiananmen Uprising. A businessman I know says:

"Asking the Chinese about the Tiananmen crackdown is like asking the Germans about the concentration camps."

- Be prepared to answer questions about your country's current policies vis-à-vis China.

Hong Kong

- Avoid discussion of the exiled Chinese dissidents' resistance to the Chinese government. The tide has turned against the dissidents in Hong Kong; the typical response to questions about them is that they can have little impact on China's or Hong Kong's future working, from outside China.

- Ask Hong Kong hosts how the predictions of pessimists and optimists on the island compare as to predictions of Hong Kong's future after 1997, what positive and negative signals are emanating from Beijing, and whether the Basic Law will be enough to protect Hong Kong from Chinese manipulation.

- Feel free to ask where Hong Kong people are emigrating, how the Hong Kong stock market reacts to events in the P.R.C., and whether Hong Kong will remain a financial hub of Asia after 1997.

South Korea

- Talk about Chinese influence on traditional Korean culture, but *not* Japanese influence. Putting down Japan is a national pastime in Korea.

- Don't opine that the Koreans seem to emulate Japan. Make no comparisons like "Korean management style seems to be similar to Japan's," even though it is.

- Talk about Korea's *influence on Japan*. Since the seventh century, a brain-drain of Korean talent has been siphoned off to Japan, including monks, scholars, doctors, artists, and musicians. Confucianism came across the Sea of Japan from Korea in the eighth century. The *geisha* house originated from Korea's *kisaeng* house. The five-note atonal scale used in Japanese music came from Korea.

- Do not refer to the Japanese atrocities in Korea during the colonial period (1910–1945), including Korean women's being taken into battle by Japanese troops for companionship. The Japanese called them "wartime ladies of consolation."

(Koreans recently sought an apology from Emperor Akihito and received it.)

- Talk about the island of Cheju (the "Hawaii of the Orient"), where women work only at "outside work" while men tend to the household chores.

- Remember not to use verbal Japanisms or Japanese words. A naïve engineer, when asked if he had learned any Korean words while he was in Seoul, replied with a smile: "*Arigoto* and *mamasan*"—the Japanese word for "thank you," and the familiar form for addressing a low-status woman, such as a brothel owner.

- Don't talk about Korean student protests, the potential for the reunification of North and South Korea, labor strikes, resignations of past presidents, resistance to U.S. troop presence in Korea, the shooting-down of KAL 007, the 1985 seizure of the American Information Library and the Chamber of Commerce offices in Seoul, or Taiwan–Korea relations.

- Mention how Seoul beat out a Japanese city to host the 1988 Summer Olympic Games, a major international "gold medal" for South Korea.

Japan

- Talk about Japanisms, such as Kabuki and Noh theater, flower arrangement, the tea ceremony, *karaoke* singing bars, and the Japanese royal family—Emperor Akihito and Empress Michiko, as well as Hirohito, known posthumously as Emperor Showa.

- Don't talk about the U.S.-Japan Security Treaty, under which Japan would provide a front line of defense against Communist encroachment in Asia. Japan spends one-tenth what the United States does, for military outlays, but pays 40 percent of the bill to maintain American troops in Japan. (The Japanese Constitution stipulates that only 1 percent of the GNP may be used for military spending.)

- Avoid mentioning T. Boone Pickens, Japan's ownership of high-profile real estate abroad, trade imbalances, Japan–Korea relations, the status of Korean residents in Japan, and compensation for the South Korean victims of atomic bombs dropped on Japan.

Singapore

- Talk about the city-state's economic prowess and multiethnic population and traditions.

- Be cognizant of Singapore-bashing in the region; Malaysia views the population of Singapore not as *Singaporeans,* but as ethnically distinct Malays, Chinese, and Indians, among other groups.

- Avoid politics, the strict social policies, and the island's small size relative to its economic achievement.

Malaysia/Indonesia

- Concentrate on questions like "Where are you from in Indonesia?" "What is the ethnic group (*suku*) of the people in your family's village?" "How many children do you have?" Foreign businesswomen will be asked whether they are married. A single woman should just say "Belum," a rough equivalent of "Not yet."

- Expect women to talk about clothing, and men, about sports and physical fitness. Population control, planned parenthood, and birth control can be discussed more openly and frankly than in other Moslem countries.

- Do not bring up the subject of the 1965 coup in Indonesia or the linkage between politics and religion there and in Malaysia.

- Do not ask questions about a Malay's income, or "What kind of yacht do you own?", or any question arising from Western notions of upward mobility.

- Avoid going into detail about belief/nonbelief in God. ("Only Communists don't believe in God.")

Thailand

- Ask about Thailand's King Bhumipol, age 63, and Queen Sirikit, Buddhism and its ubiquitous iconography throughout the country, and Thai classical dance.

- Talk politics *if* you're well-informed about the current situation; Prime Minister Chaatchai Choonhavan was democratically elected in 1988 but was forced to resign in 1990 by military men who claimed Chaatchai's probusiness government was corrupt. Having revamped his cabinet, Chaatchai is back in office (as of this writing).

- Be careful in any discussions of the AIDS epidemic in Thailand versus the country's lucrative sex industry; many higher-class Thai women vehemently denounce official reluctance to enforce Thailand's laws forbidding prostitution.

Philippines

- Be ready to engage in conversation with educated Filipinos on virtually any topic.
- Avoid talk of the continuing influence of the Marcos camp on the Philippines' politics and society, the likeliness of a military coup, Communist insurgency in Mindanao, and the future of U.S. bases in the Philippines.
- Be aware that the term "Peacetime" refers to the period before World War II (1902–1941).

Fielding Loaded Questions

As "ambassadors" of their country, Westerners should try to answer loaded questions truthfully. However, their answers should not appear overly critical of their country, its policies, or its leaders. Asians are not in the habit of criticizing *their* country, especially in the company of foreigners.

Asian business associates have asked me the following questions point-blank, in all frankness and seriousness. *What would your replies have been?*

- "We hear about racial discrimination in America, and the black people are very poor. Why is this?"
- "Can you go out at night in your town without being mugged?"
- "Is it true about American women being liberated to the point they control American men?"
- "You know so much about our country, some people here might think you are a spy. Are you?"
- "Are you going to be a millionaire?"

To this last question, posed by a delegation of Koreans, I answered: "No, but I plan to *marry* a millionaire." That got a big laugh and diffused their not-so-oblique attempt to gauge the size and success of my company.

CHAPTER SIX

Speaking Without Words: The Art of "Belly Language"

An angry fist cannot strike a smiling face.
CHINESE PROVERB

Mr. X, from NEC, made two types of mistakes in his sales presentation. We've gone over the verbal ones in the previous chapter. This chapter looks at the second category of his intercultural communication mistakes, the nonverbal ones, which were equally responsible for the Asians' exodus from the meeting room.

- He stood above his audience, looking down on them, which is not a good way for a seller to show deference to a buyer.
- He made no direct eye contact until he was irritated; then, he glared at his listeners, which is extremely rude behavior in Asia.
- He used wide arm gestures, which are not used by Asians and are felt to be threatening.
- He failed to read nonverbal signals given by his audience; they were indicating that his presentation had gone on too long and that his audience did not take an interest in his product.
- He remained haughty and arrogant in posture and facial expression, even as his audience looked at their watches and fidgeted impatiently.

Why East and West Clash When Communicating Nonverbally

Like most Westerners, Mr. X communicated in a *low-context* manner: his message was explicit, overt, and clearly sent out to his audience, but he did not depend on, or even acknowledge, the nonverbal signals, like body language and eye contact, that would have told him that the message wasn't being *received*.

Asians communicate less directly and less explicitly than Westerners. Intercultural communication pundits say that Asians' manner of communication is conducive to a *high-context* social environment. People who communicate with each other in this kind of environment assume that each of them possesses a complete knowledge of the *contextual* background information regarding the subject matter they are discussing. In high-context groups, much communication can be implied; it need not be stated explicitly. In high-context (as opposed to low-context) societies, communication between people can rely more on body movements (called *kinesics*), facial expressions, eye contact, and other nonverbal signals, to get a message across. Few words are needed to express an opinion. A slight change in an expected gesture can send a clear message, because the *context* for the message is universally understood. High-context communication environments place a premium on the personal relationship among communicators (to communicate at all, the communicators need to know each other extremely well). People from other cultures are recognized immediately as outsiders, because they are not trained to respond to the hidden cues being expressed.

North Americans learn to communicate in a melting-pot environment; explicit verbal communication is necessary, to exchange messages with people from widely varying cultural backgrounds. The *context* of the information has to be communicated before the information itself can be exchanged.

Nonverbal signals and unspoken assumptions continue to figure prominently in Asians' personal and business relationships. The best known Asian words that refer to communicating without words are *haragei* or "belly language," in Japan, and *nunchì* or "face reading," in Korea. *Nunchì* refers to the intuitive power to know what another person is thinking, by reading nonverbal cues. Koreans believe deeply in the powers of extrasensory perception and intuitive knowledge or insight; they use the term *tongchal yok,* says author Boye de Mente, to describe "the visceral feeling by which Korean businessmen often make decisions—as opposed to using intellectual reasoning or logic."

Nonverbal Expression Is Not Universal

The problem for Westerners in Asia is that East and West often don't agree on the meaning of nonverbal cues and signals. In the

Philippines, for example, a jerk of the head and chin downward means "No" and a jerk upward means "Yes." When Filipinos raise their eyebrows in response to a request, the gesture means "No." Indians (and Bulgarians, incidentally), when they mean "Yes," use a head gesture that is the same as Westerners' for saying "No." A smile or a laugh in Asia may mean embarrassment or disapproval, as well as happiness and approval, as in the West. Direct eye contact may be considered an intimidation tactic by Asians, when actually Westerners are only trying to give the Asians undivided attention.

"Nonverbals" Can't Always Be Controlled

"Nonverbals" are hard to *control*, because they are mostly automatic and spontaneous; sometimes, people simply cannot avoid "communicating." "Any action . . . if noticed and interpreted by another," writes intercultural communication expert John Condon, "'communicates'—whether or not it communicates what was intended, and even whether or not the person was aware of having communicated anything at all." When anger begins, the posture stiffens, the eyes widen and the stare becomes intense, the volume of the voice rises, and the head movements become jerky. Without knowing it, people are *communicating* that they have grown impatient and irritated. Asian counterparts, being sensitive to nonverbal signals, read the reactions as if they are lettered on a billboard: "I am impatient. I am irritated."

"Nonverbals" Seem Endless: Which Ones Can Be Believed?

How do people communicate without words? By using everything from a glance or a sniff to a pointed departure from the premises—and those are only some of the *negative* nonverbal communications. The number of nonverbals is endless.

Anyone who has been "put off" by an Asian's nonverbal behavior—or has offended an Asian with a nonverbal gesture or expression—knows how important it is to understand the meaning of local signals and gestures *before arrival in Asia*. These are the media of nonverbal communication most used by Asians:

- Facial expressions (called *shirankae* in Japan)
- Eye contact and "eye messages"
- Body language, including arm and hand gestures

- Physical touching and proximity boundaries
- The use of silence during negotiating
- Your gender (i.e., working as a woman in Asia)
- Your clothes, and what *they* say
- Written communication

Facial Expressions and the Language of Smiles

"She smiles very differently from us, doesn't she? And she is so expressive. Her face is all expression." That's how a Korean student described her North American teacher at their first meeting. People living in societies that depend greatly on nonverbal gestures and expressions must truncate their expressions, in order to conceal their most personal thoughts and feelings. The private self is hidden behind a façade of nondemonstrative and nonrevealing physical gestures and expressions.

Asians tend to control their facial expressions to a remarkable degree. The Japanese call their stony, blank face the "know-nothing face" (*shirankao*); the face is devoid of nonverbal messages other than jerky nods of understanding.

North Americans tend to deliver their most serious points with a stern and solemn facial expression. Asians, however, may deliver a serious point with a smile or a short laugh, in an attempt to soften the truth and reduce the potential for confrontation.

When Filipinos laugh during a negotiation, they may be indicating that they are stating something vital to the discussion, not something frivolous. Filipinos use a smile to apologize, to praise, or to show poise, but they also smile when they are angry or embarrassed. In Thailand, the "land of smiles," a smile or a laugh may not indicate amusement or mirth, especially during a business meeting. A short laugh may mean that a Thai is embarrassed by something that has been done or said. Thais smile at conflict rather than confront it; they are likely to smile at Westerners when disagreeing with them, which can be disarming and disconcerting for the more overtly aggressive North Americans.

Laughing and smiling may be a means of protecting visitors from bad news, or from something that the host believes will trouble them. (In the previous chapter, we discussed how Asians conceal bad news so as not to worsen someone's mood.) News of a flood or a child's death may be delivered with a sinister-seeming smile and a giggle. An Indonesian friend might mention, with a smile, that his mother has died of oral cancer. One morning, standing in front of our hotel in Korla, a desert town in the Xinjiang province of China, a United Nations consultant and I saw a tractor-wagon, loaded with masonry rock, hit a ditch and dump its contents upon its driver. Passersby dragged the driver from the rubble and set him on the hood of a car. Our hotel's concierge ran over to examine the situation and gave us the lowdown with a toothy smile: "He dead for sure. Hit his head very hard, I think." We stood there horrified at his seeming indifference, until we remembered that his smile was a shield to protect us—the honored foreign guests—from being disturbed by the event. When an Asian smiles or laughs at tragedy, words of concern, spoken in a condolent voice, are in order.

Laughter can also indicate fear, humiliation, or apology. If an Asian partner laughs during a serious conversation, or if others in the same room laugh suddenly, the *wrong* response is to blurt out: "What's so funny?" The Asians may be laughing for reasons other than amusement. The Westerner may have just committed an offense, and their laughter may be a way to courteously cover it up.

Eye Contact: Does It Mean Honesty or Intimidation?

Although, out of curiosity, Asians may stare long and hard at foreigners in a nonbusiness setting, most Asian businesspeople will not gaze at or listen to a speaker to the same degree that North Americans typically will. Westerners are taught to look at parents and superiors when spoken to. Seeing "eye-to-eye" connotes mutual understanding and trust. A person who "can't look you in the eye" is suspected of being dishonest. In Asia, NOT looking at a superior directly indicates obedience and subservience. Throughout Asia, parents discipline their children with a hard stare. Thus, from early upbringing, direct eye contact in Asia carries a subconscious connotation of provocation and condemnation.

John Graham, in a study of negotiating behavior at the University of Southern California, found that Americans, Germans, and Britishers gaze at their business partners roughly 30 percent of the time, during a negotiation. The Japanese look at their negotiating partners only 13 percent of the time, or less than half that of their Western counterparts. Graham did not test Thais, Filipinos, Malays, or Chinese in his survey. However, my own experience in communicating with people from these cultures indicates that they mirror the Japanese in their aversion to prolonged eye contact. Thais consider it rude to look directly into another person's face, because it *feels* to them like a threat. They tend to divert their eyes from contact and to conduct conversation while looking askance, or out of the corner of their eye, at a companion.

Chinese and Koreans maintain more direct eye contact than other Asians. Overseas Chinese in Hong Kong, Singapore, or Taiwan maintain about as much eye contact as Westerners.

When Asians don't look them directly in the eye, Westerners may *feel* that somehow they're not being listened to or that the Asians are not interested in what they're saying; surely the Asians are bored, preoccupied, or, worse yet, dishonest. Nothing could be further from reality. The Asians *are* paying attention.

In a negotiation between a Japanese company and one from Germany, the senior Japanese negotiator rarely glanced at the German negotiators at all, and soon began to nod off, sitting straight in his chair but seeming to fall asleep. (In my experience, at least one person on the Asian side of the negotiation table will close his or her eyes and doze off at some time during a extended presentation.) The Germans took it as an insult and walked out on the negotiation, never to return. They had expected the leader of the Japanese side to employ a hands-on style during the discussion; instead, they discovered, as others have, that a senior Japanese negotiator will often play only a sort of referee role during business meetings, merely ensuring that an agenda is followed. Underlings ask questions, formulate proposals, and basically do the work. The senior negotiator will make the opening and closing statements and that's about all. His zen-like silence and lack of eye contact mean things are proceeding effortlessly, not that the deal is uninteresting to him. The Germans learned this lesson the hard way.

Whom Can One Touch, and When?

Asian cultures are not touching cultures. Most touching is still intrasexual and intrafamilial throughout Asia. Shaking hands may

still be considered unhygienic by some Asians who will insist on
the bow when greeting strangers, but this attitude is rare among
those accustomed to meeting Western businesspeople. Japanese
spouses won't kiss or embrace in public, even if they have been
separated for weeks. A son returning from four years of school in
the United States will stand three feet away and greet his Korean
parents at the airport with a solemn bow, or maybe two or three
bows, if emotions are running high. Even close Korean relatives
rarely hug or kiss each other; they may just face one another and
tremble, says Korean author and culture expert Won-dal Yang.

Westerners, who tend to be more physically informal and intimate, may have to control a natural tendency to touch businesspeople in Asia, as part of the nonverbal communication with them.
If they do (unless the person touched is a close personal friend),
they'll sense the Asian stiffening and becoming instantly uncomfortable. Fortunately, North Americans and Asians are similar in
that they rarely touch each other when negotiating, unlike Latin
Americans, who tend to tap someone on the forearm to emphasize
a negotiating point. Both North Americans and Asians interpret
touching of this sort as a hard-sell tactic and a violation of personal
space. However, more than one American executive has ruined a
deal in Asia by backslapping an Asian partner at the banquet table
or at the conclusion of a meeting.

Proximity Boundaries: How Close Is Too Close?

There's a difference between touching and what experts call
proxemics. North Americans, whether strangers or friends, stand
about 18 inches apart when speaking to one another. The Chinese
and the Koreans stand about 24 inches apart, and the Japanese
feel comfortable standing about 36 inches apart. In other words,
North Americans' normal stance tends to crowd their Asian hosts
during initial formal meetings.

An interesting thing happens when businesspeople in Asia socialize *informally:* their proximity distance shrinks. (The North
Americans' remains about the same, give and take a few back slaps
and shoulder slams.) The Japanese and the Koreans observe clearly
different proximity boundaries for the informal setting and the
formal one. "They can get so close when drinking and socializing,"
said one consultant I know, "they make you feel uncomfortable and
glad you're wearing your deodorant." One county commissioner in
the United States, a woman who often meets informally with
Japanese delegations, says, "They [the Japanese] put their noses

right up to my breasts. It drives me crazy!" Her Japanese guests are simply observing a much tighter proximity boundary than Westerners are accustomed to in an informal setting. The next morning, back in the office, the 36-inch pattern will be back.

When Touching Taboos Break Down

Touching becomes "legal" during an informal drinking session between persons of the same sex. Asian men touch each other, and will touch foreign men, as the drinking escalates. A Thai who puts a hand on a same-sex Westerner's knee is only giving a sign of friendship.

Opposite-sex touching is a different matter. Beyond the handshake, Asian men will not touch foreign women under any circumstances, and Westerners should not touch any Asian business associates of the opposite sex who are not *very* close friends. Confucius was very clear about this. He taught that men should not pass an object to a woman directly. They should place the object down for the woman to pick up herself, thus avoiding any personal contact. An Asian's head should never be touched; the head is considered the person's spiritual center. Moslem Asians should be touched only with the right hand, if at all—never with the "unclean" left hand.

Asian Body Language

Let me see you walk and I'll tell you what you're like.

This Chinese proverb is a reminder of how one's body language reveals one's personality. Enter the foreigner, with confident gait and widely gesticulating arms, who towers above Asian counterparts, looming over them like the offensive and impolite Mr. X.

What body gestures should generally be avoided, in all of Asia? Which ones should be observed? I have divided gestures into two categories: body gestures, and arm and hand gestures.

Body Gestures: Some Help, and Some Hinder

When moving about an open area with an Asian host, visitors should avoid walking confidently out ahead of him. They should not don a hard hat and strut about like they own the place, as many North Americans do, as if by second nature. When a host *is showing* visitors the interior of a factory or a construction site, they should walk slightly behind him, especially if he is of superior status, to convey polite respect nonverbally.

When moving about a room, a foreigner who is of large physical stature must be cautious not to inadvertently exhibit disrespect to those of high status, especially elders, by either looming over them or passing in front of them without acknowledging their presence. A polite gesture is to hunch over a bit while passing a superior who is seated, as if to ask permission to pass before him. If it is necessary to pass before a seated person in the Philippines, it is polite to clasp the hands and lower the head when passing in front of the person. One hand may also be extended in the direction of passage, as if to ask, "May I pass this way in front of you?"

Offensive Feet.   Throughout Asia, the feet are considered unclean, so Westerners must be extremely careful not to point theirs at other people and to be mindful of how they sit. It's easy to be accidentally offensive. A Thai will give a dirty look to a visitor who points the soles of his or her feet in the Thai's direction, when leaning back against a pillow, legs crossed, while sitting at the dinner table. (The Thais seem to be more sensitive about feet than any other Asian nationality.) In a meeting room anywhere in Asia, the feet should stay firmly on the floor, to ensure against committing any offense. My most urgent advice is: Don't swing a crossed leg, don't tap the feet, and, for God's sake, don't prop the feet up on a tabletop in the presence of Asian hosts!

Feet should never be mentioned or talked about. Selwa Roosevelt, White House chief of protocol during the Reagan years, tells a revealing story in her memoir, *Keeper of the Gate.* An American diplomat once deeply offended a visiting Chinese delegation to Washington by discussing feet at the banquet table—a grave faux pas in China, and not all that tasteful in the West, either.

Arm and Hand Gestures

Asians make less use of their arms and hands to emphasize speech than Westerners do. In formal situations, an Asian's arm and hand gestures may be limited to movements of the fingers as they rest in the person's lap. (This is especially true for Asian women.) Wide gesticulating while talking is thought to be unrefined and rude. "Talking" with the hands, especially when communicating through an interpreter, is unintelligible to Asians. Wide arm movements intended to clarify a point (even the British do fewer of these than North Americans do) will only baffle Asian counterparts and may give an impression of anger. The Japanese usually keep the hands folded on the lap or on a table; when standing, most Asians clasp the hands in front of the body.

In the West, the hands-on-hips gesture indicates frankness and confidence. Among Asians, the gesture reflects obstinacy and may be insulting; in Indonesia, the gesture is the traditional attitude of defiance in *wayang* shadow-play theater. Another arm gesture to avoid is folding the arms akimbo. Among Filipinos, this gesture signifies arrogance and challenge; I try to avoid using it anywhere in Asia. Storing the hands in the pockets is considered bad manners.

Passing Objects. The taboo on hands hidden in pockets and the protocol of using both hands to accept and receive things probably have a similar origin. The ancient Chinese wore a loose robe that featured deep, wide sleeves in which weapons could be hidden. When both hands were used to give and receive objects, the sleeves were pulled back and proper intent was ensured. The tradition has survived, and both hands should be used to give and receive objects in Asia—even a piece of paper, a pen, or a business card across a wide table. In Korea and Japan, a person may hand something, such as a document, with the right hand, with the palm of the left hand placed under the right forearm. Objects can be passed in this way in these countries, but they should be received with both hands. *There is one exception to this rule:* Among Moslems in Asia, objects are given and received with the right hand only, assisting the right hand with the left only when giving or receiving a heavy object. The left hand is used for washing after using the toilet and for very little else.

Pointing and Calling. Asians consider it proper to point at objects and people with the thumb, *not* the forefinger. To motion a person to proceed ahead of another person, the thumb is extended and the other fingers are drawn into a fist, like a horizontal hitch-hiking sign. Filipinos sometimes point with the eyes and the chin, a gesture that can be emulated when in the Philippines.

To point to oneself in East Asia, the nose is touched rather than the chest. The ancient Chinese believed, as Chinese culture and language expert Eduardo Fazzioli explains, "that the nose was the starting point for the human body's development in the womb and therefore the origin of the individual." The Chinese character for "oneself" is a pictogram of a human face with a nose.

To call someone, the palm and fingers of the right hand are formed into a cup and the air in front of the person is scooped in a downward motion. Use of the Western-style hand wave to call someone in Asia may be offensive. Vietnamese residents of a community in California recently complained to their parish that non-Vietnamese neighbors offended them by calling them in this manner. In Vietnam, the Western-style wave to call someone is reserved for calling a dog!

How Asians Communicate Anger Without Words

When business meetings between Japanese and Chinese get heated, it is not uncommon for the Japanese negotiator to slam a fist upon the negotiating table in frustration and anger. The Chinese person's aversion to public display of anger and aggression typically compels him or her to break off the negotiation and proceed through a go-between. Like the Japanese, Korean negotiators are known to be more openly aggressive than the Chinese; as I've already mentioned, Thais, Filipinos, and Malays have a deep-set aversion to outbursts and aggressive body language.

Blow-ups rarely occur among Asians when they deal with Westerners. They may become angry and irritated, but they express these feelings nonverbally. Because displays of anger on the Asian side of the table may not be obvious, Westerners may inadvertently worsen an already deteriorating situation. Here are some telltale signs to look for:

- In Japan, a sucking of breath drawn through the teeth produces a "sah" sound. This may indicate the person is upset and running out of patience.
- The Chinese, whether in China or overseas, may show their negative response or anger by waving a hand in front of their face in a quick, fan-like motion.

Among other signs that Asian counterparts are uncomfortable, disinterested, or downright ticked off are:

- Blank expressions with no smiling;
- Disconcerted and/or impatient smiles and nods;

- Repeated glances at a clock or watch;
- Sudden unwillingness to make eye contact;
- A cessation of question asking;
- An inquiry by a lower-level functionary to an assistant or interpreter as to how long the presentation will last;
- A cold silence that is allowed to prevail in reply to a request.

The best response to these signs is to back off and call for a break, and then to drop the issue and take it up later, informally, through a go-between.

Silence: Part of the Negotiator's Arsenal

American conversational style does not allow silent periods. We have idioms to express our distaste for silence: "dead air" and "pregnant pause." We learn in sales training seminars that silence on the part of a customer is a deathknell to a potential sale. "Never stop talking" is a key component of Western sales practice, and our best salespeople often possess a so-called gift for gab. Although we sometimes say silence is golden, it makes us uncomfortable when it occurs during conversation, especially when discussing business.

Asians feel much more at ease with silence than Westerners do. Throughout Asia, businesspeople use silence as a persuasive tactic toward their Asian business associates—a "polite" reaction to an unacceptable offer. Asians, in general, feel more comfortable than Westerners do, in taking their time to collect their thoughts and formulate a clear reply. Asian negotiators may have to ponder for a moment whether they are *allowed* to answer a question, given that they may only be the mouthpiece for a cast of players not present at the meeting.

During negotiations in Asia, North Americans generally feel so uncomfortable with silence that they make unneeded concessions. Fear of silence costs Westerners millions of dollars! One Westerner negotiating in Japan repeatedly dropped his prices, because he took silence to mean a rejection of an offer. On one deal, he dropped his price $750,000 because he couldn't wait out 30 seconds of silence. His Japanese counterpart had thought his first price was fine. In Japan, and among ethnic Chinese, I've seen negotiations in which *10 minutes of silence* followed an offer.

Western discomfort with silence also breeds mistrust. When the Westerner's original price is so quickly lowered, without the Asian's even asking that it be lowered, isn't it probable that it was padded?

The key is to present an offer and wait out the ensuing silence, *without interrupting*. Interruption indicates weak resolve, flexibility in the offer, and a flawed proposal. The quiet wait, while maintaining proper manners, may be the longest wait of one's business life, but breaking the silence, I guarantee, will mean the proposed terms won't be accepted.

Nonverbal Negotiating Checklist

- Sit down at the negotiation table, rather than stand above the audience.
- Speak to the whole group. Avoid facing only one person in the Asian group, or the interpreter, while you speak.
- When listening to an Asian negotiator, don't slouch in the seat, doodle, cross the legs, or otherwise appear unattentive or disrespectfully informal, especially if you are a seller rather than a buyer.
- Handle objects such as product samples (theirs and yours) with utmost respect; pass papers, cards, and brochures with two hands while bowing slightly.
- Assign a member of your team to observe nonverbal signals on the Asian side *as you make your presentation*—nods of comprehension, facial expressions indicating interest, suspicion, or enthusiasm, and so on.
- Instruct the members of your team to control their nonverbal gestures at all times, and to give you positive nonverbal feedback *as you speak*, such as affirmative nods of agreement and approval, which will help to reinforce what you say, in the minds of your Asian counterparts.
- Instruct every member of your team to *never* break a silence and to always follow your lead before contributing to the discussion.
- Practice these routines with your team *before* arriving in Asia.

◆

What Gender Communicates:
Western Businesswomen in Asia

Female readers might think it strange to discuss businesswomen in Asia in a chapter on nonverbal communication. However, gender conditions, to some extent, the way Asian businesspeople deal with Westerners, especially females. Here's an example.

An American woman is the owner, president, and chairperson of the board of an American company. When her company hosted an all-male visiting Japanese delegation, the Japanese men wouldn't engage her in conversation during formal or informal meetings, but would instead communicate with male assistants. Their discomfort in communicating with an American business-woman was too great. A consultant to the company recommended that she visit Japan and take along a male vice president to conduct initial interfacing with the Japanese.

A female expatriate working in Asia will make as much headway as a male, but a woman sent over for an initial meeting as a representative of a company, unaccompanied and without formal introduction by an entity on the Asian side, may have trouble breaking sex-role barriers. The more internationalized the company and its executives, the less sex-role barriers will be a problem.

Why is there so much discomfort among Asian men in doing business with women? It goes back to the fact that Confucius was a chauvinist. "Women and servants," said Confucius, "are most difficult to deal with." Under his laws, men could divorce a wife if she failed to give birth to a son, if she was caught stealing, if she was jealous, if she nagged him, or if she disobeyed her parents-in-law. Women were not to speak before a man nor contradict him. They were to temper their facial expression and be sure not to show their teeth in the presence of men—for example, when laughing. (Korean women still place a hand over the mouth when laughing.) A woman may be considered an "unperson" by her husband until she produces a son. If a Japanese woman is not married by the age of 24, she has a good chance of never marrying and being labeled a social "leftover." A Korean wife is often called *anae,* or inside person, bound by tradition to remain in the house tending to the family. The Chinese character for wife is a woman with a broom in her hand. Korean women are rarely invited by their husbands to participate in business entertainment. There is one consolation, however: The Korean wife holds the purse strings of the household coffer.

"Ladies first" is not a custom in China or Korea. Some Westerners are horrified when Asian men are impolite to women. In China and Korea, men blow cigarette smoke in women's faces and let doors slam on them. In Korea, husbands get into taxicabs before wives. Women in Korea help men with their coats, and Asian women may not be introduced, even when part of a delegation. Later in a meeting, a Westerner may learn that the woman present is not a secretary but the head of the chemistry division at the negotiating company, or has some equally prestigious function.

Although Mao Tse-tung claimed that "Women hold up half the sky," working at jobs and as housewives, women are politically disenfranchised and expected to serve their husbands. Women account for only 1.29 percent of Japan's corporate managers. Most women workers are merely "office ladies" (O.L.s) who pour tea, bow to male superiors, type, and answer phones. Toshimi Kayahi Antram, author of *There's No Job A Woman Can't Do*, explains her all-too-typical experience as a young educated woman trying to get ahead in corporate Japan:

> After I graduated from Nihon University with a degree in journalism in 1975, I joined an advertising company. I requested that I be put in the creative department to work as a copy writer; however, the personnel manager said to me: "Women only work three or four years before they get married. They can't be strong soldiers to fight the company battles." So he put me in the accounts section to work as a bookkeeper. . . . Finally, after months of frustration, I took my case directly to the president of the company. He listened kindly and then smiled and said, "You know, for women, the happiest job in the world is to be a wife and mother. Women should not be so tough and aggressive like men. You'll know someday after you find the right man and settle down." . . . Not much later I took off for America.

One Foreign Businesswoman's Valuable Opinions

Probably the most frequently asked question during my Etiquette Edge seminars pertains to whether it's prudent to send a woman to Asia to represent a company's interest. "Will she be as effective as a man in male-dominated Asia?" or "Will she have problems making contacts and penetrating the bureaucracy?" After interviewing women who have worked in Asia, I can answer both questions with a resounding "Yes!"

Jackie Gannon has worked throughout the Asia-Pacific as an American businesswoman for over three years. Recently, I asked her several questions about her experience in doing business in Asia as a Western woman. I believe her comments illuminate the advantages and pitfalls of being a woman working in Asia.

What are the advantages, for a woman doing business in Asia?

Because there is no set standard for foreign women working in Asia, you can set your own standards without experiencing the same level of pressure experienced by foreign men in Asia; that is, for example, pressure to stay out late drinking and socializing with business associates. You therefore can set the agenda for how you want the business relationship to be conducted. *You* can interface the way *you* choose to and not how prescribed protocol requires.

As a woman dealing with men in Asia, you enjoy all of the advantages that you have in the West when dealing with men, for instance, using your natural charm to finesse a social advantage that may represent a business advantage as well.

As a foreign businesswoman in Asia, as long as you aren't curt, vocally feminist, or too aggressive, you will be treated extremely well; you will not be excluded or considered an outsider to the system, as is the myth. In fact, it's more like you're visiting royalty— and that alone is a great advantage.

Another advantage of working in Asia as a foreign woman, as opposed to some other overseas posts, is that bothersome sexual come-ons in the context of doing business occur very rarely anywhere in Asia, except in the Latin-influenced Philippines. The foreign businesswoman need not ever worry that a business associate would suggest bartering influence or a business opportunity in exchange for your romantic attention.

What are the drawbacks, for a foreign businesswoman in Asia?

As a foreign woman working in Asia, everybody *assumes* you're the secretary or "Office Lady," especially other Asian women. You may not receive the instant respect that you think you deserve, or that men below your station receive. On a plane, for example, you might find yourself asked to sit "with the other women." At a hotel, you may find there is little to do socially because single foreign women don't readily fit into Asian society. In this sense, it's a big advantage to be married while working in Asia, as it makes it easier for Asian men to socialize with you outside the context of business.

Hosting an Asian delegation is tough for a foreign woman, because Asian men always want to pick up the tab, which makes entertaining hard to arrange. I have to prepay all business entertainment.

You will find yourself the victim of stereotypes about the effectiveness of Western women working in Asia. But guess what? The stereotype is more likely to be held among the men of your *home office,* not your male counterparts in Asia. It is *they* who believe Western women can do no good in Asia. It is *they* who may use you as a scapegoat when things go wrong with the company's Asian endeavors, even things clearly out of your control. Don't be surprised if they blame their company's business problems in Asia on the fact that "they sent a woman to Asia and Asians don't like Western women as business partners."

What advice would you give to foreign businesswomen who plan to work in the Pacific Rim?

Build and maintain relationships with Asian business associates, contacts, and partners *independently* of your firm. Visit with their families at their homes. Confide in them and allow them to confide in you. Such an approach is protection against the failure of your firm in Asia; your business contacts will still be in place whether your firm succeeds in Asia or not.

Learn to ignore the way women are treated in Asia. You won't be successful if you can't repress all that you have learned in the West about women's rights and equal opportunity. As a foreign woman in Asia, you will NOT be treated as a woman; you will be associated with your training, skills, and job position. But you have to accept the fact that the Asian women you meet must conform to traditional roles that may be offensive to you.

Do not go to Asia without having been in your industry long enough to possess a deep understanding of your company, its product line, and your industry in general. This applies, of course, to men as well, but women have to win the respect of male counterparts in Asia before being taken seriously, and the only way to do this is by being an expert, a supplier of quality information to potential Asian customers.

If you are young (under 35), hide your age and emphasize your credentials. Know what your skill area is and wear it on your sleeve. It's okay to warn someone you "aren't a trained technician," but make sure you have a clearly defined area of real expertise or skill that identifies you.

Know something about the country in which you do business. Travel in Asia or, better yet, *live* in Asia before doing business there. It will impress your Asian partners greatly if you, for example, have lived in China for a time. Moreover, you won't be considered "just another company person" if you travel on your own in Asia in your free time during your stint there.

Probably most important of all, find a "mentor," someone on the Asian side who will show you the ropes, introduce you to key people, and answer your questions along the way. Seek out a retired Asian person who knows your industry well and is willing to share with you their years of experience.

Will an Asian Woman Be a Foreign Woman's Mentor?

Not likely. A bond of camaraderie is not easily forged between Asian businesswomen and North American businesswomen who come to Asia.

There is no dearth of women in high positions in Asian business; all across the region, with the exception of Moslem Asia, women occupy some of the highest entrepreneurial positions, albeit they are heavily outnumbered by men. Asian women who have obtained high positions and status in business have done so in the face of rigid rules and stereotypes that banish Asian women to the home and exclude them from business. Those who have climbed the corporate ladder are smart, tough, skilled, and bold in nonconforming. They covet their positions because the system doesn't allow many females to participate. Thus, an Asian woman rarely helps, or mentors, younger Asian women, much less foreign women. "It's been hard for them and they try to prevent competing women from rising by making their career mobility slower than it is already," an aristocratic and influential Thai businesswoman confided to me anonymously. No female peers helped *them,* so they won't go out of their way to help others, especially businesswomen from the West.

The best bet for a mentor, Jackie Gannon says, is a retired Asian business*man*. Older men are perfect mentors for Western businesswomen, because they are outside the companies that are potential clients and they have families at home and so will not be motivated by romantic prospects. Moreover, they are not prone to consider a Western woman a competitive threat; an Asian woman might.

Foreign Women as Delegation Leaders

Increasingly, American and Canadian women are traveling to Asia as leaders of business delegations rather than as support staff. For some, the role has been easy to fill, in part, because their Asian associates have personally witnessed their rise in rank and have come to respect their abilities through business association with them. Others report hardship in getting Asians to accept their role as lead negotiators; some even claim that they are all but ignored during business meetings.

A few tips might help foreign women setting out for Asia as team leaders.

- Before meetings take place, send an advance meeting agenda that includes short biographies of yourself and your team members. Describe yourself as "team leader," or make it apparent from your title that you are the superior-ranking delegate.

- Communicate your leadership role nonverbally, by entering doorways before your team members, for example, and sitting in the place of honor at the negotiation table (farthest from the door, with team members sitting at your sides). Communicate your leadership function verbally, by initiating and concluding all meetings with an opening and closing speech.

- Make sure your team members defer to you at all times, and ask that questions from the Asian side, if directed to members of your team, be directed to you, instead. If the Asian negotiators persist in ignoring you or refusing to acknowledge your leadership, you may find it necessary, as a last resort, to ask to continue the meeting without your team members being present.

How to Avoid the "Youth in Asia" Stereotype

Asian businesspeople tend to associate advancing age with skill and seniority; unfortunately for those of us who are young, they also tend to associate youth with inexperience and low position. They may distrust young people (under 30) at first, or refuse to take them seriously. Many consultants with whom I have spoken advise younger entrepreneurs, when visiting an Asian business associate for the first time, to take along an older "corporate personality" who will alleviate the negative impact of the "youth in Asia" stereotype.

For someone under 30, the initial objective when meeting Asian businesspeople is to impress them with an exceptional skill level and a deep commitment to the Pacific Rim market. Once a unique expertise is identified, the youth image fades quickly. Literally thousands of young Asians receive their education in the West; young businesspeople can connect with these people when they are in the West and link up with them later as each of them moves up in their respective companies. Some of the young Asians that I met five years ago are now section heads at their companies. In another 5 to 10 years, they'll be vice presidents who can offer me a direct conduit into the highest echelons of their companies.

Clothes: Personal Communicators

The clothes a person wears are another dimension of nonverbal communication. I have noticed in Asia that foreigners commit three sartorial misdemeanors:

1. Foreign women usually dress too loudly and suggestively for conservative Asia.
2. Foreign men dress like American cowboys, à la John Wayne; snakeskin boots and a Stetson should be left at home on the range.
3. Expatriates go too native in dress.

For those who are tempted to don a *sarong* wraparound in Malaysia or a *batik* shirt for a VIP diplomatic meeting in Indonesia, let this yarn, reported to the *New York Times,* be a forewarning. David Jones is president of Marketing Services International and has lived in Tokyo for 35 years. He has been known to attend *sumo* wrestling matches and receptions wearing a formal *kimono,* comprised of a baggy black silk coat called a *haori* and a *hakama,* a pair of baggy pleated trousers that looks like a skirt. When invited by the Imperial Household to meet Emperor Hirohito at a garden party, Jones wore the *kimono* outfit. "My wife and I were greeted by the Emperor," says Mr. Jones. "He was wearing a suit."

Clothing to Bring to Asia

A basic travel wardrobe is all that is needed for a short trip. Should new clothes be needed while on the road, Asia is the best place in the world to purchase them or, better yet, have them custom-made. Women should bring along two lightweight travel suits and an assortment of modest, subdued-colored blouses to wear with the suit skirts. Linen jackets will look rumpled after any amount of time in the tropics. Remember to pack a pair of low-heeled athletic shoes for walking and a pair of conservative dress shoes for business. A waterproof topcoat and/or a travel umbrella are essential. Women should not skimp on accessories or rely on fake *anything:* those Louis Vuitton bags women carry in Asian capitals are the real thing.

Men should pack one dark suit, navy or grey (charcoal can be threatening, psychologically), a cotton sport jacket, a pair of slacks, sport shirts, a light raincoat, dress shoes, and loafers for sightseeing.

I recommend "one dark suit" because it's perfect for a formal *satay* in Singapore or a banquet in China, as well as less formal business meetings and factory tours. Polyester should *never* be worn in the tropics. Western men should avoid imitating Asian associates' businesswear by having a baggy Chinese-style suit made for themselves. The suits look great on the smaller-framed men of Hong Kong, Taiwan, and Singapore, but they make Western men look like peripatetic tents. A good look for *informal* occasions and sightseeing is to wear a multipocketed safari jacket, khaki pants, and an Oxford shirt and tie. (See the Weather Planner in Appendix B, before deciding whether to pack a sweater and wool overcoat.)

Beards and Tans

Body hair on men is considered by most Asian cultures to be unsightly, and beards may not be appreciated. Thai men eschew them, possibly because Thai women associate them with old age. A Westerner may want to thin a full beard a bit.

A deep tan is hardly considered ideal in Asia, because sun is associated with outdoor work. A sun-wrinkled old face, usually that of a farmer, connotes labor and, hence, low status. A porcelain-white face is a woman's wish in East Asia.

Pacific Rim Dress Codes

China.   The Chinese were the first agricultural people to clothe both men and women in trousers. For Chinese women, the tradition lives on, at least among most women managers and officials. A foreign woman will fit in best wearing pantsuits or modest business suits; grey and dark blue are best. Sweatsuits are appropriate for *tai chi tuan* exercises at daybreak. Spike-heeled shoes, colorfully printed bags, elaborate necklaces, and designer jeans need not be packed for a trip to the People's Republic. Chinese men wear a Western-style suit with growing frequency, but the Mao jacket has made a noticeable comeback since the Tiananmen Square Massacre. Foreign men should wear a suit and tie in the winter, but this attire isn't necessary in the summer. Jackets can come off at banquets, if the room is warm.

Conservative China is not the place to flaunt wild haberdashery. Both foreign men and women should avoid loud colors.

Chinese managers are known to have been fired for manufacturing garish apparel deemed "too Western."

Hong Kong, Korea, and Taiwan. The dress code throughout the rest of East Asia, for business or for visiting homes, is a suit and tie for men, and a dress or skirt with a blouse for women. Conservative, lightweight suits are worn by men in Hong Kong; pinstripes are the mark of men in the banking sector. Korean business suits vary widely in color and quality, and Korean men have a tendency to wear blue tailored suits with white socks, a stylistic aberration better left unimitated. A nice watch on the wrist of foreign men and women is de rigueur in all of these countries.

Japan. The Japanese always "dress," even for an outing to the well-stocked fishing ponds that dot the city of Tokyo. Japanese men wear a blue serge suit throughout the year, even in broiling summer. For women, style gets tricky. *Vogue* magazine's summation of the women's fashion scene in Japan hits the mark:

Japanese style is prim, ladylike, label-conscious, and nervous. Japanese women dress each morning under the stern guidance of the country's fashion magazines and intense national pressure to look collectively correct.

Japanese women wear black tailored suits with black pumps in winter, and pastel suits and beige pumps in summer. Women wear subdued colors: pale yellow, moss green, charcoal grey, and mushroom. The style is to conceal, to call zero attention to oneself; only children and young people wear bright colors. Nancy Reagan's choice of a Bill Blass rose-colored dress suit for her lunch at the palace with Empress Michiko in 1989 was irreproachable. Don't forget to wear a slip, says *Vogue*, and *no* runs, please.

Singapore. Women in Singapore dress simply, colorfully, and with grace and contemporary style. Foreign women are expected to be fashion-conscious—conservative yet cosmopolitan—and should pack eveningwear with their meetingwear. Singaporean businessmen wear a crisp white shirt with a tie and slacks. Foreign men can arrive at a meeting or dinner engagement wearing a suit with jacket, and remove the jacket when others do (it's usually warm).

Malaysia and Indonesia. In Moslem Asia, Westerners have to be especially careful to steer clear of garish or loud colors. Foreign women can wear a dress or skirt with a blouse; short sleeves are acceptable, but a backless dress or sleeveless garments should never be worn. Both foreign men and women can wear *batik,* even to a semiformal engagement, to impress their Indonesian hosts, but women should not wear slacks or shorts. Tropical safari suits are okay for foreign men, with an Oxford shirt and somber tie for formal occasions. The dress code for men during business meetings in Indonesia is a white shirt with tie and slacks. Because of the heat and humidity in Indonesia and Malaysia, jackets are superfluous except for meetings with high government officials and receptions. For these occasions, a dark suit is necessary.

Thailand. Thai society is divided into two classes, upper and lower. At formal occasions, attire should match one's station— the richer the better. High-status Thais may overdress for the hot climate. Foreign women should avoid sheer dresses, too-short shorts, or miniskirts, all of which will offend Thailand's Buddhist code of modesty. For dinner out, foreign men can wear a nice shirt without a tie; a crisp new *batik* shirt, especially for a home visit, makes a splash. The color black is associated with death in Thailand and should be avoided in ordinary dress.

Philippines. The Philippines is a pocket of high fashion. Filipino women wear fine jewelry, behave with high social grace, and give in periodically to a bit of fashion flamboyance. Possibly because of Imelda Marcos's legacy, one can't be too dressy in the Philippines. Foreign women are free to dress up more wildly there than elsewhere in Asia. Spanish *conquistadores* in the Philippines wore their shirts inside their trousers and prohibited Filipinos from doing so; to this day, Filipino men wear a light embroidered shirt called a *barong tagalog* outside *their* trousers. The light embroidered shirt made in the Philippines is suitable for foreign men at dinner in a restaurant, but they should choose a long-sleeved shirt made of pineapple fiber rather than the short-sleeved polyester or cotton version. Most executives and Filipino men attending a formal event wear the long-sleeved model. For meetings, a jacket and tie for foreign men and a work suit for women are appropriate.

Saying It in Writing:
Brochures and Their Translation

The golden rule of communicating with Asians in writing is to do it in English *unless* a native-speaking in-house translator can translate the English documents perfectly. It's better to use English than to send a badly translated business correspondence.

Of the many translation debacles that have happened in Asia, my favorites are these. In the Japanese version of *Reader's Digest,* a Pepsi-Cola advertisement read: PEPSI-COLA TASTES SO GOOD THAT YOUR DEAD RELATIVES WILL COME OUT OF THE GRAVE TO DRINK IT. As Shuji Hayashi writes in his book *Culture and Management in Japan,* "this gruesome phrasing has all the markings of a third-rate American cultural anthropologist moonlighting as a copy writer." In another vein, the Library of Congress hired a translator to translate state documents from Chinese into English. It was discovered later that the translation read like a children's book in Chinese. In one document, "People got off the big boat . . .," rather than the "ship"!

If the Library of Congress and Pepsi can't get it right, the most earnest Western company may not either, unless all translations are subjected to stringent quality control. Most firms find it too expensive to hire a native-speaking in-house translator to review marketing materials and advertising slogans. The best alternative is to find someone to do a sample translation and then send it to a prospective translator who has a recognized respectability in the field, to have it checked over. Finally, a *native speaker* should read and review the materials and suggest changes. The person's gut feelings about the letter, brochure, or advertisement are important, whether it's funny, somber, ridiculous, too lofty, conceited, lacking in humility, or just right.

CHAPTER SEVEN

How to Survive Asian Bargaining Tactics

Without deception you cannot carry out strategy, without strategy you cannot control the opponent.
MEI YAOCHEN, IN SUN TZU'S THE ART OF WAR

"For every successful Japanese–American negotiation," says Mitchell Deutsch, author of *Doing Business with the Japanese*, "there are twenty-five failures." How many of these represent good deals gone sour for preventable reasons is difficult to calculate. One of the key causes for breakdowns in negotiations between East and West is the divergent business agendas and priorities on either side, which simply cannot be reconciled in a business agreement.

Asian commercial intentions in cooperating with North American firms often contrast with those of the Westerners much more than they compare. For instance, the Western side typically desires to sell finished products to the local market in Asia; the Asian side wants to penetrate, with the help of the Westerner's technology and marketing presence, the international export market. Or, the Western side wants to utilize inexpensive Asian labor to assemble manufactured products; the Asian side intends to assimilate the Westerner's technology, in order to eventually sell to the same markets that the Western firm currently serves. The North American side may be (quite reasonably) unwilling to:

- Adapt a product to the needs of consumers or end-users in Asia;
- Consider noncash transactions like countertrade, barter, and counterpurchase;
- Transfer high technology;
- Enter a "strategic alliance" such as a manufacturing joint venture.

154

Sometimes, the two parties can find a mutually beneficial way to collaborate; often, they part ways after two or three meetings, and each side pursues divergent business agendas. The Chinese say, about this outcome: *Tong chung yi meng* ("Same bed, different dreams"). These are strategic concerns of doing intelligent business, and it is better to part ways as friends than to enter a contract that neither side feels is in its best long-term interest.

"Asian Negotiators Are Too Frustrating to Deal With"

Numerous cases exist where a North American company teams up with an Asian company, opens negotiations, exchanges technical personnel, and hosts delegations from Asia, only to see a potential deal fizzle out. Why does this happen? What mistakes are made? The Western negotiators are likely to cast aspersions in the direction of the Asians, as though the converse could not be true. Some of the Westerners' complaints will be familiar to those readers annealed to the frustrations of negotiating in Asia.

Asians Are Slow to Make Decisions

Although the foreign team is usually empowered with high-level decision-making authority, the career negotiator on the Asian side of the table may possess little or no power to make a unilateral decision. Consensus decision making, by definition, takes more time and more investment of resources on both sides. The Western side is rarely, if ever, prepared for the time-consuming switchbacks in negotiating positions pursued by the Asian side.

Asians Ask Endless Questions

Strategic information gathering is a common feature of all negotiations with foreigners, throughout Asia. North Americans often lose their patience and get angry, when asked by their Asian counterparts to supply a continuous flow of sensitive information during preliminary negotiations. Over the course of a negotiation in Asia, Westerners will find that they have to answer the same questions, over and over, for no apparent reason. Information seems to travel in one direction—West to East. Westerners often complain of a lack of detail in information garnered from the Asian side; when the "technical exchange" is completed, they have acquired only an incomplete, and unusable, technical picture. (We'll discuss safeguards against "information rape" later in the chapter.)

Asians Want to Renegotiate a Signed Contract

Many Westerners have complained that contracts are considered flexible arrangements in the minds of their Asian counterparts. "You can expect," my Chinese consultant tells me, "that only one-third of the contractual problems will have been addressed by the time the contract is signed." The bulk of the issues will be brought up *after* the Westerners thought all conceivable problems have been solved in negotiating the contract. The Japanese even have a name for the doctrine of contractual flexibility: *jijo henko* ("changed circumstances").

Western Negotiators Aren't Perfect

In numerous cases, deals have gone awry because of shortcomings on the Westerners' part. To be fair, Asians have some valid complaints about Western negotiators.

North Americans Are Impatient and Insensitive

"The problem with North Americans," says a Thai business associate of mine, "is cultural insensitivity in conjunction with impatience." Westerners want the meeting *now;* they don't want to take time for tea. They want to do business on the first trip, although business in Asia is traditionally not done during the first visit.

Jacob J. Kaplan, a retired international consultant and former State Department official, notes:

Americans want their answers and results quickly, and in general they're used to getting them. But in other countries people tend to be more cautious; they tend to think things through a little longer. The most common mistake American businessmen make is being too impatient. "Why can't you do it my way?" they say. But when you're abroad, you can't do business *except* on other people's terms.

They Don't Do Their Homework

Westerners often open negotiations without the slightest knowledge of the market in Asia or the distribution system that serves it. They then expect it to operate like the system in their own countries. "It is annoying when these Americans come to the negotiations armed with knowledge gained only from newspaper clippings," says Hajime Karatsu, an executive with Matsushita Electric Corporation.

They Don't Respond to the Customer's Needs

Often, a Western company is unwilling to adapt its product to local needs, or to dedicate itself to learning about local customer needs. They approach the Asian market with a quick-kill attitude, without considering the customer's *ongoing* need for after-sales service and future technical training and product upgrading. In contrast, typical Japanese vendors are willing to adapt their products to fit the rules of the marketplace and the specific needs of Asian customers, no matter how difficult this may be. They are niche-market oriented, and North American companies tend to be mass-market oriented, says Andrew Grossman, a United States commercial attaché stationed in Seoul.

Their Business Style Is Impersonal and "No-Nonsense"

The Westerner believes "time is money" but seems to want to base long-term business agreements on quickly drawn contracts and not on underlying personal relationships with people whose dedication and teamwork are essential to actually implementing the contract. Most Asians resent the traditionally loud negotiation style of the West and consider the Westerners' confrontational, pugilistic, win–lose negotiating behavior insulting. They prize politeness and respect above even an attractive offer. If an Asian businessperson is insulted, he or she would rather forsake a commercial opportunity than do business with the insulter. "If a Japanese comes to you," commented an Indonesian executive, recently quoted in the *Los Angeles Times,* "they would normally give you a present, similar to an Indonesian. An American just comes to you with a briefcase, a pen, a checkbook, and a contract—everything stipulated in fine print, very fine."

They Send the Wrong Man (or Woman)

Many North American firms send the wrong person to Asia to represent their interests. This person is often the CEO. His or her frank and cocky business style may be at the root of communication breakdown and the resulting ill-feeling on both sides. Steve Jobs, cofounder of Apple Computer, was probably a bad choice as the person to represent his company to Epson in Japan. Jobs and an associate, Jay Elliot, were picked up by a Japanese chauffeur to be driven to Epson's headquarters, located two hours outside Tokyo. They soon found themselves delayed in traffic because an avalanche had blocked the road. Train routes were blocked as well. Eight hours of detours and backtracking later, they finally arrived at Epson. I'll let the reporter of this anecdote, Jeffrey Young, author of *Steve Jobs: The Journey Is the Reward,* tell you what happened:

> Waiting for [Steve Jobs and Jay Elliot] were all the Epson managers and vice-president lined up in the lobby. Steve was furious, and the first thing he demanded was food, rattling off a list of sushi. Factotums were sent scurrying to scare it up.
>
> The president of the company then took them all into their boardroom, where they had carefully set up all their latest products. A spokesman started explaining what each one was and its special features. After about a minute, Elliot reports that Steve turned to the president of the company and said, "This is shit. Don't you have anything good?" and with that he marched out. The self-effacing Japanese were shocked and had no idea how to react. The team from Apple made a hasty departure.

(For more about whom to send to Asia, see Chapter 14.)

Western Reps Often Don't Understand the Products They Sell

Given the number of Asian complaints, it would seem that few North American companies know how to educate their customers while retaining their proprietary know-how. It's one thing to want to withhold proprietary technical know-how, but quite another not to be able to address the technical needs of a customer and tailor a technical product to those needs. "The Japanese and even the Europeans can provide customers with an advisory engineer who really knows the product. The Americans often cannot," complains Chen Li-an, Minister of Economic Affairs in Taiwan. "In

Europe and Japan, the best engineers are assigned to products, but in the U.S. they just do research."

When North American and Asian Negotiators Meet

Negotiating in Asia is an infinitely more delicate and difficult task than in the West, if only because Asians define the *purpose of negotiation* and the *function of business partnership* differently than do Westerners. For the North American, the purpose of a business negotiation is to close a deal. For the typical Asian businessperson, it is to build trust and compatibility between business partners. For the North American, the function of a business relationship is to make a profit, preferably in the near term. For the Asian, it is to create a network of business ties based on obligation and reciprocity, which will pan out in the form of continuous profit over the long term. Indeed, Westerners tend to come to the negotiation table to sign an isolated deal—complete, finite, and predictable; Asians come to the negotiation table to *establish a relationship*.

Differing Perceptions of a Business Agreement

For North Americans, a business agreement is a static transaction for which a detailed contract is desired, to limit liability and responsibility for various contingencies. For Asians, a business agreement is a formalized, ongoing, dynamic relationship not so much based on price as on trust and accountability, like-mindedness, friendship, and respect. Westerners depend on a minutely detailed contract to manage every potential conflict with their partners. Contracts among Asian business associates may only be a couple of pages long.

In the West, the term "everything's negotiable" applies up to the point when the contract is signed. In Asia, the axiom continues to apply to an agreement even after the contract is signed. Many Koreans, for example, consider "paper contracts" of little lasting value. If conditions change—the political climate, the economic climate, labor relations, supplies, or price—Koreans, Chinese, and other Asians might feel little compunction about informing the Western side that the contract must be renegotiated to reflect changed conditions. Westerners expect contractual terms to remain static; much of a "good deal" is predicated on a *prediction* of changing conditions that enhances one's contractual position over the life of the agreement. Herein lies one of the great puzzles of doing business in Asia: how to strike a contract that will be honored by the Asian side and enforceable by the Western side.

More than a few of my Asian friends and associates have told me, "When we're 8,000 miles apart, any legal contract, no matter how explicit, is meaningless. What's meaningful is that you and I both give our best to solve problems and make the deal work. That's all that matters. If that's not there, then there's nothing." Western lawyers working in Asia, however, advise their clients to enter into a detailed contract, to have something to fall back on should a deal go sour. Yet, a company that files a suit for breach of contract in Asia, as many North American firms have done, will likely be blackballed in its industry, at least in the country involved, and possibly throughout Asia. The Westerners may win the battle, but they will lose the war. Asian firms suffer the same fate when they sue, which they do rarely. A Chinese proverb says: "Though starving to death, do not steal; though annoyed to death, do not file a lawsuit."

Different Approaches to Bargaining

The typical Western bargaining "strategy," if there is one, usually amounts to discussing a proposed contract, clause-by-clause, with the intention of winning concessions within each clause during the process. When the final clause is agreed upon, the negotiation is over, and the side that has won the most profit-producing concessions in the contract is considered the winner. North American negotiators concentrate nearly all of their energy on "getting the facts" and then persuading an opponent to make concessions and to accept compromises.

Not so in Asia. "In Japan, the seller and buyer . . . both maneuver carefully so there will be neither a winner nor a loser," says Shuji Hayashi in his book *Culture and Management in Japan.* "Both parties figure out the other's intentions, find a medium point where each can make a profit, and conclude a deal at that price." Westerners might consider this sort of *cooperative* bargaining a form of collusion between the buyer and seller; the fact is, however, that this form of negotiation tends to reduce the chance for serious altercation between negotiating parties and, thus, helps to lend permanency to their business relationship.

The differences at the negotiating table don't stop there. Look, for instance, at *how* we bargain. North Americans break up the bargaining process into parts. When an issue is resolved, they move to the next issue, until all of the clauses of the contract are settled. They proceed step-by-step, nailing down each clause of the contract in sequence; they measure their progress by adding up the number of resolved issues and comparing the sum with those issues still unresolved. They might say, "We're halfway to an agreement."

An Asian couldn't make that assessment. Asians tend to go from one element to the next *without* settling. They negotiate *holistically*, discussing all aspects of a contract two or three times before making concrete commitments. Meanwhile, the Westerners make concessions along the way, "baiting the hook" as part of winning reciprocal concessions from their opponents. Asians first gather information, then discuss the ways the two sides might cooperate; they discuss each aspect of a proposal, and then, at the last stage, begin the give-and-take of concession making. Westerners get frustrated when the Asian side wants to discuss the entire agreement two or more times, offering no concessions until the very end of the meeting. The Westerners have, by then, offered several concessions and are expected to offer *more* of them at the end too!

How Westerners Can Succeed When Negotiating in Asia

By recognizing a set of *strategic archetypes* used by Asian negotiators, Westerners can enhance their negotiating power in Asia. I have encountered eight strategic archetypes repeatedly in Asia, as have other Westerners. Humility, propriety, and respect mark every business encounter in the Pacific Rim, but most Asian negotiators imitate military tactics developed in China 2,500 years ago for the "art" of war. Throughout Asia, war strategy became commercial strategy. While Westerners read "one-minute" management books, the East Asians study Sun Tzu's *The Art of War, The Way of the Bushido, The Book of Five Rings,* and *The 36 Strategies.* These works remain popular and influential. The strategies they reveal are passed on through mentor–apprentice relationships; rookie negotiators are groomed continuously in Asia to function as negotiators with foreign companies. When Japanese negotiators go overseas, almost invariably they will have in tow one or two underlings who are there to listen and to draft reports on each day's negotiations. In this way, a number of strategic archetypes and tactics are passed on to new generations of negotiators. The sections below show (1) how these tactics work, (2) how to recognize them, and (3) how to gain an advantage by responding to them with appropriate counterstrategies.

Strategy 1. Playing the Orphan

Use humility to make them haughty.
Sun Tzu

Throughout Asia, one encounters business situations in which the Asian company claims to be weaker and more vulnerable than it really is. The Asian side claims it is a small or backward company, in order to elicit sympathy and to generate aid from the foreign side in the form of concessions. This seems odd to North American executives who are typically in the habit of trying to convince a negotiating partner that their company is large and powerful. Sun Tzu taught: "Even though you are competent, appear to be incompetent." The equivalent Western idiom is: "Play dumb." Sun Tzu's commentator, Mei Yaochen, elaborated: "Give the appearance of inferiority and weakness, to make [your enemy] proud." Asians may open a negotiation by dwelling on their company's vulnerabilities, small size, and other feigned weaknesses, to swell Westerners' confidence and induce them to ask for less in return for the concessions that the Westerners are prepared to request. Some Westerners might think the orphan strategy is an expression of Asian humility. Instead, the orphan strategy often conceals a hidden agenda.

For example, a claim of weakness is soon followed by a request that the foreign side ease its credit terms, to lighten the financial burden on the Asian side. Or, the Asians demand conciliatory "favors" outside the contract, again to lighten the burden on Asian side. I've heard of many cases in which a Chinese partner in a joint venture arrangement claims it is experiencing financial problems, in order to win a cash infusion from the foreign side. The cash, however, is spent surreptitiously on commodities like cotton, coffee, or sugar, which are then sold on the free market at a profit. In this way, the Chinese side capitalizes on the foreigner's "investment" before purchasing the necessary capital goods stipulated in the joint venture contract.

In another case, a Japanese firm signed a deal with an American real estate development company, but then delayed its implementation—again, claiming financial problems—until the American partner got into financial trouble. At that time, the Japanese firm began pushing for concessions in the "grey areas" of the agreement. The Japanese strategy from the outset had been to gain control of the U.S. company, even though the firm had given to the American company an impression that it was in perpetual financial trouble.

How to Respond to the Orphan Strategy

- Collect verified financial information about any Asian company that is involved in a prospective deal. Many Asian companies will provide an annual financial report, but many will not. In Indonesia, China, and Taiwan, financial information about a company may be unavailable, or only made available after extensive modification. If the company is listed for public trading, inquiry can be made, at a brokerage firm in Asia, about whether a consultant might be hired to conduct relevant research. This sort of approach can be expected from an Asian counterpart, who will do similar research on the Western firm.

- Treat the *"Asia division"*—the unit assigned to the Asia venture—as small, underfunded, and vulnerable. Lower Asian counterparts' expectations of its size and power by explaining the need for the division to generate its own profits, in order to fulfill its mandate as a division within the larger company. This will help to dislodge the notion that the resources targeted at Asia by the Western firm will be limitless.

- Enter negotiations with a set of predefined, noncash concessions that are of little value to your company and that can, if necessary, be offered in response to the orphan tactic. A relatively inexpensive communication center, for example, or a software package could be a good low-cost sweetener.

- Circumvent the Asians' use of the orphan tactic by behaving like an "orphan company" before the Asians do. Even though the Asian negotiators will know your company's financial situation backward and forward before the negotiation, humbly apologize, for instance, for your company's size and unsophisticated technology, at the outset of the meeting.

- Go to Asia on a shoestring. If you're staying at the Lotte Hotel in Seoul or the Imperial in Tokyo, you *must* be bountiful with your money. A little frugality goes a long way toward reducing the "rich foreign company" stereotype.

Strategy 2. Team-Driven Intelligence Gathering

Comparisons give rise to victories.
                    Sun Tzu

"By the comparisons of measurements, you know where victory and defeat lie," Cao Cao advises in *The Art of War*. What Asian counterparts can find out about a Western company will be used against the company during negotiations—how large or small the company is, what sort of technological know-how it possesses, and the tone of its financial muscle. A concerted effort may be underway to transfer to the Asian side as much of the company's know-how as possible, free of charge. Westerners who have negotiated in Asia report that Asians value detail in formulating their business decisions; they consider information gathering to be the heart of a negotiation. However, what they call a "know-how exchange" often becomes "information rape," with the Asian side planning to reverse-engineer a Western product from the outset of collaboration with the firm. The effort will be a concerted, team objective. If Western negotiators are not on guard against it, their firm is likely to find itself the victim of information rape.

Asians' ideal of sharing in a company's know-how without paying for it may be partially cultural in origin. When members of early agrarian society in Asia innovated, a breakthrough benefited everyone directly. No notion of proprietary know-how took root; new technology was shared by all. Knowledge was kept public, and to imitate or adopt someone else's methodology was considered virtuous, and a great compliment to the person who created it. Borrowing another person's know-how was considered to be neither thievery nor unethical. The Japanese have long conducted a policy of "selective borrowing" from foreigners. Industrial Japan borrowed extensively from the West and adapted Western production and quality control techniques to its own needs. The United States brought "marketing" to Japan in the 1950s, after World War II; no such word in Japanese even existed until then.

All of this is *not* to suggest that Asia hasn't developed technologies on its own; its well-known inventions through the centuries had dramatic effects on all of civilization. However, their revolutionary impact was felt mainly on the older European continent; their origin went largely unrecognized and unappreciated in the New World.

Today, technological innovations travel back and forth across the Pacific with amazing frequency. The flow of innovation, however, is moving faster toward the East than toward the West. Japanese companies, for example, purchased over half of the American high-technology firms that were sold during a 30-month period from 1989 to 1991, according to a study by the Economic Strategy Institute, a Washington think tank. Increasingly, North American corporations have found it necessary to forge "strategic alliances" with Asian companies (mostly Japanese), in order to acquire know-how from Asia, rather than vice versa. Facilitating the flow of technical information and human know-how has proven easier said than done.

How to Respond to Team-Driven Intelligence Gathering

- Gather beforehand as much technical information as possible, regarding the Asian company's products, by researching its patents, attending trade fairs, and participating in technical seminars. Decide exactly what technological know-how you are after. Determine how much of the "technological puzzle" you have already obtained from other sources, before writing out the technical questions that you plan to ask during meetings.

- Prepare your technical team, before arranging for any technical exchange, and debrief your negotiation team as to what information is "shareable" and what is not, before the exchange opens. Differences in personality between American and Asian "techies" can cause information to flow in one direction. North Americans have a natural tendency to expound on their scientific achievements and proprietary work, when asked. Asian scientists will not as readily reveal their achievements; they consider such behavior to be in violation of Confucian precepts about humility. Getting an Asian technician to reveal needed information can be a struggle, not only for reasons of humility but also because the technician may be under strict limitations on information sharing, imposed by and upon the Asian company.

- Assign a leader to be responsible for the exchange, to ensure that know-how is not accidentally delivered to the other side. Before independently answering a question, an engineer on your team should confer with the negotiation team leader.

- Reconvene the team after formal meetings, to discuss the technology puzzle you are attempting to assemble, and to discern the technical objectives of the Asian side, as revealed in their line of questioning. Fill in newly acquired pieces of information, and select those to be sought at the next meeting. You may have to be adamant with your hosts' social arrangements, to allow the necessary time for your team to do this in private.

- Take copious notes at every meeting; the entire technical exchange will be a waste of resources without them. To ensure continuity of an exchange over time (and allowing for changes in your technical personnel), submit technology exchange "minutes" for filing at the home office. Circulate the information gleaned in Asia, to capitalize on it to the fullest extent possible.

- Remember that certain information *is* proprietary to Asian firms and/or sensitive to their country's national security. Remain patient during a technical exchange; the Asian negotiator will have to consider the following issues before answering: Can the question be answered without violating government-imposed technology restrictions? Will a particular answer violate proprietary know-how guidelines issued by superiors? Can an answer be formulated that will be clear to the Westerners after being translated? North Americans who interrupt their Asian counterparts while they consider these issues often curtail the flow of information to their side. Don't hound an Asian partner to answer a question, if you sense a reticence to respond. Some questions that are impossible to get answered on Monday are forthrightly answered on Tuesday, after approval to do so has been received behind the scenes. Keep asking the same question in a new way on different occasions. A statement of misfact may elicit the "corrected" information that you are seeking. For example: "With all these shipping crates piled on the dock ready to go overseas, your factory must be exporting at least 50 percent of its production." Answer: "Actually, the figure is much lower."

- Formalize "turn taking." Asians may not feel comfortable exchanging information through the taking of turns. They may not feel at ease "bouncing ideas around," which is a habit of informal North American engineers at meetings.

Hiroshi Ishi of Nippon Telephone & Telegraph says:

> In my own experience, I found that turn taking is most difficult for me to learn to adapt to, in discussions with Americans. Situation-oriented nonverbal cues for turn taking in Japanese meetings are much more clear to me. In Japan, it is very rude to interrupt other persons' speaking. We have been taught to be patient, to listen until others are finished talking.

As we all know, Westerners sometimes *have* to interrupt, if they are to be heard at all. Two rules should be followed:

1. After speaking, *ask,* rather than motion with your hands or signal with your eyes, for Asian partners to "Please" add comments or response to the discussion.
2. *Wait* for the Asian speaker to formulate ideas and speak. Do not break the silence while the idea gathering is going on.

- Sidestep questions skillfully. If you cannot answer a technology-related question, answer: "This subject area is proprietary," or "This is outside the agreement we have made about this exchange," or "Our company has not released that information as of yet." Be gentle but firm, and make sure that every member of your team uses the same basic reply.
- Never expect an Asian partner to protect your proprietary know-how from being counterfeited in his or her country. Actively protect it yourself, by registering the proper patents in Asia and policing the market on your own. Should your product or technology get knocked-off or stolen, you may be able to extract royalties, but it will take a lengthy, expensive, and unpleasant lawsuit to do so.

Strategy 3. The Haughty Buyer

The customer is God.

Sellers of products and services in the West defer to their buyers to some degree, to show their loyalty to them, but buyers and sellers in the West ultimately deal with one another as social equals. Not so in Asia: buyers and sellers differ fundamentally in social status. In North America, buyers and sellers maintain a somewhat adversarial relationship; buyers ask vendors to bid against each other, to get a lower price, and sellers seek out those buyers who will pay a premium price. When monetary advantage can be found elsewhere, buyers have few qualms about terminating their relationship with a seller. Business is business.

In much of Asia, however, buyers and sellers forge longer-term bonds of trust and partnership. Sellers tend to respond to every wish and whim of their buyers. In Japan, and increasingly in Korea as well as other parts of Asia, the customer is not only king, but God. Here's the hitch, though. Asian buyers look after their suppliers in ways their North American counterparts do not. Asian sellers tend to *overserve* their buyers, because they can trust that their buyers will stay loyal to them if times get tough. A buyer might pay a price above market value, find a seller new customers, and—you guessed it—help to *protect* the seller's business from foreign competitors. In Japan, the relationship between buyer and seller is based on *amae,* the paternalistic, dependent relationship we spoke of earlier. Paternalistic buyer–seller bonds are hard to break, especially for a newcomer in the market. More than just the lowest price must be offered; the buyer must be *overserved,* in the Asian suppliers' manner.

Westerners' typical unwillingness to accept the lower-status position of suppliers in Asia and to enter into paternalistic relationships with buyers is a primary reason, though not the sole reason, that American executives often hear their potential Asian customers say, "We'll contact you when we are prepared to buy," which means, "Thanks anyway." Asian buyers are not exactly "haughty" as part of a strategy; they are demanding, and possibly condescending, out of conditioning. To sell, Westerners may have to enter *amae*-like relationships and accept the lower status. They have to satisfy what they may consider unreasonable demands, in order to lure Asian buyers—fast delivery, costly product modifications, and strictly enforced quality specifications, for example. Some companies have perished trying to meet the rigorous requirements of being sellers in Asia. Still, there are ways to lasso buyers without losing the corporate shirt.

How to Respond to the Haughty Buyer

- Don't approach an Asian customer as an equal. Remain formal, observe protocol and manners, and play what I call the

A Foreigner Plays the Haughty Buyer

An international steel manufacturer who has done business with the Japanese, Koreans, Thais, and other Asian nationalities for years visited China recently, to tour a steel factory and request a bid. He was the buyer, and a "haughty" one at that.

He was wined and dined in a huge, walnut-paneled dining room, with over a hundred company officials, at one of China's largest steel mills. An extensive tour of the factory followed, and then came honorific speeches made by the company's highest officials. Finally, the buyer-manufacturer was taken to a private meeting, with just two other people present: the factory's Westernized manager ("who was right off Madison Avenue") and the manager's female assistant. They asked to "speak frankly" with him, wanting to know how their company could win the manufacturer's large bid. What did the Chinese need to do in order to win it? The American played the *haughty buyer.*

"I am *shocked* at your organization here," he said. "No quality inspection, workers sleeping at their positions. I am *appalled.*"

The two Chinese, of course, were shocked and insulted. But the buyer let them stew for a minute. Then he said, reassuringly, that "these problems in your factory can be remedied, however, with some upgrading and discipline." Then the clincher: "If we are to do business, you are going to have to make it *so attractive* to us that we can't afford *not* to do business with you."

The Chinese team worked all night on the bid, which they submitted to the steel manufacturer the following morning. It was $40 million under the manufacturer's previous bids! You can't *always* play the haughty buyer, but on occasion it works wonders.

◆

"lowly seller." Position yourself as the seller in deferential relationships with potential Asian buyers. Always show respect for Asian company officials and bureaucrats who are in a position to influence a purchase of your goods. As a seller, never request "quick action" on a problem from an Asian official or customer. Rather, request a "favor." You'll get more done, faster, with this approach.

- Remember that sellers don't bring up business. They talk, entertain, and inform, but the buyer initiates business discussions in Asia. Unless your product is overwhelmingly essential to the Asian's needs, the prebusiness interim may be longer than you're accustomed to. Learn to wait until the buyer asks to discuss purchase of your product.

- Overserve an Asian customer, to prove your willingness to enter long-term, paternalistic relationships in Asia. Be at the customer's beck and call. Japanese customers, for example, want *anshinkan,* or "peace of mind" that the seller is never going to let them down. This takes time to foster and can be destroyed with one mistake. If there is any problem whatsoever, your company's management *must* respond immediately and in a big way, to keep the customer. Requests for information, quotations, and product brochures should be responded to immediately, not at your convenience.

- Remember that you too can play the "haughty buyer," as long as you reciprocate later, if your vendor needs a break.

Strategy 4. Outlasting the Enemy

It is easy to take over from those who have not thought ahead.
                                                  Li Quan in *The Art of War*

Asian negotiations can, as the Chinese saying goes, be like "grinding a rod down to a needle." When the Taoist concept of *wu wei* (nonassertion) is applied to business negotiation, the strategy is to seek long-term success through minimal short-term effort: state a position and wait, hoping that opponents will yield on concessions, in order to close the deal. Time is NOT money for Asian negotiators; it's a weapon. Chiang Kai-shek used it to bilk the United States out of millions of dollars in military hardware aid, without lifting a finger against the Japanese during World War II. He kept delaying any action on his verbal commitments while escalating his demands.

Asian negotiators often follow a similar tactic when doing business with foreigners. They open a negotiation, extend an invitation to visit their country, supply some technical information, and dedicate time and resources to forging an agreement. Unfortunately, the final contract remains elusive. Japanese investors, according to a number of American real estate developers I know, will sit down with them and sign on for a mutually beneficial deal, but problems set in at the last minute, when they balk and push for concessions. Then they initiate delay tactics, all the while pushing for more and more concessions in the grey areas of the contract. The foreign side often gives in, because a costly delay of the deal may jeopardize firm financial commitments.

When Asian negotiators use delay tactics that push foreigners to the brink of anger, they may be seeking more than concessions. They may be testing the Westerners' commitment to a deal or their accountability. They may want to clarify the unequal status between buyer and seller. By delaying, they send a message that their interest may be waning; the Westerners may weaken in their resolve to hold out for a stated price. I've seen this strategy used on youthful foreigners (myself included), as a way of testing their will and trying to intimidate them—to put them in their youthful place. Another possible reason for delay is that an Asian wants to kill a deal without losing face, and hopes the Westerner will take a hint and walk away as a friend, not a frustrated foe.

How to Respond to Delay Tactics

- Maintain an open time-frame when in Asia or hosting an Asian delegation in the West.

- Never attempt to speed up a negotiation by offering concessions. Instead, *slow the pace down even more* and maintain the original negotiating position.

- State your position and never change, beyond lowering your price 10 percent or so. The Asian delay boils down to a war of wills, and the first side to give in loses. Some advice from Suzy Gershman and Judith Thomas, in their book *Born to Shop: Hong Kong,* applies to large business deals as well: "Keep repeating your position and do not waver. . . . you must have a lot of time to bargain well. Wearing down the opponent is key to success."

- Understand the Asians' self-interests; they will always act to serve their interests, but they may not always be forthcoming about what exactly those interests are. Figure out what the Asian side wants: Cash investment? Foreign technology? An export outlet? Independence and clout, by associating with a foreign firm, with no real intention of doing much business at all? Many U.S. firms have entered China before these questions were answered, because the firms were blinded by the potential of capturing a new market in Asia. Go-betweens or consultants should be utilized on the Asian side, to ascertain the underlying intentions of the Asian partner.

- Determine whether a delay may be a matter of face saving rather than price. Don't depend solely on logical reasoning to substantiate a position and break a stalemate, especially in Japan; remember that Asians tend to negotiate as a team. Your logically thought-out demands may be reasonable to you, but the Asian negotiator's acceptance of them may be seen as a grave show of weakness on his or her part. "If you give an inch as a Japanese negotiator," says steel manufacturer Mike Wilkenson, who has dealt with the Japanese for years, "you go to the bottom of the pile." In other words, it's risky to knuckle-under to a foreign negotiator. Should the foreign party benefit more than the Asian side in a deal, the Asian negotiator can suffer a humiliating loss of face.

• Pull out all the stops when a deadlock occurs. From speaking with a number of Western negotiators, I conclude that this stage of a negotiation is perhaps the most critical for Westerners. At this juncture, business becomes war. The Asian side uses every tactic it can, to dislodge the will of the Westerners. The contest is no longer about who is right or what the facts are, but about whose obstinacy and stamina are greater. State your demand, give the reasons why it is important to you, and then stand behind it with your whole emotional being, as if it is the most vital thing in the world to you. Indicate that you won't back down, no matter how far you're pushed or how much time is allowed to pass. Make the issue one of honor, not of cold facts, no matter how persuasive the facts are. Say verbally and nonverbally that you *care* about obtaining this demand and won't give up an inch of it. It may sound melodramatic, but you have to be a bit of a warrior at this point, willing to risk perhaps months of preparation to get what you want and know you deserve.

Strategy 5. Hidden Identities

The inscrutable win, the obvious lose.
　　　　　Du Mu in *The Art of War*

In the city of Hefei, in China's Anhui Province, I came across two Canadian representatives of a water purification equipment company. They were to have an important meeting with local import officials the following morning, in the conference room at our hotel (the only foreigners' hotel in the city).

I met them the next day, as they emerged confidently from their meeting. I also recognized a past acquaintance, the leading official from the Ministry of Foreign Economic Relations and Trade. After he left the hotel, I complimented the Canadians on obtaining a meeting with such a prominent official, and suggested that this official's presence indicated significant interest in the water purification system, on the part of the Chinese.

"Who, him?" one of the Canadians blurted. "He said he was just our interpreter for the meeting!"

This high official had concealed his true identity, in order to eavesdrop on the Canadians in the guise of an interpreter. They had been burned by the hidden identity strategy.

Although a meeting in Asia usually begins with an exchange of business cards and handshakes, the true identities of the real decision makers on the Asian negotiating team may remain unknown—sometimes indefinitely. Ascertaining precisely who the key players are and how much influence they wield is difficult, because some persons may vanish and later reappear at a banquet or sightseeing excursion.

The hidden identity strategy may also involve sudden changes among the Asian side's negotiating personnel. The number of Asian negotiators may swell over time, while the foreign side generally depends on the same team throughout. Being forced to defend a proposal before a new team can be maddening or can lead to making extra concessions or giving up some that have already been won. More innocently, the Asian negotiator whom the company hosted in the West for a factory visit and a side trip to Disneyland may have suddenly moved to another division of the Asian company. All the concessions won with him are now gone, and the process must start all over again with a new negotiator. In China, this problem has been exacerbated by the massive reorganization that has taken place since the Tiananmen Square Massacre. It would be unfair to Asians, however, not to mention that the same problem occurs in North America, for different reasons. With the constant merging of North American companies and the high turnover of their executives, whether through departure, relocation, or promotion, the appearance of new negotiators can be difficult and disconcerting for Asians who desire to forge long-term, ongoing relationships with Western companies.

How to Respond to Hidden Identities

- Try to ascertain, before meetings open, who will be negotiating on the Asian side. Will it be a division head, a group of engineers, the director of marketing, government representatives, or all of these players simultaneously? Research the counterpart company before traveling to Asia, and solicit as much information as you can about its individual negotiators. This means reading more than the company's annual report. Sources of information about the personnel in an Asian company include consultants who have worked for it, its retired managers and executives, and foreign executives who have dealt with the company in the past. The wider your business network in Asia, the more information you will be able to get.

- Find out who are the primary players in the decision-making process; foreign representatives have to feel their way in the dark, to acquire a solid working understanding of how the respective government departments and bureaus involved in a proposed venture interlink. Factory directors will usually diagram, for the foreigner who *asks*, the interlocking governmental institutions affecting their enterprise.

- Ask your Asian counterpart to draw organizational charts for the company with which you are doing business and the industry with which you are involved. By keeping a running list of decision makers, you can make educated conclusions as to how the players interconnect. *Don't* be like the American CEO who opened discussions with a Korean manufacturer and then learned that he was already linked up with one of the manufacturer's competitors!

- Get in the habit of merely *presenting* ideas, proposals, and information during meetings. Conduct the real *negotiating* during informal after-hours meetings with the top person on the Asian side (once you've found out who this person is). Supply information within the context of the group meeting, and get down to the give-and-take of dealing when fewer players are present. In Korea and Taiwan, deals are often struck between *individual* sole proprietors of enterprises, away from the corporate conference room.

Strategy 6. The Trust Game

Honey in mouth but dagger in heart.
            Chinese Saying

A well-known American cable-television company has recently signed a deal with a comparable cable network in Taiwan. The agreement was based on a royalty to be paid by the Taiwanese company to the U.S. company, for each television show aired. To guarantee its 10 percent share, the American company requested that the contract enable it to periodically view the Taiwanese company's accounting books.

The president of the Taiwanese company took the request as a grave insult. He was livid, and nixed the entire deal, which had taken months to put together. "The American company is implying that we are liars," he railed. "If the Americans can't trust us, then we won't trust them!"

The irony is that *most* Taiwanese companies (this one included) keep two, or even three, sets of books, and a demand to have the accounting records made public, in a deal of this size, would be reasonable anywhere else in the world.

As part of what I call the trust game, the Asian doesn't want to trust the Westerner, but reacts negatively to any suggestion that the mistrust is mutual. Asians may even purposefully personalize negotiations, to give Westerners a feeling that trust has been generated and thus lure them into a deal; Westerners may find they are being called an "old friend" at the second meeting. The Asian side's personalization of the negotiation may be a good thing for the long-term relationship between the two companies. However, it may be merely a tactic to obtain proprietary information about the firm—its size and past endeavors, the price and marketability of its products, its experience in Asia, and so on. Trust has to work both ways. As T. Boone Pickens has said: "When you embrace these people [the Japanese], make sure they've got their arms around you too, and not around your neck." Ethnic Chinese often say, "Be open with us. We are your friends." They are, but they're also *business associates*.

The trust game in Asia can be especially brutal on "middlemen" and firms that share their technology. "When the hares have been killed, the hounds are cooked," as the Chinese say. That is, the middlemen are discarded once they have fulfilled their purpose. I recommend that middlemen sign a bomb-proof contract with the manufacturer they represent, guaranteeing them total exclusivity to rep the product in Asia. They should conclude the contract before they disseminate information or quote prices of equipment among potential Asian customers. Often, Asian customers will contact the manufacturer directly and attempt to cut the middlemen out. The motive may not be to avoid paying an added commission, but simply to forge a relationship directly with the manufacturer and get closer to its technology.

In another trust game, the Asian side signs a "symbolic agreement." The Asians win over the Western firm by signing a well-drafted contract, but then fail to *implement* what they have agreed to do. Some Asians may sign a "symbolic contract" knowing full well that governing bodies with oversight of the venture will not accept the conditions of the deal. Requests for major revisions in the contract arrive soon after. A recent case in Korea involved the purchase of agricultural goods from the United States. The goods were refused by Korean Customs. The Korean customer had guaranteed that the government would enact a regulation allowing the import of the goods long before the contract was signed. Unfortunately, the Korean government had been unwilling to enact the law. The deal died, along with a shipment of perishable product.

How to Respond to the Trust Game

- Understand *the nature of the business relationship* that is involved. There are two types of East–West business relationships, and it's *very* important to know the difference. The first type is cordial, polite, and respectful, yet formal and business oriented. Both players keep their cards close to their chest and toss around the words "trust" and "old friend," but their loyalty to one another is second to their business interests. The second type is a truly personalized relationship that is completely transparent and is founded on loyalty and reciprocity. Trust between the partners is never feigned. Few Westerners are party to this type of relationship with Asian business-people, unless they are linked to them through family relations. By *knowing what type of relationship you are in,* you will know when the Asians' overtures to trust are real, and when they're part of a trust game strategy. Some frank and insightful advice from a native Chinese consultant generalizes for all of Asia:

    As a Westerner you should *not* try to get too close personally to your counterpart in Asia. Pretend that there is no distance between you, but in your heart realize that there is a distance. Stay within the mainstream of your Western business style. Remain a little formal and aloof. It's to your advantage because it makes you a little inaccessible, a little different, a little more revered and respected by your Asian partner. The Chinese, for instance, might respect the Western businessperson more than his own colleagues in China. As a Westerner, if you try to equalize the relationship by overly personalizing it, the Chinese you are dealing with might be tempted to take advantage of you, because you seem willing to enter the sort of business relationship that Chinese maintain amongst themselves; that is, one based on personal ties and the secret exchange of informal favors and benefits. You will lose their respect even if you do gain a modicum of trust. The trick is to know what stage each of your business relationships in Asia has reached, and with whom to lower your guard.

- Sign a detailed contract with Asian partners, no matter how trustworthy you think they may be. The following good advice about contracts comes from Gibson, Dunn, & Crutcher, a Los Angeles law firm that handles a great deal of Asia-related business:

> Nothing is more mistaken and dangerous than the common misunderstanding that . . . high-ranking connections and toasting are the important things, with a contract being just a decorative formality. . . . [C]onnections do not last forever. The duration of a . . . venture is often 10–15 years or much longer. During this period, many things can happen to your connections. They can die, become seriously ill, be removed from their positions, or just disappear. . . . Only a good contract can endure the changes of time, personnel, and [political] climate.

You may want to use an attorney only during final negotiations, to show that you do believe in the integrity of your Asian partner, but make sure your contract is sound nonetheless.

Strategy 7. Sacrifice Something Small for Something Big

Cast a brick to attract a piece of jade.
                              Chinese Saying

In this strategy, Asian counterparts attempt to trick Westerners into trading something significant for something insignificant. An Indonesian or Chinese joint venture partner might assure a Western company of access to a large untapped market or offer unlimited numbers of inexpensive workers in exchange for cash, technology, and worker training. Many gullible Westerners have fallen victim to this strategy, believing the numbers that appear in feasibility studies presented by the Asians. The market may be both smaller than the numbers claim *and* quite inaccessible, despite promises of access to it. The building space and land offered may appear to be a real break, but would cost a bundle to upgrade.

Some Asian managers desire to link up with a foreign firm to gain the benefits that accrue to an Asian factory that forges a joint venture with a foreign company. In China, for example, these benefits can include the right to hire and fire workers, the unilateral right to buy imports without government approval, and the right to pay more to workers than regular Chinese enterprises can, thus allowing the manager to attract more workers with higher skills.

Some foreign companies have been asked by Chinese enterprises to form a joint venture but to station only one foreign manager in China—an easy way for the Chinese enterprise to enjoy the benefits of being a "foreign-invested enterprise." They sign a contract to manufacture and sell a foreign product, but the interests of the foreign partner become secondary to their own, the moment the contract is signed. A weak Asian company can obtain a new lease on life by merging with an unsuspecting, richer foreign partner. Even a near-bankrupt Asian company, by becoming a partner of a large foreign company, gains leverage over its Asian competitors. "If you forge alliances with strong partners, your enemies won't dare plot against you," Cheng Shi comments in *The Art of War*. For the foreign company, this objective on the part of its Asian partner usually leads to disaster.

How to Respond to the Small Sacrifice

- Appreciate the ultimate intentions of an Asian corporate partner and/or the government officials that oversee it. Does the firm desire to link up with your firm to acquire your technology, access international markets that you currently serve, or obtain an infusion of hard cash? Have the Asians made their agenda transparent and can you accommodate it? Some consultants recommend putting all of *your* objectives on the table at the start and letting your Asian partners know up front exactly what you want. If they can't deliver, move on to another partner without wasting time or resources.
- Do your own verifying. An Asian firm might tell you that they have a monopoly on a local market, and that they cannot adequately serve this market; do your own feasibility study to investigate this. Asians have a propensity to pad studies, especially in China and Taiwan.

- Start with a small test deal, when dealing with an Asian firm for the first time, and insist on an "organic contract"—one that stipulates a continuing collaboration between parties as a succession of performance clauses is achieved by both sides. For example, you agree to upgrade the 10-year-old technology in a joint venture factory if, and when, your Asian counterpart fulfills certain performance clauses—for instance, opens up new lines of distribution into remote areas of the country. An organic contract ensures that a partnership expands only when *both* sides attain successive levels of achievement, sharing both the risks and rewards of a venture.

- Test your Asian partners' commitment to real sharing of responsibilities by inviting them to come to the West to conduct negotiations. Your home-court advantage will be that *they* will have to return with something significant in hand to show their superiors, rather than your having to return from Asia with something to show yours. As Master Sun wrote, "Good warriors cause others to come to them, and do not go to others."

Strategy 8. The Shotgun Approach

The "shotgun approach offer" is experienced by foreign business negotiators most often when dealing with individual Overseas Chinese entrepreneurs (briefcase companies); their locale is just about all of Asia except Japan and Korea. The Westerners begin by presenting a product for sale to the Asian side, and within minutes they find themselves talking about transferring technology, transferring a management model, and setting up a manufacturing joint venture in Asia. They have been lured off course by the "shotgun strategy."

We don't need to dwell long on this tactic; most of us have dealt with it in some form on our home turf. A Chinese Malay businessperson might negotiate like the proverbial used car salesmen of the West: they want a deal, any deal, *now*. Owners of Asian "trading companies" tend to work alone and to negotiate as individual (one-person) companies.

They start by saying, "I can get you anything in Asia that you want. Bamboo furniture, tropical fish, orchids, anything. My brother has an orchid farm just near Kuala Lumpur, you know."

"Okay, okay," you say, "let's concentrate on orchids. Can you get 8,000 stems by February?"

"Well, I don't know . . . 8,000 is a lot of orchids. Let me call my brother. Maybe we start slow with about 200 per week."

Your expected sigh only triggers another onslaught.

"We should grow orchids here! Set up a greenhouse. Start small. Big profit. You make a mint. Why didn't you guys think of it? It'll be like having the right to print money!"

You sigh again and balk at the whole idea of collaborating at all.

These deal makers try to make Westerners feel guilty about not trusting them. In fact, the obstacle in the negotiation is that they can't perform on what they originally claimed they could do. Wise Westerners stay polite and collected, and they keep communication lines open. Getting irate is the only sin that Westerners can commit in dealing with these "pushy" Overseas Chinese: it robs the Westerners of face and gets their name around as a company to avoid.

PART III

THE BOOK OF "LI"
ETIQUETTE—CEREMONY—PROTOCOL

CHAPTER EIGHT

Banquets and Bacchanals

*I know all that I need to know about a foreign
business person after one meal with him.*
A CHINESE BUSINESSMAN

At a recent banquet in Macao, a Chinese businessman revealed to me the significance of dining etiquette in Asia. "Food differentiates people," he began. "If you're a person who likes sweet food, then you're like people from Shanghai. If you like hot food, you are said to be Szechwanese." He told me that I was Shanghaiese because I had been eating more sweet food than spicy food at the banquet. He had observed me as I ate from more than twenty plates of food. He then told me that he decides whether he's going to do business with a foreigner simply by watching the foreigner eat.

> If he eats slowly and savors his food, he's probably a patient businessperson. If he happily tries out food he has never had before, he's likely to be flexible in business. And if he is polite and formal at the dinner table, he will probably be careful to protect my face in a business relationship. This is a person that I would like to do business with.

In the West, we like to say, "You are what you eat." Before arriving in Asia that should be translated to "You are *how* you eat."

Food for Thought: What to Know Beforehand

Prepare for the unexpected, before dining in Asia. You might be served bat soup ("night duck" soup) in China or encouraged to try dog meat ("fragrant meat") in Taiwan, where eating dog is thought to improve sexual virility. In Hong Kong, you might savor

183

sea slugs, jellyfish salad, or glazed duck tongue. In Korea, you may be the guest of a host who likes snake meat, believed to ameliorate kidney problems, dissipation, and many other maladies. (The snake shops of Seoul were forced out of town prior to the 1988 Summer Olympic Games, as part of a campaign to show the West how cosmopolitan the city has become.) With an Indonesian host, you might be honored with beef brain curry, dried chicken blood, black dog, or beef intestines. In Japan, you might try "writhing fish" (extremely raw *sushi*) or raw *fugu* (globefish), which periodically kills Japanese who prepare it wrongly and eat a piece of its gall bladder. The strange things that Asians can make delicious to both the eye and the palate never cease to impress me—with one exception. Monkey brain, which the Thais say fortifies sexual virility, was served, in a macabre presentation, at a lunch I attended in Bangkok. I'll never forget it.

For most visitors from the West, dining in Asia is a pleasure. For some, however, it can be the hardest thing about crossing into Asian culture. Westerners might expect certain foods to be readily available. When they are not available, and the Westerners can't seem to escape foods that they abhor, they sometimes panic. For example, cheese is not served at an Asian meal; the Malays even think it's bad for the health. A fresh salad is not easily located, except in restaurants that specialize in Western food. Most Asian foods are cooked, an ancient tradition enforced through centuries, because of the health risk from eating raw food fertilized with night soil (human fertilizer). Some foreigners in Asia, unaccustomed to the foods, run out of patience. Recently, I heard an American executive in a restaurant in China yell out: "If I eat another fungus, I'll go crazy!" Most foreigners who dine in Asia get along fine; some even change to a more Asian diet when they return home. In short, you can expect your Asian host to introduce you to some of the finest, most beautifully presented food you will ever eat.

A few warnings are in order, however. Asia is no place for a person who is allergic to monosodium glutamate (MSG), a crystalline powder derived from the soybean and used as a flavor enhancer in many Asian dishes. Low-salt diets can't be maintained: soy sauce and the ever popular Korean *kimchi* are full of salt. Don't go to Asia as a business guest, if you plan to maintain a strict vegetarian diet. I was once taken to a restaurant near Chongqing, China, with a husband-and-wife team of American executives. The woman was a vegetarian, but the Chinese hosts had no way of serving her individually prepared dishes. (Chinese meals are

Coffee: The Worst of Culture Shock

Good coffee can be hard to find in Asia, and nothing makes North Americans in Asia more cranky than not being able to procure a proper cup of coffee. These are the prospects:

- In Japan, you'll find great coffee in restaurants; real cream is available too. Good coffee can be obtained from vending machines, which are seemingly located on every street corner and in every alleyway of Tokyo. Coffee-deprived foreigners are amazed when they find a vending machine dispensing hot, fresh coffee made from beans that the customer can select. The machine actually grinds the coffee beans and brews the coffee.

- In Korea, they serve good coffee but must be requested to not add sugar to it before it's brought to the table. Koreans have a terrible sweet tooth when it comes to coffee.

- In China, the coffee tastes like muddy water.

- Those who usually add cream to coffee might want to drink it black in some parts of Asia. Korean restaurants offer only non-dairy creamer, and the real cream in China and Indonesia is normally an off-yellow color. The best bet is to drink tea wherever you venture in Asia and to feel fortunate if a perfect cup of coffee unexpectedly crosses your path.

- Solution: Bring premeasured packets of coffee in your suitcase. You can make your own coffee if necessary, using the hot pre-boiled water that will be in a thermos in your hotel room, wherever you are in Asia. As a general rule, avoid drinking tap water in Asian countries.

◆

communally eaten from common plates.) The situation became serious when we were asked to pick out, before the banquet, the small (live) pig that we would like to eat. Early in the meal, we heard a harrowing squeal back in the kitchen as the pig got slaughtered. Being a very sensitive vegetarian, the woman was repulsed.

A Brief "Wok" Through Asian Cuisine

Food is frequently a topic of conversation at business banquets in Asia—more so than in the West. Some knowledge of Asian cooking will be needed, to participate in the conversation. The discussion will also offer a chance to demonstrate cultural empathy for your host's country and its history. As Confucius said, "There is no one who does not eat and drink. But few there are who can appreciate taste." To put you on the road to good taste, let's review what Asian cooking is all about.

China: Birthplace of East Asian Culinary Art

Throughout China's convulsive history of revolt and reaction against thoughts, policies, foreigners, and democracy-minded students, Chinese leaders have never once targeted the traditional aspects of their timeless food preparation. China's food epitomizes the unalterable cultural tradition inherent in Chinese wherever they live.

China developed the notion of the "balanced diet" in 200 A.D. Ancient Chinese divided all foods into two groups based on whether they embodied *Yin* or *Yang* characteristics. Author Boye de Mente explains: "*Yin* foods are thin, bland, cooling, and low in calories; *yang* foods are rich, spicy, warming, and high in calories. Boiling foods makes them *yin;* deep-frying makes them *yang.*" A Tao-like balance of both *Yin* and *Yang* foods was the ideal in one's diet. The Chinese further classified foods into five "tastes": spicy, bitter, sweet, sour, or salty. These categories corresponded both to the five primary elements of Chinese cosmology (metal, wood, water, earth, and fire) as well as to the five primary organs of the body.

The object of Chinese cooking was to enhance the unique taste of each food, rather than mix foods together or disguise their taste with sauces. Variety of dishes and harmony between them were equally important in a meal. Individual dishes were to complement each other. The best cook was one who created a dish that brought out the natural flavor of an ingredient rather than manipulated its flavor with spice or sauce. Regional cuisines grew up in China, such as Cantonese, Beijing, Shanghai, Szechuan, and Mandarin, based on what foods were available in each area and the degree of exposure to foreign influence. Asian countries have borrowed cooking ingredients from foreigners for centuries. Peanuts came to China with the Spanish. Japanese *tempura* originated from the deep-fried food recipes left in Japan by the Portuguese. Chili peppers came to Asia from the Iberian Peninsula. Even noodles came from the West, and were called "foreign hemp" by the Chinese.

The Chinese had a profound impact on Asian cuisine when they invented soy sauce (made from soybeans, wheat, and salt) 2,500 years ago. Called "meat without bones," soybean products (*tofu*) became essential in the cuisine of East Asia; they became the cornerstone of Japanese cooking, around the fifth century. From China also came tea to Japan, around 800 A.D., and with tea came the religion of Buddhism. In the tea ceremony of Buddhism, a small number of people ceremoniously ate food and sipped tea. The ritual evolved over the centuries into Japan's *kaiseki ryori* (tea ceremony cooking). It also influenced Japanese dining etiquette, not to mention tableware and dining-room interior design.

Japan: Food as Art

The island empire of Japan had few food materials to work with; they were limited mainly to fish, fruit, and an assortment of vegetables. Thus, food presentation, garnish, and adornment were emphasized early, in Japanese cuisine. Food portions were kept small but served artfully, in exquisite dishes and bowls, to enhance the food's visual appeal. Dishes were subtle and refined in taste. The Japanese call the style *sappari*—neat, clean, light, and honest. The Japanese stretched to extremes the Chinese notion of flavor separation. A sliver of raw fish (*sashimi*) is eaten with only pure white rice and a touch of soy sauce. A garnish of shaved ginger or scallion is added to a bowl of soup at the table by the diner, so as not to taint its distinct flavor during cooking. Each flavor is relished for its individuality. Dishes might be classified by seasons, as well as taste. The interior of a dining room will often be changed with the seasons. Food and mood: in Japanese cuisine, they change together.

The Worldly Recipes of the Malay

In Moslem Asia, foreign ships from around the world made their way through the Straits of Malacca, stopping often to wait for tradewinds to shift or to pay off piratical sultans. In their hulls were spices from Arabia, India, and all of the Spice Islands. By 1511, when the Portuguese took control of Malacca, the coastal towns of the Straits were probably the most cosmopolitan in Asia. To an already formed Malay cuisine, new ingredients were added—nutmeg, cloves, anise, cinnamon, and coriander.

New techniques for cooking, like *pilau* (cooking of rice with meat and seasonings), fused with native island techniques.

Today, rice remains the center of the Malay meal. A wide variety of spiced and curried dishes offsets an endless array of fresh fish, clams, and lobster. Interestingly, the Malays cook their rice to be less sticky and more absorbent than do the East Asians. They forgo chopsticks to eat with the fingers, rolling the dry rice into wetter foods and putting food into the mouth with the thumb and forefinger of the right hand. Indonesian dishes are sometimes labeled "too hot" by outsiders who try to eat spicy *sambal* (a common chili-and-spice sauce), not realizing it's to be mixed in a whole bowl of rice.

The King's Cuisine of Thailand

Thai food evolved in the king's court. The kings of Siam demanded the best in taste and presentation from both their wives' kitchens and their palace kitchen. Because the king's favor was needed for any upward move in the nobility, the career of the cook who prepared a poor meal could suffer severely. Thailand borrowed recipes and ingredients from other non-European countries (Thailand eluded European colonialism). With Brahmanic religion, however, came the cuisine of India, readily superimposed on Thailand's indigenous cuisine, which had come with ancient migrations of people from South China. To the rice-centered Thai meal were added curry sauces and spice-laden soups made creamy with coconut milk. Caramelized noodles (*mee grab*) and intricately carved tropical fruits satisfied the Thai's sweet tooth.

The Pseudo-Western Cuisine of the Philippines

The Philippines challenges the Western palate less than other Asian countries do, because of the American and Spanish colonial presence there. Asian cuisine can be avoided entirely, and replaced with beef steak, hot dogs, Coca-Cola, and ice cream. The experimental Westerner *can* find foreign flavors in the islands in, say, a bitter melon dish, a fishy-tasting *bagoong* soup, or *balut,* an imaginative dish consisting of hard-boiled duck eggs and their partly formed embryos. Rice is ever present, but the food differs from elsewhere in Asia in emphasizing sour and acidic flavors. Many dishes are cooked in vinegar or tamarind, a sour cucumber-like fruit. *Sinigang* soup cooked in sour fruits and vegetables is an illustration.

Minding Your Manners at Meals in Asia

Table manners in Asia range from the rustic to the urbane, depending on the status of the diners. A group of Chinese farm workers may surprise you, at a restaurant in Beijing, by eating with their hands and tossing duck bones into communal piles, or spitting them onto the floor. In Hong Kong, you may be invited to an evening of elegant dining at Jimmy's of Hong Kong, where the waiters wear tuxedos. The people of each "realm" of Asia cherish their own eating style and table etiquette. With one reading, it's impossible to gain a command of every particular of dining etiquette in every country of the region. I suggest that you try to master some *generic* guidelines for dining in Asia. Then, before you leave for an Asian destination, review the finer points pertaining to the places you plan to visit. I've tried to give you both in this chapter.

General Dining Guidelines

Declining Food. One of the most beguiling verbal miscues between Asians and Westerners in Asia occurs when the host and guest talk about their next meal. Asians, when asked, are trained to deny that they are hungry. Westerners are quite frank about their appetite. When an Asian invites a Westerner to have lunch, the Westerner says, "Yes, I'm starved." This may offend the host and be perceived as uncouth, because only a low-bred Asian would say such a thing. Conversely, when the Westerner prepares a meal for the Asian and asks whether the guest is hungry, the host is likely to hear, "No, I'm not really very hungry." The Westerner feels offended, having just labored over preparing or arranging dinner. A tip: Decline an offering of food once, before accepting.

Eating Fast. Some meals in Asia are rather light for Western tastes. You will embarrass your host by finishing your meal before others at your table and giving the impression that you have not been fed enough. Fast eating and lack of conversation may also indicate self-indulgence or impatience in one's character. Keep in mind the Chinese proverb: "Be quick over your work, but not over your food."

Smacking the Lips and Slurping Soup. You *can* smack your lips and slurp your soup, to show your host how much you like the fare. Recently, I served dinner to a number of friends and a prominent and well-educated couple from China. The husband had been in the United States for some time, but his wife had just arrived. Suddenly, there was a great lip smacking and sucking going on at the table, and then a belch. The Chinese man turned scarlet in embarrassment. He had forgotten to tell his wife that lip smacking and burping do not have the same meaning here as in Asia. Slurping soup is allowed, and is taken as a compliment. Asians "inhale" their soup in an effort to cool it. You can do this too. Suck noodles from your soup bowl to cool them. It's okay.

Using a Toothpick.   Toothpicks are used after the meal, but hold your left hand over your mouth while using the toothpick with your right.

Blowing the Nose at the Table.   Do not blow the nose or clear the throat loudly at an Asian table; go into the bathroom if such remedies are necessary. Koreans are especially disgusted when Westerners pull out a handkerchief and blow the nose at the dinner table.

Complaining about Food.   If you really can't stomach something, say "Thank you, but I don't have a taste for that dish," or "Thank you, but I have had enough of that one." As a guest, you will be honored with the highest-quality and most expensive dishes. In the Northwest of China, at a banquet, I was served a splendid dish by a Chinese factory host, but the dish was soaked in one inch of oil as a sign of respect and welcoming for me. Oil is rationed in China, and to use it in the preparation of food is one way that some Chinese honor foreign guests. Koreans serve live octopus with the same intent. I suppose the consolation of eating something alive is that you know it's fresh! But some people might be nauseated with something wiggling in their mouth. The octopus's sucker pads may even attach themselves to the top of the mouth. Pry the sucker off with the finger while covering the mouth with the other hand. *Keep your composure,* no matter how bizarre you think the food is. Don't make the mistake of complaining about what may be a national delicacy.

Complaining about Cleanliness.   Asia will usually meet Westerners' standards for cleanliness in restaurants, but there are always exceptions among restaurants where utensils and dishes are washed by hand. Ask for a different plate or bowl, but don't say that the one served has not been washed. Be careful not to appear overly concerned about the cleanliness of tableware. Often, porcelain dishes will have black spots in the glaze. Don't complain or ask for another dish; the spots are imbedded in the porcelain. An American I was with in China complained about these spots, saying that the dishes had not been washed. Everyone was embarrassed.

Eating with the Fingers.   In general, keep the fingers off the food, if possible. Spear fruit with a fork or pick it up with chopsticks. Don't eat the skin of fruits. Peel apples and pears; a knife will usually be provided. Skins are thought to be dirty—again a tradition that originates from the use of night soil as fertilizer.

Paying the Tab.   In Asia, there is no such thing as "Dutch treat." You won't hear the Western-style phrase "We should have lunch sometime," implying that the cost of the meal may be shared. The person who invites the other pays the bill. If you invite someone out, then you pay the entire tab. If the origin of the invitation is unclear—for example, at an office staff dinner in a restaurant, then the superior person will pay. In a less-developed Asian country, that person may often be you, because you are foreign and have more money. Don't do what a colleague of mine did in Bangkok, after dinner with a Thai official who had invited us to dinner. At the end of the dinner, he removed his wallet from his back pocket and said, "We would like to pay our share." In the West, this gesture shows someone isn't niggardly. In Asia, it may be construed as not appreciating the host.

One last note: As someone's guest, avoid ordering only the high-priced items on a menu. You can expect the same consideration when hosting Asians.

Mind Your Chopsticks

The Chinese started eating with chopsticks about 4,000 years ago, when they began to cook chopped, bite-size foods. Utensils similar to a knife and fork had been used by the Chinese before chopsticks, but soon became associated with earlier, more primitive cooking. Chopsticks came to be thought more sophisticated and elegant, because the diner has to do less work when the food is served.

Before arriving in Asia, be able to manipulate chopsticks with some deftness. Those who can, earn ego-boosting praise at the banquet table from their Asian hosts. Most North Americans can handle chopsticks perfectly well, because of their high exposure to eating Asian-style in restaurants, but some improvement can always be made. The worst thing that could happen is that your host pities your ineptness with chopsticks to such a degree that the waiter is asked to bring out a knife and fork for you.

Be prepared to use chopsticks everywhere in Asia, outside of Thailand. You will find a knife and fork on the Malay dining table, whether you are in Singapore, Malaysia, Indonesia, or the Philippines, but you are just as likely to confront chopsticks offered by ethnic-Chinese hosts in these places. In China, Taiwan, Japan, and Korea, and among Chinese hosts in Singapore, expect to use chopsticks, although silverware is often used in restaurants in Korea, and many Koreans eat their rice with a spoon. If you want chopsticks in Korea, you can ask for them. They're called *jŏt garak*.

The Thais use a fork and spoon, not chopsticks. They are proud of their Thai nationality and rather sensitive about the heavy Chinese influence on their customs, so it is important to remember this difference, when dining with Thais. Chopsticks are not used in Thailand at all, except in some Chinese homes; *don't* ask for them. Recently, I was in a top Bangkok restaurant with several American managers, all happily ordering from their menus. Before I could stop him, one of the managers called out confidently to the waiter, "Please, bring us chopsticks. We can use them!" At first the waiter thought he was kidding. Then, with a rather nasty expression, he went back to the kitchen to dig some up. He had to wash six pair, one for each of us. In a Thai restaurant in San Diego, I noticed that the menu stated the Thai attitude about chopsticks succinctly: IF YOU *INSIST* ON USING CHOPSTICKS, WE CAN OFFER THEM TO YOU.

There are some rules for using chopsticks in Asia. Because the chopstick is a sign of heaven, it is loaded with symbolism. One chopstick stuck in a bowl of rice is used at a typical funeral meal throughout East Asia. If you leave your chopsticks upright in a bowl of rice, it symbolizes death. Use the chopstick-rest at the side of your plate, and don't lay your chopsticks on the table after using them. Try not to drop chopsticks; it connotes bad luck.

Do not point with your chopsticks. A person who points with a fork is considered rude; pointing chopsticks at somebody is equally impolite. Many people recommend using the reverse end of chopsticks for grabbing food from communal plates on the banquet table. I suppose this would be more sanitary, but I have never seen a Chinese person reverse chopsticks at any banquet, and thus, I don't either. If your hosts do it, however, you should too.

You can signal that you are finished eating by placing your chopsticks across your rice bowl. Another signal is to leave food on your plate and put your chopsticks on their rest.

Asia's Code of Rice

Rice symbolizes purity in Asia, because it is grown with nothing else in the paddy. "Fan" refers to rice, rice muffins, and rice soup in China. In Korea, rice is called "pap." A Chinese person eats nearly a pound of rice every day, and three out of five people on earth eat rice as the main item in their diet. Rice is considered "the sweat of fellow men," so don't leave an uneaten heap of it on your plate when you're finished eating.

Rice is served with the meal throughout Asia. In China, it may be brought out at the end of a banquet, with rice soup and rice muffins. This is a way of saying, "Although we have dined extravagantly, we still eat rice like common people." Recently, however, that tradition seems to be fading. Rice may be conspicuously absent from today's Chinese banquet table. If you ask your hosts about the custom's being discontinued, they will take it that you want rice and it will be brought out immediately. If you don't want it, don't ask about it.

The role of rice in a meal varies from country to country. In Japan, rice is kept clean and pure throughout the meal. It is eaten alone, and should not be mixed with other foods. Even *sushi* (raw fish) should be dunked in the soy sauce so that the fish gets soaked but the rice remains dry and white. In China, Korea, and elsewhere in Asia, you can freely mix your food with rice in your rice bowl. The style of eating among Malays and Thais is to use a spoon to scoop morsels from dishes into the rice bowl first, before eating them. Everything is mixed with rice.

Toasting and Speeches

The Westerner always experiences a sense of alarm when he or she realizes it's time to make a toast to an Asian host during a banquet. I'm afraid there's no alternative: you must toast the host and *each member of your delegation* should do so at each banquet. The problem is that the Asian side sometimes wants to toast you under the table, until everyone is smashed. (We'll talk more about drinking alcohol in the next chapter.) For now, how do you make a good, believable toast to your Asian counterparts?

The first unknown is whether you should stand up or remain seated, when making your toast. This will be readily resolved by your host, who will *toast you first*. As the honored guest, allow the host to toast you first. Don't beat him or her to it. If the host stands when toasting you, that's your cue to stand up and be toasted. (Everyone in the room will stand up too.) If the host remains seated, which seems to be the current trend in most of Asia, then you can remain seated for all subsequent toasts.

You will probably have to toast someone through an interpreter. That's not easy; inform the interpreter beforehand that you would like to make a toast to so-and-so. Then stand up (if your host did for you) with your drink held in your right hand with your left hand supporting the base of the glass. If you're toasting with *sake, maotai, soju,* or whatever, make sure that everyone has a full glass before you toast, or you'll be standing there twisting in the wind as each person's glass is filled—not a good feeling. You can make your toast just after the waiter or waitress makes the rounds, or request the interpreter to have each glass filled because you would like to make a toast. The Japanese will initiate introductions and hear speeches before the meal begins. Most other Asians toast throughout the meal.

What do you say in your toast? The first rule is to be sincere and not sound canned. Spouting off about mutual cooperation sounds artificial as hell, and the Asian side can sense it, even through the interpreter. Get some of your personality into your toast, and cite your positive personal experiences with the people on the Asian side. Don't focus too much attention on any one person. You can, however, highlight the capabilities of the key person who has put a deal together or has been instrumental in introducing two companies. Try not to degrade the toasting tradition by toasting the chauffeur or the waiter on toast number 20. By this time, the ritual will seem ridiculous (intoxication will be widespread), but try to maintain respect for it.

A good first toast would be to the *company* that you are meeting. You can modify the following toast to fit any occasion:

> On behalf of my company, North American Incorporated, I would like to thank Asian Incorporated for honoring us with this fine banquet. We look forward to our discussions tomorrow and believe that our two companies can build on the friendships that we share.

Then say "bottoms-up" in the local language, which should not be hard, if you were listening when you were toasted. In China, it's *gambei*. In Japan, use *kanpai*. In Korea, it's *konbae*.

Another toast, to an individual, might be:

> We would like to make a toast to the director of Asian Incorporated—Director Wang—whose diligent efforts and agreeable personality have made mutual cooperation between North American Incorporated and Asian Incorporated profitable and enjoyable.

You might be wondering how to resist the bottoms-up part of the toasting ritual, especially if you plan on negotiating with a clear head after a lunchtime banquet. Good luck! It's not easy getting a banquet crowd in Asia *not* to drink alcohol, but you can try. Although you are required to *gambei* a couple of times, you can "make a deal" with the table to practice "no bottoms-up" for the rest of the banquet. I play it up by getting the head negotiator on the Asian side to shake on it, making it fun, and holding the Asians to it. You can accept toasts by drinking a few sips out of your cola glass or wine glass, but be prepared for pressure and prodding to empty your glass of high-octane alcoholic beverage. There is no easy way out.

In a large, multi-table banquet, the president on each side will sometimes have to stand up and give a short speech to the whole crowd. This is not a toast, and a drink does not have to be raised. A Western president can use the company-to-company form on page 194, but might elaborate on the future of the mutual collaboration and cooperation. If you have to give a speech before a podium at a very large banquet in Korea or Japan, bow to the chairperson on the Asian side before going behind the podium to begin, and bow to your audience before speaking. Anywhere else in Asia, you can skip the bow. In your speech, you don't have to begin with the gender-leveling "ladies and gentlemen." "Ladies" are not frequently referred to in public, in Asia. Start with "Distinguished guests, ladies and gentlemen . . ."—a nice blend of Asian and Western styles.

Getting Seated at the Banquet

Many Asians will not be offering you a chair, for seating at the dinner table. In most restaurants throughout Asia, you will sit in a chair, but be prepared for regional variations in seating. Koreans traditionally sit on cushions when eating; men sit cross-legged and women, usually side-saddle. Be careful not to step on the pillows. The Japanese kneel when eating, which can be excruciating for Westerners, after 20 or 30 minutes. Thai hosts may take you to a traditional restaurant, where they sit in the lotus position (cross-legged). Thankfully, however, most Thai restaurants serving foreigners have a deep space cut away underneath the tables, so you won't have to sit cross-legged.

Smoking at the Dinner Table

Don't smoke at a banquet table unless your hosts do. Most often, they will. In Indonesia you will have to get used to the heavy odor of clove (*kretek*) cigarettes, which remain the smoke of choice there. You will be offered a cigarette whenever somebody lights up. You should extend the same courtesy. Western women should not smoke at an Asian banquet table, unless an Asian woman is doing so. The same rule applies to drinking alcohol. This may sound chauvinistic and it probably is, but there is little point in a female's bucking the tradition by openly smoking and drinking in Asia. Follow the lead of the Asian women who are present—they may turn out to be more liberated than you'd expect. Among Moslem Asians, no one, male or female, should ask to smoke or to drink alcohol.

Talking Business over Food

Asian attitudes vary, regarding the Western practice of the "power lunch"—talking business over a meal. A Thai may get irritated when business is brought up during lunch; a Filipino might expect it. The Filipino would be horrified, however, if you were to bring up business during dinner. Asian Moslems can't stand talk of deals at the dinner table; the Chinese accept it, if it's done indirectly. A good policy is to avoid talking business during a meal unless the host initiates the discussion.

Business *ideas* (as opposed to specifics) will often be discussed at an Asian banquet. The occasion is often used to drop subtle hints to the foreigner about the sort of business deal that the Asian side is seeking. You may have to be on your toes to decipher what is being expressed, which can be tough if you're feeling the effects of too much local brew.

At a banquet in the Xinjiang Province of China, a bureaucrat on the Chinese side asked politely whether the visiting American CEO was interested in, of all things, raisin-drying technology.

Because he was running a company that specialized in cotton production, the American said, "No," and quickly forgot about the question. It was discovered later that the Chinese lacked the authority to approve a purchase of cotton-spinning machinery at the time, but were actively seeking to purchase raisin-drying technology. The Chinese bureaucrat was giving the American a lead on a significant sale, but the hint was missed. I saw the same thing happen when a high-technology company in Malaysia asked if any of us would be interested in "dog chew." The company had a connection to a company that was selling dog food at an extremely competitive price. We returned home, found a buyer, and put a deal together. The moral is, keep your ears open at banquets.

The Confucian Banquet
(China, Hong Kong, Taiwan, Singapore)

Whether your host is an ethnic Chinese person from China, Singapore, Malaysia, Thailand, Hong Kong, Taiwan, or the Philippines, you should be versed in the ways of the classic Chinese banquet, which originated in ancient China. The Chinese banquet will be arranged for one of three places: a restaurant, the dining room of a company, or the dining room at a hotel. I have never heard of one being given at an Asian host's home. Usually, you will be picked up by your host and brought to the banquet location. Wait in an adjacent room or lobby for all of the guests to arrive, before entering the dining room. As the guest of honor, you will enter the dining area first. If you are hosting the banquet, then insist that your Asian counterpart enter first.

The banquet table will be large and round, with a lazy susan in its center. Wait to be told where to sit. The guest of honor sits facing the entrance to the dining room, at the right of the Asian host. The right side is the honored position. In ancient times, the Chinese prince-heir would sit at the left of the emperor; as delegation leader, you can generally expect the Asians' head person to be seated on your left, and number two person on your right. Often, Asians and Westerners will be seated in an alternating fashion. (In Korea, the host may sit opposite the guest's place of honor.) If the Asian host's wife is present, she will sit opposite her husband, but foreign wives will usually be seated next to their husbands. If you are fortunate enough to have been invited to an official VIP banquet, expect seating to be prearranged and marked with name cards inscribed in English.

Placed before you on the table, you will find a small dish, a bowl, a porcelain spoon, and a pair of wooden chopsticks. A waitress will be making her way around the table, pouring wine into one of three glasses at each place. The tiny porcelain shot glass is for the strong toasting liqueur—usually the high-proof spirit *maotai*, made from sorghum and wheat germ. A friend of mine powered a Diahatzu microvan around Beijing using *maotai* for fuel. It's that strong. Your largest glass is for cola or beer, and the middle-size one is for wine. If tea is served, it will arrive after the meal.

Start some conversation with a compliment about the center display. Thinly sliced strips of colorful "thousand-year-old duck egg" are often arranged to render a dragon (symbolizing China) or a fish (symbolizing abundance). You might want to demonstrate your knowledge of the duck egg dish, which is made from eggs that are covered with ashes, lime, and mud, and then put in a jar for a month or so. The eggs come out multicolored but none too appetizing. Follow your host's lead, however, if he plucks off a piece of egg from the display and eats it. Recent economic cutbacks in China have curtailed the big rotten-egg displays of the past. In other parts of Asia, you may see center displays created from vegetables and other, tastier materials. Before the first dish arrives, when the aroma of the kitchen has reached your table, you might say: "My forefinger is trembling." The Chinese expression indicates that you anticipate something wonderful.

After the wine is poured, there will be an opening toast. Sometimes your host will order *maotai* or an equally strong local liqueur to be poured for the first toast. Whether you are standing or sitting for the toast, hold the thimble-sized cup in one hand while gently supporting it with the fingers of the other, under its base. The dinner will not begin until there is a toast. Then your host will beckon the guests to eat by saying "*Chíng*" ("Please") or "*Chíng yong*" (literally, "Please use"). Pluck food from the communal plates nearest you. Don't twirl the lazy susan around, looking for something you like. Try everything. Take one or two bites at a time from a communal plate, and put them on your plate. To show your cultural knowledge, find a nice morsel with your chopsticks and place it on your neighbor's plate. He or she will do the same for you. No serving spoons will accompany the banquet dishes, so use your chopsticks.

Don't mix the various foods. Appreciate each dish for its uniqueness. Don't use the fingers except with barbecued ribs or hunks of bony mutton. Remove small bones from the mouth with chopsticks. When one side of a large communal fish has been finished, it will be turned over by the Chinese, working together with chopsticks and spoons.

Pace your eating and drinking by participating in the conversation. Keep the conversation alive, when dining with ethnic Chinese hosts. Use safe rapport subjects (see Chapter 5). You will enjoy 10 to 20 different dishes, before the fruit's arrival indicates that the meal is over.

The soup will come at the close of a meal, rather than the beginning. Some soups can be rather exotic. If you are served sharkfin soup, you are being honored as a respected guest. The turtle soup will be the real thing and not mock turtle soup. I have seen it refused by Chinese guests who can't eat chunks of an innocent turtle. Bird's-nest soup is made by simmering real birds' nests—the product of swallows that vomit up fish to form their nest. Chicken stock and ham are added, but this dish might be too much for you.

If you plan to stay in Asia for a week or more, you may want to honor your ethnic Chinese hosts with a banquet comparable to the one they have given for you. Solicit (through your Chinese interpreter) the assistance of a facilitator from the Asian side, to help you find the right restaurant. There are four classes of banquets; you can see what will be served by obtaining a banquet menu card from the restaurant. Prepare to pay for the banquet before you eat. The price is usually around $100–$150 for five people.

After the hot towels are delivered, Chinese banquets end quickly and will usually NOT be followed by additional entertainment.

Dining Korean-Style

When Westerners talk and laugh garrulously over a dinner table, a Korean might consider their behavior offensively noisy and crass. Eating is a solemn act in Korea, usually done quietly and with respect for the food on the table. Too much talk at a meal is an offense to the food and to the private art of eating. Because Koreans have faced famine repeatedly throughout their history, the Korean banquet is a more solemn and quiet occasion than elsewhere in Asia. To some Westerners, the banquets may seem dull. Check yourself, when you feel you have to fill up silences. Endure them with a smile.

The dinner table is not a place where the traditional Korean family comes together. In many Korean homes to this day, two (or more) tables are used to serve a meal, with family members divided among them. Elders and youths are usually separated. The wife may even stay in the kitchen to eat. In the context of business entertainment, husbands and wives in Korea may not socialize together. Not long ago, Korean men brought a "little wife" to official functions, out of fear that their rustic real wife might commit a blunder and embarrass them in front of a foreign guest. Expect the banquet in Korea to be mellow and subdued and to involve little business discussion. Enjoy being wooed by the sound of the classical flute, hour-glass drum, and zither. The waitress may wear traditional *han-bok* dress, which dates back to the Lyi Dynasty in Korea.

The Korean banquet layout is more individualistic than in communal China. A set of bowls filled with different dishes is arranged in front of each person, with a bowl of rice in the center. Coffee and tea are served. Almost everyone drinks the rice wine, *soju*, with meals. The drinking water at the table is usually a tad yellow, and I avoid it. There will be no lazy susan, but a large, flat dish will feature various condiments in small trays. The rectangular Korean table stands about 10 inches above the floor and is surrounded by colorful silk pillows to sit on.

If you are served Chinese-style in Korea, take the food you want from an assortment of dishes and place the morsels on your own plate. Keep your rice bowl centered in front of you; it is the center of the Korean meal. You will find a large porcelain spoon placed between you and the rice bowl, parallel to the edge of the table. Use it for rice and soup. Serve yourself and begin eating without being urged. Feel free to take more of what you like. You don't have to wait to be offered more, and Koreans will appreciate it. The soup will arrive after the meal, as in China.

Let your host pour your tea, wine and *soju, as well as your soy sauce*. Pour for your neighbor all of these as well. Some Koreans will give you fancy metal chopsticks that may look elegant but are harder to use than wooden ones. You can impress your Korean host by using both your spoon and your chopsticks with the same hand. Scoop up some rice with your spoon and put it in your mouth. Then take hold of some other food with your chopsticks and eat that. Then dip into your soup with your spoon, all the while holding your sticks and the spoon with the same hand. Try it alone, before auditioning in front of your host.

Korean cooking features many sauces, a welcome change if you have been in China, Taiwan, or Hong Kong. Other specialties include charcoal-fried fondue, braised ribs, *jujube* porridge, *bulgogi*, and *kalki*. *Bulgogi* consists of thinly sliced, marinated beef, cooked in a garlic and ginger sauce on a cone of iron. *Kalki* is marinated beef ribs. *Bibimpap* is a bowl of rice with condiments and a raw egg on top. *Naengmyon* is a dish of spicy cold noodles. *Tofu* is called *tobu* in Korea. And then there's *kimchi*, Korea's homegrown specialty.

The city of Seoul consumes 100,000 tons of *kimchi* cabbage every fall, most of it put in jars, salted, and mixed with turnips, garlic, ginger, white radishes, zucchini, and pumpkin before being buried (to prevent freezing) for fermentation. Some say the whole country smells like *kimchi* or the garlic that's in it. Koreans serve *kimchi* with everything. You don't have to like it, but eat it at a banquet as a gesture of respect and politeness. Mix it with rice. Dip it in your soup to cool it. Eat a small piece periodically throughout a meal.

Korean restaurants are an odd combination of the Orient and the Occident, because of the U.S. presence in Korea since the 1950s. The menus are usually bilingual, and knives and forks are familiar. Your party may not all be served at the same time, if you have ordered different items from the menu. You will be served when your particular meal is cooked. The bill may arrive very early in the meal, which might seem rude to a Westerner. A race to the cashier may follow dinner, as counterparts all want to play the role of gracious host. To avoid this, if you want to be the host who pays, excuse yourself before the end of the meal to go to the restroom, and then pay surreptitiously. When you pay for the dinner at a restaurant in Korea, say that your Korean guest can have the honor the next time around.

When you are finished eating, place your chopsticks back on their rest and your spoon behind the bowl. You can also leave some food on your plate. Banquets in Korea are at an end when the fruit is gone. Incidentally, fruits are packed with symbolism in Confucian Asia: oranges mean happiness; pomegranates connote fertility; apples signify peace; and pears symbolize prosperity.

The Japanese Banquet

As elsewhere in Asia, you will be given a hot, damp towel (*o-shibori*) to clean your hands before eating in Japan. You may be given a menu, but the best method is to let your host order the meal for the whole party. Your meal will arrive on your own individual tray. The tray will contain a bowl of rice on the left and a bowl of soup on the right, both covered with lids. Remove the lid from the rice bowl and place it on the tray beside it. Remove the lid from the soup and place it on the right, next to the bowl on the tray. With your chopsticks, mix a bit of the green-colored horse radish (*wasabi*) with some soy sauce. The strips of raw fish (*sashimi*) can be dipped in the sauce. Most Westerners are well-acquainted with *sushi* bars in North America, but I will remind you that *wasabi* is deceptively hot and can creep up on you unexpectedly. The correct way to eat *sushi* in Japan is by picking up the wrapped fish with the fingers, not with chopsticks.

Eat the rice between bites of other food. Hold your bowl of rice at chest level and scoop it out with your chopsticks. Slurp the soup (the louder the slurp, the more complimentary) from the bowl, held with the right hand. Don't pour anything over the rice or mix food in it. Think of it as a palate cleanser between bites from different dishes.

Dining in Moslem Asia
(Malaysia, Indonesia, Singapore)

If you are dining with Moslem Asians, it is likely that you are attending either a meal at the home of a Malay or a buffet-style banquet. Although you may be invited to a strictly Malay banquet in Southeast Asia, it is more likely that you will attend a banquet at which many ethnic groups will be represented. At this type of dining affair, diversity is the watchword. While chicken, tomatoes, and cucumber are common to the diet of Malays, Chinese, and Indians, many foodstuffs are eaten by only one of these ethnic groups. Indians eat lentils, potatoes, carrots, milk, and mutton. The Chinese enjoy duck, eel, and peppers. Malays eat bananas, bread, fruit, and curried beef.

The Malays set a Western-style table with a fork and spoon but no knife (knives are considered weapons). A glass of water or juice will be found to the left of a plate of rice. The left hand is used to handle the glass. At the beginning of a meal, you will be asked by your host: "Will you please join me?" That is your cue to begin eating.

If you are invited to a traditional Malay meal, you may want to imitate your hosts and eat with the right hand, without a fork or spoon. Do not eat with the left hand, as it is considered unclean. To eat with the hand, scoop up a little food with the fingers of the right hand. Do not get the palm soiled. Bend over the dish slightly. Push the food into the mouth with the thumb. The tongue can receive the food, but do not make sucking noises or lick the fingers.

The left hand may be used for serving and passing dishes of food. Food is passed around the table from right to left and is served with spoons. Refuse a second helping by spreading your hand over your plate and saying "No, thank you."

Eating in Indonesia is considered private and will be accompanied by very light conversation. At meals, men and women may be separated. The same custom was once practiced in China. Expect to be served warm beer and Turkish coffee and, of course, Chinese tea. Dinner and party speeches are expected in Indonesia, as elsewhere in Asia. *"Silakan Minum"* is the verbal signal to begin eating or drinking. Leave food on your plate or you will be given more.

Most Indonesians entertain businesspeople in restaurants, rather than in their homes, which are often small and cramped. Never attempt to pay the bill if an Indonesian invites you to dinner. Don't participate in the American custom of leaping for the tab.

Banquets in Thailand and the Philippines

A banquet in Thailand will likely take place in a teak-paneled dining room that doubles as a performance hall for classical Thai dancers. The dancing provides entertainment before and during dinner, which is usually scheduled around 8:00 P.M. You will be seated at a low table closest to the action. After you've finished, don't change your seat to sit closer to your Thai host. This sort of leveling will make your host uncomfortable. Remember that you are the honored guest.

When they are translated into English, some dishes in Thailand sound horrifying: eggs in horse urine, mouse droppings, and elephant's penis soup, to name a few. Don't be alarmed, however. Most Thai food is mild, relatively less exotic than these dishes, and always delicious. *Kaeng* refers to a spectrum of dishes served in heavy sauce, including many soups and all curries. Mix *kaeng* dishes with rice, rather than eating them alone. Most side dishes are called *krueng kieng,* or cooked food that arrives at the table dry, without a sauce. The yellow color of many Thai dishes comes from tumeric, and red chilies make some of the dishes spicy-hot.

The Thais use a fork and spoon rather than chopsticks. Use the spoon with the right hand. Use the fork to push food into the spoon and carry it to the rice bowl, where it can be mixed with rice. Serve yourself more rice from the bowl on the table or request it from a server. Call waiters or waitresses to the table with the palm-down scoop; you can address them in a quiet voice as *"Nong"* meaning "little sister (or brother)."

Thais don't bother with graciously placing tidbits on your plate, like the Chinese do, and Thais eat rather quietly. The food is superb, but talking about it endlessly is not done in this part of Asia. The quantities of food may be smaller than you are accustomed to or have experienced elsewhere.

A Filipino banquet is usually informal; at a large banquet, a buffet serving style may be used. Dinner will consist of two or three courses, starting with soup and ending with a dessert. Liquor and wine may not accompany dinner, but you will likely be asked to have a drink in a bar before sitting down to dinner in a restaurant. Many Filipinos use spoons and forks rather than chopsticks. Use your fork to push food into the spoon for eating. After the banquet, you may be taken dancing at a nearby discotheque or in an annex adjacent to the banquet room. You may even be asked to sing your favorite song to the other guests. For advice on post-banquet revelry, read on.

CHAPTER NINE

Singing (and Drinking) for Sales

It is better to play than do nothing.
CONFUCIUS

You get through to a man's soul at night.
JAPANESE PROVERB

Recently, a Hong Kong banking institution merged with two others, one Japanese and the other American. The president of the Hong Kong institution had to visit the president of each partner bank, to have the contract signed. He went to New York first. When he landed at La Guardia Airport, nobody was there to pick him up, so he took a taxi to Manhattan and found himself a hotel room. The next morning, he called his American partner, who said to come over to the office. The Hong Kong banker took a taxi to the bank, went up in the elevator, and waited 10 minutes for the American to get out of a meeting. They shook hands, said hello, and sat down to sign the papers, which had been laid out on a conference table ready to sign. After the papers were signed, the American bid the Hong Kong president bon voyage, and that was that. A few days later, the man from Hong Kong made his way back to La Guardia en route to Tokyo to meet his Japanese partners.

When he deplaned at Narita Airport, he found a man holding a placard with his name on it. This man said he was to be the Hong Kong banker's driver during his stay in Tokyo. The next stop was a luxurious traditional inn (*ryokan*) just outside the city. The Hong Kong banker recalled that he had mentioned he would like to stay in a *ryokan,* when he had first met his new Japanese partner over a year before. An hour after he was settled in at the *ryokan,* his partner showed up to pick him up. There was then a banquet at a fabulous Tokyo restaurant, drinking and singing at a singing bar, and then he was driven back to his *ryokan.* He had a great time.

On the following day, he was taken on a tour of Tokyo's Modern Art Museum (he had mentioned his interest in Impressionist art at the banquet) and was given time for shopping in the Ginza. That night, at a company party, he was introduced to over 20 people who work for the Japanese company. On the third day, the papers were signed ceremoniously and the man from Hong Kong was driven back to Narita; a Japanese company vice president accompanied him almost to the door of the airliner. The Hong Kong bank president understood one reason for the success of the Japanese in conducting international business.

Asians value getting to know their business partners before doing business with them. They foster trust and friendship with their business counterparts through business entertainment. The Japanese spend more on business entertainment than they do on national defense (1.5 percent of GNP versus 1 percent). In 1989, Japanese companies spent $36.6 billion entertaining corporate clients at restaurants, golf courses, and bars, for an average of $18,700 per company. The frugal Chinese spend 500 million *yuan* on business banquets every year, and the Koreans are just as bacchanalian. How do Asians justify these huge expenditures? They save on legal expenses that would otherwise arise from conflicts between business partners. They know their customers intimately and they trust their partners. Through business entertainment, business relationships are built and maintained over years.

Participating in After-Banquet Fun

North Americans are perfectly willing to conduct their business coolly and clinically, without much human touch. If a deal sours with someone, the typical reaction is to bring in a lawyer and crank up a legal proceeding. There are perks and power lunches and networking parties, but these business bonding interactions differ fundamentally from the Asian notion of business relationships. A business relationship in Asia, once forged, will likely live for a lifetime. It is a permanent bond between people, not necessarily between companies. Anyone fortunate enough to have built up a number of business relationships in Asia is well aware of how important it is to maintain these bonds by participating in business socializing while in Asia. Much actual business takes place at informal nighttime drinking sessions. Important introductions can be obtained at a company party. Most importantly, the casual atmosphere of camaraderie that pervades social gatherings offers a chance to relax, express oneself, and clear away some of the cultural differences with Asian business partners.

Whether you are invited out drinking, to a singing bar, or to a small party among Asian friends, make certain that you attend. Don't shy away from any social event, fearing you may have to sing, dance, play the piano, or drink too much. This chapter will prepare you for what to expect when the banquet's over and it's time to go out on the town with your Asian hosts.

Where You Will Be Entertained

It's difficult to say where you will be taken by your Asian host. The type and intensity of entertainment that you experience will depend on your standing in your company, the size of your company, and whether you are a buyer or a seller. The longer you are in Asia and the closer your friendship with your Asian host, the more you'll see of what I describe here. My purpose is to furnish an overview of the possibilities.

One thing is certain: the business entertainment that you experience after the banquet will involve drinking alcohol, unless your Asian host is a Moslem. (We'll talk later about how to avoid drinking too much.) Other forms of entertainment won't involve drinking, but most of them fall within the category of "sightseeing," which we'll get to later as well.

After the banquet, one of a numbers of things could happen. First, you may be invited to a company party at the office or in a lounge at a nearby hotel. Most Asians have small homes that could not accommodate a large party. Many of the people at such a party you will have already met during negotiations. A second possibility is bar hopping—moving from singing bar to singing bar until everyone is inebriated and it's three in the morning. A third possibility is a night at a discotheque, a mode of business entertainment that has gained in popularity, especially among younger Asian businesspeople.

Depending on how friendly you are with your Asian host, you may end up avoiding bars and alcoholic drinking altogether, and spend time instead chatting in tea or coffee houses (called *tabang* in Korea and *kissaten* in Japan). I have spent wonderful afternoons lounging with Asian hosts over coffee and cashews. A slower mode of business entertainment facilitates communication between partners. The more you can encourage it, the better. Mention of the more illicit nighttime activities that you might encounter is saved for another chapter. Whatever you are treated to, the time out on the town with your Asian host is a time to express otherwise unexpressed ideas to each other.

General Guidelines for Business Entertainees

Don't Expect to Be Entertained Initially.   Unless you represent a very large company that the Asian side has solicited for a meeting, you should not expect instant VIP treatment. If you contact an Asian company through the mail and arrange to meet with a vice president when you arrive in Kuala Lumpur or Jakarta or Taipei, the meeting will be cordial but a banquet will not have been planned. Nobody will be on hand at the airport to pick you up and pay for your hotel room, unless you have been expressly *invited* by the Asian side to visit the company as a guest. If you place a large order during your first meeting, or indicate that such an order is in the works, a banquet will suddenly be scheduled. The Chinese procedure for initial meetings is representative. The Chinese will not entertain you before being formally introduced to you and conducting an initial business meeting with you, at which time they will ask, fairly bluntly: "What have you got in mind for our two companies to cooperate in business?" They want to know whether it's worth dealing with you. They want to hear your ideas about possible cooperation and only then will the ritual of business entertainment begin. If they like what they hear, they will invite you to a banquet that night.

Have Your Calling Card Always at Hand.   Whether you are wandering about Tokyo's nightspots in the Roponggi or those in Malacca, Seoul, or Bangkok, having your calling card on hand. Having your name and your company's name translated into the local language on your card will impress your Asian acquaintances and make it easier for them to understand the business you are in. Some of your informal conversations may turn out to be profitable, if you wield an Asian-language business card. It seems that every time I go out to a coffee house or a *sushi* bar or a *sul-jip* wine shop in Asia, if I have my calling cards, I come home with new connections made in Asia. You can, too!

Appreciate the Drinking Ritual.   As a group, Asians are probably the most Dionysian people on earth. Making exception for Asian Moslems and for Thais, who abstain from drinking alcohol because the Buddha discouraged it, drinking for Asians is nothing less than a national pastime. Asians drink a lot of alcohol, especially when entertaining foreign guests.

A first rule is not to drink alone. Drinking is a social event, and you should use the opportunity to get personal with your business counterpart, expand your network of connections, and show off the real you. Your counterpart will certainly feel free, during a drinking session, to show you his or her true self—to a degree that might take you off guard a bit. Asians are physiologically less tolerant to alcohol and tend to get intoxicated more quickly than Caucasians. You can expect a Japanese counterpart to arrive at a stage of chumminess before you do. If the chumminess progresses to intoxication, the unrestrained bonhomie exhibited may be disconcerting to you. Because Chinese hosts will drink with you only in groups, individual opinions and proclivities usually remain concealed. With ethnic Chinese elsewhere in Asia, however, drinking is a chance to build trust and knowledge of each other. A Korean counterpart may become a bit sentimental and somber, after drinking. It can be challenging for a happy-go-lucky Westerner to maintain composure, through an evening of teary-eyed ballads and gushy reminiscing.

What may really surprise you is Asia's tolerance of public drunkenness. Malaysia, Indonesia, and the Philippines do not tolerate or accept public drunkenness, but Korea and Japan have no social rule that castigates a person who is publicly counting pink elephants. Instead, drunken behavior is accepted as part of the goings-on of daily life. On the streets of Tokyo and Seoul, men in suits fall all over themselves, stone-drunk, trying to flag a taxi and get home. Other people hardly notice. As a visitor who might be surprised by this behavior, remember not to pass a remark (like, "Boy, he's drunk") or make a gesture to your host implying pity or disapproval. Such behavior is totally accepted.

Appreciate the Local Drinks.   Every country takes pride in its beverages. Asian countries are no exception. The region's most famous alcoholic beverages are *sake* (a rice wine) in Japan, *soju* (another rice wine) in Korea, and *maotai* in Chinese areas. Of those, *maotai* is, by far, the highest in alcohol content—106-proof—and the toughest to appreciate, whether you are feigning to like it or not. On a flight to Seoul recently, a small bottle of *maotai* leaked through a man's carry-on bag. Within minutes, the entire cabin filled with the ineffable odor of the liqueur. It's that strong!

Foreigners sometimes forget to exhibit respect for a local brew. Don't plug up your nose, at the smell of *maotai*. Don't flinch when hot *sake* hits your palate, or decline with distaste when a Korean offers you a glass of milky white *makkolli* as a gesture of accepting you into the brotherhood. Remember that these are national drinks that carry deep cultural significance.

Sensitive-tongued foreigners need not worry, however. One of the legacies of European imperialism in Asia is the modern beer brewery. The Chinese character for "beer" means "humble mouth liquor," a reference to the ignoble barbarians from the West who drank it. Because the Dutch, British, and Germans all left beer-making know-how in Asia, some of the tastiest beers in the world are available to visitors. If you show a preference for beer or whiskey (called Scotch, no matter what, in Asia) over the local wine or liqueur, your hosts will offer it to you. On some occasions, however, you will have to accept the local beverage. Most are fine, once you get used to them.

Except in high-class restaurants, you will not be served in Asia the mixed drinks that are common in the West. Singapore has Singapore Sling, Thailand has daiquiris, and Hong Kong features gin and tonic, but, in most of East Asia, the emphasis will be on drinking "neat," as the British say. Ice is rarely added to Asian alcoholic drinks; you may have to leave your "on the rocks" preference at home. *Soju* is not normally mixed, though I have found it does blend well with the Japanese soft drink called Pocari Sweat, which is available everywhere in Korea. Have a can of this nearby, to dilute your drink when the walls start to spin a little. An open bar at a party in Asia may offer a variety of your favorite mixed beverages, but usually you'll be drinking the hard stuff straight.

Pace Yourself When Drinking.   Be careful; pace yourself. A good system for any visiting delegation is to keep track *of each other's* drinking, to prevent anyone from getting obnoxiously intoxicated or sick, which is always embarrassing and repugnant, wherever you are. American businesspeople in Asia often drink too much and, being extroverted and gregarious to begin with, can turn into adolescents. This sort of behavior, whether in a bar, on a bus, or at a party, is considered rude and crass by the more introverted Asians. To Filipinos, excessive alcohol intake symbolizes "greed" and is thought to indicate a lack of breeding.

Consider Abstaining: Advice for Women.   Most Asian women drink less alcohol than do Asian men. A visiting woman from the West may want to follow suit. At parties in Korea, women often limit themselves to soft drinks, and I have seen the same conduct in Thailand. Few Filipino women will accompany their husbands in drinking alcohol. Women are totally excluded from Korea's *makkolli* drinking ritual, which we'll get to later. In Japan, women coworkers at a company party drink with the group. However, as a general rule, foreign women should follow the lead of the Asian women present at a function, before accepting an alcoholic beverage, and they should never drink to excess, even if the male attendees do.

Decline to Drink, Politely.   When you want to say no to drinking alcohol in Asia, remember the words of the poet Baudelaire: "A man who drinks only water must have something to conceal." Do not use an oblique "no" when you decline: claim it's "doctor's orders" or that you are having some stomach problems. Ask your host to fill your cup with cola rather than something hard.

Don't Be Afraid to Talk Business over Drinks.   At drinking parties, go for business concessions on your contract. If they are available, this is the setting in which you'll win them. This is a particularly valid reason for participating in any drinking outing that your Asian counterpart invites you to.

Prepare to Perform.   In China, Malaysia, and Indonesia, the demands on the foreigner to contribute during festivities are minimal. You're not going to have to stand up and sing or dance—or drink much, beyond a few ounces of *maotai*—in the People's Republic. Everyone else in Asia, you can and should prepare to share some of your hidden talents. Paul Crane writes: "To refuse to add to the entertainment of the group leaves a bad taste for all, and spoils the *kibun* [mood] of the group."

You can reduce your anxiety about participating, through preparation. First, ask yourself whether you have any entertainment skills that could be sharpened before your trip to Asia—a song you used to sing, or a tune you could once play on the piano or guitar. If you play the harmonica, bring one along. Do you know any card tricks or magic? Can you sketch a caricature? Can you juggle? Any of these will help make you the life of the party, and you will not soon be forgotten by the Asians you meet. If you can offer nothing else, bring a Polaroid camera and a stack of film, and pass out party pictures. They will go over very well.

Don't Advertise Your Talents.   Even if you can belt out an aria à la Pavarotti, don't tout your talent to your Asian hosts. Your ability will be exhibited everywhere you are taken, turning you into a visiting opera singer rather than a businessperson. If you were once a concert pianist, don't tell anyone. Near the end of your stay, you might ask whether there is a piano at the party and commandeer it for a while. It's better to surprise your Asian host, if you have true artistic prowess.

I recommend this approach because of a terrible experience I once had in Taiwan. In a coastal town on Taiwan's Riviera, our delegation was attending a huge local dance, with music by a 10-piece band and attendance by all of the town's dignitaries. We were standing among the 500 or so guests, talking with our hosts about how good the band was. I mentioned that one of the members of our delegation, and myself, had played guitar when we were younger. Instantly, our host informed the master of ceremonies of our talents. Unable to refuse, we were then led up to the stage and handed electric guitars. We struggled through a version of "I Heard It Through the Grapevine." Our interpreter translated the lyrics from another microphone. The guests applauded graciously, but it was an exasperating experience for which my colleague will never forgive me. Later, I asked the interpreter how she translated the lyric. She said that, in Mandarin, the lyric started with, "I heard it from the grapes," and got even stranger after that.

Singing Bars, Discotheques, and Other Meeting Places

In an earlier chapter, I mentioned Japan's singing bars (*karaoke*), where people go after work, sing love songs to each other, and get smashed. One thing that makes the *karaoke* bar seem so intimidating when it is shown on television is that it looks fully lighted. Actually, the room has been lighted to shoot the videotape, and the singing bar is usually quite dark and very comfortable. But that doesn't mean you won't have to sing.

A man at NYNEX International told me a funny story about his singing experience in Japan. He was asked to sing while in a *karaoke* bar with a Japanese host. He declined, giving the excuse that he didn't speak Japanese. His hosts had prepared well, however. They had taken him to a bar equipped with a video machine that automatically translates a song into virtually any foreign language! Having run out of excuses, he had to sing for his sales.

Unfortunately for terrible singers like me, the singing bar concept has spread throughout the Asia-Pacific, with the expansion of Japanese business. Even worse, non-Japanese Asians everywhere have taken to the idea, and love to entertain foreign businesspeople in *karaoke* bars. They now exist in Singapore, the Philippines, Hong Kong, Taiwan, and even in teetotaling Malaysia! (In Malaysia, however, *karaoke* bars are smaller and move private than elsewhere in Asia. Malays often meet here with their family members and, for example, "sing to their mother," as a Malay friend once told me.)

In a *typical* singing bar in Asia, a gigantic video screen, at least five feet wide, is at the front of the room. On the screen, a music video plays, at moderate volume, and the images are some of the most sentimental imaginable. As the song is played, the lyrics can be heard *and* read as subtitles on the screen. They are translated into Japanese, Chinese, and English. (I'm sure other languages are available as well.)

The person chosen to sing sits on a leather bar stool to the right of the screen, at the front of the room. He or she holds a microphone and sings along (solo) with the music while reading the lyrics. Luckily, nobody in the bar really listens, unless the singer is really good. Most of the songs played in a *karaoke* bar have been heard many times before. My only advice to foreign singers is to make a sincere effort and keep the showboat to a minimum. There's no crime in singing out of tune, but unrestrained exuberance at the microphone is out-of-place.

Do I *Have* to Sing?   Most North Americans dislike singing alone but don't mind singing along with a group. East Asians are exactly the opposite. In the West, people tend to sing together. In Asia, groups of people ask individuals to sing alone. It's not the singing that seems to interest most Asians; the important thing is the emotional experience of hearing an individual express himself or herself through a song. I think what Lee O-Young says about Koreans applies everywhere in Asia: "[Koreans] seem more interested in *asking* someone to sing than in the song itself."

At a party, you might be asked to sing an American song *without* electronic accompaniment. It's easier to decline in some countries than in others. A Filipino or a Thai won't press the issue, but a Japanese or a Korean may, if the party is really swinging. If you want to arrive completely armed to avoid any mishap, you might want to rehearse a chestnut like "Yesterday" or "The Girl from Ipanema" beforehand.

The singing has a couple of rules. Do not sing unless you are asked to. To do otherwise would be blatantly boastful and might be taken as effrontery. Asians usually choose singers democratically, so you may feel teamed-up on. Politely decline and always hesitate before you sing. Be as humble as possible, but voice strong objection if you are *repeatedly* asked to sing. Asians always politely decline to sing, if asked; actually, they want to sing, and they would feel rebuffed if they were not asked. Repeat all of your requests for others to sing, as many times as it takes. Asians usually decline invitations before accepting them.

Drinking Games and How to Avoid Them

Beyond the toasting ritual practiced throughout Asia, only in Korea will the foreigner encounter a *de rigueur* drinking game. Other drinking games exist in other places, but they will not be practiced in the presence of foreign guests who are not very close friends. A word about Korean drinking protocol is in order.

Drinking, Korean-Style.   A Korean ballad wails: "There is no one to offer me drink, so I am sad." Drinking is a social ritual in Korea, and part of business ritual as well.

After a banquet, your Korean host might take you to a *makkolli jip* (drinking house). If you are invited to one of these traditional drinking places, make sure that you partake in the drinking. To refuse an offer of a local brew—like *munbaeju,* a time-honored liquor that the government has dubbed "an intangible cultural treasure"—might be taken as an insult by your Korean host. *Makkolli* is an opaque, bland, white, mildly alcoholic beverage that is made from fermented rice and has little taste. Even the Korean tourist office describes the taste of *makkolli* as "not too unpleasant"; the drink is popular because it's part of indigenous Korean culture and affordable. The more traditional the Korean, the more intense will be the preference for *makkolli* and for another home brew called *sujonggwa,* which is made from the fermented scorched rice left on the bottom of a pan, sugar, water, dried persimmons, and ginger. *Sujonggwa* is served often, following a meal. These drinks are completely natural and unadorned. Drinking them usually fosters a "good old boy" bonhomie among men, so they should never be refused.

If you are taken to *bulgogi* and *kalbi* restaurants, be prepared to find yourself in a friendly drinking bout. Also, don't be surprised if you find yourself bowing and exchanging oversentimental words of close friendship with your inebriated Korean host. These are all part of the ritual. *Soju,* the clear rice wine, may be served in traditional ceramic cups made of Korean celedon, to enhance the tie with the past.

Now for the drinking game I warned about. After introduction, Korean parties will break up into groups of people conversing while they hold drinks—usually *soju,* plum wine, beer, wine, whiskey, or, in a traditional bar, one of the home brews I mentioned above. Once the meal starts, watch out. Gary Steenson, a member of the U.S. Consulate, explains:

> [W]hen someone finishes his own first drink, he holds up his glass upside-down (to demonstrate that it is empty), and then hands it to another diner, while at the same time offering to fill it with a bottle of whatever is close at hand . . . .

The person who hands over his glass can't get another drink until the refill content of his glass has been drunk and the glass returned to him. The guest of honor can expect to be the center of attention during the game.

Steenson continues:

> Within 20 minutes to half an hour, everyone at a table for eight or ten has drunk from someone else's glass and passed his own to another man, at least once, and usually several times.

The party won't be over until everyone has passed his cup to everybody else. Wives are usually excluded from the ritual, so foreign women may not be included. Besides parties and banquets, this game will be played at the *kisaeng* house, Korea's version of the *geisha* house. It's not a ritual for someone with a microbe phobia, but there is no easy way to avoid participating in the game, other than saying you are under "doctor's orders" not to drink. The players will then skip you when passing glasses. You can also drink a sip, pour the remainder into a water glass, and then pass the glass on. Your reticence, however, may dampen the mood of the party. Don't decline on grounds that germs may be on the passed-along glasses! Leave a dinner or drinking party looking sober, even if your hosts do not. Your sobriety can do your solid reputation no harm.

Drinking, in Japan. Each December, the managers and employees of Japanese companies participate in forget-the-year drinking parties, called *bonenkai;* in January, a similar round

Should You Pour for Your Partner?

A point of protocol anywhere in Asia is to keep an eye on your neighbor's glass and fill it when it's empty. Pour for your neighbor when his or her glass gets low. Do not fill your own glass, but wait for your neighbor to fill it for you. In Japan, hold your glass up with both hands as it is filled. (You can leave it on the table anywhere else in Asia.)

When you pour, hold the bottle in your right hand, supporting your right wrist with your left hand. You can even lightly touch, with your left hand, the elbow of the person you are pouring for. Don't fill a glass that is not nearing empty. The person may be signaling that he or she has had enough, by leaving the glass partly filled. Keep your glass half-full, if you do not want to drink anymore.

◆

of New Year's parties is called *shinnenkai*. At these gatherings, salarymen and salarywomen attempt to win approval of their superiors by giving performances, such as singing *karaoke*, dancing traditional dances, or performing magic tricks. In addition, office staff members in Japan often meet after work for mandatory drinking parties called *enkai*. Even female employees with children at home must attend and drink. Although you will probably never witness a *bonenkai* or a *shinnenkai*, you may be invited to an after-work *enkai*. Short speeches and toasts start the festivities. Subordinates (*kohai*) pour beer from large bottles into small glasses for their superiors (*senpai*). You may find that the Japanese get quite drunk at the *enkai*. There is no doubt that status boundaries come down and everyone experiences a feeling of company camaraderie. If you commit a blooper, blunder, or faux pas at an *enkai*, you don't have to worry about apologizing the next morning. Participants expect even their superiors to commit gaffes at these informal drinking sessions.

A few rules for pouring and drinking alcohol in Japan are in order. Wait for your host to lift his glass or thimble-sized *sake* cup (*sukazuki*), before you pour. Hold the *sake* or beer bottle with two hands. Don't pick up a bottle and pour yourself a drink in Japan. That's rude. Those near will be just waiting for the chance to fill your glass; let them. Lift your glass, preferably with two hands, before they pour for you. Some Japan experts recommend that when you've had enough to drink, your glass should be left full, and the Japanese won't bother you to drink more. However, the Japanese consider it less rude to pour what's in your glass into an empty ashtray or a flower pot than to simply leave it full. Another way is to place your hand over your glass so that it cannot be refilled and then turn your glass upside down when you've drained the contents. All of these methods will work. When the bottles are drained, someone will offer a final toast and ask that the group proceed to a singing bar.

Drinking Taboos in Malaysia and Indonesia. Business ice-breaking in Moslem Asia is accomplished through conversation in the office, not over drinks in a bar. As you become more acquainted with your Moslem host, you can expect to be invited to the person's home for dinner; this invitation will usually come long before any suggestion that you meet somewhere for a drink.

Saturday Night Fever: Asia's Discotheques

North Americans who have not traveled in Asia, or have not been there for many years, may not realize how cosmopolitan, or "Western," Asian capital cities have become. As part of socializing with Asians, you will likely find yourself in a familiar surrounding—the discotheque.

Discos frequented by businesspeople of your high caliber in Asia differ in many ways from the Western notion of the disco as a "meat market." High-class discos in Asia are truly for socializing, dancing, and having a good time with friends. Foreign businessmen should not appear "on the prowl" for local girls, when taken to discos by an Asian host. That's not to say that the atmosphere is not conducive to romance, but prurient desires should be relegated to a lower priority than meeting people and making new friends. The Asian disco is no place to forget to show respect for Asian women. An American executive I know committed the unforgivable faux pas in Japan. Scanning the young, costumed Japanese waitresses, he turned to his Japanese counterparts and said: "They're so cute. You just want to wrap one up and take her home." In Japan, women are revered, even if they are *geishas*. The foreigner's blunder was in the worst taste, though the comment was allowed to pass without incident.

Dancing, for Asians, is social, and not simply a way to meet available members of the opposite sex. When you are invited to "go dancing at a disco," it doesn't mean your Asian host thinks you need a sexual companion. Expect the event to be of a social nature: you can make new friends, expand your network, and show off your skills on the dance floor. A night at a disco is another chance for you to deepen the bond between you and your Asian business counterpart. You will soon find out that most of the clientele at a top disco in Asia are worth knowing from a business standpoint. Large parties of people at a disco are often the staff of a local company, meeting business clients. They are not just "young people" out having a good time. (Don't forget your business cards.)

Discotheques in Singapore are representative of the best discotheques in Asia, and most of what applies to them will apply to discos throughout the region.

In Singapore, discos are centered around the Orchard Towers area, often hidden in the basements of high-rises. New discos come and go, and two or three discos are always the "happening" ones at any given time. Your host may take you to the disco featuring "ladies night," where the crowd will be largest because women are admitted free on that night. (If you're unhosted, you can find the right spot by reading "This Week in Singapore" or asking a young-looking taxi driver.) The music is always well-chosen dance hits. The indigenous or foreign rock bands are usually quite good musically and they imitate the latest tunes with uncanny accuracy.

You will probably arrive at the disco after dinner, at the appropriately late hour of 10:00 or 11:00 P.M. If you're out alone or with Western friends, don't go home early, discouraged that no one is out at the discos at 10:00 P.M. Things actually get going around 1:00 A.M. Once inside a disco, you will notice that the atmosphere is sophisticated, personal, and fun-filled. There is much less sexual display than in a Western dance bar. However, the music may be very loud and bass-y, which can extinguish any hope of communicating with your host, especially if there is a language barrier between you. That is why singing bars are often located in, or adjacent to, popular discos. Your host will beckon you to sit in a singing bar, where talking is possible. In this intimate setting, you may want to broach that sticky clause in the contract negotiation discussed earlier in the day, especially if you are out with an individual rather than a group. Such business discussion is welcome at informal meetings of this sort, late at night, free from the formality of the office.

Back at the bar, you may find yourself in a mind-teasing drinking game played with the fingers, a variation of Stone Paper Scissors. I've seen middle-aged businessmen playing it, and a good way to break in to meet some new people is to ask how to play the game. Soon you'll find yourself one of the crowd, invited to go out the following night to "an even better disco" with your new friends.

You can sit at the bar, in a booth, or at a small table. Starting at the bar, you will meet someone, usually a male, who will bring you into the fray. Asian women are socially approachable, but they respond better to a new face if introduced by their male friends. Once you are in a group, you will find yourself possibly at one of the booth areas. Often, two men, or two women, will go out and dance together. Don't be offended if someone of the same sex asks you to dance. Do it. It is acceptable and has nothing to do with being gay or lesbian.

It's perfectly all right to dance up a storm, but don't get obnoxiously drunk. Not only will such behavior embarrass your host, it virtually nullifies constructive communication between people who speak different native languages. When trying to communicate in loud places, you have to speak loudly and clearly, mouthing each word to help your Asian host to understand you. Many people whom you meet in a disco will speak only rudimentary English. Singapore and the Philippines are unique in this respect: business socializing is conducted in English; you have to drop your required "Hello, I am from America" accent. The communication pace picks up and you have to be on your toes to keep up. Educated Singaporeans are especially articulate and witty. Another reason not to drink too much is that it's easy to get lost in the dust.

The evening is over when the lights go on at 3:00 A.M. The guests sit for a bit and then leave. Make sure you get the phone numbers and names of your new acquaintances. They should receive a copy of your hotel card and your business card. (You should memorize or write down your hotel address before going out, to ensure that you make it home.) Return all phone calls, should friends call when you're away from the hotel. Also, when returning to your hotel, don't be annoyed by the 20-to-50 percent surcharge on cab fare after midnight in Seoul, Singapore, and other Asian cities.

Not all of the dancing you do in Asia will involve modern gyrations to throbbing disco beats. Before going to Asia, you may want to brush up on your Fox Trot, Waltz, and Charleston. On a trip to Shehezi in Xinjiang Province in China, our delegation was invited to a local dance. I was expecting a discotheque, where couples would be dancing to rock and roll. No such luck. The "dance" was held in a underground bomb shelter (the town isn't far from the Soviet border) and featured a nine-piece polka band. Over 1,000

Chinese swirled around the enormous, smoke-filled dance hall, elegantly two-stepping and waltzing. Almost immediately, we were recognized as honorable foreign guests. A man approached with a gorgeous Chinese girl in a bright red silk dress, the only daring dress in the crowd, and said in broken English that the girl was his girlfriend but that she was mine to dance with for the rest of the evening. The band started up and 1,000 Chinese watched the foreign guest stumble around the dance floor with the most beautiful girl in Shehezi. I couldn't two-step and couldn't waltz. It was humiliating. Moral: If you're a 1960s generation North American who never learned a traditional dance step, you might want to learn a couple of steps before going to Asia. They can come in handy.

CHAPTER TEN

The Rites of Asian Gift Giving

Man with buttoned-up pockets, no one will do you a favor. Only a hand will wash a hand; if you want to receive, you must give.

CHINESE PROVERB

Two instances of corporate gift giving—an ultimate gift-giving disaster, and an unparalleled gift-giving success—will say more about giving gifts to Asians than any introductory background I could give in general terms.

The Gift-Giving Disaster

A friend of mine, a consultant, brings Asian and American companies together to do business. In conjunction with an educational institution, his company was host to a delegation of 20 business-people from the People's Republic of China. He made arrangements for an elaborate banquet at a local Chinese restaurant, and purchased expensive photobooks of the Pacific Northwest to give to each member of the Chinese delegation. He had the books wrapped in appropriate paper and, at the end of the banquet, his company presented them to the Chinese, permitting them to take the gifts home unopened. He knew that the proper protocol in Asia is to not open gifts in view of the giver.

At this moment, the members of the educational institution announced that they too had gifts for the Chinese. After passing out 20 additional gifts, they urged the Chinese to unwrap them. The mood in the room turned icy. The Chinese balked, but finally gave in and starting unwrapping. Out came 20 inexpensive laminated photographs mounted on wooden plaques. "It looked like something you'd find at a carnival," recalls the consultant. The Chinese were instantly embarrassed, and found it impossible to feign appreciation in order to save face for the givers of such chintzy gifts. The earlier good mood of the evening was irretrievable.

The Gift-Giving Success

To my mind, Robert W. Frye, chief of protocol for AT&T, wins the trophy for the best gift ever given to a corporate client. The gift was not given to an Asian client, but an Asian would have appreciated Frye's well-planned gift as much as the Italian client-recipient did. Frye tells the story:

> When the vice president of Italy's IRI was coming to the U.S., I had lunch with one of his assistants at the Inter-Continental in New York. I asked him what the VP particularly liked, and it turned out he was an avid cyclist. I contacted his wife and asked her to give us the exact model number of his favorite bike. She had to go out to their garage to get it. Then we contacted the manufacturer, obtained a copy of the mechanical drawing for the bike and had it etched on a lovely piece of stock crystal. He was absolutely amazed when our CEO presented it to him. I think he'll always remember AT&T, don't you?

You bet he will! If only more Western companies would put that kind of effort into gift giving to Asians, there would be fewer disasters like the one I described above.

Jumping onto the Gift-Giving Merry-Go-Round

In dependent business relationships throughout Asia, one method by which a person might build business ties is through the giving of gifts. When someone gives a gift or grants a favor to another person, the receiver keeps track of what is received and reciprocates with a gift or favor of equal value in the future.

When and how does a foreigner fit in?

Asians understand that gift giving in the West doesn't carry the connotations that it does in the East. They don't expect foreigners to participate in gift giving to the degree that Asians do. However, a wise Westerner will not miss a golden opportunity to build lasting reciprocal business relationships in Asia. The favors and gifts exchanged can be as simple as sending product information to a business associate in Manila just because he might be interested, or as complex as finding an apartment in Cambridge for the Harvard-bound daughter of a Japanese manager who is in charge of approving proposed sales to Japan.

Westerners who become part of a network of Asians who are all doing favors, so that they can later solicit assistance, may feel overwhelmed—*overobligated.* A consultant friend of mine has complained that his Asian associates' requests for favors have become ridiculous: job hunting for a Yale-educated Thai; sponsoring a Chinese woman (an associate's sister-in-law) who wants to leave the People's Republic; and introducing foreign men to the sister of a Taiwanese business associate, because she wants to marry an American and move to the United States. Many prominent Asian businesspeople feel equally overwhelmed, and will often refuse gifts from businesspeople to whom they do not desire to be indebted in the future. No one *wants* to enter into relationships of obligation and dependence, unless a clear and worthwhile advantage is to be gained.

Westerners who may feel that informal obligations not specified in a contract sap too much time and energy should remember that they may find it necessary to *cash in* gifts and favors to Asian counterparts at some future time. For example, if favor-giving relations are maintained with an official at an Asian Customs House, and a delay in unloading a shipping container has been announced, asking a "favor" of the official will get the goods unloaded. This beats complaining directly to the "top man," as is the practice in the West. Problems get resolved much faster in Asia when people there are *obligated* to "come through," because of reciprocal relationships nurtured through gift giving and favor granting.

Corporate gift giving varies from country to country in Asia. Here's an overview of how—and why—Asian businesspeople give gifts.

Giving Gifts Asian-Style

Business gift giving is probably more prevalent in Japan than anywhere in the world. The custom began in the early Japanese village, as a method of sharing resources. *Sake,* rice cakes, and the first harvest of the season were ritually offered to the gods during ceremonies. The gods then bade the villagers to share the rest among their less-endowed neighbors. Gift giving, an act of *giri* (obligation building), requires a reciprocal gift of similar value, some time in the future. *Giri* obligations go way back in Japanese history.

The Japanese family has for centuries given "incense money" (*koden*), or a donation, to a family that has suffered a death. The bereaved family records the amount of money given, and, when they attend a funeral for a member of the donor-family, their *koden* is the exact amount in return. A family might also donate labor to another family, for example, to repair a barn after a storm. Again, the *exact* amount of labor and materials is then to be returned in the future. Gift-giving etiquette has become a mark of high social character; a person said to be *giri-gatai* is responsible and trustworthy in keeping reciprocity balanced. A person who is too cheap has a negative blemish on his or her personal character and social standing in the community.

Most gift giving between Japanese businesspeople and companies takes place twice a year (specific dates are given later) and is important for building *giri* bonds with business counterparts. A special gift may elicit a special favor—a promotion, or entrance to a better school for a son or daughter. Anyone ready to label gift giving as not-so-subtle bribery would be correct. The art to giving gifts in Japan is to let no person *appear* to be playing favorites or becoming heavily influenced by gift-giving friends. *Honne* (what's privately true) and *tatamae* (what's publicly said) characterize gift giving in Japan. *Tatamae* is satisfied because the gift giving appears benign; yet its purpose is to perpetuate sub rosa arrangements and commitments that are never openly revealed.

Cash gifts don't play a pervasive role in Japan (they do elsewhere in Asia). The Japanese value "presents" and not cash gifts, because money doesn't buy *status and prestige* in a company, which most Japanese covet more than a higher income level. True prestige means being given a company car and driver, for example, or a membership to a prestigious golf club. Money alone can't buy these things. Only high status at a company can.

Korean businesspeople adopted the Japanese pattern of corporate gift giving during the years of Japanese occupation. Gifts are exchanged during *Chusok* (the autumn harvest festival) primarily, but the Koreans exchange gifts year-round, to help facilitate daily business. Cash gifts to influential government decision makers are common; few foreigners participate directly in these gifts, but many do so indirectly, via go-betweens. (More will be said later about "greasing palms.")

Formal gift giving in Malaysia and Indonesia takes place mainly among friends when visiting each other's homes, but ethnic Chinese and Malay Moslems participate in the giving of cash gifts (bribes that are hardly even disguised) as part of everyday dealings in these countries. I mentioned earlier the animosity that prevails between Malay government officials and the predominantly ethnic-Chinese business community. For the Chinese to get official approval of virtually anything, they have to offer cash "presents," bribes, or kickbacks to Moslem officials.

Cash bribes often facilitate Mainland Chinese deals too; reciprocal favor granting is the cornerstone of *guanxi* (connection making). In a country that prides itself on its egalitarian socialist ideology, the prevalence of *guanxi* is ironic. Coercive gift giving was discouraged after the Communist Liberation, but bribe taking ballooned with the free-market reforms under Deng Xiaoping. The Chinese expect foreigners to exchange gifts (given to the company, not individuals) when they visit China. In Taiwan and Hong Kong, expectations are the same, but gifts can be given to individuals rather than to companies.

Thai businesspeople give gifts during Thailand's New Year's (in April) and on their friends' birthdays. Filipino business associates give gifts in a similarly informal manner, mostly during the Christmas season. Giving gifts is not part of doing business in Singapore. Birthday presents are given to close friends and small items from the West can be given upon arrival.

Giving gifts is a chance to exhibit knowledge of Asian culture, as well as personal grace and tact. Here are some rules to remember.

Guidelines for ALL of Asia

Research the "Perfect" Gift. Imitate Robert W. Frye by giving a gift related to an Asian partner's profession or (better yet) hobby. A good strategy is to add to a collection. Asians take note of visitors' tastes and interests. I received a name stamp, called a "chop" in Korea, after mentioning, in the most offhand and brief way, that I did not have one. Another time, in China, I mentioned that a woman friend enjoys working with silk. *Voilá!* Ten meters of raw silk appeared as a gift the following day. Birth dates and hobbies of an associate's children should be noted, for future gift giving.

Purchase Gifts in the West.   Never give a gift that is readily and inexpensively available in Asia. "Made in Taiwan" or "Made in Singapore" knockoff-items may be good imitations, but they make headlines about your level of taste and generosity. Shop for logo recognition and stay away from "oriental" gifts like lacquerware, porcelain china, statues of Buddha, or jade jewelry. You run the risk of giving an item of Chinese origin to a Japanese person, or, God forbid!, a Japanese item to a Korean. Many Asian-style antiques were originally designed for Western tastes and do not please the Asian eye. If you are flying blind and know little about your Asian host, stick with what *you* know. As an amateur photographer, I might give my Asian host a Bret Weston print. A music-lover might know the best collection of Bach on compact disc. I once shopped with a technology transfer expert, for gifts for a group of visiting Chinese scientists. We gave them a number of the best technology books from the M.I.T. bookstore.

Don't Spark a Gift War.   Avoid giving grandiose, extravagantly expensive gifts. How will your hosts feel, receiving a $1,500 silver set, when they have brought a bottle of *maotai* in return? Try to reciprocate gifts with selections that are of comparable, or less, cash value. Don't one-up an Asian business associate by giving a more expensive gift in return. And don't give a luxurious gift *expecting* that it will be answered in kind.

Always Wrap Your Gifts.   Never give a gift unless it is wrapped and accompanied by a suitable card. If you purchase a gift at a prestigious store such as Tiffany's, have it wrapped in the store's logo box and wrapping paper. Don't unwrap a gift *unless you are asked to do so.* Just place it at your side, thank the giver, and bow, if you are in Japan. If you *are* asked to open a gift, don't pull and tear ferociously and shred the wrapping; read the card, and then delicately pry the paper open and reveal the gift to onlookers.

Appreciate Lingering Superstitions about Gifts.   Most tabooed gifts in Asia carry negative symbolism, are homonyms of morbid words, or are items associated with the funeral ceremony. (Inappropriate gifts are mentioned in individual-country sections, a little later.) In general, avoid giving an item that represents division, conflict, or disunity. For example, never give a knife to an Asian, unless you want to sever the relationship. Scissors and letter openers are risky choices as well. Giving flowers has some hazards. White flowers are for mourning in Japan, and a potted plant given to a Japanese person in a hospital implies that he or she is "rooted in illness." Steer clear of giving the Chinese flowers, too. They are mainly brought to people's hospital rooms and to funerals.

Observe Five Asian Gift-Giving Customs

1. Allow your host to organize a special time and place, to exchange gifts with you.
2. Do not open your gift in the presence of the giver, unless you are asked to do so.
3. Always refer to a gift you have received, at a later date. This, among other things, helps to build continuity in the business relationship.
4. Never give a gift without alerting your host that you are going to do so; for example, inform your host that you will be bringing over a gift to his office before leaving for the airport. If you are giving to a group, the whole group will then be present, which is important.
5. Give an individual a gift only in private; give to a group during a scheduled group gathering, when everyone is present. Remember that the worst mistake you can make in Asia is to rob someone of face—in this situation, by giving gifts to the others and forgetting one person in the group.

Be Prepared for Many Types of Gift Giving. Gift giving is a pervasive way to maintain human relationships at all levels of Asian society. Be prepared to give not only to a high-ranking Asian counterpart, but to people occupying lower levels in the hierarchy. To be safe, always pack three types of gifts before leaving for Asia: expensive, "perfect" gifts bought especially for your most prestigious partners; food gifts and other middle-range consumer goods (pen sets, paper weights, picture books, high-quality calendars, expensive liquor) for, say, the managers at the Asian company with which you do business; an assortment of inexpensive novelty items (books, tee shirts, notebooks, toys, games, cartons of cigarettes—all *made in North America*) for workers at the factory or for the children of Asian friends. Corporate logos can appear on small, novelty-type gifts to individuals, or on large gifts given company-to-company, but the logo should be used sparingly, to keep the gifts from seeming promotional.

Always Bring a Gift to an Asian Home.   When invited to the home of an Asian, arrive with a gift. Gourmet-quality foods purchased in the West are your best bet. Fresh fruit is a good gift, but only the Philippines allow its importation. (Nice fruit baskets can be bought locally in Aisa.) A friend of mine who lives in the Pacific Northwest brings smoked salmon to Asian friends, which is always a winner. Boxes of chocolate and other sweets get good response. Offer gifts with both hands, and don't expect them to be opened in your presence.

Always Send Thank-You Notes.   You don't have to respond with a formal thank-you letter after receiving a gift from an Indonesian, and you shouldn't expect a thank-you note to be sent to you by a Korean, but it is wise to observe the Western custom *whenever* an Asian gives you a gift. Don't imitate the German executive who stopped giving gifts of food and drink to Koreans during the *Chusok* holiday, because he never received a thank-you note. He ended up losing many of his Korean customers.

Don't Spoil Everything with Your Card.   *Never* use red ink! In China, when someone wants to sever a relationship forever, a letter is written to the person in red ink. In Japan, funeral notices are red. During a recent seminar on Japanese business, a participant told a story about how his company selected and addressed Christmas cards to its Japanese joint-venture partner. The cards were red. The participant, who is Japanese-American, stopped the mail just in time: "We almost sent 500 funeral cards to our Japanese partner!" You can expect to receive Christmas cards from Asian business associates. They often observe the custom for foreigners, even though they may not celebrate the holiday themselves.

Refuse Gifts Delicately.   Some gifts can't be accepted, either because they are too difficult to transport (like a Chinese porcelain vase), illegal to bring into one's home country (for example, a *bonsai* tree into the United States), or too valuable to be in compliance with corporate rules. Selwa Roosevelt, who handled protocol at the White House for seven years during the Reagan Administration, once had to persuade an Indonesian official not to give President Reagan a Komodo Dragon, a 10-foot-long, man-eating lizard! A refusal of a gift can be taken as an insult by the giver. If you cannot accept a gift, thank the giver first, then explain why you can't accept, and finally, offer a possible alternative. One alternative to personally accepting a gift is to have your firm accept it from the giver directly. Check with headquarters before making any decision; nobody needs a Komodo Dragon running around corporate headquarters.

Gift Giving in Confucian Asia
(China, Taiwan, Hong Kong, Korea, and Singapore)

Businesspeople in China exchange gifts twice a year, on National Day (October 1st) and during the Chinese New Year holidays, in February. Foreigners are not expected to send gifts or cards during these holidays; as elsewhere in Asia, Westerners should give gifts when visiting an Asian counterpart or when hosting an Asian delegation. (Businesses located in Asia should participate in holiday gift giving as local firms do.)

The Chinese often give to foreigners gifts that are charged with symbolic meaning. A company I worked for in China once received a set of eight porcelain horses as a gift. We smiled politely, wondering, "Why horses?" The giver, it turned out, had any one of three reasons—and maybe more—for selecting the miniature animals as a gift. Traditionally, horses are considered valuable in China, because they can always be sold for a good price. In Chinese myths, horses represent the Yang male principle, and a set of eight horses, like the one we received, represented those of King Mu, who ruled China in the tenth century.

Gift Giving in China

- Give gifts to the group; give to the Chinese company, organization, or institution that you are involved with, rather than to an individual at the company. You can, however, give one substantial gift to the group and small items, like tee shirts, pen sets, or cartons of cigarettes, to *each member* of the group.
- Expect your gift to be declined once, twice, or even three times, out of politeness, though this Chinese behavior is becoming less common. The Chinese expect you to humbly refuse a gift once, then accept with thanks.

- Wrap all gifts. You may want to wrap them in red paper, the color of luck. But remember, no red ink.

- Give a pair of Mandarin duck pillows for a wedding gift; they make a good (and common) present, and they symbolize marital bliss. Try to give *a pair* of something as a wedding gift; the symbol of marriage in China is two identical characters for "happiness," side-by-side, called "Double Happiness" 喜喜. Place a "Double Happiness" card on your gift; you can obtain one at any Chinese stationery store.

- Be sensitive to the "spiritual pollution" factor, when gift giving in China. Be careful not to give risqué clothing, racey fashion magazines, provocative video tapes, or anything else that may be considered morally degenerative.

Tabooed Gifts.   Many North Americans are fascinated with white wolves. A woman friend of mine loves them and suggested that I give a photobook of them to a visiting Chinese delegation from Hong Kong. She picked out a beautiful tabletop photobook of mountain wolves. Fortunately, I balked at the idea, sensing something sinister in the wolf's symbolism. Research revealed that the wolf is a symbol of cruelty and greed, in Chinese myth, and a lecher is referred to as a sex-wolf (*se lang*). Another warning involves the tortoise, a symbol of immortality in China. A "tortoise-master" is a father of a prostitute, a "black tortoise" is a pimp, and the animal has also been used to symbolize the penis. Thus, giving a replica of a tortoise, on a woman's brooch, for example, is hazardous. A fish (*yu*) is better, because its name is a homonym for "abundance, affluence" (*yu*). Never give the Chinese straw sandals (a bad omen because they are worn at funerals), the likeness of a badger (a symbol of cunning), or the likeness of a heron or stork (in Hokkien culture, the heron symbolizes a woman's death).

Giving a clock is a no-no in China. In Mandarin, the phrase "to give a clock" is a homonym for "to attend a dying parent." Receiving a gift of a clock would be considered a bad omen. Joseph Dorto, chief executive of Virginia International Terminals, had 20 clocks engraved for his Chinese customers. He opted to scrap the clocks, when he learned that the time when someone is given a clock in China is thought to be a prediction of the time of the person's eventual death!

A gift to someone other than the leader of the group should be given *through* his or her superior, not directly. Secretly given gifts from foreigners to underlings can get them into trouble. During a

Auspicious (and Inauspicious) Numbers

3 Three is a lucky number in Thailand. You might give three books, or three bronze elephants, or three music cassettes. In Hong Kong, the word for "three" sounds like "life" and is considered lucky.

4 In Japan and Korea, do not give four of anything: the word for "four" (*shī* in Japanese and *sa* in Korean) is a homonym for death. Some older hotels in Korea have no "fourth floor." Hospitals and hotels in Japan often have no rooms numbered "4," and dishware, a common wedding gift, is sold in sets of 3 and 5, but not 4. Try to give odd numbers of items in these countries.

8 In Hong Kong, the word for "eight" sounds like "prosperity" and is considered lucky.

9 The word for "nine," in Hong Kong, is a homonym for "eternity." Hong Kong businesspeople are known to pay upward of $10,000 for license plates with eights and nines in them. Auspicious plates are advertised in the daily newspapers.

◆

stay in Urumchi, I befriended our Chinese driver and wanted to give him some cassette tapes of Western music. It would have been inappropriate for me to give the tapes to the driver directly. I went to the leader of the Chinese delegation and gave the gifts to him, to give to the driver. It all went as planned until, at four o'clock the following morning outside our hotel, I heard Grace Jones's music blaring at full volume from the driver's Toyota Landcruiser. The ribald lyrics rang out like gunfire in a desert. The appropriateness of a gift should be certain, before it's too late.

Giving in Taiwan and Hong Kong

Gifts can be given to individuals in Taiwan and Hong Kong. Beyond that difference, the rules described above for gift giving in China apply to gifts to Chinese people outside the Mainland.

In Taiwan, a small gift should be given at the end of a first formal visit. Top-quality tea, specially packaged by a local store, is a nice gift, when visiting a Taiwanese home. Because designer goods are not readily available in Taiwan, and are expensive when they are available, they make excellent gifts.

In Hong Kong, every conceivable imported product can be found. Western liquors are plentiful, as are Western designer goods, at inexpensive prices. The best bet is to bring as a gift something that a Hong Kong resident would not have seen be-fore—perhaps something made in a home-state or one's own town.

Giving Gifts to Koreans

Koreans have no qualms about accepting gifts (including cash) from other Koreans, but they can be quite sensitive about receiv-ing gifts from foreigners. By all means, let a Korean host give the first gift; thereafter, follow the guidelines for all of Asia, pre-sented earlier. Koreans do not want other Koreans to think they are manipulated by non-Koreans who are willing to pay them off. They flinch when foreigners offer them expensive gifts, because they may then be exposed to peer criticism, which can be nasty in Korea. Give to a Korean privately and with utmost tact, and ob-serve these protocols:

- Bring a relatively small gift to Korea, on a first formal visit.
- Never send a gift; give only when visiting Korea.
- Present a gift in private, with both hands, while apologizing for the gift's insignificance. Do not ruin the *kibun* (mood) of the recipient by making him or her feel suddenly indebted to you.
- Calendars make excellent gifts; they are valued highly as status symbols and they can be shown off to colleagues. A first-rate calendar gives a Korean prestige.
- Upper classes in Korea have a taste for imported whiskey (and little taste for their domestic brands). Johnny Walker Black Label Scotch can't miss, for a Korean man, but don't give any type of liquor to a Korean woman.
- A gift may be delivered secretly to you by your Korean host—it may be left in your hotel room, for example.

The guests at a Korean wedding bring a cash gift which they put in an envelope and leave on a special table placed at the entrance of the wedding hall. Each envelope is inscribed with the Chinese character for "happiness" 喜 . Westerners, who may feel uncom-fortable giving cash to a newlywed couple, can give a wrapped gift, such as crystal or an appliance. The gift should be left on the table where other guests have left their envelopes. To a Korean funeral, attendees bring a white envelope with 20,000–50,000 *won* inside ($30–$70). This envelope should be inscribed with the Chinese character for "sorrow" 哀 , and placed on a table set up for that purpose. An envelope of money should never be handed directly to anybody. Inscribed envelopes can be obtained from a stationery store or local calligrapher.

Gift Giving in Japan

Japanese businesspeople exchange gifts during *Chugen* (in July; no fixed date) and *Oseibo* (in December, at year's end). Store windows throughout Japan fill up with a wild array of exquisitely displayed items. Cash gifts to employees at *Chugen* usually equal four to twelve times the value of one month's salary. Most households count on the extra "gift" money for economic survival. Gift giving to corporate clients is not limited to *Oseibo* and *Chugen;* small gifts of cooking oil, soy sauce, fruit, tea, and cookies are given to loyal customers year round.

The ulterior motives behind Japanese gift giving are hardly hidden, which is one reason gifts are wrapped and not opened in front of the giver. Gift giving is a shadow art of influencing others who are in a position to give later help. It's an insurance policy of sorts; in case of some unforeseen emergency, such as a blunder committed on the job, a person may be protected because he or she can cash in on a past gift or favor, to gain forgiveness from a superior.

For many Japanese, the custom of corporate gift giving has become a burdensome formality; some even consider it feudalistic. Many companies now prohibit corporate gift giving completely. For most, it is a formality that involves giving something of sufficient monetary value to fulfill an obligation. A Japanese executive who goes overseas will buy a quantity of the same item and give one to each person to whom *giri* is owed. *Taraimawashi* refers to the widespread practice of passing on a gift received—when the gift has no conceivable use to oneself—to another person to whom one owes *giri*. (Gift giving between individual Japanese friends, however, is based less on obligation than on *ninjo,* or personal feeling. The monetary value of the gift is not as important as its emotional content.)

The bigger the gift one gives, the more influence one can wield over the receiver. Thus, "present" giving in Japan can get extravagant. Westerners should be cautious not to give large, influence-buying "presents" unless they are positive they can come through, should the gift be accepted. For example, a present for a key Japanese executive might be to place a condominium at his or her disposal during an extended stay in the United States. If the offer is accepted, the condo had better be ready and available! An offer of a "present" should be made through a go-between, never directly. Here are some more tips for giving gifts in Japan:

- Give a very small "gift of encouragement," within 24 hours of arrival. Do not give a larger gift until it's time to leave and gifts have been received from the Japanese.

- Avoid bows or garishly colored wrapping paper. The centuries-old Japanese art of wrapping dates back to the *chimaki,* rice dumplings wrapped in bamboo leaves and exquisitely presented. Have all gifts to Japanese professionally wrapped at the store where they are purchased.

- Don't give *Satsuma-yaki,* expensive antique Japanese pottery made for export during the Meiji Era. It's appreciated in the West but not widely liked in Japan.

- Give money in envelopes at weddings and funerals, and to children at New Year's.

- A foreign woman working for a Japanese corporation in Japan may want to surprise her male superiors by giving them each a box of chocolate (called "duty-chocolate" in Japan) on Valentine's Day. The same gift can be given to one's sweetheart, but almost every female worker in Japan gives such a gift to her male manager on February 14.

Gift Giving in Moslem Asia
(Indonesia, Malaysia, and Singapore)

The giving of gifts (*hadiah*) is an integral part of Malay social and business life. Among Moslems anywhere in Asia, Westerners should be prepared to give to many—and often. More important than the size and expense of gifts to Malays is the gifts' message: the receiver's needs and wants have been given thought, and the giver is willing to sacrifice something to give the gift. As Li Wang says: "To be a gift, the object must have . . . value to both giver and recipient." This doesn't mean giving up a retirement watch or a family heirloom, but it does mean sensitivity to Malay hosts' tastes and preferences.

In his book *Dos and Taboos Around the World,* Roger Axtell tells about a company that found the "perfect" gift for a delegation of Moslems from the Middle East, who were visiting the West: a sterling compass, to help the delegation face East, toward Mecca, Islam's Holy City, at the daily call to prayer. To avoid giving very imperfect gifts:

- Do not give Moslems pork, liquor, ashtrays, knives, or toy dogs.
- Expect rather lavish gifts at a first meeting.
- Do not expect your gift to be opened in your presence or to elicit a formal thank-you. However, expect to be asked to open a gift presented by hosts after a business meeting or a speech.
- Bring to a Malay home a food gift wrapped in white paper.
- Be careful not to admire something in a Malay's home; the host might ask that it be accepted as a gift.

Gift Giving in Thailand and the Philippines

The rite of gift giving in Thailand and the Philippines is quite Westernized and free of most of the formalities that make it dicey for foreigners elsewhere in Asia. In general, Westerners visiting these countries should play Santa Claus, and bring gifts to *everyone* who is a consistent contact, including the person who delivers mail, the security guard at the front gate, the officious receptionist at the front desk of the hotel that is home for six months out of the year, and so on. Most gifts can be small—books, food baskets, company calendars, pens, calculators, and the like.

Christmas is the season for gift giving in the Philippines. At Christmas time, Filipino employees receive bonuses of roughly two months' pay, and businesspeople exchange gifts called *pasalubong.* In Thailand, gifts are exchanged between businesspeople at Thai New Year's, in mid-April.

Because the people who do business together in Thailand and the Philippines are often relatives, most of the gift giving is done between families and close friends. These tips will help an outsider:

- Pay ordinary attention to wrapping; it's not as important in the Philippines and Thailand as it is elsewhere in Asia.
- Give status-symbol gifts to Filipinos: handbags by Gucci, designer jeans, and wristwatches carrying reputable brand names.
- Expect gifts in the Philippines to be hidden away and opened later, out of sight of the giver.
- Look for symbolic gifts: white elephants symbolize royalty in Thailand, as do umbrellas (nobles were once sheltered by them). Pewter elephants and nice umbrellas make fine gifts.
- Bring an envelope containing 100–200 *baht* ($4–$8), when attending a religious ceremony of any kind in Thailand. The gift is for the host at the ceremony, to "make merit" with the spirits.
- Send a gift of crystal, an appliance, a vase, or wine glasses ahead of time to the bride's house (or the groom's if he originated the invitation), when invited to a wedding in the Philippines.

When Gifts Become Graft

The definition of bribery in Asia is like the classic definition of pornography: Nobody can tell you what it is, but they know it when they see it. In 1977, when a Congressional subcommittee heard about U.S. multinational firms' payments to officials and politicians in foreign countries, they knew they had seen it. The result was the Foreign Corrupt Practices Act, a hastily written, insufficiently debated, and poorly drafted piece of legislation that forbids American companies (and their subsidiaries) to influence foreign buying decisions by making payments of gifts or money to foreign officials, politicians, or their political parties.

"Bribing was wholesale," recalls former Senator William Proxmire, the author of the bill, when he looks back on the early 1970s, an era of multinational bribing. "The Lockheed Corporation paid a bribe to Japan of more than $1.5 million." Indeed, Lockheed had spent $25 million in bribes, to sell airplanes in Japan, Turkey, Italy, and the Netherlands; Japan's Prime Minister Tanaka received $1.6 million in kickbacks. However, Lockheed was a scapegoat. Exxon and Northrop Corporation had spent

"Tea Money": When and How to Tip in Asia

Japan: Tipping is not a widespread practice. Don't tip taxi drivers. Expect to pay a flat fee to airport porters. Restaurants add a 10–16 percent combined tax and service surcharge. Money gifts for hotel maids can be left in the room, in a special envelope (ask at the desk for one). Write the maid's name and your name on the envelope.

China: Until recently, tipping was rarely done. With times now hard, bellhops and porters often expect tips. Taxi drivers can be tipped 5 percent of the fare. Don't tip in restaurants. Appreciation can be shown by writing nice comments in suggestion books or by giving novelty gift items.

Taiwan: Tipping is relatively rare, but porters accept 15 Taiwan dollars (50¢) per bag. Let taxi drivers keep the small change; no tip is necessary.

Hong Kong: "Tea money" greases the system in Hong Kong: tip everyone. Most restaurants will add 10 percent to the bill; if it's not added, tip 10 percent. Tip a taxi driver 10 percent, or round off the fare to the nearest unit of 10. Porters and bellboys get HK $7–$14 ($1–$2).

Singapore: The government frowns on tipping. Restaurants add a 10 percent service fee. Tip cab drivers who go out of their way to help you locate a destination, but don't feel obliged to tip anyone else.

Korea: Don't tip individual taxi drivers, waiters or waitresses, or porters, unless they go out of their way to give assistance. Usually, no tip is needed, because a 10–20 percent service charge and tax is added to hotel, restaurant, and shopping bills. Tip a Korean hotel maid by leaving 3,000 *won* ($5) under the pillow for every four days that you stay.

Malaysia: Expect a 15 percent service charge and tax to be added to all bills. Leave more, if the service is exceptional. Tip taxi drivers 10 percent; they now accept tips (in the past, they did not). Tip porters and bellboys 1 *ringgit* (70¢) per bag.

Thailand: Porters get 5 *baht* (20¢) per bag (there will be a fixed fee at the airport and train station), and bellboys get 25–50 *baht* ($1–$2) for a whole transport. A good restaurant may add 10–15 percent to the bill; in a dive, there's no need to tip. Tip a taxi driver 10 percent, but agree on a total fare with a *tuk-tuk* driver before climbing into the three-wheeled motorized transporter. Don't give anyone a 1-*baht* tip; it would be an insult.

Indonesia: Tip 10 percent at a restaurant when no service charge is added. Let a cab driver keep small change under 1,000 *rupiah* (50¢). Tip a cab driver 2,000–4,000 *rupiah* ($1–$2) for a long journey. Porters and bellboys get 500–600 *rupiah* (50¢–60¢) per large bag.

Philippines: A 10 percent fee will usually be added to a hotel or restaurant bill; leave 10 percent for a waiter or waitress if the fee isn't added. Taxi drivers get 6–10 *pesos* (25¢–45¢). Tip porters 6 *pesos* (25¢) per bag. Washroom attendants get 5 *pesos* (20¢).

◆

much more to influence foreign decision makers, and hundreds of other companies were doing the identical thing around the world. In most foreign countries at that time, the practice of offering kickbacks and pledging cash gifts in exchange for business was simply part of the modus operandi for selling, an important component in a company's competitive advantage overseas.

Until the Act was ratified, little energy had been spent debating the ethical issues involved, when multinational firms swayed foreign decision makers by handing over sums of cold cash. The following statement by A. Carl Kotchian, president of Lockheed from 1965 until 1977, probably expresses the collective sentiments of overseas marketers until the Foreign Corrupt Practices Act was passed:

> I knew that if we wanted our product to have a chance to win on its own merits, we had to follow the functioning system [in Japan]. If we wanted our product to have a chance, we understood that we would have to pay, or pledge to pay, substantial sums of money in addition to the contractual sales commissions. We never *sought* to make these extra payments. We would have preferred not to have the additional expense for the sale. But, always, they were recommended by those whose experience and judgment we trusted and whose recommendations we therefore followed.

A company guilty of paying off foreign politicians with cash or gifts can now be fined up to $1 million; culpable employees can be fined up to $10,000. Nearly every publicly owned U.S. company has drafted gift-giving policies for overseas representatives. Any rep should know his or her company's rules before giving or receiving gifts. A tax advisor should be consulted on the current limit of personal liability in accepting a gift from a foreign business partner. The rep's company may be able to accept the gift— as a corporation—and store it at the company.

Robert and Nanthapa Cooper, in their book *Culture Shock,* write about Thailand: "Bribery is as invisible as the spirit world." The statement could be applied almost anywhere in Asia. Few methods seem to exist for obtaining favorable bureaucratic decisions in Asia, other than offering a commission, kickback, or rebate. Even when a bribe is paid, a Western company is likely to eventually become the victim of a bribe given by a competing company. Here are some ideas on how to deal with direct and indirect requests to fill Asian pockets.

Greasing the System with "Commissions"

Asian officials may be part of the educated elite, but they usually pull down a lower salary than their private-sector counterparts. For this reason, they sometimes drag their feet, unless properly motivated with a small cash incentive.

The "grease" may be as innocent as a strategically given air conditioner, or as unabashed as a handbag full of cash. Price kickbacks are a ubiquitous and traditional method. Of the 50 representative offices selling medical instruments in Beijing, the most successful ones routinely hike their commission rate to 15 percent by increasing prices. They share the difference with Chinese officials who are in a position to facilitate deals. The success of Daewoo, the Korean corporate conglomerate (*chaebol*), was built on the bribes that its founder, Woo Jung Kim, doled out to government officials. Things have changed in Korea since that time, but cash in a white envelope still lubricates an otherwise unyielding bureaucratic machinery.

Westerners should *never* become involved directly in the paying of commissions; handling of the actual commission paying should be left to an Asian joint-venture partner, or a distributor. Often, local or native managers receive an inflated salary, which enables them to "tip" all of the people who help prevent a business from being strangled by delivery delays, approvals, and so on. Gifts and favors should not be given indiscriminately. A favor-inducing gift has to be given to the right person—the person in the loop of decisions that affect a particular venture—if it is to have a beneficial effect. Finding out exactly who this person is, before making a move, is critical. At a Korean *chaebol*, the person may be a general manager directly responsible for approving the purchase of a product—NOT the president of the company. Conversely, at a small company, gifts *should* be given to the president, because he or she will wield unilateral power over purchases. An Asian go-between will know best. Once a personal tie is formed with the go-between, he or she can make most commission decisions.

The "Professional" Go-Between. Go-betweens can be hired as business facilitators in any Asian country. They help get goods off a dock, they lobby a key government official for special consideration of a proposal, and they use their personal connections to help make foreigners' business run smoothly. They should always be paid "on spec"—when the job is done.

Other Ways to Influence a Deal.   Any benefit that a Westerner can bring to an Asian company will factor into the decision-making process regarding the product and the attention the business receives. Possible offers are: to upgrade a local factory, by bringing in needed office equipment; to set up a welfare fund for workers; or to sponsor star workers with scholarships for overseas training. All of these perks can nudge a decision maker without money changing hands.

Receiving Gifts in Asia

In *36 Strategies,* a famous Chinese book of war tactics written 2,500 years ago, two of the battle strategies suggest the use of gifts to influence an adversary. Chin-ning Chu, author of *The Chinese Mind Game,* tells us that, in the first strategy, one defeats an enemy by "capturing" its chief. One does this by luring the chief away from his forces and giving him the thing that pleases him, whether it be money, power, or prestige. The pleased chief will then become manipulatable and, thus, a less formidable enemy. Some company-to-company gifts from Asians may connote, as Richard Ricci warns in his book *Living in Korea,* "advanced thanks for favorable consideration—subtle encouragement to act in the interests of the gift giver." You may feel taken advantage of when money arrives in a white envelope to thank you for services rendered or to attempt to favorably influence a decision you have to make, for example, whether you will hire a job applicant or give a passing grade to a student. Matthews Masayuki Hamabata, an author who returned to Japan after being educated in the United States, offers a revealing illustration in his book *Crested Kimono:*

> [I] had developed a close friendship with Mrs. Itoo and her only daughter, Sanae. We had been meeting frequently to discuss the prospect of an American college education for Sanae, and in fact, I had helped Sanae with her [college] applications . . . . Just as we

were about to part company, Mrs. Itoo handed me a small, carefully wrapped box and a card . . . . On the subway ride home, I discovered that I had received a Valentine's Day card and a box of chocolates . . . . Delighted with my gift, I opened the box . . . and out fell 50,000 yen (then about $250) in five crisp, 10,000-yen bills. I was, at once, shocked, insulted, and hurt. "Who do the Itoos think they are? They can't buy me or my services!"

After talking with his friends, Hamabata realized that the Itoos were only trying to repay a debt of gratitude (*on*), by giving a gift imbued with inner feelings (*ninjoo*); the gift was also an acknowledgment that the Itoos needed Hamabata and valued their relationship with him. He concluded that since the gift was given to him *after* he rendered his services, it could not be construed as any kind of bribe. But what about gifts presented before a service is rendered, before a decision is to be made?

How should Westerners deal with receiving truly coercive gifts? When a gift arrives from someone who is attempting to "encourage," for example, a job offer, the request can be sidestepped by giving the person a return gift *before* the person approaches, job application in hand. The same method can be used to avoid any unreasonable request made in the guise of a gift. It's a good method, because it preserves face for the person seeking the favor. Many Asians refuse gifts (by sending them back to the giver) because they realize they are thinly veiled bribes. This response is risky: the services of the giver may be needed in the future.

The second strategy that Chin-ning Chu describes is called "the beauty trap": one fosters a more cooperative relationship with an adversary by treating him to the services of a desirable female companion who is specially trained to please him. A bond of trust is forged between adversaries, and crucial concessions may then be easier for the giver to obtain from the receiver.

The next chapter describes how to elude the treacheries of "the beauty trap."

CHAPTER ELEVEN

Love, Sex, and the (Naughty) Foreigner in Asia

We were honored to be dinner guests of a well-connected Colonel in the Bangkok police department. We had met the Colonel on the plane from Hong Kong, and he had invited us to a traditional Thai meal at the Indra Hotel, one of the best hotels in Bangkok. Well into a most enjoyable evening, my colleague, an American loan broker, turned to the Colonel and asked rather bluntly whether "prostitution" in Thailand had been officially legalized. We told the Colonel how we had been openly solicited, ever since exiting Don Muang Airport earlier that day, by Thai men selling female companionship.

"No, no, no," the Colonel said, "but prostitution is so widespread in Thailand that we cannot enforce any law against it."

With the red papaya devoured, dinner was suddenly over. The Colonel bid us farewell at his Mercedes, parked in the hotel garage. Before driving off, he said something in Thai to our driver, a detective with the Bangkok police force. They exchanged knowing smiles.

With the Colonel gone, the detective drove us to Phatpong, Bangkok's sex-and-sin district ("Colonel's treat," the detective grinned), for a tour of the city's sex clubs. Upon entering the first club, we were dumbfounded to find a woman on stage engaged in a live recreation of a triple-x-rated version of the lewd nightclub scene from "The Deer Hunter."

Welcome to "sex entertainment" in Asia.

Asia's "Floating World" of Business Entertainment

Unless they are doing business in the People's Republic or Singapore, or with Moslem Asians, Westerners can expect sex entertainment to be part of socializing with an Asian business partner, by the second or third meeting. I don't mean that *having sex* is part of the routine of being entertained, but a "sex club" may well be on the list of places where an Asian host entertains. Whether in Phatpong in Bangkok, Itaewon in Seoul, Shinjuku in Tokyo, or Ermita in Manila, the type of sex-oriented entertainment— whether a floor show, hostess bar, or *geisha* house—will depend on the personality and status of the host.

It's important for Westerners *not* to appear horrified, in the presence of a host, by the sleaze-for-sale extravaganzas for which these districts in Asia are famed. Female visitors, who are usually invited on such tours if their delegation includes men, may find the experience especially trying. The guests should remain gracious, even as a group of drunken office workers stumbles by and a *mamasan* grabs the nearest arm and whines hoarsely: "I have beautiful girl . . . she give you everything . . . massage whole body . . . love you long time . . . forever."

Those who do extensive business in Asia, or live there as expatriates, can anticipate being offered, sooner or later, to indulge in sexual favors procured by the host. Visiting Westerners typically react to Asians' fondness of sex entertainment in one of two ways: either they find it morally reprehensible, or they run amok in the sexual opportunities being offered. One hears two types of stories (always "second-hand," of course), the first about the puritanical wife of a foreign executive, being dragged along for an evening of pornographic floor shows with the guys; the other about foreign men (even Congressmen!), spending every drunken evening in Asia in the arms of a different call girl.

Avoiding either extreme in viewpoint, this chapter deals with the subject of Asian sexual entertainment candidly, accepting the practice as the animal lover must accept bullfighting in Spain. It's part of the indigenous culture and, no matter what one may think about it, it won't be vanishing any time soon.

Serious pitfalls await the Western businessperson who chooses to partake of Asia's supersensual "floating world." Some of these may not be clear to the naked eye (so to speak). Here's some advice on the hidden drawbacks:

- *Damage to Your Reputation.* Whether your weak spot is alcohol or sexual companionship, Asian hosts will indulge you, if they feel it's in *their* interest. Be careful, or you'll find yourself labeled, which can do your reputation, and that of your firm, long-term harm.

- *Damage to Your Ability to Expand Your Business Network.* Once your reputation for being promiscuous spreads, many conservative, more traditional, Asians may shun you or, at least, mistrust you. Your ability to build business relationships in powerful circles of older businesspeople may be stymied.

- *Exposure to Criminal Elements.* Crime and drug abuse permeate Asia's sex industry and represent indirect threats to any foreigner who appears to have money. A foreigner's activities in these areas can also result in a potentially scandalous incident—the most direct route to persona non grata status in the local business community.

- *Risk of Contracting Sexually Transmitted Diseases.* Sexually transmitted diseases are rampant in most of the region's sex districts. One disturbing estimate says that 70 percent of the 1 million prostitutes in Bangkok carry a sexually transmitted disease. Thailand and the Philippines are in the throes of the AIDS epidemic.

The Beauty Trap

Beyond these risks, there is a purely psychological victory for the Asian side, when Western businesspeople succumb to sexual favors and inducements. Asians have, for centuries, shown a willingness to cater to the prurient desires of foreigners, in order to forge a deal. Asian businesspeople are aware of the power inherent in a gesture of sexual gift giving; in the context of business entertainment, the practice is nothing short of an obligation-creating tactic in the guise of a trust builder.

Here's a typical scenario. Mr. X, the representative of a North American company, visits a Korean supplier for the first time. Because his company is a potentially major source of income for the Korean firm, Mr. X is taken to a *kisaeng* house by his Korean hosts. He is serenaded by traditionally clad young Korean girls who bounce in his lap and giggle demurely at his jokes; the *soju* serves as an aphrodisiac. Mr. X is assured that his favorite hostess will accompany him to his hotel. Intoxicated, and feeling a little pressured by his Korean hosts, the neophyte Westerner smiles contentedly and accepts the offer. Off to the hotel they go.

Passions spent, Mr. X passes out and the girl vanishes. In the morning, Mr. X wakes up hung over and discovers himself the victim of a sudden attack of guilt about his promiscuous behavior. What about his wife at home? Has he lost credibility with his Korean hosts? And so on.

He's an emotional wreck. Perhaps none of this would matter, except that Mr. X is to negotiate the fine points of a contract throughout the entire day. His performance won't be up to par and he may even feel that the Koreans "have something over him," which could oblige him to play a soft hand in negotiating the contract.

Moral of the story: The preservation of mental alertness and business reputation in Asia should take precedence over any desire to experience an Asian sex partner or please one's hosts by accepting offers to do so. Phillip Crane has written that, in dealing with Koreans, "to refuse wine, women, or bribes because of one's beliefs and standards is to gain respect and a hearing." The same response can be expected from other Asians as well.

The following sections will make it easier for Westerners not to register surprise or shock when they're introduced to amorous business entertainment throughout Asia.

Business and Sex in Confucian Asia (China, Korea, Taiwan, and Hong Kong)

Although Confucius was somewhat of a prude, proclaiming that boys and girls should not be permitted to sit together after the age of seven, the Chinese did enjoy a vibrant erotic-comic literature that came to full blossom in the 16th and 17th centuries. Some of the notable titles included "The Carnal Prayer Mat," recently translated into English, and "The Life of the Lord of Perfect Satisfaction." (The Chinese have always had a knack for titles.)

Some of the earliest known sexual paraphernalia was developed in China, and included numerous instruments of arousal and an early condom (a "sheep's-eye-ring") made from the hairy ring of muscle around the eye of a sheep. It had to be softened by soaking it in a cup of tea—difficult foreplay indeed!

The sexual puritanism of the Mao era virtually stamped out anything remotely pornographic in modern China, including the ancient novels mentioned above. Mainland Chinese tend to perceive human nakedness as crass and rather uncivilized. Even Chinese newlyweds are said to wear undergarments when sleeping.

In China, sex has no part in the entertainment of foreign guests. A lone prostitute may prowl the lobby of the Friendship Hotel, hoping to serve a foreigner who is on an expense account, but no Chinese host will unexpectedly invite a Westerner to a hostess bar or a tour of the local red-light district. They simply don't exist in China for foreign consumption.

Korea is an entirely different story.

Korea's *Kisaeng* Houses

Korea's modern sex industry, which started in the late 1950s, grew up around the U.S. military presence. Now, on the steep alleyways of Itaewon in Seoul, high-heeled call girls and *mamasans* roam among intoxicated servicemen, tourists, diplomats, and businesspeople. A Westerner may be asked to accompany a Korean host on a walk through Itaewon, but a night out with a Korean businessman on an expense account will more likely lead to a *kisaeng* house (the country's version of the *geisha* house), or its modern equivalent.

At one time there existed one *kisaeng* house for every ten males in Korea. Most of the *kisaeng* houses were set up along ancient highways throughout the country, to service traveling officialdom. The attraction of the *kisaeng* house, like that of the *geisha* house of Japan, is mainly nostalgic; it is a fading institution that once thrived, when Korean society had a wealthy, elite class of men to support it.

Traditionally clad, shy, young girls sit down at the sides of each guest, take drink orders for the table, and serve whatever food and drinks are requested. They sing traditional songs, dance traditional dances, and lead in the toasting of the guests. Although some kissing of clients might take place, the event usually involves no sex. An Egyptian scholar has commented that the *kisaeng* house is "not a pleasure party, but a torture," because so much unconsummated teasing takes place. An equally disgruntled American consulate official summed up his experience in the *kisaeng* house when he told me: "The girls put food in your mouth and make you sing. It's really awful."

Kisaeng houses are, however, part of a tradition of male entertainment in Korea and visitors may be invited to go to one. Anyone accepting the invitation should make sure that ample resources are available to return the favor, during a long-term stay in Korea. The cost of visiting a *kisaeng* house ranges from $300 to several hundred dollars for drinks, girls, and a floor show, which includes the traditional song and dance. Westerners should not attempt to enter a *kisaeng* house without Korean colleagues; they exist for Koreans, not foreigners.

A "room salon" is a modern variation of the *kisaeng* house. Women in modern dress, and of a higher social class than the *kisaeng* girls, service wealthy Koreans and foreigners as well-paid call girls. The women often attend parties given by Koreans in honor of their foreign guests from abroad.

Taiwan's Piano Bars and "Barber Shops"

Taipei's late-night district, dubbed "Buffalo Town"* by the locals, features discos and bars populated by foreign expatriates who dance to some surprisingly good rock ensembles from the States. Visiting foreigners usually enjoy the taste of home in Buffalo Town, but, unless a host is young and somewhat hip (many businesspeople are, in Taiwan), Buffalo Town will not be an option for business entertainment.

A host may, however, take visitors to a hostess bar, often called a "piano bar" on its streetside neon sign. A piano bar is a combination singing bar and hostess bar. Small rooms for conversation skirt a dance floor, a stage for a singer, and cocktail tables. The Asian host will likely be a member of a club located in the piano bar. Visitors will be asked to sing, and girls will have drinks with the group. More intimate talk happens in the little rooms. Visitors who don't plan on accepting any sexual favors arranged by their host should decline to move off with anyone into one of the small rooms. (The waiters in piano bars double as playmates.)

*Un*hosted Westerners should be careful about entering piano bars; they are not regular drinking bars. I naively sat down in one—called the King Long Dong Hotel Piano Bar—with a colleague recently, and we ordered beer. Suddenly, the club owner came over and declared ruefully: "This is a high-class place. Five hundred dollars for each American. Girls included. You can sing if you want. The watermelon is free." Neither of us realized it was a "club" and not just a hotel bar. Some smooth talking got us out for the cost of the beer.

Special Warning: Westerners who need a haircut while in Asia should go to a barber shop located in a major tourist hotel. The streetside "barber shop" in East Asia serves as a traditional front for a prostitution house. Wandering around Taipei, one might see a sign next to a barber's rotating lamp that reads: FAR EAST BEST TONSORIAL PARLOR—SPECIAL TREATMENTS. This is *not* the best place to get that new feather cut.

* "Buffalo" refers to hairy Anglo men.

Hong Kong's "Discreet" Sex Entertainment

Hong Kong's approach to prostitution originated with the arrival of a puritanical Victorian mentality, which the British brought to Hong Kong after the Opium War. The act of "solicitation," the prostitute's selling of her body, was offensive to the British. If the transaction was part of a gratuitious gift from a business associate, there were fewer qualms. The hostess bars and strip joints of Wanchai and Tsimshatsui still draw tourists in search of sleaze, but most sex entertainment among businesspeople in Hong Kong takes place in "members only" clubs.

A foreign man with extensive business ties in Hong Kong will almost certainly, eventually, be treated by a male Chinese counterpart to an evening at a social club where he is a member. Female companionship will be included. The entertainment is expensive, but the foreigner never sees the tab. A typical evening begins with a bottle of brandy, served in an ice bucket at a private booth. A young Chinese woman wearing a tight-fitting silk dress (*cheongsam*) sits down and politely converses for as long as the guest wishes. The *mamasan* keeps track of the time spent conversing, and adds up the fee. It's calculated almost like a telephone bill, only the guest really can reach out and touch someone—but not *inside* the club. It's inappropriate to touch a hostess while inside the bar.

If the guest convinces himself that he must "know" the girl biblically, the next step is to inform the *mamasan* of a wish to take the girl to the guest's hotel. The Asian business host will have arranged everything beforehand and paid the "release fee." Guests don't *have* to take a girl home; they can just drink and talk, and say goodnight. Such virtuous behavior will do one's reputation no harm.

Sex and Business in Japan

Yoshiwara, Tokyo's renowned sex-and-sin district, created a scandal among respectable Japanese when it was the first district in the city to rise up from the ashes, after the earthquake and fire of 1923. Amazingly, an identical rebirth occurred in 1945: Yoshiwara was the first district to be rebuilt in Tokyo after World War II, even before funds were provided for rebuilding schools and hospitals!

Japan's tenacious sex industry, which continues to thrive, ranges from rickety "love hotels" to expense-account *geisha* houses. Between those extremes, there are hotel bars, which have virtually eclipsed the *geisha* houses as destinations for Japanese men in search of sexual companionship, and the more raunchy, but less expensive, sex clubs. Japan also features bathhouses (*sopurando*) where massage and "special services" are available. Some are specifically for foreigners; others carry a "No Foreigners" sign out front.

Love hotels (*rabu hoteru*) cater to young couples seeking a few hours of privacy. Their architectural kitsch seems beyond the realm of the possible. A popular spot in Tokyo's Roppongi district looks like a Disneyland version of a medieval castle, with crenelated towers, mock balconies, and ubiquitous air conditioners, to keep the couples cool.

The *Geisha* House

A *geisha* house can be recognized, in any large Japanese city, by its window filled with red lanterns. Often, four or five *kimono*-clad *geishas* (courtesans highly trained in the arts) stand in the window wearing wigs and white face makeup, primping themselves, and casting faint smiles to passersby.

A guest who is invited to accompany a Japanese host to a *geisha* house should feel honored. The gesture will cost hundreds, if not thousands, of dollars. The *geisha* house is not a brothel, and it's unlikely that there will be any pressure to experience the sexual services of a professional *geisha*. Even a Japanese client cannot have sex with a *geisha* unless he signs a contract to keep her as his mistress, or succeeds in sweeping her off her feet through flirtatious conversation.

Through the *geisha*, a Japanese man experiences all the suggestive sexuality that may not be present in his relationship with his wife. The *geisha* sings to him, dances, pours the *sake*, and indulges him in coquettish conversation. A Japanese man's obligations to his wife and family have been traditionally considered separate from his passionate extramarital relationships with mistresses and *geishas*. (Japanese women were not permitted to maintain a separate existence, outside the family.) Times are changing, however. When it surfaced that Prime Minister Sosuke Uno had retained the services of a part-time *geisha*, the outcry from Japanese women voters was instrumental in causing a humiliating electoral defeat for the Liberal Democratic Party, which forced Uno to resign.

The Sex Club

Visiting foreigners can easily locate a sex club in Japan; much-perused photographs of available girls are posted out front. In the days of legal prostitution in Japan (1193 to 1956), the girls themselves were *publicly* displayed outside. Japanese businessmen, often with foreign counterparts (*gaijins*) in tow, frequent the sex clubs of the Kabuki-cho district in Tokyo probably more than any others.

The typical Japanese sex club can be pretty sleazy, and often features Filipino women (their passports are controlled by the *yakuza*, Japan's version of the mafia), who dance lewdly on strobe-lit stages. In his book *Bicycle Days,* John Burnham Schwartz describes a macabre true-to-reality scene in which a gaggle of Japanese managers in a sex club play the children's finger game called "Rock Paper Scissors," to choose which one of them is to go on stage to participate in sexual acts with the performers. In his culture-revealing book *Behind the Mask,* Ian Buruma describes a Japanese sex club performance as a sociological phenomenon:

> The girls shuffle over to the edge of the stage, crouch and . . . slowly move around, crablike, from person to person, softly encouraging the spectators to take a closer look. To aid the men in their explorations, . . . magnifying glasses and small hand-torches . . . pass from hand to hand . . . [But] instead of being the humiliated subjects of masculine desire, the women seem in complete control, like matriarchal goddesses. The tension of this remarkable ceremony is broken in the end by wild applause, and loud, liberating laughter. Several men produce handkerchiefs to wipe the sweat off their heated brows.

Warning: Foreigners impelled to visit a Japanese sex club might be offended by the sadomasochistic burlesque. Declining such entertainment is difficult, however, because a host may give little warning before pulling a guest into a sex club during an evening of general drinking and carousing.

Thailand's Demimonde (and Its Pitfalls)

To the first-time visitor to Bangkok, the capital of Thailand may seem like an enormous brothel. From the moment one emerges from Customs at the airport, one is solicited continuously by the male representatives of women whose bodies are for sale: the taxi driver, then the bellhop, then the *tuk-tuk* driver. The offers never stop. Foreign women in Thailand are considered potential customers too. When a woman friend of mine, who works for the United Nations, arrived in Bangkok, a young man attached himself to her as a "guide." When they arrived at her hotel, the woman tried to pay the man a tip and bid him farewell. The man, however, wanted to accompany her to her room and stay the night, "at a very low price." To quote Robert Elegant, "Venus . . . is an equal-opportunity employer" in Thailand. My impression of the city was sealed recently, when I looked under my hotel bed as I packed to leave Bangkok for Singapore. I noticed that the bed was supported by five casters, not the usual four—one on each corner and one in the middle.

Not long ago, a mob of Thai women protesters at the Bangkok airport raised placards, in view of arriving tourists, reading: "Go Home Sex Tours!" Unfortunately, tourism (much of it sex-motivated) is Thailand's biggest source of foreign exchange. The country's sex industry took off during World War II, was given a boost by the Korean War, and crescendoed during the war in Vietnam. Now there are over 20,000 bars and nightclubs in Bangkok, employing 1.5 million women. The district of debauch is called Phatpong, not far from Krung Thep train station. Outrageously kitsch floor shows are the destination of typical late-night outings with Thai business associates. (There isn't much alternative nighttime entertainment in Bangkok, besides classical Thai dancing.)

Poor, landless parents send their daughters to Bangkok, to work for a pittance in these clubs. In the Northern Thai village of Baan Joom in Phayoa Province, as many as 90 percent of the girls enter the flesh trade after completing their six years of compulsory education. Women-trafficking involves influential people and even the police; the punishment for trafficking offenses is often light.

Inside the clubs, the dancers wear numbers so that clients can pick out a dancer they like, without pointing. Even in a sex club, pointing in Asia is rude. Some of the girls wear a different colored number to denote a "special service"—for example, *bali bali,* a bubblebath massage in which the girl uses her whole body to "massage" the body of the client, with both of them covered in soap bubbles.

Tips for the Single Traveler

- Look as low-roller as possible. There's plenty of crime in any Asian sex district, and, especially if tipsy, you're easy prey. If unhosted when visiting these areas, dress casually in pants and a pull-over shirt. Don't go there with a Rolex watch, a Nikon camera, a passport, or more than $50 in cash.
- Leave valuables in the safe back at the hotel, especially if you board a bus for a side trip to, say, Chiang Mai in Thailand. Buses, especially in Thailand, but elsewhere as well, are often "hijacked" between check points. Thieves climb on board and take wristwatches, cash, and traveler's checks.
- Clear your room of valuables before bringing anyone home. Cameras, jewelry, and wallets have been known to grow legs, after the foreigner slips into unconsciousness.

◆

AIDS in Thailand

I would remain prudish, like other authors on this subject, and advise simply abstaining from partaking in Thailand's "floating world," in order to eliminate any chance of contracting AIDS there, IF I believed that few foreign businesspeople visiting Thailand would consider purchasing the services of a sexual companion, in light of the prevalence of the HIV virus among prostitutes there. The reality is that organized sex tours and visiting businesspeople support Thailand's thriving sex industry into the 1990s, in the face of bleak AIDS reports emanating from the country. I don't mean to be brash, but thousands of foreigners have sex in Thailand every year, most of it safe, some of it unsafe.

In conjunction with intravenous drug use, especially in Thailand's urban slum areas, AIDS has spread like an unseen plague. In one slum, where 2 percent of the population tested HIV-positive in 1987, over 90 percent tested positive in 1990! Drug use was the main factor in infecting people; unprotected homosexual and heterosexual sex was a distant second. AIDS is now widespread in Thailand and, because Thai prostitutes often travel with their foreign companions to as far away as Singapore, AIDS is a threat in upwardly mobile Bangkok as well as in the slums of Chiang Mai, Pattaya, and Phuket. A person sampling Thailand's well-advertised sexual merchandise should practice *extreme* caution. As a Malay taxi driver in Singapore told me:

"In Bangkok, if you wear a *cone-dome,* you live; if you don't, you no live."

Sex Entertainment in the Philippines

Sex entertainment in the Philippines will consist mainly of visiting the sex clubs with a Filipino host. Wives are often included; it's all part of Manila nightlife.

The AIDS scourge has come ashore in the Philippines, so all cautions mentioned earlier apply to accepting sexual favors.

In the World of Suzy Wong: Relationships with Asians

What happens when a Western businessperson gets romantically involved with an Asian? It happens often, especially between Western men and Asian women, for two reasons:

1. More men than women are hired to represent Western companies in Asia;
2. A strong mutual attraction exists between Western men and Asian women, but not between Western women and Asian men.

North American men are often attracted to the smaller physical size of Asian women; indeed, many believe that they are more "feminine," compared with "liberated" Western women. In general, women in Asia *are* trained to take care of men, as part of their culturally accepted role in society. Confucian philosophy stipulated, in the "Three Obediences for Women," that before marriage a woman is to obey her father; after marriage, her husband; and after that, her first-born son.

Many Asian women perceive North American men as physically strong and socially assertive, at least when compared to Asian men, who are often shy and not aggressive socially with women. Foreign men usually approach women freely in social situations (often too freely), and some Asian women find this attractive. There are other attractions as well. By marrying a foreigner who holds a foreign passport, an Asian girl can freely leave her country and obtain a visa to live elsewhere. Dubbed "white hunters," many young women (and young men) in Asia have pressured visiting foreigners into wedlock. "This girl comes over to my apartment and does my laundry and everything, and won't leave," an American engineer complained to me in Taipei recently. In Xinjiang, China, I was asked once to marry a Chinese girl who wanted to leave China to study architecture; it was a favor my host was doing for his superior—finding a way for the superior's daughter to escape the desert and live in America. I declined gracefully.

A Korean woman may desire a Western husband so she won't have to move in with a cantankerous Korean mother-in-law, as is the custom in Korea to this day. A poor girl may latch on to a "rich foreigner" as her best avenue toward bettering her lot. Whatever the attraction between Western men and Asian women, it exists, and it's strong—so strong, in fact, that it often destroys expatriate marriages. In Taipei, a self-help group of foreign expatriate spouses has been convening for some time, assisting its members in dealing with straying husbands. The bitter truth is that an Asia post is no place to shore up a marriage.

When a Western man settles down and marries an Asian woman, a number of problems can arise. First, the man usually comes to the relationship possessed of a certain steryotyped image of the Asian woman—she is a subservient, sensual, *geisha*-like China doll; she's Suzie Wong herself! It comes as no surprise that this image is indelible in the Western male psyche; every bestselling novel and blockbuster movie dealing with Asia reinforces this stereotype, including novels such as *Shogun* and movies like "Platoon." Western men typically marry an Asian girl who fits their notion of the supersensuous Asian woman. I call this the *fishnet stocking syndrome.* They marry the tight-skirted, long-haired, dark-skinned, red lip-glossed girl—the "tart with the heart." The hilarious aside about their choice is that Asians of middle or higher status consider this sort of Asian girl quite unattractive. A lower status girl offers the foreigner nothing in the way of family business contacts, but she usually wins over her new family when she comes to the West. Why? Because she's *trained* to serve men (including her new father-in-law, who typically adores her), and commits herself wholeheartedly to her new family, which is usually much appreciated by her new in-laws in the West.

For better or worse, a handful of North Americans doing business in Asia have discovered synergy in combining romantic objectives with their business objectives. By marrying an Asian, they have become members of a network of Asian businesspeople linked through family association. These men and women have expanded their business contacts in Asia through marriage. As a Westerner becomes more involved in Asian business, romantic partners from his or her own culture may become less attractive as potential mates. A business associate of mine, who does business with Asians and who is married to an Asian woman, explains:

> After my first marriage had ended, I decided to marry an Asian woman. I was very calculating. I wanted to do business there. Marrying an Asian woman was a natural thing for me to do. If you are going to spend your life pursuing Asia business, you really have to be with somebody that will understand you, and understands Asia. My experience with most American women is that they don't always understand Asia, and they are not able to tolerate me in what I'm doing internationally. So I found somebody who was already there.

It isn't easy for a non-Asian to marry an Asian of high status who offers family business connections. Most marriages in Asia are arranged by families, based on whether the union is suitable to the families that will be linked by the marriage, not on considerations of love. About one half of Japanese marriages are arranged, often with the help of one's boss. (When marriage troubles arise, it's often the boss who receives a phone call from a distraught spouse seeking advice.) A marriage affects many people, and the choice of a mate is made by consensus, not by love-struck individuals. Marriages in Korea, for example, are arranged by a marriage broker armed with photo albums of single boys and girls. Horoscopes and other shamanistic divining methods help the broker match suitable mates. The families involved are well-educated graduates of some of the best universities in the world, but these modern urbanites still adhere to ancient marriage traditions.

In general, East Asians maintain strict rules regarding the purity of their race—another reason why foreigners rarely marry into well-placed families. High-status families do not condone such ties and, unless they desire to cut themselves off from their families, young Asians almost invariably accept a pact put together by their parents. There are expections, especially if the union is considered a good political move: an upper-class person may be married off to a politically prominent or extremely wealthy foreign family.

For Koreans, anyone who is not full-blooded Korean is totally unacceptable as a mate. To this day, orphaned Korean babies are brought to the United States by Project Hope. They are not *pure-blooded Korean* babies, but babies whose ethnicity may be mixed—the product of Korean girls' fraternizing with American GIs or visiting Japanese. Japan has experienced more racial mixing than Korea and is not as stringent about keeping the race pure.

Coming Home to North America

What happens when a Western man brings an Asian woman back to North America? The Asian woman becomes the victim of the same sterotyping that she has dealt with from her new husband. American society tends to label Asian women as weak, dependent, subservient—"China dolls." Some Asian women who come to North America get the feeling that Westerners believe that all women who come from Asia are prostitutes. Merce Willard, probably the most famous television journalist in the Philippines—"the Jane Pauley of the Philippines"—tells a revealing tale. She was out with friends at a nightclub in Portland. An American man nuzzled up to her and said: "Where are you from?" "Portland," she replied. He said: "No, where are your parents from?" When he was told that she is Filipino, he said knowingly: "Yeah, I've been to Alongapo" (which, located outside Subic Bay, is probably the biggest brothel in the world). To Merce, this was profoundly insulting, but typical of the way North American men lump Asian women into the category of personal sexual playthings. More than any other problem, the Asian woman who relocates to North America finds this image hardest to deal with. However, once these images are dissolved in the Western male spouse, mixed marriages between Asian women and North American men have a high degree of permanency.

Is it the same for Western women who marry Asian men?

Western Women Enter the Dragon as Wives

Western wife/Asian husband liaisons usually start in North America when an Asian man is attending a university. Or, they begin when the Western woman is working in Asia, often as a teacher of English. North American women may find Asian men sensitive, sublime, and intimate companions, free of the hazards of Western machismo. They might also find them more loyal as spouses. Indeed, Japan has one-fourth the U.S. divorce rate, and other Asian countries have even lower rates.

One of the problems, however, that Western women have to deal with in meeting and dating Asian men—especially when in Asia—is that Asian men are often put off by North American women because they are larger physically than most Asians, including Asian men, and thus sexually intimidating. Also, because North American women are generally much more aggressive socially than Asian women, they are all the more intimidating for the typically shy and reserved Asian man.

Interestingly, the problems for the Western woman who marries in the West are greater than those for the woman who marries in the East. The Western woman discovers that her role in the marriage undergoes a profound change when her husband re-enters Asian society. She finds out that the rigid social roles for married men and women that exist in East Asia cannot be easily circumvented. For an Asian husband to be a success at his job, he has to work incessantly and often drink with coworkers until late at night. He increasingly commiserates with his drinking buddies rather than his wife. The couple spends less time together. Their intimacy fades, as does their ability to communicate. The wife grows bored and, if she lacks a command of the local language, isolated and increasingly lonely. Her friendships with Asians may remain shallow, unless she has perfect language capability. Soon, she returns home, without her Asian husband.

Marriages in which the Western woman is living *in Asia* at the time she meets an Asian man are usually more permanent unions. The wife will know the local language, she will have been assimilated into the culture, and she will have learned to deal with the social role of being an Asian wife.

Meeting the Right Person

A single person working in Asia will find that the best method of meeting potential romantic partners is through introductions by other Asians who are good friends. These "introducers" will take it upon themselves to find members of the opposite sex compatible mates. Actual introductions will happen at parties and other social events.

It's important for Western men to avoid trying to meet Asian romantic partners in the *fishnet stocking syndrome* that I mentioned earlier. One of the common mistakes Western men make in Asia is to meet a girl of low status in a hostess bar or club and then bring her to a social or business-related gathering where high-status Asians are present. That's a real gaffe.

By making friends and subtly mentioning a wish to meet some-one who can be dated, Westerners will make more headway than by hanging around in bars and discos.

Another tip is hands-off, until a relationship has been forged. Asians are sensitive about physical contact in public; a partner will be humiliated by overintimacy in the presence of others. In a city like Bangkok, where so many women work as prostitutes, a Thai woman of high status must attend to her reputation constantly, by maintaining an air of respectability. No public affection can take place in Thailand between men and women, even between husband and wife, without the woman losing face. When a Thai woman visits a man, especially a Westerner, she will bring along another female, to safeguard her reputation.

As part of socializing on more intimate terms with people in Asia, Westerners will almost certainly be invited into someone's home, or possibly even be brought into the family structure as a godparent or a sponsor of a young person going to college in the West.

As foreign businesspeople build friendships among Asian business partners, they see more of everyday life in Asia—religious ceremonies, weddings, and funerals. Each of these events carries a particular set of protocols, many of which are described in the next chapter. Westerners need to be aware of how they are expected to fulfill new roles as close friend, confidant, or relative, of an Asian family.

CHAPTER TWELVE

Etiquette Minefields: Homes, Shrines, and Ceremonies

The host is happy when the guest is gone.
CHINESE PROVERB

The back of the head of a departing guest is beautiful.
KOREAN PROVERB

We return now to the art of Asian business entertainment. Socializing with Asian business partners will hardly be concluded with sumptuous banquets and nights out on the town. Asian hosts may well want to show off the cultural sights in the area as well. Such tours are always fascinating, but their pace can be wearing and they can be a test of patience well before approaching the negotiation table.

Some people enjoy business sightseeing; for others, it's a chore. A common complaint among foreign visitors is that, sometimes, sightseeing with Asian hosts simply outlasts the foreigners' stamina. Fulfilling their stereotype in Asia, most North Americans want to curtail the cultural part of their trip and get down to business in a hurry. Unfortunately, saying "No" to sightseeing can be taken as an insult, unless one has been taken ill. Even if visitors *are* feeling under the weather, Asian hosts may perceive their refusal to see the sights as an act of Asian-style humility; Asians make it a habit to decline hospitality, as part of being polite to each other. That was the case a few years back, when I was a member of a delegation traveling in Asia (the exact locale doesn't matter).

For hours on end, with a winter breeze blowing, we had been wandering down a cliff trail past enormous Buddhas carved into

259

stone. A member of the delegation started feeling feverish. I informed the interpreter on the Chinese side (our go-between) that the delegation wished to proceed directly to our hotel after the day's sightseeing, rather than stopping for dinner on the way back. The request seemed reasonable enough, but when delivered to our hosts, it fell on quite deaf ears.

Did our hosts think we were just being polite by declining to accept their dinner invitation?

Midway through the five-hour drive back, over terrible roads, we stopped to eat a five-course meal in an open-air roadside restaurant. It was 37 degrees Fahrenheit *inside* the dining room! Strangely, the ill delegate felt fine the next morning. However, four days later *I* developed walking pneumonia.

In retrospect, my guess about our hosts' motives is that our presence in Asia was seen as an opportunity for them to enjoy themselves at their company's expense. Many Asian businesspeople do not have the opportunity to enjoy the "good life" except when entertaining a foreign delegation, and those hosting us were not about to give up a perk because a foreign visitor felt sick.

This Business of Sightseeing

The lesson in my anecdote is: prepare for a full and often exhausting sightseeing itinerary when visiting Asian business partners, *especially if your company is being pursued as a customer by the Asian company.* If your company has initiated the meeting, with the intention to win a customer in Asia, a succession of day-long cultural expeditions is not part of the protocol.

The best way to prepare for sightseeing in Asia is to bring along the right clothes, some knowledge of the area to be visited, and an open mind. They will have little choice in what they see, but wise Westerners come prepared to visit the host's home, tour a local shrine or sacred site, and participate in a festival, ceremony, or social event, such as a wedding, baptism, tea ceremony, or possibly a funeral (attendance at funerals is usually reserved for close friends of an Asian family).

The information and advice in this chapter are intended to build confidence and poise for engaging in these nonbusiness activities, whether as a well-mannered spectator or as a seasoned participant. The activities may be nonbusiness, but their tether to the negotiating process and the ultimate purpose of the visit is loosened, not severed. Some general sightseeing rules apply to any excursion, alone or accompanied by an Asian host.

Guidelines for Gracious Guests

Don't Be an "Ugly" North American.   Something awful happens, when some North Americans spend time in Asia. They tend to get cocky. They get loud and offensive. They get an idea that they're somehow superior to the locals. Asians are polite and subservient, they discover, and often this contrast goes to their heads. Asians working at bars and hotels are used to serving Westerners; they tolerate their obnoxious behavior as long as the tips keep rolling in.

This awful phenomenon in its quintessential form occurs among U.S. servicemen in Korea and the Philippines. Recently, I accompanied an American marketing director on a business trip to Korea. On our first evening in Seoul, we took a taxi to the outdoor market in Itaewon. The first foreigner we saw was a U.S. serviceman. He was drunk, and grabbed a Michael Jackson tee shirt off one of the stalls. "How much is this, *mamasan?*" he yelled at the grandmotherly Korean vendor.

"Three thousand *won,*" she said.

"Too f–cking much!" the serviceman screamed, and threw the shirt in her face.

We were appalled. Not ten minutes later, we saw another serviceman getting into a taxi with his buddies, wearing an enormous inflated condom on his head. Would they act the same way in St. Louis, San Diego, or Baltimore?

In most parts of Asia, Westerners will never know when they have been offensive. In Thailand, for example, bad behavior won't elicit a negative response because Thais hold harmony to be their most important value; they won't argue with someone or cause the person to lose face in any way. (That doesn't mean they agree or think the behavior is right.) Recently, I was on a city bus in Taipei, laughing and joking with a group of American expatriates and students. Suddenly, a Taiwanese man rose up in front of us and began screaming at us in English: "You Americans think you can have your party right here on a bus. You are rude. Why don't you all go home!"

Gulp.

A woman in our group jumped up immediately and began apologizing (in Chinese, which surprised him) for our behavior. She explained that Americans *are* rude and loud and that we would all get off at the next stop. We did.

North Americans are "ugliest" when suffering from what I call *travel insanity*. After a week or so on the road in Asia, most of them, of any age or temperament, begin to show some signs of intolerance for dealing with the headaches of travel in Asia. I once stood in the Beijing airport with an American executive who, when he was momentarily separated from his wife, began screaming, to bewildered Chinese strangers: "Where is my wife?!" "She'll show up; calm down, you're in China," I said. He screamed in my face: "You've lost my wife in China!"

I've seen Australian, Canadian, and English travelers blow up in the same manner. But I've *never* seen an Asian behave comparably when visiting North America.

Avoid Being Overtly Critical.   Common decency dictates not being critical of a foreign place, when speaking with locals who call it home. Unfortunately, North Americans find a lot to complain about in Asian cities, from traffic, humidity, and thieves to disagreeable odors, horn-honking, and general inefficiency. Gracious guests try not to complain or to reveal that they are disgruntled and uncomfortable. I've seen Westerners look so morose that their Asian host concluded they must be "mentally depressed." North Americans are sometimes rightly perceived as incessant complainers. If critical comments must be made, they might be prefaced with: "My only criticism about such-and-such is . . . ."

Respect Religious Taboos and Superstitions.   The surest way to offend an Asian host is to try to persuade him that his belief in animistic spirits or dead ancestors is naive superstition. For some of us, Asia's ancient and culturally ingrained religious practices challenge every resolution to experience the region with an open mind.

The sacred is everywhere in Asia. One sees spirit houses on pedestals outside buildings and on street corners in Thailand, where the *phra phum* (spirit of the land) is said to reside. Building shrines dot the landscape (and the topless bars!) in Hong Kong, with their burning incense a potential fire hazard. In Japan, the deceased founders of a company watch over it from company "shrines" of Shinto origin. The Taiwanese worship so many gods (mostly to ask for help in making more money) that they can't believe it when Christians tell them that they worship only one god. They reply that the Christians' God must be very powerful, to be able to offer all that their numerous gods can offer. In their minds, the more gods a person worships, the better the chances that one of them will come through!

Divination in Asia goes back to the Shang Dynasty (1766–1122 B.C.), when the Chinese used "dragon bones" to tell fortunes. One's questions concerning weather, sacrifice of animals to the gods, harvest of crops, conduct in war, or one's personal luck, were addressed to the oracle bones. Superstition, divination, and religious ceremony continue to condition many facets of daily life in Asia today.

Here are some examples of situations that will require poise and open-mindedness:

- A Japanese partner requests to have a Shinto priest conduct an elaborate ceremonial ritual inside a new joint-venture factory, whether constructed in Japan *or* North America;

- A Hong Kong Chinese financier says "No" because the building proposed for his purchase faces a mountain, or a body of water, from an inauspicious direction;

- An Indonesian partner asks to have a new offshore oil rig consecrated by a holy man, flying above the rig in a helicopter, with a severed bull's head and an assortment of ritual objects.

North Americans have funny variations in their acceptance of Eastern mysticism. After a seminar at NYNEX International, an Asian-American representative of the company came up to me and said she did not believe in the *I Ching,* the Confucian Book of Change that has been used in fortune telling for 2,500 years. However, she continued, she *did* believe in *Feng Shui,* Chinese geomancy used to place objects and structures in proper alignment with their natural surroundings. She had recently paid a *Feng Shui* artist to rearrange her furniture, at home and at her business office in Thailand.

"Business has been better ever since," she said delightedly. "But I do *not* believe in the *I Ching.*"

Dress Appropriately. To supplement the discussion of business attire in Chapter 6, I must mention something about sightseeing attire. The first rule for visiting homes and shrines and attending ceremonies is to dress conservatively, avoiding loud colors and suggestively cut dresses. Shorts should be worn only for going to a beach and for hot-weather outings in Indonesia. A tight-fitting leather skirt can be a disaster. One of the most embarrassed persons I've ever seen in Asia was wearing one when her Thai hosts took her to a restaurant where she had to sit on the floor—a spectacle indeed.

The most horrific insensitivity to local protocol that I have witnessed in Asia involved attire. At the Beijing airport, a group of European and Australian girls had just deplaned wearing braless tanktops, and denim shorts cut off about as high as they can be cut off. Their Chinese tour organizers were stunned and embarrassed. This occurred in 1985, during China's campaign against "spiritual pollution"—decadent influence from the West.

Decline Offers Delicately.   Some Asian hosts will ask visitors to participate in something that falls outside their zone of comfort: eating live lobster, praying to Buddha, or accepting one of the host's wives as a sexual companion (all actual cases in Japan, China, and India, respectively). Laughter would be rude, as would a reply like: "Are you kidding!" In Indonesia one says, "*Bukan adat kami*" ("It is not our custom"). When the going gets too weird and the visitor wants to politely refuse participating in an activity that makes him or her uncomfortable, the same phrase in English should be used anywhere in Asia.

Watch Where the Camera Is Pointing.   Sightseeing tours in Asia may include military airfields, dams, power plants, and other strategic installations. Before clicking away with a Nikon, visitors should ask whether it's all right to photograph. Often, it isn't. What's *verboten* can sometimes be surprising. In Taiwan recently, I was reprimanded for shooting a photo inside a Circle K food store, probably because it was a copy-cat store and not a legal franchise.

When visitors rudely point a camera at the locals, they embarrass their host. Koreans are especially sensitive about having their picture taken by North Americans, as are the native peoples of Thailand. To photograph someone, arrangements should be made through the host. Two *always* rules are:

1. Ask permission before snapping photos in temples, churches, and mosques;

2. Unload film from a camera, before going through security checkpoints (cameras are often opened, to check for explosives).

Don't Deride Bad English. A common sight in Asia is a sign, brochure, or product name translated into hilarious English. It can be difficult not to chuckle aloud at these charming grammatical bloopers, thereby insulting one's host. For example, in the Temple of the Reclining Buddha in Bangkok, a sign warns: IT IS FORBIDDEN TO ENTER A WOMAN—EVEN A FOREIGNER IF DRESSED AS A MAN. The sign above a bar in Tokyo advertises: SPECIAL COCKTAILS FOR LADIES WITH NUTS. A sign for donkey rides in North Thailand reads: WOULD YOU LIKE TO RIDE ON YOUR OWN ASS? It's better not to comment on such translations, rather than to risk offending the host.

Visiting the Asian Home

An Asian's home is usually *not* where foreigners are entertained. Entertaining guests can be expensive and is felt to infringe upon the private sanctity of one's home; the proverbs at the outset of this chapter clearly reflect these pervasive attitudes. The Japanese seldom, if ever, invite foreigners to visit them at home; nearly all foreigners who visit Japanese homes do so as part of an organized tour. The same is true in Korea and China. However, many Western businesspeople have been treated to a visit to the home of an Asian associate who has become a close friend. Because an Asian home is a minefield of potential mishap for unaware foreign visitors, these general rules should head any list of dos and don'ts for a visit:

- Never call on an Asian home unannounced—as many of us feel free to do in the West—except in a clear emergency.
- Bring a gift, such as food or flowers, on any visit to an Asian home. If you *must* visit a home unannounced, bring along a nice store-bought gift, as insurance against violating the code of privacy. See Chapter 9 for specifics on gift giving at the Asian home.

- Don't expect the host to conduct a tour of the house, as is the Western custom; this practice is rare anywhere in Asia. The Japanese entertain visitors in a room reserved just for that purpose, so they won't have to show guests their entire house.

- Be yourself, unless you brag a lot, tell jokes incessantly, or talk and laugh loudly.

Visiting a Chinese Home

Chinese counterparts will rarely entertain foreign business associates in their home. Because of a scarcity of housing in the People's Republic, most Chinese live with three generations of their family, in a cramped apartment that they would be hesitant to show to a foreign business partner.

A visit to a Chinese home in the P.R.C. will likely be an arranged visit to a "typical Chinese residency," as part of a tour of the work unit (*danwei*) where the proposed company is to be located. Such a home visit may also be included as part of a day's sightseeing with Chinese hosts. Usually, the resident will be taken by surprise, which is embarrassing to the visitors, who feel they are intruding; essentially, they are. Break the ice by saying admiringly to the Chinese resident: "You eat in the East and lodge in the West!" ("You are well-off and possess the best of all worlds"). He or she will serve green tea in glasses and bring out chairs for everyone to sit down. Compliment the nice television (especially if it's a color set; they are hard to come by in China), as well as the wall photos of family members, and the quaint and comfortable furnishings.

Try *not* to ask to use the bathroom, because it will probably be located at the end of the apartment complex and will be of the nonflush, porcelain-footpad variety, without a supply of toilet paper.

If traveling through an Autonomous Region of China where one or more National Minorities live, make sure to request that the hosts stop at the home of a native family. Traditional homes, such as the tent-like *yurts* of the Kazak people of Xinjiang Province, are selected for such tourist stops. These visits are fascinating and can revitalize the most wearied business traveler. There are many such minority peoples in Taiwan, as well.

While out walking in a Chinese town or city, you may be engaged by a local resident who wants to practice "Voice of America" English by asking you to visit his or her home for a cup of tea. It's

Mind Your Shoes
(Better yet, mind your *socks!*)

Always wear new, clean socks in Asia; visitors are asked to leave their shoes at the door of a home, restaurant, temple, or inn. Often, slippers will be provided for use inside a home or hotel. At a traditional inn in Korea (*yogwan*) or Japan (*ryokan*), carry your shoes to your room rather than leave them unattended, especially if they are expensive. It's unlikely they would grow legs in Japan, but in Korea their disappearance is possible.

In traditional Asian restaurants, shoes are taken off and can be stored in cabinets near the dining table. Asians (especially Koreans) sometimes wear their shoes with the heels crushed down, so the shoes can be removed quickly. Western men might want to take a pair of loafers to Asia, for their off–on ease when slippers must be worn.

◆

polite to accept these offers, if you have time; however, adamantly refuse to stay the night in a Chinese person's home: it is *illegal* for non-Chinese foreigners to do so. Neighbors are suspicious in China and will likely talk of the visit. An overnight stay would jeopardize your new friends politically.

A Westerner is most likely to visit the home of a Chinese person while in North America; typically, the invitation will come from an Overseas Chinese family that has emigrated from Hong Kong or Taiwan. Before asking a Mandarin-speaking interpreter to join you on the visit, remember that most Hong Kong Chinese speak the Cantonese dialect and most Chinese from Taiwan speak the Taiwanese dialect. Another interpreter may be needed.

You will probably be asked to remove your shoes in the foyer. If an older person is present, greet him or her first, with a bow. (The same protocol applies to goodbye.) Don't expect a refreshing, mixed, alcoholic drink when you arrive. A sweet and fruity liqueur or rice wine may be all that is offered.

As you make your way through the chinoiserie decor, you may want to compliment the pair of bronze Mandarin ducks on the hearth (they symbolize conjugal bliss), or the lotus-blossom painting, or the ubiquitous carved wall-hanging with two jade fishes in its center (it symbolizes luck and prosperity for the household). These items, as well as the family photos hanging on the wall, are all tinder for sparking conversation. Remember, however, that many experts insist that no object in a Chinese home should be praised too admiringly; the host may be impelled to give it to the admirer as a gift. (I have never experienced this or heard of its happening to businesspeople.)

Chinese friends may refer to their children with nicknames that might seem insulting in translation, like Little Dog, Little Pig, and so on. Feel free to address Chinese children the way their parents do. In the presence of visitors, most parents will call their children by their formal names, but many will introduce them as "Little" (*Xiao*) So-and-So. Thus, a child named Lu Fang may be called Xiao Fang. Listen carefully to how children are addressed when *first* introduced. It might cause a laugh if you suddenly adopt a nickname halfway through the evening and say, to a child, something like: "Where do you go to school, Little Pig?"

Visiting a Korean Home

Korean family relations have been a source of strife for individual Koreans for centuries. "It is easy to rule a kingdom but difficult to rule one's family," says a male-biased Korean proverb. The typical Korean family may not enjoy being together much. Their living rooms are constantly filled with neighborhood visitors— perhaps to defuse internecine conflicts threatening to explode in the household. Family members watch each other's *nunchi* (mood) carefully, so as not to ruffle any feathers. Guests are welcome in the Korean home because they break the monotony of strict and authoritarian Korean home life. In some traditional Korean homes to this day, the wife serves the food and then leaves the husband to eat alone. Not too long ago, wives would serve the meal and eat only the leftovers after their husband had eaten!

Korean homes are usually small, so consider it an honor to be invited into one as a guest. Remove your shoes before entering the house; the *ondol* floors are covered with an oiled paper and are kept immaculately clean.

When invited for dinner in a Korean home, arrive punctually with a food gift. The cue to move toward the dinner table is the arrival of hot towels from the kitchen, for cleaning the hands. Sit down on the cushions at the low table; the warm floor is heated from below. The host will probably surprise you with utterances about the insignificance and low quality of the food served. My reply to this attempt to lower expectations and preserve face, anywhere in Asia, is a light and humorous comment, like: "But the food looks so good, I can almost taste it with my eyes."

When you feel your legs going numb, grin and bear it. The last thing you want to do is stretch out your legs under the low table and upend the entire meal. (It's easier for this to happen than you would think.) As when dining in restaurants with Korean associates, you may find Korean family members rather taciturn at the dinner table. Don't add to the awkwardness by filling every silence.

Inside a Japanese Home

The traditional Japanese house is a small, uncluttered space containing a minimum of low storage furniture. The interior is a manifestation of the Zen-Buddhist notion of *shibui*, the expression of spirituality through minimal aesthetic means. Emphasis is on compactness, portability, and modularity; open space is partitioned using movable paper-covered doors (*fusuma*). Should you receive the honor of being invited to visit a Japanese home, here are some essentials to keep in mind.

Most Japanese homes are entered through a gate with a nameplate (*hyosatsu*). In the entryway (*genkan*), take off your shoes and place them with their toes facing the direction from which you came. Upon entering the house, you will notice that the floor is covered with finely woven straw mats (*tatami*), about six feet long and three feet wide. Rooms in Japan are measured by determining how many *tatami* are needed to cover the floor.

Inside most Japanese homes, interior decoration will be limited to an arrangement of small objects, such as a hanging scroll, sculpture, and flowers, in an alcove called a *tokonoma*. The arrangement is changed with the seasons. Don't walk up and stand in the *tokonoma* to admire the scroll and flowers.

Kneel on the cushion shown to you (usually the place of honor next to the *tokonoma*), with the feet close together under the buttocks. Should you be seated in a short, legless chair with a back, men can sit with their legs crossed and women with legs to one side. Anyone who enters the room will kneel and bow to you. Scoot off the cushion and return the bow; don't stand up, as is the Western custom. When the host invites you to relax, adjust yourself into the cross-legged position (*aqura*). Women sit side-saddle, never cross-legged.

After you are served dinner, don't offer to help in the kitchen; the cooking area, a private place, is not for public perusal. When tea is served, the evening is coming to a close. Don't tarry; leave before the host drops a hint that it's getting late.

Japanese Bath Etiquette.   Should you be spending the night, you may want to use the bath (*furo*), a deep tub for soaking only.

Lather up in the small shower area while sitting on the stool. Rinse off and then get into the tub. It may be hot, but don't cool it by adding cold water. Leave the water in the tub, when finished soaking. Replace the wooden cover and leave it for the next person. (Everyone in the household soaks in the same water.)

Visiting Homes in Moslem Asia (Indonesia, Malaysia, and Singapore)

The first thing to remember, when visiting Moslems, is that they strictly observe regularized prayer. Moslems pray to Allah five times daily—at dawn, at noon, before and after sunset, and at bedtime. When invited to a Moslem home, always let the host set the time of arrival, which will likely be 30 minutes after sunset. You can arrive 10 to 15 minutes late, at an Indonesian or Malaysian home; the hosts may even expect you to. Remove your shoes before entering a Malay's home.

Once inside a Moslem's house, abstain from smoking; if you must smoke, ask permission. Do not expect an alcoholic beverage to be served; accept tea or fruit juice—with the right hand, never the left.

You may espy the family *Koran,* the Islamic book of scripture, on a table or reading stand. Show your knowledge of how sacred the holy book is to a Moslem by *not* walking up to it and thumbing through its pages. Look at it and ask about it, if you like, but ask permission before touching it, and touch it only with the right hand and with utmost respect.

If you are served dinner in a Moslem home, expect to sit on cushions on the floor, men cross-legged and women side-saddle. If you eat with the fingers, use the right hand. If you don't, it's all right to ask for a spoon and fork, but *not* a knife. (Utensils may be set out for your use; for Malay dining etiquette, see Chapter 8.) As in Japan, don't offer to help with the dishes; most middle- and upper-class Malays have servants who will clean up. You may be asked to sing and play with the kids, if they are present. Do not overtly praise a Moslem's beautiful child, however, or you might bring the "evil eye" upon the child, and, with it, misfortune.

When you need to use the bathroom or take a bath while staying at a Moslem's house, here's what to expect. The toilet (*W.C.* or *way say*) and the bath (*bak mandi*) will be in separate rooms. (I describe Malay bathrooms on page 274.) If you are staying overnight and want to take a bath, *don't* go into the bathing room (*kamar mandi*) and hop into the three-foot-high tub. Fill the scoop with water from the tap and splash the water over you while standing *next to* the tub, which acts as a catch-basin. If the tub gets too full, you can scoop some water from it. In some areas, and when the weather is hot, the water may not be heated.

Visiting Homes in Thailand and the Philippines

The rules of visiting a Thai person at home begin before entering the house. First, there is the exchange of shoes for a pair of slippers that will be found outside on the doorstep. Next, there is the entry *without* stepping on the threshold of the front door. A benevolent spirit, whose job is to keep out bad spirits, lives in the threshold.

Once inside the house, the host's joyful children will run to greet you and take your hand. Remember to thwart the Western instinct to pat kids on the head, because the head is considered a Thai's spiritual center and touching the head is tantamount to jostling the soul.

Inside a home in Thailand are images of the Buddha and of Thailand's beloved king and his queen. Images of the king are not to be touched or commented on without the utmost respect. Refer to the king as His Majesty King Bhumibol Adulyadij. He was coronated on May 5, 1950. The Buddha images are not merely creative interior decoration. Usually placed in high positions inside the home, they are objects to be revered and always handled with respect and care. At all times, keep your head respectfully lower than the head of a statue of the Buddha (no easy feat for tall visitors). Author Michael Crichton, in his book *Travels,* narrates his experience of Thai sensitivity about the height of the Buddha. Crichton went to a movie theater that was showing a Peter Sellers movie called "A Girl in My Soup."

> To watch the movie was a bizarre experience. Peter Sellers would stand up from a table, and suddenly the Buddha statue in his wall niche would explode like a black-ink sparkler, which continued until Sellers sat down again. Then you could see the peaceful Buddha once more. The Thai censor had inked out the image of the Buddha, frame by frame, whenever Peter Sellers was higher than the statue.

Inquire about the significance of a Thai's religious artworks, as long as you don't do so in a skeptical manner. Another conversation-starter is to ask a male Thai whether he underwent *phansa,* the three-month monkhood that half of all Thai males undergo early in their careers. Most Thai men, especially harried officials and businessmen, covet fond memories of their *phansa* experience, and enjoy reliving it by telling about it.

Dinner at a Thai home will usually be served buffet-style, if guests are coming. Prepare to sit on the floor to eat, however. When sitting cross-legged, try not to point the sole of the feet at anyone sitting across from you; it demeans them.

Another very different type of Thai home, which you may visit, is that of a monk. If you visit a Thai temple (*wat*), you may be taken inside a monk's house, and some important rules govern your time there. First, remember to *wai* when greeting a monk. Rehearse the gesture, as described in Chapter 4, until it is smooth and comfortable. You don't have to shake hands, but, if the monk initiates a handshake, don't grip in a too-familiar Western manner. When admitted to the house, be careful not to stand or sit in a higher position than the monk, or to press against him or touch his head. It is expressly forbidden for women to touch monks; foreign women may not be permitted to enter the monk's home at all. To hand something to a monk, set the item down near him. He will pick up the object, reducing the risk of being touched by a layperson.

Visiting the Filipino Home.   Upper- and middle-class homes in the Philippines are the most Western-like in all of Asia. Not much will come as a surprise during a visit to one. I mention here only a couple of things.

Some Filipinos, especially those living in the countryside, remove their shoes before entering their house. In urban areas, shoes are usually worn inside the home. Don't arrive with a gift of food or wine, when invited to dinner at a Filipino home. It may be interpreted that you think the host will serve too little food! You will sit at a table to eat, and seating is usually informal. Servants probably did the cooking, and compliments about the food are not necessarily considered compliments to the host. Instead, focus your praise on the host's choice of furniture, flower arrangement, artworks, taste in music, and so on.

Visiting Sacred Places in Asia

Typically, Westerners who go to Asia worship one God (if they worship at all). They are familiar with one holy book and a formal place of worship. In Asia, monotheistic Westerners often react with suspicion toward Asians' religiosity, which includes animism, ancestor worship, Shamanism, polytheism, monasticism, and two kinds of monotheism. Too rare is the foreigner who accepts Asian religion with an open and interested mind.

The Chinese Buddhist Temple

Remove your hat and sunglasses before entering a Buddhist temple anywhere in Asia, and put out your cigarette. If asked to participate as a worshiper, you may do so if you choose. You will be given a handful of incense sticks to place upright in the urn at the entrance to the temple.

If asked to pray to the Buddha, kneel before the altar on one of the red pillows, and bow the head each time the monk beats his drum. Make a wish with each successive obeisant bow of the head. Follow the lead of other worshipers, and expect a crowd to form as you pray; few Chinese will have seen a *waibing* (foreigner) kneel and pray in a Chinese temple. Try to be as sincere as possible; your host will appreciate it—not to mention Buddha. Once, I put real gusto into the prayer bowing. My amazed Chinese hosts said: "Buddha will look kindly on you because you were so sincere."

As you make your way through the temple, ask about the significance of the many different postures of the seated Buddha. Each signifies a different stage in his life and teaching. Incidentally, the swastika symbol you will see on, or near, the Buddha does not mean that Buddhists are Nazis; it is used to mean "ten thousand," a number that the Chinese associate with infinity and immortality. ("May the ten thousand things go according to your wishes!") Ten thousand is used the way we use "a million," the ultimate extreme quantity. The swastika is also used to denote the "seal of the heart of the Buddha."

You may also be asked to have one of the astrologers read your fortune; they usually sit at small tables set up near the entrance to temples. The small fee will be paid discreetly by your hosts.

Visiting Mosques

Few mosques in Asia are open to foreigners. If you get the chance to visit one, some rules are strictly enforced. The entrance to a mosque or Hindu temple will have a place for you to place your shoes. You may be asked to wash your hands and face in an adjacent tiled washing area. Foreign women should not shake anyone's hand inside a mosque, or the worshiper's washing ritual will

The "Throneless" Asian Bathroom

Half of the world's population uses the squat-style toilet. Many Southeast Asians use a Western toilet by climbing on top of it and squatting. Prepare to use squat toilets in Asia, when you are away from your hotel, especially when sightseeing.

In a Japanese bathroom (*furoba*), you may confront the squat toilet too, especially in rural areas where it will be unlikely that the toilet is connected to a sewer. (Only six out of 10 homes in Japan have flush toilets connected to sewers.) A wooden cover must be removed before use. Squat facing the wall, toward the hooded end of the porcelain fixture. *A special note:* Inside a Japanese home, special slippers are to be worn in the bathroom. A pair will be placed outside the door. Put them on and leave your house slippers in their place, which serves to notify others that the toilet is occupied. Remember to *change back to your slippers* when you come out. It would be considered a formidable gaffe to wear toilet slippers back to the dinner table, for instance.

In Indonesia, the bathroom (*way say*) may lack toilet paper. Malays wash rather than wipe, using the water dipper to splash themselves. Bring your own tissue when sightseeing there. In fact, this is a prudent policy everywhere in Asia.

◆

have to be repeated. Greet the man at the door of the mosque with a formal *salaam*. You may be asked to put on one of the robes that will be at the door, before going in.

Inside the mosque, notice the emphasis on repeating geometric patterns in carved stone or painted tile. The interior of the temple will be devoid of religious iconography or human representations, because Moslems believe it is blasphemous to mimic the work of Allah. You will see no representations of Allah himself. Mosque interiors are designed to foster uninterrupted prayer, done while kneeling on rugs, facing east, toward the holy city of Mecca.

Visiting a *Wat* in Thailand

A *wat* (temple) in Thailand is also a community center. The central area (*bot*), where the image of the Buddha sits, is the most sacred part of the temple; shoes are removed before entering it. As in the Thai home, step over the high thresholds when making your way through the *wat*. Inside a temple, *never* climb on a statue of the Buddha, for example, to have your picture taken. A number of tourists have ended up behind bars for doing so.

Speaking of Religion . . .

Most Asians love to talk about their faiths. The trick is to ask non-insulting, yet compelling, questions about a particular religion. Here are some good conversation-starting questions that will elicit enthusiastic responses from a host, after you have determined which religions are personally practiced or culturally present:

About Shintoism

- Without a founder, and with no official sacred scriptures, how was Shintoism preserved through the ages?
- *Shinto* means the way of the *kami;* are *kami* gods or ideas?
- Why does a *torii* gate stand at the entrance to all *Shinto* shrines?

About Buddhism

- What are the Four Noble Truths that the Buddha discovered?
- What do some of the Buddha's hand positions (*mudra*) signify?
- What is the difference between the Theravada and the Mahayana doctrines of Buddhism?

About Confucianism

- Is Confucianism a religious doctrine or a philosophy for living?
- What is meant by the Confucian concept of *jen* (virtue); are people born with it, or must they cultivate it?
- What did Mengtzu (Mencius, c. 371–289 B.C.) add to Confucian philosophy?

About Hinduism

- What does *samsara* (birth and rebirth) mean?
- What is meant by the Hindu ideas of *dharma* (duty), *karma* (the accumulated consequences of our actions), and *moksha* (release from rebirth on earth)?
- What are Hinduism's four paths to enlightenment?

About Islam

- What is the significance of making the pilgrimage (*hajj*) to Mecca?
- What are the Five Pillars of the Islamic faith?
- What is the difference between the Sunni and the Shi'ite sects of Islam?

About Catholicism

- Is Filipino Catholicism completely Christian or are vestiges of pre-Spanish Filipino culture still present in it?
- Is the system of godparenthood strictly of Christian origin in the Philippines, or did it have an indigenous pre-Catholicism origin?
- Are Christian Filipinos all Roman Catholics, or do other sects exist too?

If you attend a sermon in the central *bot,* don't be surprised to see worshipers gossiping, slurping tea, or chewing betel nuts as the abbot speaks. Men and women sit side-saddle with legs off to one side or tucked under the buttocks. Don't sit cross-legged and don't remain standing in the *bot;* polite form dictates that visitors be lower in height than the monks up in front.

If you ask to make an offering, you will be given three incense sticks, flowers, a candle, and a piece of gold leaf. Light the candle and set it amidst the others. Place the flower in the water vessel. Light the incense with the candle. Stick the incense in the sand urn, and press the gold onto the Buddha image. While kneeling, *wai* before the Buddha and make some wishes. It can't hurt!

Holiday Events and Ceremonies

Most Chinese holiday celebrations are based on the Chinese Lunar Calendar, developed during the Tang Dynasty 2,000 years ago. The calendar marks the changing agricultural seasons. Many Chinese festivals celebrated today originated as ancient agricultural holidays. For example, Chinese New Year, observed throughout Confucian Asia and by Overseas Chinese everywhere, was a time, during the bitter weeks of winter, when farmers could relax and celebrate because work was not possible.

Chinese New Year (*Xin-nian*), wherever it is celebrated, lasts two weeks and is also called "Spring Festival." Families reunite and dine at sumptuous banquets. The spirits of ancestors are invited into homes, their pictures are rehung, incense and candles are lit, and red banners carrying words of luck are hung on doors to keep away evil spirits. The streets fill with paper lanterns and teams of outlandishly colorful dancers. Children receive red envelopes filled with luck money, and firecrackers scare away evil spirits. On the fourth day after New Year, paper money is sacrificed and more firecrackers are exploded, to welcome the gods back to earth after their sojourn in heaven.

The Dragon Boat Festival, also known as the Double Fifth Festival because it falls on the fifth day of the fifth moon of the lunar calendar, follows the first harvest, but actually commemorates the death of Chu Yuan, an early Chinese poet. Chu Yuan martyred himself in protest of a corrupt king, by throwing himself in the Han River. During the festival, many Chinese eat *Tzungtzu,* a kind of dumpling, in his honor. Teams from Hong Kong, Singapore, Taiwan, and other Overseas Chinese communities compete, in 42-foot boats, in regattas held in Hong Kong and Taiwan in late May or early June.

There's little reason to mention other of the numerous holiday ceremonies in Asia. If taken to one of them by an Asian host, Westerners are spectators rather than participants. The important thing to know is *when* the major festivals occur, so as not to schedule business meetings during these times. (The holiday calendar in Appendix F is included as a guide.)

One Asian holiday that expatriates should be aware of, because they may be indirectly involved, is the *Ching Ming* (clear and bright) Festival in China, which is celebrated in the first week of April. In Taiwan, it is called the Tomb Sweeping Festival and is celebrated on April 5, because the date coincides with that of the death of Chiang Kai-shek. Entire families make their way to the resting places of their forebears and celebrate the family lineage. Distant family members reunite to make small sacrificial offerings at dawn, in homage to their ancestors. They place flowers on graves, burn paper money as offerings, and sweep clean the tombs of deceased family members. Part of the *Ching Ming* ritual will involve the most revered object in the Chinese home—the ancestral tablet, a wooden plaque that carries all of the names of a family's lineage. Anyone allowed anywhere near this object must treat it with extreme respect and care.

In Korea, a similar holiday is called *Chusok;* it is the most important Korean festival. Here too, families visit the graves of their ancestors to pay filial respect.

Should you be invited to join a family in any of these solemn festivals, wear subdued casual clothing, bring paper money and cooked food to sacrifice, and don't drink alcoholic beverages, speak loudly, or talk of things other than the ongoing legacy of the host's family.

Attending a Wedding in Asia

Chinese Weddings.* Bring a wrapped gift to a Chinese wedding, with a card congratulating the couple and containing a phrase like "May your marriage last throughout your lives." Present the gift to the bride and groom; they will be receiving

---

* The protocols apply to Chinese weddings in general, whether in China, Taiwan, Hong Kong, Singapore, or elsewhere.

guests at the door, which you will find covered with red paper banners that carry the "Double Happiness" character.

Chinese weddings are formal-dress affairs. Men should wear their best suit (but not a tux) with a colorful tie, preferably good-luck red; women can wear their best dress, but no miniskirts. Traditionally, Chinese brides wore bright red dresses, often adorned with an embroidered phoenix pattern. Grooms wore ornate suits with a dragon pattern on them. Nowadays, however, Chinese (as well as Korean) brides usually wear white, Western-style gowns, and grooms wear tuxedos.

A "witness of marriage," often a leader at the couple's work unit (*danwei*), conducts the marriage rite. The words spoken change with the political climate: during the Cultural Revolution, newly-weds were instructed to be diligent in studying Mao Tze-tung's thought; now, they are wished good luck, prosperity, and a healthy, preferably male, baby. This correlates with China's current one-child-per-family policy.

Weddings in Korea.   The Korean wedding is a combination of the Chinese and Japanese marriage rites, an amalgamation of Shamanistic, Buddhist, and superstitious traditions. The bride wears a white wedding gown but changes into traditional garb to pay respects to the parents in a separate part of the wedding hall. The Korean wedding is somber; the bride does not smile during the ceremony.

The Japanese Wedding.   If you receive an invitation to a Japanese wedding, return the enclosed card promptly, with a note of congratulations, whether you plan to attend or not. Men should wear a formal dark suit; women, a nice dress of any color but white, which will be worn by the bride. Bring a gift of money ($50–$100 worth of crisp *Yen*) in an envelope (*shugi-bukuro*), which you can purchase at a stationer. Your name should be written on the outside and on the inside, as well as your address, and the amount enclosed. (Ask a Japanese friend or colleague to help you do this correctly.) Cash-giving guests usually receive a noncash gift in return, of about the same monetary value as their estimated cash gift, based on their economic position and status.

Don't drink and eat until the first speeches (made by the match-maker) and toast are finished. Other speeches will follow throughout the ceremony. Don't smoke or move about the room while a speech is in progress, and don't smile when photographs are taken of you. You'll be the only person who does. Japanese often joke about the way foreigners mug the camera.

Weddings and Baptisms in the Philippines. Accept the honor, if you are asked to sponsor a baptism or attend a wedding in the Philippines. Because the marriage rite in the Philippines is a Catholic ceremony as performed in the West, there is no need to describe it here in detail. However, foreigners often act as *sponsors* of weddings. For this role, there are a few things to mention.

A sponsor of a Filipino wedding becomes an instant godparent of two mature godchildren, the bride and the groom. That is, the sponsor becomes a member of a tight-knit family. Be prepared for later requests, from these new relatives, for help in anything from finding jobs to financial assistance. During the wedding, the sponsor will stand at the altar. Bring a working lighter, in case you are named candle sponsor too. Make a donation to the church, when the collection plate is passed. Congratulate the groom, and express "best wishes" to the bride. *Peso* bills are usually pinned to the groom's shirt, to symbolically start the couple off in life, so bring a pocket full of Filipino bills.

Should you sponsor a child's baptism, another common role played by foreigners, here's how it's done. Pay the church fee when you register for the baptism with the family. You will have a say in the elaborateness of the ritual, because you are paying. Bring a nice gift for the child, such as clothing, silverware, or gold earrings. If chosen as the godmother, you may also be asked to pay for the child's baptismal dress. If the godchild is female, then the godmother will hold her during the baptism; if male, then the godfather will hold him. Coins are tossed over the guests afterward, for good luck, so bring 50 pesos worth of *centavo* coins.

Attending a Funeral in Asia

To help you prepare for the unexpected in attending an Asian funeral, let me say only that the level of solemnity and formality at a funeral rite in Asia varies widely. In Japan, you can expect a quiet, tearful funeral; in Thailand, a funeral is a rather festive affair.

At a Thai funeral, you will find people chatting, laughing, and telling jokes. This is because sorrowful emotions have already been expressed at home before the funeral rite. A funeral ceremony is considered a joyous occasion because the deceased has already embarked on a new life in a continuing cycle of lives. He or she has been reborn.

Funerals in China.   Traditional home funerals in China are such raucous affairs that they disgust many modern Chinese. The body is laid out in "longevity clothes" in the home of the bereaved, or just outside the house, while friends and relatives gather to talk and joke, all rather loudly and somewhat disrespectfully. White lanterns marked with blue characters, denoting the family name and that of the deceased, are hung on the outside of the house. Guests play drinking games and often gamble at *majong*, the purpose of the gathering being to keep the deceased company on his or her way to the spirit world. The guests bring money and food as offerings. Fireworks are set off at 12 midnight and 6 in the morning. Nobody laughs, but the loud talking continues incessantly until the funeral celebration ends the next morning.

Funerals in Japan.   In Japan, funerals are formal affairs. Men wear dark suits with black ties. Women wear a black dress with a black purse; pearls are the only acceptable jewelry. Go to the stationers to buy an envelope (*koden bukuro*) for condolence money. Write your name on the outside of the envelope. Write your name and address in the book placed at the entrance of the place of the funeral, and leave your envelope. The others present may go through a bowing ritual while on their knees, first bowing to the bereaved family, then offering a prayer with hands in front of the face. They will then offer incense. This ritual is rather involved; take a cue from those paying their respects, before performing any ritual yourself.

When mourners leave, a small packet of salt is given to each person. Have someone sprinkle the salt on you before you enter your house. The purifying salt is intended to remove any supernatural entities that might be clinging to you, after exposure to the dead.

The Art of Tea

Tea drinking in Asia, with its centuries-old procedures and rites, originated in China. The tea plant is a native of South China, where it was first used medicinally in the treatment of rheumatic fever. Tea did not become a beverage until the fourth century; in the eighth century, as the Japanese cultural historian Kakuzo Okakura says, in *The Book of Tea:* "It entered the realm of poetry as one of the polite amusements." The "code of tea" was first described by a poet named Lu Wu in the eighth century, in his epistle to tea, *The Holy Scripture of Tea,* called the *Ch'a Ching* in China. In the book, Lu Wu explains the ritual of the tea ceremony and the delicate utensils used.

The tea-drinking ritual was quickly spread to Korea by Buddhist monks, during the Yi Dynasty in the late fourteenth century; it was resisted by Korea's Confucian emperors. Korean tea rooms (*tabang*) have traditionally been informal meeting places for young and old. A romantic date or an evening of entertainment might begin in a *tabang.* Poets have composed masterpieces in them, and, in the Korean psyche, they are associated with Korea's independence movement against the Japanese, because Korean resistance patriots would meet in them to discuss and organize the revolution against Japanese colonial rule. Unfortunately, by meeting there too frequently, the patriots made it easy for Japanese police to round up resistance leaders. (All of this background makes wonderful conversation with a Korean host at a *tabang* or a banquet.)

At the close of the fourteenth century, tea drinking was refined into a ceremony in the Japanese home and monastery. The Japanese tea ceremony (*cha-no-yu*) comes from ideals of Buddhism, including poverty, austerity, and simplicity, which are all means to spirituality. The Japanese continued to ennoble tea during the fifteenth century, finally creating, as Kakuzo Okakura tells us, Teaism—a "religion of aestheticism . . . a cult founded on the adoration of the beautiful among the sordid facts of everyday existence."

Only in Japan is the ancient Asian tea ceremony still formally practiced, and schools still teach "the way of tea" to large numbers of Japanese and tourists. The ceremony is a kind of social sacrament, involving, in the words of the Japanese cultural historian E. F. Bleiler, "a submission of one's self to the ways of the fathers." Moreover, it's a lot of fun.

The decor of the tea room, the utensils, and the actions and conversation of the participants are all governed by stringent ancient rules. The ultimate purpose of the ceremony is to reenact an ancient rite exactly as it has been performed for 500 years, to allow participants to experience a deep sense of identification with a cultural past.

The ceremony itself emphasizes the ideal of *waki,* a way of life synonymous with poverty and limitation, but productive of spirituality that is attained without material possessions. The tea master uses a precise number of rudimentary utensils: a small furnace, ladle, tongs for charcoal, slop bowl, trivet, water vessel, kettle and stand, tea caddies, and ceramic tea bowls. The utensils embody another important ideal, *sabi,* which connotes the timeless simplicity and purity of Japanese objects—an aesthetic of economy. Like these objects, the tea ceremony and the tea room are devoid of ostentation or decoration. Tea rooms are designed to imitate the quiet simplicity of the Zen monastery.

Being a Guest at a Japanese Tea Ceremony

In its most traditional form, the wooden tea room is entered by way of a path through a *bonsai* garden. Bow to the picture or flower arrangement in the entryway. The host will usually enter the tea room last. Men should wear a suit and tie; women, a conservative dress of subtle color, suitable for kneeling on the floor. Seat yourself quietly on the *tatami,* on your knees (women sit side-saddle) where directed, and remain silent. Listen to the gentle murmuring of the boiling water in the ancient-looking kettle. Watch the kimono-clad tea master steep the powdered green tea, a bitter blend called *matcha,* and serve sweetcakes. (Some tea ceremonies also include a meal.) Sip the tea, holding the tea bowl in both hands. Diana Rowland, author of *Japanese Business Etiquette,* explains a common tea ceremony:

> [the thick tea is] passed from guest to guest in one big tea bowl. The ritual of drinking is to place the silk cloth, if passed with the bowl, on your left palm, set the bowl on the cloth, and steady it with your right hand . . . . You should take three and a half sips, then set it down. With your little cloth, wipe the edge of the bowl where you drank from it, turn it so that the design faces you again, and pass it to the next guest.

Later, compliment the exquisite interior of the tea room. Bow to the tea master when leaving, and express thanks for such a beautiful tea ceremony.

Shopping: What to Buy and When to Bargain

As part of sightseeing with an Asian host, visitors will likely spend time roaming a local market or outdoor bazaar. Knowledge of local crafts and indigenous products will be appreciated by your

Local Specialties

China: Porcelain, mohair sweaters, *maotai,* lacquerware, and hand-woven wool carpets.

Hong Kong: Tailored clothing and shoes, designer goods from factory outlets, jewelry (forget the knockoff watches), luggage, jade, and products from China sold at three stores: Chinese Arts & Crafts, Ltd., China Products Company, and Yue Hwa Chinese Products Emporium, Ltd.

Indonesia/Malaysia: *Batik* clothing, decorative masks, wicker-work, kites, silverwork, carved-wood decorative objects such as masks and artificial fruit and vegetables, and *kain songket* cloth (in Malaysia).

Japan: Tea sets, *kimonos,* bamboo products, rustic ceramics, Imari chinaware, *sake,* pearls, dolls, cherry bark products, silk screen paintings, cloisonné, authentic looking plastic food made for restaurant displays, and reproductions of Ukiyoe woodblock prints.

Korea: Antique art (very reasonable and plentiful in the Insadong district), black and mother-of-pearl lacquerware, fur and leather coats, celedon pottery, brassware, *ginseng,* and calligraphy brushes and utensils.

Philippines: Handicrafts, canework, shell hanging-lamps, wood carvings, and clothing like *borong tagalog* and *barong polo* shirts made of pineapple fiber.

Singapore: Clothing and crafts from India and the Middle East (found on Arab Street), designer clothing, gold and jewelry, Turkish and Oriental carpets, *batiks.*

Taiwan: Ming and Han jade antiques (some real, some fake), hand puppets, old coins, temple carvings, porcelain, ceramic ware, furniture, painting reproductions, jewelry, custom-made shoes and clothes such as a form-fitting *chipao* (silk dress; *cheongsam* in Cantonese) for women.

Thailand: Silk goods, leather products, children's clothing (very inexpensive), luggage, sapphires.

◆

host, and a request for advice on the best place to purchase a particular specialty will make a good impression.

Bargaining over prices is standard procedure in Thailand, Korea, and Hong Kong, but is done less in Malaysia, Indonesia, and the Philippines. It is *not* done in China, Singapore, or Japan, except in the street markets, like Arab Street in Singapore. In shops and boutiques, refrain from showing off any bartering ability.

CHAPTER THIRTEEN

Hosting an Asian Delegation

*Americans think that if they give me a few
gifts, take me to some shows, and get me
drunk, I'm going to do business with them.*
A FILIPINO BUSINESSMAN

North Americans who have experienced first-hand how Asians entertain foreign businesspeople in Asia assume, often falsely, that such entertainment is all that is needed to massage an Asian business guest into doing a deal. Their routinely hospitable gestures often appear empty to the Asians because, by themselves, the gestures do little to personalize the relationship between Asian guest and Western host.

Friendships are rarely forged; bonds of trust do not become strong. "The American tries to do business real quick. He thinks that if he does this nice stuff for me, that I'll do a deal with him. But it doesn't work like that!" As this Filipino testifies, many North Americans hosting Asians ignore the fact that a deal cannot be done with Asians "real quick," without a requisite personal connection between the partners.

Sumptuous entertainment is no substitute for building relationships, both business *and* personal, with visiting Asian guests. Though a host will want to fill every minute of their visit with sightseeing, meetings, and informal talks, there should be no assumption that unbridled entertainment will land a deal.

Hallmarks of the Gracious Host

When hosting Asians, the ultimate purpose is to foster long-term bonds between the visitors and *individuals* working for the North

American company. There was a time when Asian companies came to North America as captive buyers of capital goods and technology. Hosting a buying mission from Asia was considered merely a bothersome formality, by most Western firms. Asian companies now come to the West as international technology vendors, financial joint-venture partners, and acquisition-seeking corporate conglomerates. It's now common for a North American company to host Asians as part of pursuing a financially and technologically richer Asian partner. This reversal of roles has created a sea change in the art of hosting Asian delegations. It is vital to *court* Asian customers while they are on the home turf. Before business can be done, a host must entertain appropriately, foster intimate discussions, and observe rules of protocol followed by the equal, and often stronger, potential Asian partner.

The heightened importance of hosting foreign customers has impelled many blue-chip companies in the West to hire the services of a permanent in-house Chief of Protocol, whose job is to ensure that foreign guests receive the same attentive treatment that North Americans receive when in Asia. This chapter covers all the necessities for hosting an Asian business delegation—from arrival gate to departure gate—like a Chief of Protocol.

The First Unknown: Who Is Pursuing Whom?

No one has set down in stone the rules of hosting Asians; the protocol of hosting varies widely, depending on which firm—the Western or the Asian one—is pursuing the other as a customer or partner. If the Western firm is the pursuer, the Asian delegation will probably have been invited to come to the West as honored guests. If an Asian firm solicits a visit to a company in North America, the requirements of playing the role of gracious host are less extreme.

Attend to Business Courtship

In Asia, the business courting process that precedes substantive contract negotiating can take months or even years. If the Asian company being hosted is extremely attractive as a funder, customer, or strategic partner, the host company may not want to stop entertaining the guests (while building friendships with them) to discuss business, unless *they* initiate such a meeting. If they *don't* initiate business talks, they simply return to Asia having made some good friends at the host company. If the Asian partner is pursuing the host company, the entertainment can be less extensive. The primary purpose of hosting is to build long-term business relationships.

For our purposes here, let us assume that you are hosting a delegation from an Asian company that is, more or less, your company's equal. The delegation has warmly accepted the invitation to come to North America and begin discussing a joint project. You plan to show them all the hospitality you can, without going overboard and risking looking too eager for a deal.

In this most typical case, your job as a host is to choreograph your guests' entire stay, build in free time for them, and make their sojourn in the West perfectly comfortable, safe, and memorable. You want your guests to feel looked after, but not oppressed by your attentions to them.

Guidelines for Good Hosting

Find Out Who Is Coming, and Why.   The company positions of the members of a delegation will depend entirely on the nature of the visit—that is, whether a deal is being negotiated, a group of engineers is coming to be trained, and so on. It's important to find out all that you can about the delegation *beforehand*.

You can, and should, ascertain who will be in attendance, and each person's status and function in the Asian company. (You will be asked to supply the same information, when visiting Asia.) Knowing who each person is, in relation to the others present, helps in seating people at banquets and meetings. You may ask that each person's business card be sent ahead, to assist you in making name tags and place tags. The cards will help you to discern the power and influence each person wields in the Asian company.

Delegations from China may be the most mysterious, in terms of individual job function and decision-making power. You might receive a four- or five-member delegation, including a director, a department manager, a Communist Party official, and an English-speaking interpreter, without knowing which player will eventually be granted decision-making authority over the planned venture. A good rapport subject, when socializing with any visiting delegation, is the nature of the Asian firm's internal decision-making structure and the bureaucratic agencies that affect it.

Allow for Varied Exposure to the West. Depending on the Asian company's level of international orientation, your guests may range in their knowledge of the West—and its customs—from completely unfamiliar to seemingly more familiar than you are. I've had a Moslem Asian, wearing a white *sarong* and dangling his bare feet, sit cross-legged before me at a negotiation; and I've hosted a Japanese person who attended the top university in my area and understood America's economy and government policy far better than I do. An important rule is: Remain adaptable and tolerant.

You may want to inquire as to whether members of the delegation have been to North America before, to assist you in planning an itinerary for their stay. Since some hotels and many restaurants have sections for smokers and nonsmokers, you should ask whether the delegates smoke or not. If it is possible to ascertain what, if any, sports activities they participate in or would like to attend, this will help you plan their stay attractively.

Train Company Representatives to Host Properly. Four central players on your side must be readied to properly host an Asian delegation. These people are:

1. The CEO or vice president of the Asia division, who must be prepared to greet, toast, and negotiate with the visitors;
2. One or more interpreters, who must be trained to translate, perhaps from a dialect, diverse conversation during meals, sightseeing, factory tours, and meetings;
3. A chauffeur (or chauffeurs), who must be hired and briefed on general Asian protocol;
4. A master of ceremonies, or coordinator, who must be ready to choreograph the entire visit, from invitation-making to final gift-giving presentations. (I'm assuming here that this person is you.)

Beyond these four, you may be introducing a number of other company people to your Asian guests. Should they be attending a banquet or working shoulder-to-shoulder with Asian engineers visiting your factory, they too should know the essentials of Asian greeting ritual, and of verbal and nonverbal communication.

One obvious area of potential disaster, when novices are permitted to meet Asian guests, is in safe rapport, described in Chapter 5. Someone on your staff may deride King Bhumibol in a conversation with a Thai, or decry Korean unification as unthinkable to a Korean, or express, to a Japanese executive, the opinion that Japan should pay more for U.S. military protection. The worst parallel incident for me was when my glib, English-bred driver drilled a visiting Chinese delegation about the prevalence of abortion in China. I don't need to describe the arctic breeze that blew across the banquet table in response; I kicked myself for not briefing the driver beforehand, on rapport no-nos with P.R.C. visitors.

The wrong words can be a wrecking crew for the best preparations. Jump into the dialogue as quickly and graciously as you can, using bulldozer politeness and sensitivity to clear away the debris. To spare you disasters, of words or of protocol, I've made a conscious effort to gather here every piece of information and advice—and experience, mine and others'—that will prevent potential mishaps. No author starts plugging his book in Chapter 13, so take my urging at face value: be sure that everyone who will be involved in one-on-one contact or group meetings reads all the sections in which I've discussed anything about the Asian delegation's country of origin. Create some awareness on the premises by posting some information about the visitors at frequented spots, before they arrive, or gather an assembly and get an attitude of hospitality going. But, more than anything, have key people *read everything that's here.* I've had my share of disasters; I don't wish them on anybody.

Help Prevent Blunders by Asians.   Almost invariably, one or more members of a visiting Asian delegation (in addition to the interpreter) will speak some English and claim to understand the ways of the West. You may want to surreptitiously consult with this person about Western mannerisms and customs that the delegation may not be aware of—and probe the person's actual knowledge at the same time. Should they dine out at the hotel café, for example, do they understand that their waiter will expect a 15 percent tip? Do they have the appropriate attire, should they want to use the pool or recreation room? If they doff their shoes before entering the hotel room, will they remember *not* to leave them outside their door unattended, or they may be stolen? About bathing, do they know how to best use the fixtures? Are they aware that hotel staffs in the West get upset when Asians pour water over themselves to bathe while standing in the middle of the bathroom? Brass plaques once were displayed in hotel bathrooms in Hawaii, forbidding Japanese visitors from practicing this custom.

Everyone on your side has to work to prevent verbal mishaps by the Asians, who will often attempt to make speeches and engage in conversation using untrained or nonidiomatic English. North American English, unfortunately, is chock-full of sexual slang, erotic allusions, and bawdy innuendo. Be on guard to step in and defuse a guest's verbal firecracker. Take, for example, the Japanese executive who stood up to toast the wife of his American partner: "I'd like your wife, bottoms up!"

Agree on Who Pays the Bill.   Who pays will depend on who is courting the other's business. If you are pursuing your guests' company to become one of your new customers, you can't expect them to shoulder the costs to meet and cavort with you in North America. If the relationship appears to be strategic for both sides, then the costs can be shared: your company covers all of your guests' expenses minus airfare. Should you meet an Asian informally, on a return flight to the West, for example, you need not pay for his or her accommodations during a later, invited visit. However, the "whoever invites, pays" rule applies to dinner out and entertainment.

In China, sellers pay their own way, and so do potential joint-venture partners, unless a deal is much desired. A Chinese official once described this to me quite frankly: "If our two companies enter a deal, we pay for all of the banquets, hotel rooms, and your driver while you are in China. If we don't sign a deal, then you pay." Hospitality, like legal statutes in Asia, is largely situational.*

A key point to remember: Never allow a female member of your side to host Asian men at dinner and attempt to pay the bill, unless she pays it inconspicuously beforehand. For her to openly pay the bill is bad form because it can humiliate Asian guests, especially Filipinos, who are usually less egalitarian than Westerners on the issue of which sex pays.

Deal Overtly with "Security" Issues.   The exchange of sensitive technology between foreign companies presents a number of security issues for both sides, especially if North Americans are hosting a delegation from a Communist country. To prevent any unforeseen security problem on your side, you may want to inform the local office of the FBI of the visit, especially if your guests are

---

* If you are hosting an ethnic-Chinese delegation, you can name yourself humorously, "the lord of the eastern road," if you plan to pay for *everything*. The origin of this saying is in Chinese literature, where the west is the symbol of the guest and the east is the symbol of the host.

coming from the People's Republic and you are dealing with technology transfer. With P.R.C. visitors, it is also unwise to ask an individual member of the delegation to meet with you privately. The meeting might raise suspicions regarding the person's ideological firmness among his or her fellow delegates, who might be alarmed by apparent close association with a Westerner.

Setting a *Full* Itinerary

As host, you set the itinerary for a visiting delegation's entire stay. Don't expect your guests to arrive in Joliet, Jersey, or Jackson Hole with a list of sights they'd like to see and things they'd like to do. Have no fear about planning a full schedule for your Asian visitors. They will be quite acquainted with full-schedule business entertainment. The first rule of hosting is: Never leave your guests on their own.

There is a question of *when* to host an Asian delegation. Try to avoid Asian business holiday periods, of which there are many that involve annual family reunions and religious ceremonies that your Asian partner may not want to miss. One obvious mistake would be to invite an ethnic-Chinese delegation to North America during the Lunar New Year, the two-week time of festivals and family gatherings in early February. Business communication grinds to a halt during this celebration. (See Appendix F for a list of Asian holidays, before you set your hosting dates.)

Fax your completed itinerary to your Asian guests before they leave, to assist them in planning their wardrobe. If golf or other recreation is planned, describe the activity and mention that all equipment will be rented for their use.

Your Asian guests may visit more than one client, while in North America. Don't be offended by this arrangement or inquire as to whom they are meeting. Offer your assistance in arranging their transportation and accommodation for the remainder of their stay in the West. They will decline your help, unless they have encountered a serious problem.

Hosting an Asian Spouse

Rarely will an Asian businessman bring his wife to North America on a business trip, unless both are well acquainted with the West and she has a distinct reason for coming—to visit relatives, for example.

However, should an Asian spouse be brought along, you have to develop a list of activities for her while in North America. Assign a woman to serve as her personal guide, preferably the CEO's wife or a female executive at your company. Don't allow an Asian female guest to travel about unescorted, especially in a large city. Imagine the implications should she become lost or injured.

Arrival and a Welcoming Banquet

Your CEO may or may not meet the delegation at the airport, but, as coordinator, *you are required* to be on hand. Meet the delegation after it has cleared Customs; carry a placard on which their company name is printed in both their language and English. Remember to go through the appropriate greeting ritual described in Chapter 4. Have a company (or rented) van waiting out front, with a non-Asian driver, hired for the entire stay, at the wheel. Be cognizant of seating in the van. The Asian leader should sit ahead of the others.

Hotel Arrangements

Some hotels are more accustomed to serving foreigners than others are. Many are now Asian-owned and are very well-equipped to deal with visiting Asians: they feature Asian restaurants and room service menus, *karaoke* bars, and fully stocked Asian-language bookstores. An example is the Japanese-owned Otami Hotel in Los Angeles.

Always preregister your guests before they arrive, to spare them the bothersome formality and to ensure that the rooms are properly reserved. If the delegation is small, each member should have his or her own room; if large, two men per double room is an appropriate arrangement. Married couples get a double room (two double beds).

Accompany your guests to their rooms with the bellhop and your interpreter. Tip the bellhop on the sly and send him off. *You* should show your guests their rooms, using your interpreter to describe its accoutrements, which you will have checked earlier. Demonstrate the light switches, table lamps, phone system, and video message board on the television (get their names on it, to welcome them and to announce meetings if they are to be held at the hotel). Show them how to call for room service, where to find hot water, ice, and vending machines, and how to ring up security. Go through the hotel brochure to acquaint them with the hotel's additional services; you may want to go the extra mile and have the hotel map labeled in their language.

A basket of fruit, candy, cookies, or liqueurs, with a card from your company, should be waiting in their rooms. So should a can of high-quality green tea. Make sure the hotel delivers a thermos of hot water to each room every morning and evening, with clean porcelain teacups.

Give your guests a complete list of necessary phone numbers, in case they have questions or a problem. They should be able to reach you, as hosting coordinator, at any time of day or night.

Another nice touch is to have a copy of an appropriate Asian-language newspaper delivered to their hotel room each morning, even if the edition is a few days out of date. You might also find out whether a local cable-television company airs news in their language; in Southern California, the news is telecast in Japanese and Chinese.

Other Hotel Tips.   Always see guests to the elevator, if not to their room doors, before leaving them for the evening. You don't want them to have to deal with lost keys, with unlocking a newfangled door lock, and so on—or with trying to get the assistance of the concierge, who doesn't speak their language. I have heard many stories of deals falling apart because somebody lost face due to being put on a subway or expected to get their own taxi, to get back to their hotel.

Before you leave them for the night, review briefly the itinerary for the next day and the time when you will pick them up. Tell them that you have asked the hotel to call their rooms at a certain time in the morning, to wake them up.

The Opening Banquet

On the night of your Asian guests' arrival, you should arrange a banquet party at a fine restaurant that serves the cuisine the Asian delegation is accustomed to; that is, Japanese for Japanese, Szechuanese for Chinese from the Szechuan area of China, Cantonese for the Hong Kong Chinese, and so on. Consult the manager of the restaurant to make sure that the food to be served corresponds to the cuisine in your guests' region of Asia. Malay cuisine may be difficult to arrange. If so, a buffet-style banquet might be the best way to go, including *labeled* dishes and omitting pork and shellfish.

Invite *all* of the people whom the Asians will have met before, and have them share in the initial greeting proceedings, before dinner. Continuity of personnel is the key in dealing with Asians over the long term. If someone on your staff, whom the guests had met before, has transferred to another company, be forthcoming about the move; don't leave the person's absence a mystery. Your Asian guests will surely wonder why someone with whom they had built up a business relationship is suddenly missing.

Hire interpreters for the welcoming banquet, and seat one at each table. After everyone is seated, and as serving of the meal begins, your CEO should stand, make a short speech, and toast the visiting company. Keep the speech under three minutes. The group should applaud the speech and the guests being toasted. Next, the leader of the visiting delegation will rise and give a short speech, but may not raise his glass in a toast. Make sure your group applauds after his speech, too. Eating can then begin.

Remember that Moslem Asians will not be drinking alcohol (serve them juices and tea); a toast to them is unnecessary. Because the Asian's speech will not include jokes and may seem rather stiff, warn your CEO not to precede him by rousing the crowd into uproarious laughter. The CEO should keep the greeting speech light but solemn, compared to a similar speech for North American guests. Always mention, in the original itinerary sent to your Asian guests beforehand, that there will be *three-minute* dinner speeches.

The First Day: Sightseeing

Any foreigners visiting North America arrive with a mental list of sights they would like to see and things they would like to do. For first-time Asian visitors to America, the list invariably includes Disneyland, in California, or Walt Disney World and Epcot Center, in Florida. If you are located near either theme park, put a Disney tour at the start of your itinerary.

As a sightseeing destination, city zoos are also a good bet, but utilize a vehicle tour of the zoo if one exists, or you'll wear your guests out. Remember, they are probably jet-lagged this early in their stay. Among other ideas for sightseeing, depending on your regional location, are:

- Indoor shopping malls, unless your guests are from Japan and Hong Kong and have probably seen their share of department stores;
- Rodeos, animal shows, and local fairs;
- A local church, temple, or mosque, especially if your guests are religious;
- A nearby university campus, library, and main laboratories, if a visit can be arranged;
- A nearby state park or wilderness area, especially where mountaintops offer scenic vistas;
- Art, science, history, or space museums;
- The "downtown" area, with stops at key points of interest, including districts with large Asian populations where the signage is multilingual;
- Sporting events, especially recreational ones, like a triathlon meet, a skiing competition, or a baseball game. A special treat might be to visit a team practice, at an ice hockey rink, for example, and arrange for your guests to meet some of the players.

Depending on the season in your location, you may invite your guests to play golf or tennis, or to go jogging early in the morning in a local park. All of these recreations are good ideas, as long as you don't allow yourself to become overly competitive with your Asian guests. Don't birdie three holes in a row or whip someone in straight sets. An Asian won't do this to you when you visit Asia. *Warnings:* Avoid extreme sports like white-water rafting, wrestling, boxing, snow skiing, and trampolining; they aren't worth the risk of someone's getting hurt. Don't subject your guests to potentially dangerous environments like high-crime areas at night, hard-rock concerts, or off-roading strips.

The results can be calamitous. Take, for example, a visiting Japanese delegation that was invited by their American counterparts to view the Napa Valley wine country from a hot air balloon. The balloon was caught by an ill wind, snapped its moorings, and rose aloft without its American pilot. The four Japanese in the basket could operate the radio but couldn't speak English. From the ground, the American balloon pilot tried to talk them down,

Photographing the Delegation

Informal photos should be shot randomly during sightseeing. You may want to videotape activities as well. When photographing group shots, however, formality is the watchword. Make sure the leader of each side stands at the center of the shot, and allow time for the Asian group to position themselves according to rank. You may want to choreograph your side the same way. Don't demean your guests by asking them to wear company shirts or caps, or to hold things.

A visiting delegation from China refused to wear green company hats, in a group photograph at an American firm's headquarters. The Chinese took the caps that were handed to them, threw them on the ground, and stomped on them. Everyone was dismayed and embarrassed. It turned out that the U.S. company was about to portray the Chinese on film as cuckolds! (A man wearing a green hat is the symbol of the cuckold in China.)

◆

but to no avail; he couldn't speak Japanese. By luck alone, the balloon came down in a wheat field, spilling its Japanese delegation onto the ground unscathed. Let this be a lesson.

Take a Tip from Your Guests about What to Do

Remember that little things may interest your guests more than the big impressive landmarks that they have probably seen on television anyway. As part of sightseeing, point out some of our peculiarities, and ask what your guests are most surprised by when they visit North America. They're likely to mention strange things like: drinking fountains, junk food, ocean sports, bananas, chewing gum, avocados, weird hairdos, the ubiquity of television, how people smile and say hello on the street, and the availability of imported products at reasonable prices. Their comments will surely give you ideas to add to the itinerary as you go.

Dining Out

Asian guests may not be acquainted with the vast number of choices North Americans are required to make, when ordering in a restaurant. You may want to order for your guests, when dining out, after confirming that the basic ingredient in the entrée is acceptable. American breakfasts epitomize the problem. Don't permit a waiter or waitress to engage the Asian delegation in the

20-questions ritual of how they want their eggs, what kind of toast they want, and whether they want bacon or sausage. Order a standard breakfast for each person, including yourself, omitting any taboo foods. At a Mexican (or other ethnic) restaurant, it does little good for a waiter to pass out individual menus; most Asians will not know the names of any of the selections. Again, order for the group after confirming that they like the basic ingredient of the dish.

Other tips about meals are the following:

- Meals are not for negotiating business; hold off on initiating business talk until inside the meeting room;
- Don't lopside the table: invite an equal number of diners from your side and theirs;
- Don't bluntly ask your guests the familiar Western premeal question: "Are you hungry?" You're liable to hear the reply "I'm not very hungry," even though your polite guests may be famished.
- Arrange to pay the bill discreetly, before the meal.
- Keep the conversation alive, using safe rapport topics listed in Chapter 5.

Sensitive Rapport Topics

If you expect to discuss politics with your guests, you may want to brush up on your government's current foreign relations policies, especially those concerning your guests' country. A common habit among Westerners is to criticize their own country's government too freely, which can surprise and even unsettle an Asian guest.

A productive topic for conversation, should the discussion turn to politics, is your home country's political and economic system. Few Asian businesspeople understand the North American bureaucratic system of city, county, and state jurisdictions, because Asian state bureaucracies are set up differently. Your minicourse in the U.S. system of state administration, and how it affects business, will be much appreciated.

Another productive area of conversation might concern North American cultural diversity. Few Asians realize that there is a massive difference between doing business with an American, for example, in New York City, and an American on the West Coast. An enlightening discussion might be to dissolve your guests' possible stereotypes about North Americans by describing to them the host of nations represented in an average telephone directory.

Day Two: Business Discussions

A schedule for business discussions (given that you intend to discuss business at all) should appear on the original itinerary sent to your Asian guests. Negotiations are best held at the hotel where your guests are staying, because the location allows them to periodically rest in their room, conduct private meetings among themselves during the day, and retrieve needed presentation materials that they may have forgotten. As a second choice, a meeting room at your company is perfectly suitable. In either case, a hostess should be hired to serve green tea in teacups (lidded if possible), fruit juices, and soft drinks at intervals throughout the day.

Open the first business meeting of the visit with a speech. Start with "Since our last meeting . . ." and continue on to a review of the business relationship with the Asian company up to the present. Describe the activities of your company since your last meeting. Allow the Asians to make an introduction as well. This exchange builds continuity in your business relationship and gets things off to a good start.

Expect your guests to give your negotiating team wrapped gifts about halfway through the scheduled negotiations. Don't unwrap them unless they insist; thank them sincerely the following day. (The names of your negotiating team should have been included with your itinerary, to help your guests bring the correct number of gifts.) Break for lunch at a preset hour, to avoid the "Are you hungry?" routine.

Most Asian negotiators expect long meetings, but remember that Asian Moslems may adhere to a strict prayer schedule and Malay guests may be accustomed to bathing frequently throughout the day. I recall a strange meeting with a ethnic-Chinese visitor from Malaysia. After dinner, we brought our Malay guest (call him Mr. Wang) to a beach house near San Diego, to continue our negotiations for the importation of orchids. In the midst of negotiating, Mr. Wang rose suddenly and asked where the bath was. The head of the delegation and the owner of the house pointed to the bathroom, rather puzzled. Mr. Wang went into the bathroom and started showering. The Americans sat there totally bemused. A few moments later, Mr. Wang emerged, hair wet, looking refreshed, sat down, and continued his discussion. The Americans stared at him open-mouthed. I interjected that Malays bathe often, because it is very hot in Southeast Asia. Mr. Wang agreed and continued on.

Can a Visiting Delegation Make Decisions?

The more international the Asian company, the more decision-making power the persons you are hosting will possess. Some may even be given unilateral autonomy to sign deals while in North America. Small companies, however, may need to discuss issues with superiors at home, before anything can be finalized. Because many Japanese companies missed out on lucrative real estate deals in the mid-1980s, having moved too slowly to sign agreements, savvy Japanese companies tend to move faster now by granting decision-making autonomy to delegations that visit North America. Perhaps companies in other Asia-Pacific countries will follow Japan's lead.

After the Meeting: Bright Lights, Big City

Evenings are important times to build informal communications with your Asian guests—to "get to know each other." In some cities, filling the nights with rewarding business entertainment will be easier than in others. No matter how difficult it is, however, to find good entertainment in your area, entertain your Asian guests *every* night of their stay.

Build your nighttime entertainment schedule from the following list of ideas:

- A Broadway play or, better yet, a musical (outside of New York, check all available road companies);
- A ballet or modern dance performance;
- A classical music concert;
- A concert by a famous singer;
- A harbor cruise, after dark;
- An outing at a well-known jazz club or intimate jazz loft.

Let me offer a warning about comedy performances. Stand-up comics can be exceedingly profane in language and confrontational in their treatment of an audience. A night at a Comedy

Store or the Improv is highly unwise. One hosting horror story, which I'm ashamed to even know of, occurred when an American computer company treated a Moslem delegation from Jakarta to a night at the Improv. It was the week when Salman Rushdie, author of *The Satanic Verses,* came under fire from Islamic fundamentalists. A comedian took off on the theme, to the offense of the delegation, which asked to leave the show early. Even under the best circumstances, language barriers make comedians difficult for your guests to understand. Avoid comedians entirely.

Build in Free Time.   On the final day of hosting a P.R.C. delegation, we were on our way to pick them up at their hotel, early in the morning, to take them to the airport. Suddenly, before us on the road, we saw seven Chinese men running across four lanes of highway, from the entrance to their hotel to a shopping mall on the other side. Traffic swerved around them. "What in God's name are they doing!" I cried.

Then I realized that, in all our efforts to entertain the delegation, we hadn't allowed them one free moment to go shopping for friends and family while in America. They were rushing to a shopping mall, lest they return home empty-handed. Now I remember to arrange a time for uninterrupted shopping by Asian guests. The Japanese even have a word—*omiyagé*—for a gift brought back from a foreign place and given to someone important.

Handling Minor Expenses.   On a free-time shopping expedition, your guests can purchase to their heart's desire and at their own expense. However, you should insist on covering the cost of *all* of their incidental gift purchases during sightseeing activities. Refuse to allow them to pay for a poster, tee shirt, postcards (carry some stamps with you), or mementos, with their own money. In fact, don't let them even *touch* cash. You pay the cashier while they go to the next store. (You might recall that cash is thought to be dirty in Korea.) You will receive identical treatment in Asia; even in cash-poor China, a young person will accompany you everywhere with *Renminbi* currency for your gift-buying pleasure.

The Visit to Your Home

A great way to end a stay for your Asian guests is to give them a glimpse of how you personally live at home, or how North

The Drawbacks of Cocktail Parties

Habitually, Westerners throw a cocktail party, in order to get acquainted with new faces and to introduce friends to other friends. Most Asians, however, eschew the cocktail-style social gathering; it is not part of an Asian's normal social or business life. Asians usually socialize in groups of people who are well-acquainted beforehand, and some find cocktail parties downright disconcerting. Thais, for example, find it bizarre to eat while standing, or walking, as is done at this Western function. Cocktail parties are a bad idea for entertaining Indonesians, for the obvious reason of alcohol consumption restrictions in Moslem Asia; besides, Indonesians don't like eating while standing. Other Asians believe cocktail party entertaining crass and depersonalizing because the host and guest alike are expected to serve themselves or to ask a bartender for a drink, with no chance for the guest to politely decline repeatedly. Indeed, the very purpose of the cocktail party is to facilitate conversation; and for many Asians, too much talking can be construed as pompous, uncouth, and conceited.

◆

Americans live at home. Inviting Asian guests over to dine and to meet the kids can go a long way toward personalizing a business relationship. Dinner at the home of the CEO offers a good environment for long goodbyes as well; you might place it on the itinerary as the wrap-up, on the night before the delegation is taken to the airport to catch their flight home.

Dinner with the Family

Serve what you wish for dinner, unless you are entertaining Moslem Asians. If your guest is Moslem, a good solution is to serve the meal buffet-style, omit pork or separate it into a buffet tray, and explain each dish to your Moslem guest.

Don't express your bonhomie by saying "I hope you're hungry." An Asian who would answer "Yes, I'm starving," would be considered low-class, rustic in upbringing, or simply rude. You may find it difficult to get some Asians to move toward the table for dinner.

Seating. Remember that the highest ranking person sits opposite the door. If you sit at a rectangular table, the top-ranking persons from each side sit at mid-table, facing each other.

Talking at the Table. Dinner conversation should center around people, especially family members. Questions about your family members may be a bit personal for you ("Do you plan on having another child soon?"), so be prepared. Frank questions might also include financially sensitive issues like whether you rent or own your home, and what you paid for it. Remain open and frank, rather than threatened or embarrassed. You may want to warn your spouse about this, before your guests arrive.

The Gift-Giving Ceremony: A Final Touch

A special gift-giving ceremony should be the final event on the itinerary, and a good place to do it is in the home, after dinner. Remember to give small gifts (so as not to cause problems with the airlines or Customs) of comparable value to the gifts received from your guests. In addition, give one or more of the following:

- An address book of the people your guests met in North America;
- A photo album of their stay;
- An edited videotape of their stay, including sightseeing tours.

Long goodbyes can ensue after gift giving. Then you, as coordinator, and the driver can take the delegation back to their hotel.

The Final Day

You and the driver pick up the delegation at the hotel. You should have already paid the hotel in full. (An American I worked for suffered through the humiliation of a credit-card authorization scene, as his delegation waited in the lobby to go to the airport.)

The coordinator should then accompany the delegation to the airport, right up to the gate, and remain until the guests' plane is in the air.

Then congratulate yourself for a hosting job well done!

CHAPTER FOURTEEN

Out on the Rim: Living, Working, and Traveling

Three great decisions will determine how much, and in what ways, living in Asia will affect you: where you live, where you travel when you leave the place you live, and how far native you decide to go.

JAMES FALLOWS

Living in Asia affects people in different ways. To James Fallows's list of variables, I would add another: How Asia affects you will also depend on your *attitude* when entering Asia—whether it is open and accepting, or closed and condescending.

The purpose of this chapter is to help with personal preparation for living and working in Asia. I will highlight some of the assets and drawbacks of living in Asia's capital cities, and will offer some advice on how to avoid the culture shock most foreign expatriates experience when they relocate in Asia. In the closing pages, you will find tips for easier, safer traveling in Asia, gathered from my own hard knocks of the road and skies, as well as those of my friends, associates, and other vagabonds of the Far East.

Let's start by taking a glance at the Asia Post—its hidden fortunes and potential perils.

The Asia Post: Glamour or Peril?

An Asia posting can be made or marred by the city in which one must live. Asian capitals range widely, from those that feature all the comforts of home, such as Tokyo, Hong Kong, and Singapore, to hardship posts like Beijing, Jakarta, and Taipei, which lack the most common necessities of life one is accustomed to.

Before our armchair tour, let me warn you that much of "idyllic" Asia, shown in travel magazines, has been turned into an environmental wasteland, an "industrial sewer," as a British steel-maker described it to me recently. Taiwan, Korea, parts of the Philippines, much of China, and Thailand's urban centers have fallen victim to human abuse of the environment. As multinational business moves through the Asia-Pacific in search of lax environmental regulations, Asia's pockets of paradise will become increasingly scarce.

Occupying the bottom position on the Asia comfort continuum is the People's Republic of China, at least in the minds of the intrepid expatriates who have lived there. Their complaints about the high costs, pollution, and scarcity of imported goods in Beijing, Chongqing, and Guangzhao have only been augmented by their new dimension of frustration and anxiety, brought on by the Tiananmen Square Massacre.

Life in modernized Taiwan can't be said to be much better than that in China. Taipei's 2.5 million residents endure Mexico City-style traffic jams (thankfully, Taiwan's drivers don't honk horns incessantly as Seoulites do) and a vile, throat-singeing smog that is the worst in all of Asia. Expatriates living in Taiwan have a not-so-funny one-liner about the island's fouled air and water: Every year you live in Taipei takes a year off your life!

Hong Kong, on the other hand, remains one of the finest cities in which to live, in the entire world. Hotel rates and office rents went down after the 1989 turmoil in China; so did tourism. Skilled workers are hard to find, because those with money or brains have either left the island or are preparing to leave, before the curtain comes down in 1997.

For non-Chinese speakers looking to get to know the Chinese mind, I highly recommend a stint in Singapore. Because English is spoken there, an expatriate can make friends easily and become quickly acquainted with Chinese idiosyncracies. Singapore's only drawbacks are its strict civil code ($500 for jaywalking, and strict laws prohibiting smoking in public places) and its small size.

South Korea is less comfortable than Hong Kong, and the tense political atmosphere and monthly threats against Americans are a source of stress and anxiety for expatriates living there. Across the street from the Hotel Lotte, the perpetually blackened American Information Services building stands surrounded by helmeted riot police, who give this city its ambiance of imminent violence. During a recent leisurely walk through the markets of Insadong in Seoul, a U.S. serviceman from Iowa stopped me and said: "Always take a taxi here. Never walk alone. You're just *asking* for it."

Indonesia, Malaysia, and Thailand are often called tropical paradises. With its fun-first approach to life and business, Thailand is the only country in this group that's really "tropical," in the non-climatic sense. To non-Moslems, Indonesia and Malaysia will seem rather strict and uncomfortably authoritarian. Another serious drawback in Moslem Asia is the petty and not-so-petty corruption that preys on foreign businesspeople.

For pure comfort, Japan dominates in the region. Visitors can walk around Tokyo at any time of day or night, without fear of being assaulted in any way. The trash cans are so clean, strangers are inclined to ask whether they are for trash, before tossing something into them. The Japanese one meets on the street enjoy conversing with foreigners, though many Westerners in Japan claim that non-Japanese, especially foreign women, are systematically excluded from the highest social circles. I have met as many converts to Tokyo life as I have people who came to despise the place and its residents. Job opportunities for Westerners in Japan are plentiful, allowing spouses to work if they desire, and wages are high. Relative to Paris, London, or New York, the incessantly heard stereotype of "expensive Tokyo" is, I believe, unfair. A delightful dinner in central Tokyo can be had for $6–8 at a small, conveyor-belt *sushi* bar. A Japanese stamp for a letter going overseas costs 50 cents, slightly less than in the United States.

The "Livability" of Asia's Capital Cities

To help with decisions on where to relocate in Asia, I've defined a set of criteria for measuring the overall "livability" of an Asian city. Whether the city is amenable as a home and workplace depends on a number of factors. For the purpose of this admittedly nonscientific analysis, I have judged each Asian capital in five categories:

1. Business and communication services;
2. Cost of living, including rent;
3. Traffic congestion and smog;
4. Entertainment and nightlife;
5. Proximity to interesting cultural centers like museums, monuments, temples, and ancient palaces.

The results might be a surprise. (See page 306.)

In the category of *business and communication services*, every Asian country can now be said to be *on-line* in the global communication network. All top-end hotels, even deep in the interior of China and Indonesia, feature "business centers" where one can find computers, fax machines, and copying services. I should warn, however, that China's telecommunication network remains woefully insufficient to handle its long-distance volume and is a source of frustration for those trying to call to, or out of, China. The same situation exists in parts of Indonesia.

In judging Asian cities for their *cost of living*, I used a simple relationship criterion: What do you get for how much money? That is, an apartment in Hong Kong may cost the same as one in Tokyo, but the one in Tokyo will be tiny and cramped while the one in Hong Kong may feature awe-inspiring views of Repulse Bay. Looking at rents, which are a good indication of overall cost of living in Asia, a nice apartment in the Roppongi, in Tokyo, could cost $9,000 a month; the same amount will rent a five-bedroom house in Seoul. In China, most executives live in one of the "expat villages" or in hotel rooms with connecting offices, all priced at around $150,000 a year for an office and connecting bedroom. In Taiwan, apartments are reasonable but look like dilapidated cell blocks. Kuala Lumpur ("K.L." in local parlance) is the most amenable Asian capital, in terms of cost of renting a nice home in a safe area; the cost of living there is one-third less than that in nearby Singapore.

No city was a big winner on *traffic congestion and smog*, although Taipei and Bangkok came in tied for last. Hong Kong and Kuala Lumpur feature the least offensive traffic and smog; Hong Kong's streets are often jammed, but with the Star Ferry leaving every five minutes from Kowloon, an efficient subway system, and low-priced taxis, getting around in gorgeous Hong Kong is one of life's pleasures.

The *entertainment and nightlife* trophy goes to Tokyo for its long list of nighttime activities, including Kabuki and Noh theater, art and fashion shows, musical concerts, and discos. The staid cities of Moslem Asia—Kuala Lumpur and Jakarta—are more wanting for after-hours fun, with the exception of a few discotheques in the large hotels.

Westerners' proximity to *local cultural centers* is important, because the Westerners often lack the time to travel from one Asian country to another. Vacation time is usually used to return to North America to visit friends and family members. Beijing is a big winner here, with its rich array of awe-inspiring sights, like the Summer Palace, the Forbidden City, and the Great Wall of China,

to name three that could fill a whole week of continuous sightseeing. Seoul and Jakarta offer the least in sights, though unremark-
able Jakarta is a jumping-off point to the exotic tribal regions of
Indonesia.

The "livability" tourney put Hong Kong in first place. The island's premier standing may be short-lived, because management
by the Mainland may tarnish "the pearl" after 1997. Tokyo placed
second by a neck and, as the Japanese learn to better mix and relate
with foreigners as equals, Tokyo will get even better as an Asia
post. Singapore came in third. It appears unlikely, however, that
the city-state will replace Hong Kong as a hub for the region's business activities. Most emigrating Hong Kong Chinese avoid going to
Singapore because of its restrictive civil and commercial laws.

Asian Cities' "Livability" Ratings

Rating scale: 1 (lowest) to 10 (highest)

	Business Services/ Communications	Cost of Living (e.g., Rent)	Congestion/ Pollution
Hong Kong	10	9	10
Tokyo	10	8	9
Singapore	10	9	9
Bangkok	7	8	5
Kuala Lumpur	6	10	9
Beijing	5	6	9
Manila	7	8	7
Seoul	8	8	6
Taipei	8	7	4
Jakarta	6	9	6

	Entertainment/ Nightlife	Culture/ Side Trips	Total Rating (1–50)
Hong Kong	9	9	47
Tokyo	10	9	46
Singapore	6	6	40
Bangkok	9	8	37
Kuala Lumpur	3	8	36
Beijing	5	10	35
Manila	7	6	35
Seoul	7	5	34
Taipei	7	7	33
Jakarta	4	5	30

AsiaShock: A Special Kind of Culture Shock

New arrivals in Asia, who may find themselves living in cramped quarters, often feel a sense of isolation, both geographically and socially. One U.S. Consulate circular gave this description of one of the Asia posts that rated low on the livability scale:

> Foreign business people have to agree to live in hotel rooms (usually without cooking facilities) for several years, to eat all their meals in restaurants, and to forgo accustomed sports activities, recreation, and cultural entertainment. The normal friendships and circle acquaintances among host nationals that expatriates in almost any other assignment would develop as compensation are largely barred to the foreigner. So he leads a somewhat isolated existence, artificially isolated from local culture and society.

Once relocated in Asia, the newcomers usually react to their surroundings in predictable ways. I call this the *AsiaShock Response,* a pattern of reactive behaviors that progresses through five stages. The pattern starts with anxiety and frustration over the way things are done in the local culture. If one reaches the fifth and final stage, the result is retreat, or disengagement, from the culture.

AsiaShock is a unique form of culture shock because there is usually an *ethnic difference* between resident Westerners and local inhabitants. Ancient values and ways of social organization remain in place in Asia, even though Western culture has made its presence deeply felt. A *language barrier* further isolates foreigners, as do ingrained attitudes that tend to exclude foreigners from mixing intimately with indigenous members of Asian society. The Westerner who journeys to Asia to live hardly enters a melting pot of diverse ethnic groups, which an Asian finds instantly in Los Angeles, Vancouver, or New York.

The Slippery Stairway into AsiaShock

From observations of North Americans in Asia, I have identified the following five progressive stages for the AsiaShock response.

1. Frustration with Culture

For Christ's sake, you're a taxi driver; can't you speak a word of English?

Almost all visitors to Asia experience the first level of Asia-Shock—exasperation with, and intolerance of, local methods and mannerisms. They can't stand the food. The language barrier annoys them. They order a "tenderloin steak" and get a dish of carrots with strips of fatty beef, which sends them into orbit. An American manager I was with in Singapore became irritated when the coffee did not arrive promptly: "When I'm in Denny's, even in Singapore, I expect a little service, dammit!" Unfortunately, in Singapore, even at Denny's, the coffee comes with the meal, not when customers first sit down.

2. Unwillingness to Understand the Rationale Behind Local Methods

If there's a more inefficient way of doing things, these people will find it.

Without understanding the *rationale* behind a behavior or method, Westerners tend to go "on automatic," labeling the behavior (and soon the entire culture), as inefficient, backward, and inscrutable.

Here's an example. I was in a taxi, speeding to Changi Airport in Singapore, at six o'clock in the morning. I was drowsy and a little hung over. Suddenly, a shrill pulsing sound emanated from the dashboard. It wouldn't stop!

"What is that noise?" I asked, angered.

The driver didn't answer. The shrill pulsing continued for 20 minutes, until we got to the airport. I was about to verbally tear the driver's head off, when he said calmly, "That pulsing meant that I was over the speed limit."

He had broken the speeding law (which could have cost him his license) for 20 minutes, in order to get me to the airport on time. And I was just about to bawl him out like an ugly American, because I didn't understand the *rationale* behind the method.

3. Ethnocentricity

These people are born lazy; they're indolent by nature.

To be ethnocentric means to judge a society in terms of one's own cultural standards and values, rather than the society's intrinsic cultural standards and values. European colonists thought native Malays were "lazy" when they sat around all day. They failed to realize that Malays work early in the morning and in the evening, to avoid the heat of midday. Today, many Westerners label Asians dishonest because "they never say what they mean." A bald lie is rarely told by Asians, however; Westerners simply fail to comprehend the face-saving circumlocution that Asians use to substitute for frankness.

4. Racism

I've never met a smart Japanese. As a group, they're invincible. But as individuals, they're like robots.

A fine line separates ethnocentricity and racism. The former becomes the latter when suspicion or contempt is felt for Asians merely because they are Asian. No longer does the Westerner deal with *individual* Chinese or Japanese or Malays; they become conveniently labeled as "Chinamen," "Japs," and "Coolies."

5. Avoidance of the Culture

The ultimate outcome of full-blown AsiaShock is separation from the local culture. This stage could be called *Foreign Club Syndrome*. At a foreign club in any city in Asia, the conversation will be about how tough it is to do business in Asia, how deals fall through, and how nothing can get done; like a bunch of fishermen are talking about the fish that got away. Disengagement from the culture because of business failure happens because the foreigners have not become members of an indigenous business network. A consultant friend of mine warns:

If you spend time in a foreign club you've blown it. What you've got to do is be out in the culture with the people so that they're telling you jokes about other North Americans, instead of being one of the Americans who's the brunt of the jokes, but doesn't know it.

Global companies need to view AsiaShock as a business risk; it's a costly drain on resources but it can easily be avoided.

Avoiding AsiaShock

The length of time that AsiaShock is experienced depends on *the mindset when first entering Asia.* If an entry attitude is open, curious, and accepting, AsiaShock will still be experienced, but the distress won't last long. Open-minded Westerners will adapt quickly to new surroundings and learn to function within a foreign cultural context. However, if their entry attitude is apprehensive or suspicious, they will remain in a state of AsiaShock for a longer period of time. People who enter Asia thinking they're superior, maintain prejudices when they get there, and stay closed to learning the methods of a foreign culture, hit AsiaShock and often remain in it indefinitely.

Successful acclimation to an Asia post requires adjustment of one's "cultural frame of reference." The way things are done in Asia is not as irrational as it may seem at first glance. Patience is needed, when trying to get service or make travel arrangements, and some destressing remedies should be invoked when patience runs low. Recently, after experiencing frustration with the slow pace of getting things done in Indonesia, the director of Asia marketing for American Plant Growers, Inc., suddenly understood that he had to either adapt to the slower pace or risk losing his marbles. I was rather proud of him when, in a spasm of enlightenment, he realized:

> You can't go into Asia with a typical Western attitude. When in Asia, you simply can't have everything that you are accustomed to. There are times when you "want American." You think about how much you want to bite into a big steak or tune in CBS News on the television. The problem is that you may not be able to get those things in Asia. That takes some adjusting to.

Much of the acclimation process can take place before moving to Asia. Knowing what (and what not) to expect in Asia will cut the time needed to adjust. Let's confront some aspects of living and working in Asia that have been known to put North Americans on the road to frustration and intolerance.

An Overwhelming Workload.   Probably the hardest reality for Westerners to adjust to in Asia is the long working hours, which usually entail giving up most, if not all, recreational activities. Koreans work 12 hours a day on weekdays and 5 or 6 additional hours on Saturday—more hours per week than workers in any other country. To self-motivated Westerners, work-style in Asia may seem regimented: desk-side calisthenics, 5 P.M. national anthems, and de rigueur after-hours drinking sessions with co-workers (to show loyalty to the company) can put Western workers and their spouses on edge.

Feelings of Isolation and Exclusion.   Westerners who live in Japan say there are three types of people in Japan: the Japanese, foreign "guests," and "outsiders." It's extremely difficult to maintain the status of a well-treated "guest" for very long in Japan; one then receives condescension, as an "outsider." Because of attitudes that isolate foreigners physically and socially, North Americans often experience feelings of exclusion and loneliness. For instance, the Chinese frown on foreign men (especially blacks and Middle Easterners) dating local women and mixing socially with Chinese. Foreigners seeking social interaction are relegated to foreign clubs, which are off-limits to native Chinese. Even Westerners who have lived in Asia for years and know the ropes and the language complain of being unable to shed their outsider status; the result is that they tend to socialize among themselves rather than as members of the local business community, worsening the problem of disengagement from the local culture.

Different Business Ethics.   Some North Americans find it difficult to accept and adjust to the arbitrary nature of the supply and service system in Asian countries, when they discover how many of the necessities of living, and of prosperous business, are sought and obtained through the "back door." Frustrations flare, when Westerners witness special advantages being given to ethnic Asian expatriates who maintain informal reciprocal relationships with officials. In some Asian cities, North Americans discover that they have to pay artificially inflated prices for items and services just because they are non-Asian foreigners.

Dealing with the Home Office.   A common complaint cites the difficulty in getting headquarters to listen, respond, and lead, in the management of the Asian subsidiary. Some systemic problems are hard to explain to the boss in the home office; the heat for snafus burns the Asia installation when, in fact, a strategic error has been made by headquarters. This problem exacerbates turnover and breeds an impression among workers and customers that the parent company is unstable and undependable.

Invasions of Privacy.   A foreigner's privacy often remains unrespected in Asia. Sometimes, especially in East Asia, there is a disregard for confidentiality in business dealings. Telex and facsimile messages may be considered public domain; papers left on a desk may be fair game for reading by visitors to the office. Malay workers know everything about everybody and love to gossip. Their questions may seem an intrusion and their knowledge of one's business affairs may be disconcerting.

Fear for One's Health.   Westerners living in Asia face particular feelings of isolation, and even fear, because they are far from home and local medical facilities are often lacking. Outside the major cities, few other foreigners may be available for psychological support. A local doctor in Korea may prescribe ginger for indigestion, licorice as a pain killer, and tiger balm for muscular pain. Parts of Asia have high rates of hepatitis, tuberculosis, and other transmittable diseases, an additional source of concern.

These and other factors make it difficult for foreign firms to persuade good managers to relocate in Asia.

The Asia Posting: Promotion or Purgatory?

In the past, North American companies have not made it attractive to executives to relocate in Asia and remain there. Rosalie Tung, an Asian management expert, has recognized a need for longer-term overseas assignments for U.S. businesspeople, to lend American overseas affiliates more continuity and credibility. The rapid turnover of businesspeople sent to Asia stems, she says, from "the concern among expatriates (particularly those from U.S. multinationals) that a prolonged absence from corporate headquarters may negatively affect their chances of promotion within the corporate hierarchy." The necessity for international experience among top managers is often stressed, but too many managers have returned from overseas postings to find that top slots have been filled by their underlings while they were away. James E. Challenger, president of the outplacement firm of Gray & Christmas, Inc., in Chicago, says of working overseas, "I advise everyone against it. It's one of the most dead-end things you can do."

Things are changing for the better, however. Companies have discovered that to forget about their overseas staff while they're away is tantamount to losing them to hungry placement companies when they return. Dow Chemical, 3M, and Bechtel now have policies for placing people in the promotional pipeline when they return from stints abroad. The remaining problem is that Westerners who agree to work in Asia want to return to the West in three to five years, max. Hence, by the time a businessperson forges a productive network in Asia, an unconnected neophyte is on board as a replacement. Nothing threatens the delicate relationship between the Asian company and its foreign counterpart more than turnover. Worker loyalty wanes, when workers perceive heightened risk in working for a company that often replaces its production manager. A five-year contract has to be the minimum, to instill continuity into an Asian venture.

Choosing the Right Person. The person chosen to send to Asia depends on the sort of business that is involved. Most consultants and guidebooks do not make this business-type distinction. Too many companies depend on language skill as a hiring criterion, and place too little emphasis on experience with the Asian market. Christine Houston, vice president and partner of the placement agency Korn/Ferry International, says of hiring for a Japan post: "If I'm looking for a Westerner, he should have some experience in Japan or with a Japanese firm, know the language and basically be willing to go." Language fluency is not a requisite for success in Asia, although it helps immensely to forge informal relationships that can result in sales. Skill and experience in the specific industry and market in the targeted Asian country are paramount.

For example, a company that is selling agricultural products will need a person skilled at dealing with protectionistic trading practices—a tough negotiator who can penetrate an exclusionary business–government decision-making hierarchy. A company investing in Asia will need someone who can delicately and diplomatically negotiate joint-venture agreements, including financing, land use, and labor management. A firm that is merely conducting import/export trading won't need to worry about delicate diplomacy but will face tactical negotiating on the basis of low price and quality inspection. The best route is to fill the job, not the cultural niche.

One other consideration must be acknowledged before hiring someone to work in Asia: Does he or she possess an extraordinarily *patient* disposition? Here's what a U.S. commercial officer in Seoul told me about hiring for patience:

> Some people have infinite patience. Nothing surprises them. In Korea, you have to *expect* that the cars will swerve without signaling—you have to *sense* that they will. Same thing in doing business. You have to be unflappable. Many foreign business people here get mad. They bad-mouth the locals. They want trade sanctions imposed. They're tough, impatient, sue-'em types. They go Section 301 when disputes arise, and sometimes they win. They phone the President of the United States and the Secretary of State to get things done. Sometimes it works. But if you *can't* call the President, you're better off being patient and working within the system.

Arthur Klauser, who serves as a member of the board of trustees of the Mitsui Foundation, adds to the list of desired expatriate attributes a sense of humor and a liberal arts education:

> If I've gotten anywhere at all, it's not because of my business school or my law school backgrounds (although I don't deride them at all), but because of [my interest in] other people's cultures. If you can get on that wavelength, you've got the battle half won.

Klauser chides Western corporations for overlooking their best candidates for overseas positions:

> Unfortunately, our hiring apparatus, particularly in the private sector, is still caught up in looking for specialists like lawyers, engineers, and finance types. When they come across someone with a language or humanities background, they throw the curriculum vitae into file 13. This is not helping us to be competitive.

Working in Asia

Most of the approximately 250,000 Canadians and Americans currently living and working in Asia fall into one of three groups: managers and workers in Western affiliates, employees of Asian companies, or members of the diplomatic corps and military services. The following observations are addressed to those in the first and second groups, who should be prepared to be a boss (a manager) in Asia or to work as an employee reporting to an Asian boss.

Managing at an Asian Subsidiary

Make the Firm Attractive to Skilled Workers.   Domestic firms in technically advanced Asian nations currently face a shortage of low-cost labor as well as technically skilled workers. For foreign companies trying to hire skilled locals, the competition for talent is fierce throughout Asia. Labor is so short in Japan that foreign firms there have been forced into hiring job hoppers away *from each other.* By understanding what Asian workers are looking for in a company, and how foreign companies are perceived, Western managers can enhance the attractiveness of their company to job seekers.

   The advantages of working for foreign companies start with their hiring package: they typically offer higher pay, better working conditions, and more training. These aspects should be highlighted in job description advertising. Unfortunately, Asian college graduates usually seek a *prestigious company* rather than a *career position* that will make use of distinctive skills. Large domestic companies are more desirable than foreign companies, because the latter may not be there tomorrow. The short-term business mentality that guides many Western companies has prompted them to pull out of Asia when the cost of labor rises or growth targets go unmet. Korea, for example, witnessed an exodus of over 100 foreign companies in the first nine months of 1990, because of a 60 percent rise in Korean wages over the 1987 level. The short-term nature of foreign corporate commitment in Asia has caused many skilled indigenous workers to avoid the career risk incumbent in working for a foreign-owned company. This impression can be countered by emphasizing a long-term commitment to the market and plans to expand in it over time.

   Often, managerial positions at foreign affiliates are reserved for foreigners, while Asians remain in secondary positions.* This imbalance adds to skilled Asians' uncertainty in working for a foreign company; career advancement may not be realized. Most consultants recommend relying on local staff as much as possible. Locals can best handle most labor issues and bureaucratic red tape, and can better resolve conflict in the workplace. I would add that the shift from foreign to domestic management should be tied to a performance clause in the labor contract, to further reinforce career confidence among Asians in the company's employ.

   Use "Family-Style" Management Methods.   Western personnel management methods may seem cold, clinical, and depersonalizing to Asian workers, especially in light of the social benefits and support that companies in most Asian countries offer their employees. To cite an example, women in Japan tend to perceive the prospect of working for a Western boss as a socially risky proposition. John Eleman, who has worked in Japan for six years, explains:

> A [single] woman in Japan evaluates the companies she might work for, knowing that, in almost all cases, her [future] husband will come either from within the company or from a company of

---

* This tendency does not apply in Japan, where nearly two-thirds of the foreign affiliates are run by Japanese CEOs.

similar social status. In the case of a man outside the company, she will meet him through a meeting arranged by her manager. No woman can lightly enter a job where she might have an American for a boss. What if he doesn't know what to do? And it is likely that he won't.

Western managers in Asia need to foster "family oriented" corporate culture in their companies, by participating in the lives of their workers. Here are some basic suggestions:

- Attend weddings.
- Bring flowers to people who are sick.
- Participate in religious celebrations and funerals.
- Never favor Western colleagues in the company, professionally or socially, to the exclusion of Asian colleagues.
- Treat workers as family, as Asian managers do.
- Ensure that workers enjoy their work by allowing them to socialize during work, with each other and you.

The Thai word for work (*ngan*) also means party. Thais know the difference between work and a party, but they want work to be as pleasant as possible. Worker–manager affinity can be generated by creating more than mere economic incentive for workers. Celebrate together on holidays and birthdays, and at the start of each new phase of the factory's expansion and performance. Especially in Indonesia and Thailand, if the job gets dull, burdensome, or boring, productivity will plummet and turnover will skyrocket. In many Asian countries, a long midday break for workers is practiced religiously; in the Philippines it's called a *merienda*. In China, the midday break for workers is guaranteed in the country's constitution.

When hiring, managers must keep in mind an Asian's attachment to group. Using a local person to help with hiring may avoid creating intrafirm conflicts among worker factions that are based on kinship ties, school background, regional dialect, and so on. Conversely, nepotism, offering jobs only to the workers' relatives and friends will backfire for productivity. To attract good workers, employee benefit packages that match, or surpass, domestic plans may have to be offered. A negative attitude toward nepotism can be communicated frankly to workers, without rejecting the well-entrenched practice altogether. "Merit first and then family members, please" can be an announced policy while still accepting job applicants, who will often be relatives.

Deal with Quality Problems Creatively. North Americans have made it a ritual to identify Asian workers as the source of quality problems in their Asian affiliates. Quality control is a problem of management, not workmanship. Management is responsible for structuring the tasks of production to foster high quality in the end product. Quality problems can be dealt with by segmenting the manufacturing process and putting small groups of workers in charge of each segment. When the process of quality is broken down, the process becomes measurable and workers become accountable. A most unique solution to quality problems was described by a consultant to an American diamond company. The company set up a diamond-cutting plant in the Philippines, to sell diamonds to Cartier for use in wristwatches. The task seemed impossible—to make instant diamond cutters out of unskilled Filipino workers. First, the diamond-cutting process was broken down. The chip diamonds that went into the watches each took 25 to 30 separate cuts. Each worker was trained to do three cuts and to inspect them for quality; in that way, everybody was held accountable for a fraction of the manufacturing process. No one had to be trained for start-to-finish cutting. Quality control became a simple problem to solve.

Another problem inherent in quality control in Asia involves keeping Asia-style groupism from vulgarizing the quality control procedure. For instance, the quality check person should not be from the same region, family, or social group as the person doing the work to be checked. The inspector is liable to favor someone from his or her own group or be reluctant to reject that person's work because of inferior workmanship. Recruiting from an array of villages, families, and social groups should be a rule, no matter how much the Asian staff lobbies for recruits from their own groups. Control of the "mix" of a staff in Asia will require almost continuous cross-checks of personal background.*

Resolve Conflicts While Preserving Face. To resolve conflicts in the Asian workplace, managers can appeal to emotions and not merely address facts to prove a position or make a gripe. Conflicts should be resolved outside the company, using a human touch, because word of a firing or an internal conflict at a company travels fast and wide. The T. Boone Pickens approach to conflict resolution, going in front of television cameras to deride a partner,

---

* I am indebted to Steve Willard of Willard and Associates, in Portland, Oregon, for contributing to these remarks about quality control in Asia.

doesn't work *unless* you're T. Boone Pickens. Even then, it may be futile.

Westerners take criticism and deal with conflict differently than do Asians. Westerners might experience an altercation, yell at each other, and then make up and go have a drink together. If two Asians have a conflict that erupts into yelling at each other, the two probably will never speak to each other again. A manager must remain extrasensitive to keep conflict below the surface, and must clothe reprimands of workers in the most tender terms. Criticism and firings must not rob a worker of face. Never "dress down" a worker in front of his or her coworkers. Workers who are castigated in public in Thailand, Indonesia, Malaysia, and the Philippines will often vanish without a trace rather than suffer a loss of face in the eyes of their coworkers. A manager who robs a worker of face may discover that other workers suddenly react sluggishly to commands. An offended worker may pass the buck to underlings, when the boss requests something in the future.

Workers should not be bluntly asked to offer constructive criticism of management, unless in private. Asian workers learn that making suggestions is synonymous to questioning the authority of their superior, for which they can be dismissed.

A common mistake among North American managers is to use a snide remark to reprimand poor performance. This approach doesn't work. To reprimand a secretary, an insensitive boss might quip, "You've forgotten how to spell my name already? I hope you're not getting senile." A better way: "Here is my business card for anyone who needs to know how to spell my full name."

To reprimand an Asian worker, a manager should arrange to see the person alone, at a time when production is going fairly *well*, not badly. The manager should bring up a couple of positive issues first, and then segue to the point of contention indirectly: "Keep up the effort to improve your English spelling. It's important for the home office, okay?" Should the problem continue, a follow-up meeting can be held for the sole purpose of talking about the problem: "Here is an English dictionary that might help you. I may also hire an English tutor for you as well."

Before becoming irate and firing someone, a manager should remember the pervasiveness of Asian groupism. A gauntlet brought down on one worker may inadvertently offend an entire faction inside the company, which may take revenge by circumventing the manager's authority in the future. For instance, when a Filipino is fired or accused of lying, stealing, or cheating, shame comes to his or her entire family and allied kin, who could number into the hundreds. This explains why incompetent workers and managers often hold on to their positions indefinitely: to fire them would bring shame upon numerous people, some too important to embarrass. In this vein, a person who may force other connected persons to leave should not be fined. Instead, the person can be skipped at the next round of promotions or wage hikes, giving a hint to leave; most times, a departure will come soon after.

Behave Like a "Corporate Guest." As the "new kid on the block" in an Asian country, a Western company should conduct the requisite public relations, to give the firm clout in the bureaucracy that surrounds it. This includes fraternizing with employees and government officials. Most of all, the company needs to expand its network of contacts *outside* the foreign community. Ways to do this quickly include:

- Attend trade shows and conferences;
- Join trade and industrial associations;
- Publish a company newsletter announcing employee accomplishments, R&D activities, and expansion plans;
- Sponsor community events and recreational activities;
- Sponsor grass-roots environmentalism, and so on.

Working for Asians: Dealing with Your Japanese Boss

Japanese companies rarely fill top management slots in their overseas Asian subsidiaries with foreign locals, as American and European companies usually do. One reason is that *gaijin suketto* (foreign helpers) often remain in Asia for a year or two and then rotate back to the West, a waste of the company resources needed to train and groom them for select positions. Asian firms are aware of the fact that annual job turnover in the United States is 40 percent per year (20 percent for salaried workers) and that foreign workers generally do not stay at jobs with an Asian company in Asia for long. George Fields, chairman and chief executive officer of ASI Market Research (Japan) Inc., concurs. He says that the Japanese define a foreigner as "someone who will always go home to where he came from. Foreign labor in Japan is temporary, by definition. You stay as long as you're useful." Those who do stay often complain about a discriminatory "glass ceiling" that restricts their upward movement into positions of leadership at Japanese companies. Even so, approximately 40,000 Americans and British work at present as employees of Japanese companies in Japan.

Some tips for working for a Japanese company—whether in Japan, or in North America—are in order.

1. Employees don't have much autonomy, no matter how high they are on the totem pole. I know a regional manager for NEC in the United States who is required to obtain approval from Tokyo for virtually his every move, including attending a conference or making a sales presentation.

2. The Asian employer will make judgments about applicants' character based on religious preferences, home life, and family background, as part of the interviewing process. Personal information is used to make assessments about whether an employee can be trusted and counted on to exhibit loyalty to the company. Numerous lawsuits have been brought against Japanese companies in the United States by plaintiffs who claim they have been discriminated against based on their sex, age, and ethnicity.

3. Promotion is based more on seniority than on merit. Valued higher than unique talents may be an exhibition of unflinching corporate loyalty, even at the expense of spending time with one's family. Getting promoted by an Asian boss depends on diligently and quietly performing a function at the company, until the boss takes notice. Westerners, who are typically conditioned to make their contributions public and to demand recognition for them, have found this system intensely frustrating. Connie Kang, an assistant metropolitan editor at the *San Francisco Examiner,* sheds light on the subject:

   [In] Confucian-steeped cultures, talking about your virtues is a shameful thing. You're supposed to expect people in positions of authority to recognize your abilities and appreciate you, rather than you having to go to them and . . . ask for a raise, ask for a promotion.

   Asians working for North American firms have had to learn how to state their demands more forthrightly, to gain recognition. North Americans working in Asia must learn how to win favor with their Asian managers by humbly and energetically performing their designated job roles, without seeking laurels for every action.

4. Communication habits must be adjusted to conform to those of the Japanese; the alternative is endless frustration. (See Chapters 5 and 6 for specifics on communicating with Asians.) John Nevin, chairman of Firestone, which was purchased by Bridgestone of Japan in 1988, explains:

> I'm seen as terribly abrupt and abrasive [by the Japanese]. If you're very direct, you're admired in American culture. The Japanese culture is much more subtle. I can never get them to tell me what they actually mean, and they may think I'm rude and crass.

5. Employees must be prepared NOT to fit in with coworkers or management immediately. They should participate in socializing with Asian colleagues as often as possible, but not pressure them for acceptance as "one of the guys," especially if the employees are female. Clifford Clarke, president of IRI International, a cross-cultural management consulting firm in California, explains:

> Since the Japanese think Americans are motivated pretty exclusively by titles and lots of money they give high titles and lots of money and think guys will be happy. But what they miss is that Americans are also motivated by inclusion.

Employees may not feel that they are receiving enough feedback and direct guidance from tight-lipped managers, who may be expecting self-directed performance from them. Informed socializing is the best way to break down communication barriers and get constructive criticism.

Traveling in Asia: Tips for "Occidental Tourists"

In Anne Tyler's novel, the concern of the "accidental tourist" is to visit someplace without feeling that home has been left behind. Visitors to Asia can forget this notion. No place can be more disorienting and disconcerting to the traveler than Asia. To help lessen the impact of Asia travel and make it safer and more comfortable, take heed of the following tips and advice.

Before You Leave for Asia

If you plan to relocate, living and working in Asia, the first step is to contact the American Chamber of Commerce in New York.

The Canadian consulate in Los Angeles informs us that such services are not made available by the Canadian government to Canadian firms; much valuable information, however, can be obtained by non-U.S. firms from the U.S. Government Printing Office (phone: 202/783-3238). The Chamber publishes current information about living conditions in Asia and operates a regional support office in every Asian capital. These field offices can assist in getting settled and networking among other North Americans after arrival. The Chamber can also help with contracting local support groups such the Foreigners' Community Service (FOCUS) in Korea and the Kaisha Society in Japan.

Know the Exchange Rates.   I have two tips regarding currency exchange rates. First, bring along $50–$100 worth of *each currency* you will be using during a trip. You'll save time at crowded airports and you can save money, because you'll have the chance to search out the best exchange rate, which won't be offered at the airport. Second, get acquainted with exchange rates *before* you arrive. You should have a "feel" for an exchange rate, even if you don't know the exact per-dollar amount.

I try to calculate the approximate amount of local money that is equal to US $10. In that way, I have a reference point for how much my purchases cost, which can prevent rip-offs. Upon arriving in Hong Kong recently, drowsy after 10 hours of flight, I paid HK$200 for a taxi ride to the Peninsula Hotel (the normal fare is HK$35) because I got the exchange rate screwed up in my head. Hong Kong drivers often count on foreigners' disorientation. You can't really blame them. They're attempting to make a quick buck, in order to emigrate before the Chinese take over in 1997.

Countries, Currencies, and Exchange Rates

		$1 equals
China	Yuan	5.7 ¥
Hong Kong	Hong Kong Dollar	7.23 HK$
Indonesia	Rupiah	1,860 Rp
Japan	Yen	132 Y
Korea	Won	725 W$
Malaysia	Ringgit	2.7 M$
Philippines	Peso	24.8 ₱
Singapore	Singapore Dollar	1.82 S$
Taiwan	New Taiwan Dollar	27.7 NT$
Thailand	Baht	25.4 ฿

Don't Go on a Shoestring.   Roughing it in Asia to save money does little to enhance anyone's business reputation; where you stay is an important factor in the impression you make among Asian counterparts. If you're a visiting customer staying at a top hotel, you may enhance your attractiveness to an Asian supplier, who may then soften the asking price. A note on hotel rates: the top-end Okura or the Imperial in Tokyo charges about $180 a night for a single; the Hotel Lotte in Seoul is about the same. At the lower end are the surprisingly comfortable YMCAs, which are about $25 a night for a single, throughout Asia. I don't recommend going any lower than that, however, as the following anecdote will suggest.

A cab driver picked me up in downtown Singapore late one night. I said to the driver, "190 Waterloo Street," the address of my very modest hotel, where I was forced to stay because of the unavailability of rooms in Singapore during the high tourist season. The driver snapped back knowingly: "You should meet nice girl . . . ."

I was astonished. My low-budget travel book had recommended the hotel "if you really want to splurge."

At the hotel, the driver said: "Have a nice massage."

What to Bring on a Trip to Asia.   For traveling to Asia on business, limit your luggage to *two* pieces: a suit bag that can be hung up, and a high-quality briefcase. We've talked about what clothing to bring, in Chapter 6, so I'll skip that here. The following list includes a number of items you'll be glad you brought along:

- Sunglasses with retaining strap
- Penlight for reading
- Breath mints
- Aspirin
- Toilet paper
- City maps in English
- Inflatable seat pillow
- Blindfold and sleeping pills
- 100-watt light bulb, in a plastic bag (to light dimly lit hotel rooms)
- Traveler's dictionary of the local language and one of technical terms, if needed
- Blood-type identification card (Know your blood type before leaving for Asia, in case you need a blood transfusion. You

don't have to worry about tainted blood, as it is now screened in most of Asia.)

- Earplugs (Don't forget these. In China, loudspeakers follow you everywhere, even into your train compartment, where their incessant chattering starts at 5:00 A.M.; on airplanes, Korean mothers allow their children to run up and down the aisles, screaming and laughing, as passengers try to sleep.)

- Voltage converter (See Appendix D, before using your appliances. I once blacked out an entire hotel in Guangzhao, when I plugged a 120-volt battery charger in a 220-volt outlet.)

- Water purification tablets (You can drink the tap water in Tokyo, Hong Kong, and Singapore; anywhere else in Asia, drink bottled water or purify your water.)

- Antibiotic (Before leaving for a month in Asia, I called a doctor and asked for a prescription for penicillin, in case of an ear infection or bad cold. He refused, saying: "No doctor will prescribe an antibiotic for precautionary reasons." So I went to my pharmacist for advice. He said: "Go to a fish store [he meant a store that sells *pet* fish] and get tetracycline. It's exactly the same stuff I sell and almost as good as penicillin. You just have to take more of it." I went to a fish store and bought tetracycline. It's used as a curative for pet fish.)

What to Bring When Moving to Asia.   AsiaShock can be reduced by bringing along things that may not be readily available in Asian countries. (A friend of mine living in Taipei recently begged me to bring her Tequila and refried beans, both hard to find in Taipei.) Scarce items may include special appliances, reference books, large-size garments, special cosmetic products, health products, athletic equipment, computer hardware and software, and Western-recipe cooking spices.

What Not to Pack.   Depending on where you visit, prohibited items include such things as "seditious and treasonable materials," narcotics, pornographic materials, and toy guns that look like the real thing. From studying Customs regulations in Asia, I have compiled a list of items *not* to bring to any Asian country: controlled drugs, reproductions of copyrighted material such as video tapes, laser disks, cassette tapes, large sums of cash, cigarette lighters in pistol or revolver shape, firearms and explosives, animals, birds or their byproducts, weapons, poison, and pornographic materials, no matter how mild.

A Warning about Drugs. Asia is no place to experiment with drugs, especially as a businessperson with the reputation of your firm riding on you. Singapore and Malaysia maintain the most extreme drug laws. A Singapore visa states in red block letters: DEATH PENALTY FOR DRUG TRAFFICKERS. They mean it. It's a serious offense to possess, consume, or transport controlled drugs. In Singapore, you get 20 to 30 years in jail and 15 strokes of the *rotan* (an evil little whipping instrument) for trafficking more than 10 grams of marijuana, 6 grams of opium, or 10 grams of heroin. If you're caught with more than 15 grams of heroin or 30 grams of morphine, the penalty is death. Mere *consumption* of these drugs can get you 10 years in jail and a $10,000 fine. If someone lights up at a party, LEAVE.

Getting Around in Asia

Throughout Asia, you should negotiate the fare with a driver before getting into a taxi. A driver's estimate is usually pretty accurate. (See Chapter 10, regarding tipping taxi drivers.) In Japan, don't grab for the door handle of a taxi when it pulls up in front of you. The door opens automatically and can smash an outstretched hand. In Korea, even with the threats to Americans, walking may be safer than taking a cab. Korean taxi drivers drive like hornets and are often fatigued. The traffic accident rate in Korea is 30 times the world average, and the traffic accident fatality rate is 6 times the world average! Personally, I recommend renting a car in Asia, except in Japan and Hong Kong, where you would have to drive on the left side of the road. You can obtain an international driver's license through the American Automobile Association. Rental rates are reasonable throughout Asia.

Before leaving your hotel by taxi, have the concierge write down the address of your destination and the address of your hotel, in the local language, to ease communication with your taxi drivers. To serve this purpose, an American executive brought along a matchbook from his hotel. His Japanese driver looked at the matchbook, nodded, and took the American to the outskirts of Tokyo—to the matchbook factory!

Airtips. After Latin America, the Asia-Pacific is the most dangerous place to fly in the world. Twenty-one percent of all fatal airline accidents occurred in the region between 1969 and 1988. According to a Condé Nast "Traveler" special report published in 1990, Philippine Airlines, Korean Air, Cathay Pacific, and CAAC (China's national carrier) are among the world's poorest performing airlines, for fatalities caused by accidents and terrorist attacks.

As travelers, we can do little to change this state of affairs, but some tips for an airline trip to Asia can give other comfort.

- Never buy airline tickets in Japan; the charges are exorbitant. Get them at bargain prices in Hong Kong or Bangkok.

- Don't fly on stand-by; many of Asia's airports are located one hour or more from downtown.

- Get to the terminal early, if possible, and reserve a bulkhead seat (if you are traveling economy); this location transforms a normally cramped seat into one with the leg room of first class.

- Always pick up a wheeled luggage carrier before tiring yourself out walking, or running, miles in the airport.

- Reduce jet lag by drinking fluids; skip beverages containing alcohol and caffeine. Arrive a day "early" (if a meeting is scheduled), to allow time to acclimate. Some people starve themselves for sleep, in order to adjust to the time change. I don't think this is wise, because it tends to make people irritable and drawn-looking when they arrive.

- Try to learn the names of the airports you plan to visit.

Will the REAL Frequent Flyer Please Stand Up?

Can you match these cities and their airports?

1. Tokyo	A. Kai Tek
2. Bangkok	B. Changi
3. Singapore	C. Bai Yun
4. Jakarta	D. Hanada and Narita
5. Taipei	E. MIA (acronymn)
6. Seoul	F. Sukarno-Hatta
7. Guangzhao	G. Chiang Kai-shek
8. Hong Kong	H. Don Muang
9. Kuala Lumpur	I. Kimpo
10. Manila	J. Subang

Answers: 1D; 2H; 3B; 4F; 5G; 6I; 7C; 8A; 9J; 10E (Manila International Airport).

Daytrips in the Capitals of Asia

Bangkok: The Grand Palace, the National Museum, the Royal Barges, Thompson's House, Thieves' Market, Phatpong, the canals (klongs) via long-tail boat.

Tokyo: Roppongi district, Tokyo Tower, Imperial Palace, Tokyo National Museum, Ginza district. (Remember to venture down into department store basements, where specialty foods are sold.)

Jakarta: Central Museum, Jaya Ancol Dreamland (a recreational complex), Tainan Mini Indonesia Indah (a cultural exhibit).

Singapore: Mount Faber, Jurong Bird Park, Arab Street, Tiger Balm Gardens, day trip to Indonesia, Malaysia, or Sentosa Island.

Seoul: Mary's Alley in Insadong district, by day; Itaewong district, by night; Korean Folk Village, just outside Seoul, National Museum, Kyongbok Palace, the observation deck of the Daehan Life Insurance Building, from which you can see North Korea on a clear day.

Hong Kong: Star Ferry, Victoria Peak, day trip to People's Republic or Macao.

Beijing: The Forbidden City, Temple of Heaven, the Old Observatory, the Summer Palace, the Great Wall of China, Beijing Hotel, Mao's Mausoleum.

Taipei: National Palace Museum, Museum of the Tiananmen Square Massacre, day trip to the island's northeast coast.

Kuala Lumpur: National Mosque, Batu Caves (near K.L.), National Zoo, Lake Gardens, National Museum.

Manila: Corregidor (World War II installations), Intranuros (the old Spanish walled city), Rizal Park, American Memorial Cemetery, Ayala Museum.

◆

Daytripping in Asia

Be sure to take advantage of *any* free time you have in an Asian capital, to see local sights and experience the culture close-up. "Better to have seen once than to have heard a hundred times," an ancient Chinese proverb counsels. If you get the chance, spend at least one night at a traditional inn. In Tokyo they're called *ryokan;* you'll learn to bow and remove your shoes, and you'll sleep on a *futon.* In Korea, they're called *yogwan;* you'll sleep under an *ibol* quilt, on a traditional *yo* mattress placed on an *ondol* floor, and your head will rest on a husk-stuffed pillow. You can find inns in the Undang, Taiwon, and Daeji districts of Seoul.

Be sure to bring along the daytrips list of not-to-miss sights for the business traveler on a tight schedule, on page 327. Each itinerary can be done in one *full* day of sightseeing.

Time Difference

(Example: Los Angeles time is 15 hours *behind* Bangkok time. At noon on Friday in L.A., by counting 15 hours *ahead*, we find that it is 3 A.M., Saturday morning, in Bangkok.)

	L.A./Vancouver	N.Y./Montreal, Quebec, Toronto	London
Bangkok	−15	−12	−7
Beijing	−16	−13	−8
Hong Kong	−16	−13	−8
Jakarta	−15	−12	−7
Kuala Lumpur	−15.5	−12.5	−7.5
Manila	−16	−13	−8
Seoul	−17	−14	−9
Singapore	−15.5	−12.5	−7.5
Taipei	−16	−13	−8
Tokyo	−17	−14	−9

Weather Planner

	Jan.	Feb.	Mar.	Apr.	May
Bangkok					
Average temp.	80°	82°	84°	87°	86°
Days of rain	1	3	4	6	17
Beijing					
Average temp.	31°	32°	42°	57°	68°
Days of rain	3	3	3	4	6
Hong Kong					
Average temp.	60°	59°	64°	71°	77°
Days of rain	6	8	11	12	16
Jakarta					
Average temp.	79°	80°	81°	81°	81°
Days of rain	17	19	14	11	8
Kuala Lumpur					
Average temp.	81°	81°	82°	82°	82°
Days of rain	13	16	16	20	15
Manila					
Average temp.	76°	77°	80°	81°	82°
Days of rain	5	3	3	4	10
Seoul					
Average temp.	21°	32°	40°	51°	60°
Days of rain	8	7	7	8	9
Singapore					
Average temp.	80°	81°	81°	82°	82°
Days of rain	16	11	14	15	14
Taipei					
Average temp.	60°	63°	67°	70°	75°
Days of rain	8	15	11	14	11
Tokyo					
Average temp.	39°	39°	45°	55°	62°
Days of rain	7	8	13	14	14

Temperatures are stated in Fahrenheit readings.

June	July	Aug.	Sept.	Oct.	Nov.	Dec.
85°	84°	84°	83°	83°	80°	78°
18	19	19	21	17	7	3
76°	80°	80°	69°	58°	41°	31°
9	13	11	7	4	2	2
82°	83°	83°	81°	77°	70°	63°
21	19	17	14	8	6	5
80°	80°	81°	80°	80°	79°	79°
7	5	4	5	7	12	13
81°	81°	81°	81°	81°	81°	81°
12	11	13	17	19	20	17
82°	80°	80°	80°	80°	78°	77°
16	21	22	21	17	12	9
70°	77°	64°	56°	49°	40°	32°
10	16	12	10	6	9	8
82°	82°	82°	82°	81°	81°	80°
14	13	14	13	16	18	19
80°	85°	79°	74°	70°	65°	61°
13	9	11	10	8	7	7
70°	76°	79°	73°	62°	52°	42°
16	15	13	17	14	10	7

Air Distances (in Miles)

	London	New York	San Francisco/ Los Angeles	Honolulu	Beijing
London	—	3463	5442	7225	5059
New York	3463	—	2248	4958	5942
San Francisco/ Los Angeles	5442	2248	—	2558	5139
Honolulu	7225	4958	2558	—	4398
Beijing	5059	5942	5139	4398	—
Bangkok	5917	7526	6888	5730	1779
Taipei	6075	7782	6776	5046	1065
Jakarta	7261	10,030	8965	6705	3223
Hong Kong	5981	7013	6009	4824	1071
Manila	6666	8489	7291	5294	1764
Seoul	5507	6868	5955	4539	594
Singapore	6733	8288	7343	5836	2417
Tokyo	5192	5887	4486	3350	1131
Kuala Lumpur	6540	9379	8771	6801	2687

Bangkok	Taipei	Jakarta	Hong Kong	Manila	Seoul	Singapore	Tokyo	Kuala Lumpur
5917	6075	7261	5981	6666	5507	6733	5192	6540
7521	7782	10,030	7013	8489	6868	9516	6739	9379
6888	6280	8965	6009	7291	5955	8764	5473	8771
5730	5046	6705	4824	5294	4539	5836	3350	6801
1779	1065	3223	1071	1764	594	2417	1131	2687
—	1568	1432	924	1372	775	885	2476	730
1568	—	2358	502	718	919	2611	1308	1996
1432	2358	—	2011	1723	3271	550	3581	730
924	502	2011	—	691	1300	1389	1555	1553
1372	719	1723	691	—	1621	1483	1858	1530
775	919	3271	1300	1621	—	2893	719	2853
775	2011	550	1389	1483	2893	—	2860	197
2476	1308	3581	1555	1858	719	2860	—	3298
730	1996	730	1553	1530	2853	197	3298	—

Electrical Currents

Country	Available Current
China	220–240 volts, 50 cycles.
Hong Kong	200 volts, 50 cycles.
Indonesia	110–127 volts, 50 cycles in most places.
Japan	100 volts, 50 cycles.
Malaysia	220 volts, 50 cycles.
Philippines	220 volts, 60 cycles; in Manila hotels, 110 volts, 60 cycles may be available.
Singapore	220–240 volts, 50 cycles.
South Korea	100 volts, 66 cycles.
Taiwan	220 volts, 50 cycles.
Thailand	220 volts, 50 cycles.

North American Government Offices in Asia

City	Street Address	Telephone
American Consulates		
Bangkok	95 Wireless Road	*(011-66-2) 252-5050
Beijing	3 Xiushui Bei Jie, Jianguomenwai	(011-86-1) 532-2033
Hong Kong	26 Garden Road, Central District	(011-85-2) 523-9011
Jakarta	Medan Merdeka Selatan 5	(011-62-2) 136-0360
Kuala Lumpur	376 Jalan Tun Razak	(011-60-3) 248-9011
Manila	1201 Roxas Boulevard	(011-63-2) 818-6674
Seoul	82 Sejong-no, Chongno-Ku	(011-82-2) 732-2601
Singapore	30 Hill Street	(011-65) 339-0251
Tokyo	1-10-5 Akasaka, Minato-Ku	(011-81-3) 224-5000

There is no U.S. consulate in Taiwan. For business assistance, contact:

The American Institute in Taiwan, Trade Center, 32nd Floor, 333 Keelung Road, Section 1, Taipei 10548 Taiwan

City	Street Address	Telephone
Canadian Embassies		
Bangkok	Boonmitr Building, 138 Silom Road, 11th Floor	(011-66-2) 234-1561
Beijing	10 San Li Tun Road, Chao Yang District	(011-86-1) 532-3536
Hong Kong	One Exchange Square, Connaught Place, 11–14th Floors	(011-85-2) 810-4321
Jakarta	WISMA Metropolitan, 5th Floor, Jalan Jendral Sudirman	(011-62-2) 151-0709
Kuala Lumpur	Plaza MBF, 172 Jalan Ampang, 7th Floor	(011-60-3) 261-2000
Manila	Allied Bank Centre, 6754 Ayala Avenue, 9th Floor, Makati	(011-63-2) 815-9536
Singapore	IBM Towers, 80 Anson Road, 14–15th Floors	(011-65) 225-6363
Tokyo	3-38 Akasaka 7-chome, Minato-Ku	(011-81-3) 408-2101

There are no Canadian embassies in Korea and Taiwan.

*Numbers in parentheses are, respectively, the international circuit, the country code, and the city code. For calls made within the city listed, these numbers would not be needed.

Asian Business Holidays

	January–March	April–June
Taiwan	Foundation Day (Jan 1) *Lunar New Year* (Jan/Feb) Youth Day (Mar 29)	*Tomb–Sweeping Day and the Death of Chiang Kai-shek* (Apr 15) Dragon Boat Festival (late May or Early June)
China	New Year's Day (Jan 1) *Lunar New Year and Spring Festival* (late Jan and early Feb)	Labor Day (May 1)
Thailand	New Year's Day (Jan 1) *Lunar New Year* (Jan/Feb) Magha Puja Day (Feb)	Chakri Day (Apr 6) *Songkran Water Festival* (Apr 13–15) Coronation Day (May 5) Visakha Puja (celebrating Buddha's birth, enlightenment, and entry into nirvana—May/June)
Hong Kong	New Year's Day (Jan 1) *Lunar New Year* (2–4 day celebration in early Feb)	*Ching Ming* (early Apr) Easter Weekend Queen's Birthday (Apr 21) Dragon Boat Festival (late May)
South Korea	New Year Holidays (Jan 1–3) *Lunar New Year* (Jan/Feb) Independence Movement Day (Mar 1)	Arbor Day (Apr 5) Children's Day (May 5) *Buddha's Birthday* (May) Memorial Day (June 6) Farmer's Day (June 15) Constitution Day (June 17)
Japan	*New Year's Day* (Jan 1) Bank Holidays (Jan 1–3) Adult's Day (Jan 15) National Foundation Day (Feb 11) *Vernal Equinox* (around Mar 21)	May Day (May 1) Constitution Memorial Day (May 3) Children's Day (May 5) *(Many firms close from Apr 29 to May 5)*

July–September	October–December
Confucius's Birthday and Teacher's Day (Sept 28) *Mid-Autumn Moon Festival* (Sept/Oct)	Double-Ten National Day (Oct 10) Taiwan Restoration Day (Oct 25) Chiang Kai-shek's Birthday (Oct 31) Sun Yat-sen's Birthday (Nov 12) Constitution Day (Dec 25) *Christmas (Dec 25)
Founding of the Communist Party (July 1) People's Liberation Day (Aug 1)	National Day (Oct 1)
Queen's Birthday (Aug 12)	Chulalongkorn Day (Oct 23) Loy Krathong Festival of Lights (Oct/Nov) The King's Birthday (Dec 5) Constitution Day (Dec 10) *Christmas* (Dec 25)
Mid-Autumn Moon Festival (late Sept or early Oct)	*Christmas* (Dec 25) Boxing Day (Dec 26)
Liberation Day (Aug 15) Thanksgiving (Sept/Oct)	Armed Forces Day (Oct 1) National Foundation Day (Oct 3) Hangul Day (Oct 9) *Christmas* (Dec 25)
Respect for the Aged Day (Sept 15) Autumnal Equinox Day (around Sept 23)	Health and Sports Day (Oct 10) Cultural Day (Nov 3) Labor Thanksgiving Day (Nov 23) *Happy New Year's Holidays* (Dec 28 for 5–10 days)

	January–March	April–June
Philippines	*New Year's Day* (Jan 1)	*Maundy Thursday* (3 days before Easter) *Good Friday* Labor Day (May 1) Independence Day (June 12)
Singapore	New Year's Day (Jan 1) *Lunar New Year* (Jan/Feb)	Good Friday Labor Day (May 5) Wesak Day (celebrates Buddha's birth, enlighten-ment, and entry into nirvana)
Indonesia	New Year's Day (Jan 1) Good Friday (Mar or Apr) Iaul Adha: Moslem Day of Sacrifice (Jan) *Maulid Nabi: Mohammed's Birthday* (Jan/Feb)	Feast of the Ascension (40 days after Easter) *Waicak Day* (celebrates Buddha's birth, enlighten-ment, and entry into nirvana; in May)
Malaysia	New Year's Day (Jan 1) Taipusam (Jan or Feb) *Lunar New Year* (Jan/Feb) Federal Day (Feb 1)	*Prophet Mohammed's Birthday* (Mar) Labor Day (May 1) *Wesak Day* (May/June) King Vang di-Pert van Agong's birthday (June 4)

Note: The italicized dates should be avoided as hosting dates, if at all possible.

Source: Adapted from information on Asian holidays in *The Traveler's Guide to Asian Customs and Manners,* by Elizabeth Devine and Nancy L. Braganti (New York: St. Martin's Press, 1986), and *The Business Travel Guide To ASEAN Nations,* published by Executive Squire Limited, 1979.

July–September	October–December
Philippine-American Friendship Day (July 4) Thanksgiving (Sept 21)	All Saints' Day (Nov 1) National Heroes Day (Nov 30) *Christmas* (Dec 25) Rizal Day (Dec 30)
National Day (Aug 9) Hari Raya Haji (Sept/Oct)	Deepavali (Nov) *Christmas* (Dec 25)
Independence Day (Aug 17) Mi'raj Nabi Mohammed (Aug) *Idul Fitr* (2 days of celebrating the end of Ramadan) (Aug/Sept)	*Christmas* (Dec 25)
National Day (Aug 31)	Deepavali (Oct/Nov) *Christmas* (Dec 25) Hari Raya Haji (Dec)

Filmography

The following Western feature films may be useful in broadening your perspective on Asian culture, history, and social values. I have ranked them 1–4 (with 4 being the highest ranking), according to the degree that they acquaint the viewer with Asian customs, values, history, and personality.

Shogun	4
The Last Emperor	4
Empire of the Sun	4
The Seven Samurai	4
The Year of Living Dangerously	3
The Good Earth	3
Tai-pan	3
Black Rain	3
The Killing Fields	3
The World of Suzy Wong	3
Love Is a Many Splendored Thing	3
Teahouse of the August Moon	3
The Bridge on the River Kwai	3
The Mikado	3
The Sand Pebbles	3
The Quiet American	2
Oil for the Lamps of China	2
Midway	2
The Year of the Dragon	2
Good Morning Vietnam	2
The Yakuza	2
China Rose	1
Apocalypse Now	1

To obtain a list of nonfiction films dealing with Asia-related subjects, contact the International Documentary Association in Los Angeles, California; telephone: (213) 284-8422.

Annotated Bibliography

Adams, Edward B. *Korea Guide.* Seoul International Tourist Publishing Co., 1976. An illustrated overview for the traveler to Korea.

Axtell, Roger E., ed. *Do's and Taboos Around the World,* 2nd edition. New York: John Wiley & Sons, 1990. A good collection of entertaining blunders and bloopers, some of which occurred in Asia.

———. *Do's and Taboos of Hosting International Visitors.* New York: John Wiley & Sons, 1990. Some essential advice for anyone preparing to host international guests.

Barme, Geremie, and John Minford. *Seeds of Fire: Chinese Voices of Conscience.* New York: Hill and Wang, 1988. An anthology of dissident writings from China that may interest political afficionados.

Benedict, Ruth. *The Chrysanthemum and the Sword: Patterns of Japanese Culture.* New York: New American Library, 1946. The classic, and readable, ethnography of Japanese culture, by one of America's great anthropologists.

Blofeld, John. *City of Lingering Splendour: A Frank Account of Old Peking's Exotic Pleasures.* Boston: Shambhala, 1989. A lyrically written account of one man's experience in Peking during the early 1940s.

Buruma, Ian. *Behind the Mask: On Sexual Demons, Sacred Mothers, Transvestites, Gangsters, Drifters and Other Japanese Cultural Heroes.* New York: Penguin USA, 1984. A penetrating exploration of Japanese society that obliterates many Western stereotypes and myths about Japan.

Chambers, Kevin. *A Traveler's Guide to Asian Culture.* Santa Fe, NM: John Muir Publications, 1989. A handy primer that can enhance one's appreciation of Asian cultural sights.

Chao, Buwei. *How to Cook and Eat in Chinese.* New York: Vintage Books, 1972. Includes an interesting commentary on Chinese table manners and banquet etiquette.

Christopher, Robert C. *Second to None: American Companies in Japan.* New York: Fawcett Columbine, 1986. A literate, journalistic exposé of the American corporate experience in Japan.

Chu, Chin-ning. *The Chinese Mind Game: The Best Kept Trade Secret of the East.* Beaverton, OR: AMC Publishing, 1988. An inquiry into the origin of Asian negotiating tactics; provocative, yet somewhat impractical for business readers.

Condon, John C., and Mitsuko Saito, eds. *Intercultural Encounters With Japan: Communication-Contact and Conflict.* Tokyo: The Simul Press, 1974. A classic compendium of research on Japanese values and business psychology.

Cooper, Robert, and Nanthapa Cooper. *Culture Shock! Thailand.* Singapore: Times Books International, 1982. Not necessarily for the businessperson, but this is a readable and fully illustrated description of Thai character, customs, and ceremonies.

Cormack, Annie. *Everyday Customs in China.* Edinburgh: The Moray Press, 1985. Contains interesting descriptions of Chinese rituals, including weddings and funerals.

Crane, Paul S. *Korean Patterns.* Seoul: The Royal Asiatic Society, Korea Branch, and Kwangjin Publishing Co., 1978. A bit dated now, but this small volume by a missionary has withstood the test of time for its concise portrait of Korean personality.

Crichton, Michael. *Travels.* New York: Alfred A. Knopf, 1988. An anthology of travel pieces by the author of *The Andromeda Strain;* a few selections deal with Asia.

Dalton, Bill. *Indonesia Handbook.* Berkeley: Moon Publishers, 1977. A budget traveler's guidebook that contains a concise introductory overview of Indonesian history, politics, and religion.

De Mente, Boye. *Chinese Etiquette and Ethics in Business.* Chicago: NTC Business Books, 1989. You may find a few tips in this book, but the material is somewhat dated and poorly organized.

———. *Korean Etiquette and Ethics in Business.* Lincolnwood, IL: NTC Business Books, 1988. This book contains a few useful tidbits on Korean history and etiquette, but it's poorly organized and incomplete. Contains a useful glossary of terms.

Devine, Elizabeth, and Nancy Braganti. *The Traveler's Guide to Asian Customs and Manners.* New York: St. Martin's Press, 1986. This is a good country-by-country listing of cultural dos and don'ts, though it offers little for the businessperson.

Draine, Cathie, and Barbara Hall. *Culture Shock! Indonesia.* Singapore: Times Books International, 1986. Probably the most complete description of Indonesian ethnic groups, values, customs, and manners. Unfortunately, the book lacks a much-needed index.

Eberhard, Wolfram. *A Dictionary of Chinese Symbols.* London: Routledge, 1983. An indispensable compendium of animistic, Buddhist, and Confucian symbols in Chinese art, religion, and literature.

Elegant, Robert. *Pacific Destiny: Inside Asia Today.* New York: Crown Publishers, 1990. A colorful tour through modern Asian society and politics, by a foremost journalist.

Ellison, Katherine. *Imelda: Steel Butterfly of the Philippines.* New York: McGraw-Hill, 1988. Through this biography of Marcos's First Lady, we get a first-hand glimpse of Filipino society.

Engholm, Christopher. *The China Venture: America's Corporate Encounter with the People's Republic of China,* updated edition. Chicago: Scott, Foresman, 1991. For the executive or trader doing business in post-Tiananmen China.

Eu, Geoffrey, ed. *Guide to the Orient.* Singapore: APA Productions (HK) LD., 1987. A well-researched, well-photographed armchair travel guide to all of Asia.

Executive Squire Ltd. *The Business Travel Guide to ASEAN Nations: Indonesia, Malaysia, Philippines, Singapore, Thailand, Hong Kong.* Executive Squire Ltd., 1979. This handbook may be hard to find, but it contains useful addresses, phone numbers, and logistical information for the traveler in Southeast Asia.

Fairbank, John K., ed. *Chinese Thought and Institutions.* Chicago: University of Chicago Press, 1957. A weighty textbook that explains the relationship between Chinese philosophical thinking and Chinese government bureaucracy.

——— et al. *East Asia: Tradition and Transformation.* Boston: Houghton Mifflin Co., 1973. The standard textbook overview of East Asia from Peking Man to post-World War II modernity.

Fallows, James. *More Like Us.* Boston: Houghton Mifflin Co., 1989. Useful to the Asia hand for its discussion of Japanese management practice and attitudes toward the West.

Fazziole, Edoardo. *Chinese Calligraphy.* New York: Abbeville Press, 1986. A beautifully published book of Chinese characters, with notes on their derivation.

Fieg, John Paul. *Interact: Guidelines for Thais and North Americans.* Chicago: Intercultural Press, 1980. A detailed exploration into Thai values and character; of great use to businesspeople, though the book is hard to find and of low publication quality.

Finney, Paul B. *The American Express Business Traveler's Guide.* New York: American Express Publishing Corp., 1988. A handy guide to the world's business centers, including important telecommunications information.

———. "Minding Your Ps and Qs Abroad." *Travel & Leisure,* December 1989, p. 81. Some salient tips on proper conduct in Asia.

Fun With Chinese Characters. (The Straits Times Collection.) Singapore: Federal Publications PTE Ltd., 1983. An enjoyable primer for those wishing to learn to recognize Chinese characters; includes illustrations.

Gershman, Suzy, and Judith Thomas. *Born to Shop: Hong Kong.* New York: Appletree Productions, 1990. Advice on hard-nosed (and other) tactics for bargaining, some which could be applied to business negotiations as well.

Giles, Herbert A. *The Civilization of China.* London: Williams & Norgate, 1911. Authored by one of the founders of the Wade–Giles phonetic system for translating Chinese, this thin volume epitomizes the West's impression of the Chinese at the turn of the century.

Greanias, George C. *The Foreign Corrupt Practices Act.* New York: D.C. Heath and Co., 1982. A good overview of the evolution and content of the laws pertaining to bribes and gift-giving by U.S. companies doing business in foreign countries.

Halberstam, David. *The Reckoning.* New York: Avon Books, 1986. The classic, fully readable exposé of the U.S. auto industry battling its competition in Japan.

Hamabata, Matthews Masayuki. *Crested Kimono: Power and Love in the Japanese Business Family.* Ithaca, NY: Cornell University Press, 1990. A revealing inside account of a third-generation Japanese-American's reentry into Japanese business and life style.

Hayashi, Shuji. *Culture and Management in Japan.* Tokyo: University of Tokyo Press, 1988. An eclectic but insightful study of Japanese values and their effect on management practice in Japanese companies.

Hendon, Donald W., and Rebecca Angeles Hendon. *World-class Negotiating: Dealmaking in the Global Marketplace.* New York: John Wiley & Sons, 1990. Contains some useful comparison data about negotiating tactics around the world.

Howe, Russel Warren. *The Koreans.* San Diego: Harcourt Brace & Jovanovich, 1988. This book is certainly the best written book on modern Korean society and culture, though it does not cover Korean business practice.

Jang, Song-Hyon. *The Key to Successful Business in Korea.* Seoul: Yong Ahn Publishing Co., 1988. A classic work by Korea's leading international business consultant. Absolutely essential for anybody doing business with, or managing, Koreans.

Kane, Robert S. *Asia A to Z.* New York: Doubleday, 1963. A dated, but well-written reader, exploring the cultural sights and history of all the countries of Asia.

Karnow, Stanley. *In Our Image: America's Empire in the Philippines.* New York: Foreign Policy Association, 1989. The best available exploration through Philippine history and the U.S.–Philippines relationship.

Kermadec, Jean-Michel Huon De. *The Way to Chinese Astrology: The Four Pillars of Destiny.* London: Unwin Paperbacks, 1983. An esoteric introduction to Chinese astrology, with a concise explanation of Taoist concepts and Confucianism.

Kim, Kyong Dong. "Koreans: Who Are They?" in *Doing Business in Korea,* Arthur M. Whitehill, ed. London: Croom Helm, 1987. An informative essay in a rather eclectic anthology of articles about how to do business Korean-style.

Macintoch, Charles A., trans. *Tao: A Rendering into English Verse of The Tao Teh Ching of Lao Tsze, B.C. 604.* Wheaton, IL: The Theosophical Publishing House, 1974. A pocket-size volume of epigrams from the founder of Tao religious philosophy.

Maraini, Fosco. *Meeting With Japan.* New York: Viking Press, 1960. Probably the most beautifully published book on modern Japanese society from an American publisher. Unmatched in readability, erudition, and illustration. (The book is out-of-print, but can be found at many used-book stores.)

Marsh, Robert M. *The Japanese Negotiator: Subtlety and Strategy Beyond Western Logic.* Tokyo: Kodansha International, 1988. An expertly presented analysis of Japanese negotiating behavior and strategy; of great help to Western negotiators.

McWhirter, William. "I Came, I Saw, I Blundered." *TIME,* October 9, 1989, p. 77. Relevant for anyone who has become frustrated in dealing with Asians while maintaining a Western pace and attitude.

Minoru, Tanaka. *Bushido: Way of the Samurai.* (Translated from the Hagakure.) Justin F. Stone, ed. Santa Fe, NM: Sun Publishing Co., 1975. A window on the Japanese psyche, this is a readable translation of the classic code of the Samurai.

Moore, Frank J. *Thailand—Its People, Its Society, Its Culture.* New Haven: HRAF Press, 1974. A dated, but concise overview of Thai culture, customs, and etiquette.

Moran, Robert T. *Getting Your Yen's Worth: How to Negotiate with Japan, Inc.* Houston: Gulf Publishing Co., 1985. An enduring work on how the Japanese behave in negotiations and why.

Morris, Peter T. *Chinese Sayings: What They Reveal of China's History and Culture.* Hong Kong: Po Wen Book Co., 1981. A handy and readable anthology of proverbs anybody can use to impress Chinese friends or associates.

Murphy, Michael. *Golf in the Kingdom.* New York: Dell Publishing Co.: 1972. An enduring work of fiction-like nonfiction that probes the art of golf from a "Zen" perspective.

Nagel's Encyclopedia Guide: Thailand. Geneva: Nagel Publishers, 1973. An award-winning tourists' guide that explains Thailand's complex history in a nutshell.

Naisbitt, John, and Patricia Aburdene. *Re-inventing the Corporation.* New York: Warner Books, 1985. This well-known book about corporate change contains a useful chapter on Japanese corporate organization.

————. *Megatrends 2000: Ten New Directions for the 1990's.* New York: William Morrow and Co., 1990. Contains an eye-opening chapter about the miraculous growth of Pacific Rim economies and makes a convincing case why corporate America should become more involved in Asia.

Nakane, Chie. *Japanese Society.* Berkeley: University of California Press, 1970. An excellent academic monograph that explores Japanese character and social mores.

Nakatani, Iwao. *The Japanese Firm in Transition.* Tokyo: Asian Productivity Organization, 1988. The most concise and readable description of the evolution of Japanese management methods since World War II.

Norbury, Paul, and Geoffrey Bownes, eds. *Business in Japan: A Guide to Japanese Business Practice and Procedure.* New York: John Wiley & Sons, 1974. An informative early guide to business practice in Japan that, for the most part, still holds up today.

Okakura, Kakuzo. *The Book of Tea.* New York: Dover Publications, Inc., 1964. A timeless classic on the pseudo-religious tea ceremony in Japan.

Osman, Mohd. Taib. *Malaysian World-View.* Singapore: Southeast Asian Studies Program/Institute of Southeast Asian Studies, 1985. A rough outline of Malay values and personality; available in college libraries.

Pan Am's World Guide: The Encyclopedia of Travel. New York: McGraw-Hill Book Company, 1976. A monumental collection of country facts and travel hints for 141 countries; if you find this one in a used-books store, don't hesitate to buy.

Prestowitz, Clyde V., Jr. *Trading Places: How We Allowed Japan to Take the Lead.* New York: Basic Books, 1988. The best case yet for distrusting Japan as a trading partner.

Pye, Lucian W. *Asian Power and Politics: The Cultural Dimensions of Authority.* Cambridge: The Belknap Press of Harvard University Press, 1985. Authored by a foremost orientalist, this pithy volume explores the nature of social and political power in Asia, and sheds light on bureaucratic decision making there.

————. *Chinese Commercial Negotiating Styles.* Boston: Oelgeschlager, Gunn, & Hain, 1982. The classic treatise on Chinese negotiating behavior—a must for the Asia negotiator.

Rahula, Walpola. *What the Buddha Taught.* New York: Grove Press, Inc., 1959. A readable explanation of the major tenets of Buddhism.

Rieber, Beth. *Fromm's Dollarwise Guide to Japan and Hong Kong.* Englewood Cliffs, NJ: Prentice-Hall, 1986. This complete travel guide is hard to beat for getting oriented in Japan and Hong Kong.

Riesman, David, and Evelyn Thompson Riesman. *Conversations in Japan: Modernizations in Japan: Modernization, Politics, and Culture.* London: Allen Lane, The Penguin Press, 1967. A provocative reader of erudite conversations between Japanese intellectuals and David Reisman (coauthor of *The Lonely Crowd*) and his wife in the 1960s.

Roces, Alfredo, and Grace Roces. *Culture Shock! The Philippines.* Singapore: Times Books International, 1985. Detailed advice on Filipino special occasions and daily life.

Roosevelt, Selwa. *Keeper of the Gate.* New York: Simon & Schuster, 1990. Blunders and bloopers at the White House, described by the chief of protocol during the Reagan years.

Rowland, Diana. *Japanese Business Etiquette.* New York: Warner Books, 1985. The most complete and concise book about how to conduct yourself when dealing with the Japanese.

Rucci, Richard B., ed. *Living in Korea.* Seoul: American Chamber of Commerce in Korea, 1987. Essential for those planning to live in South Korea.

Schwartz, John Burnham. *Bicycle Days: A Novel.* New York: Summit Books, 1989. A picaresque novel, in the voice of a Japanized American living in Japan, that strips Japanese culture of some of its protective shielding.

Seligman, Scott D. *Dealing with the Chinese.* New York: Warner Books, 1989. Though it was penned before the Tiananmen Uprising, this is the most current, accurate, and complete guide to etiquette and general business protocol in the People's Republic available today.

Singapore: Official Guide. Singapore: Singapore Tourist Promotion Board, 1990. A handbook available upon arrival at the Singapore airport; explains Singaporean cultural events, ethnic makeup, and Customs regulations.

Smith, Arthur H. *Chinese Characteristics.* New York: Fleming H. Revell Co., 1894. A witty and generally insightful 19th century commentary on Chinese cultural idiosyncrasies, some of which is still valid today.

Smith, Jeff. *The Frugal Gourmet Cooks Three Ancient Cuisines: China, Greece, and Rome.* New York: William Morrow & Co., 1989. This cookbook not only contains the best Chinese recipes, but also surprisingly well-researched historical passages pertaining to Chinese culinary art.

Sparke, Penny. *Modern Japanese Design*. New York: E. P. Dutton, 1987. A nice tabletop photobook with concise descriptions of the Japanese home and tea ceremony.

State Bureau of Foreign Experts, P.R.C. *The Foreign Experts' Handbook: A Guide to Living and Working in China*. Beijing: New World Press, 1988. Published by the Chinese government, this book contains the laws and regulations applicable to expatriates moving to China.

Steenson, Gary P. *Coping with Korea*. Oxford, England: Basil Blackwell, 1987. A concise guide to essential Korean social etiquette, written by an American commercial officer.

Steinberg, Rafael, and the editors of Time-Life Books. *The Cooking of Japan*. New York: Time-Life Books, 1971. A fully illustrated guide to Japanese culinary art as of the early 1970s.

————. *Pacific and Southeast Asian Cooking*. New York: Time-Life Books, 1972. Probably the best introduction to South Asian cuisine, with color illustrations.

Takeo, Kuwabara. *Japan and Western Civilization*. New York: Columbia University Press, 1983. A fascinating collection of essays exploring the clash of values between Japan and the West.

Thorp, Robert L. *Son of Heaven: Imperial Arts of China*. Japan: Son of Heaven Press, 1988. A museum-quality art catalog of Chinese imperial artworks, with commentary on their significance.

Toyne, Brian, and Peter Walters. *Global Marketing Management: A Strategic Perspective*. Boston: Allyn & Bacon, 1989. A solidly researched textbook for anyone seeking a background in international marketing.

Tuchman, Barbara W. *Stilwell and the American Experience in China, 1911–1945:* New York: Bantam Books, 1970. A brilliant narrative history of General Stilwell's dealings with Chiang Kai-shek that underscores some Chinese negotiating tactics still in practice today.

Tung, Rosalie. "Corporate Executives and Their Families in China: The Need for Cross-cultural Understanding in Business." *Columbia Journal of World Business*, Spring 1985, p. 22. A factual evaluation of the West's cultural gap in dealings with Mainland China.

Tzu, Sun. *The Art of War*. Thomas Cleary, trans. Boston & Shaftesbury: Shambhala, 1988. The most readable translation of the classic book of Asian war strategies, with an informative introduction.

Waley, Arthur. *The Opium War Through Chinese Eyes*. Stanford, CA: Stanford University Press, 1958. A splendid and engrossing story of events leading to the outbreak of the Opium War between China and the British.

Watanabe, Teresa. "Asians May Like Americans But They Respect the Japanese" *Los Angeles Times,* May 21, 1991, p. H8. Thought-provoking commentary on reactions to two megarivals in Asia.

Wheeler, Tony. *South-east Asia on a Shoestring.* Australia: Lonely Planet Publications, 1985. For the traveler on a budget who wants to experience indigenous culture close-up.

Whitted, Gerald W., ed. *New Horizons World Guide.* New York: Pan American Airways, 1961. A now-dated guide to 96 countries, including seasonal temperatures and useful country facts.

Whole Earth Review. *Access to Japan.* Sausalito, CA: Winter 1990. A stellar compendium of cutting edge articles, book reviews, and Japan-related sources.

Wilen, Tracey. "Tips from a Woman's Side of the Conference Table," *U.S.–Japan Business Review,* May 6, 1991, p. 6. Valuable advice for businesswomen; much of it applicable beyond Japan.

Wolferen, Karel Van. *The Enigma of Japanese Power: People and Politics in a Stateless Nation.* New York: Alfred A. Knopf, 1988. An illuminating appraisal of modern Japanese politics and society; a must-read for Japanophiles.

Woo, Kon Yoon. *Korean Public Bureaucracy: A Behavioral Perspective.* Seoul: Kyun Kwan University Press, 1982. An abstruse but revealing psychological analysis of Korean personality.

Wu, K. C. *The Chinese Heritage.* New York: Crown Publishers, 1982. A not-so-easy-to-read tome that finds the origin of Chinese values in the distant dynasties of the past.

Yang, Won-dal. *Korean Ways: Korean Mind.* Seoul: Tamgu Dang, 1982. The numerous short chapters of this book explain Korean character by exploring the culture's music, poetry, and history.

Zilong, Jiang. *All the Colours of the Rainbow.* Beijing: Chinese Literature, 1983. A wonderful collection of biographical sketches of representative individuals of modern Chinese society.

Index

Address, title and, 90–91
Air distance, 332–333
Analects, 25
"Asia fever," 83–85
Asian-American population, 5
"AsiaSpeak," 109–111

Banquets:
  business discussion, 196–197
  seating, 195–196
  smoking, 196
  see also specific customs of specific
    countries
Bargaining tactics, survival of, 154–180
Body language, *see* Nonverbal
  communication
Bowing ritual, 91
Brochures, translation of, 153
Buddhism, 27
Buddhist Temples, 273
Buffalo Town, 247
Business cards:
  printing of, 101–102
  use of, 90
Business entertainment, 205–206
  drinking, *see* Drinking
  guidelines of guests, 208–214
  participation in, 211–212
  type of, 207–208
  see also Discotheques; Sex
    entertainment; Singing
Business groups, membership and, 57–58
Business practices, commandments of,
  52–75
Business relationship, development of,
  67–72, 206, 284

Catholicism, 27–28
China:
  banquets and, 197–199
  business and sex, 246
  business holidays, 336–337
  cuisine of, 186–187
  culture capsule, 36–38
  dress code, 150–151
  funeral customs, 280
  gift giving, 229–231
  greetings and introductions, 92–93

  home visit in, 266–268
  living in, 303
  modern growth of, 17
  protocol, 24–25
  shopping in, 283
  tipping, 237
  topics for rapport, 125–126
  wedding customs, 277–278
Chinese New Year, 276
Cold calling, 86
Collective, significance of, 53–57
Commissions:
  go-betweens, 239–240
  guidelines of, 239
Communication:
  nonverbal, *see* Nonverbal
    communication
  problems with, *see* Communication
    obstacles
  skill development, 111–125
Communication obstacles:
  confrontation vs. compromise, 107–108
  frankness vs. face, 106–107
  intercultural errors, 8, 9, 11
  intercultural skills, 10
  personality clashes, 108–109
Confucian Asia, *see* China; Hong Kong;
  Korea; Singapore; Taiwan
Consultants, role of, 87
Corporate hierarchy, plugging into,
  60–61
Crested Kimono, 240
Cultural literacy quiz, 30–31
Culture Shock, 238
Cultures, *see specific types of cultures*

Decision making, 61–63, 155
Dining practices, 183–184. *See also*
  Table manners
Discotheques, 217–220
Discussion, promotion of, 116–124
Dos and Taboos Around the World, 235
Dragon Boat Festival, The, 276–277
Drinking:
  business discussions and, 211
  business entertainment and, 206–207
  games and avoidance of, 214–217
  pace of, 210